ALL OVER AND OTHER

WARREN ELLIS – Writer

JOHN CASSADAY – Artist

LAURA DEPUY – Colorist
with **DAVID BARON** and **WildStorm FX**

JENETTE KAHN President & Editor-in-Chief   PAUL LEVITZ Executive Vice President & Publisher
JIM LEE Editorial Director - WildStorm   JOHN NEE VP & General Manager - WildStorm
SCOTT DUNBIER Group Editor   RICHARD BRUNING VP - Creative Director
PATRICK CALDON VP - Finance & Operations   DOROTHY CROUCH VP - Licensed Publishing
TERRI CUNNINGHAM VP - Managing Editor   JOEL EHRLICH Senior VP - Advertising & Promotions
ALISON GILL Executive Director - Manufacturing   LILLIAN LASERSON VP & General Counsel   BOB WAYNE VP - Direct Sales

THE WORLD STORIES

ALI FUCHS and BILL O'NEIL — Letterers

ED ROEDER — Cover, Logo and Book Design

JOHN LAYMAN — Editor

PLANETARY CREATED BY WARREN ELLIS AND JOHN CASSADAY

PLANETARY: ALL OVER THE WORLD AND OTHER STORIES
Published by WildStorm Productions. Cover, design pages and compilation © 2000 WildStorm Productions.
Planetary and all related characters and elements are trademarks of DC Comics. All Rights Reserved.

Originally published in single magazine form as PLANETARY #1-6 and PLANETARY Preview. Copyright © 1998,
1999 WildStorm Productions, an imprint of DC Comics. Editorial Offices: 7910 Ivanhoe, #438, La Jolla, CA 92037.
Any similarities to persons living or dead are purely coincidental. PRINTED IN CANADA.

DC Comics, a division of Warner Bros. -A Time Warner Entertainment Company.

DEDICATIONS

This one is, as ever, for Niki and for Lilith, who put up
with me and make it all worth doing. And it's also for
Mike Moorcock, an inspiration, who, in saying the following,
defined my approach to writing: "Death is no obstacle."
— Warren Ellis

A great many friends in my life have come and gone. There are some who will
always be close to me and near in my mind and heart. They provide me with
all colors of kindness, inspiration and support. Kyle, Russ, Ben and, of
course, Heather. "No man is a failure who has friends."
Thank you for everything. This is for you.
— John Cassaday

To Mom and Dad for their support;
to the Tarts for their passion;
and to Randy for his.
— Laura DePuy

Planetary Consciousness
Introduction by Alan Moore

Writing this in the last guttering stub of the Twentieth Century, aware of you reading it in the fresh-lit flame of the Twenty-First, it's difficult not to be struck by the Janus-like view that we have of the landscape from here, stretching a long way behind us and further in front. Not only the much broader landscape of human and global affairs, but also the landscape of that smaller world that we know as the comic book field.

While the boom-and-bust sweep of the last decade will almost certainly not prove the end for the comic strip medium, it nevertheless remains difficult not to emerge with a sense that while comics may not have collapsed into rubble forever, still something has changed. Something's gone. Not a market, a format, a style or a thing of the hard and material world of brute commerce, but something more abstract and rarefied, some phantom essence.

The thing that has changed may not be in the comics themselves, but instead in their audience. Could it be rather that people have changed in the accelerated and furious rush of these last hundred years while the comics that they read have changed more slowly or, in many cases, not at all? One of the field's defining axioms in this century has been that people want not change, but the illusion of the same. This is a fallacy based on a purely short-term observation. While it may be true that people don't want change, it's also true that what we want and what we get are very different things. The Twentieth Century gave us nothing else but constant and tumultuous change and did not think to ask us if we wanted it or not. We both knew change, and were ourselves changed in the torrent of events. The underlying human tastes and audience demands on which we built the comic field have altered in the flux of things, within the readership if not within the books themselves. The way that people think and see things has moved on. The massive scaffolding of values where the comic field was raised seems now deserted, seems redundant.

Comic book creators moving through this wasteland between centuries are, it would seem, subject to twin, conflicting impulses. On one hand is the reckless New-Year's-resolution urge to plunge headlong into the future, as of course we must, while on the other hand we have the weighty knowledge of the glittering rubble that we leave behind us, at our backs. With so much of great worth there in the long back yard of comic history, we are obliged to ask ourselves if there might not yet be buried treasures, items fit for salvage. Many of us seem to have the feeling, only mistily defined, that it is some element in comics past that will provide the key with which we can unlock the medium's future. As if in order to move forward, we must also somehow simultaneously move back, however paradoxical that may appear. Which brings us, by a somewhat drawn-out route, to *Planetary*.

Warren Ellis and John Cassaday have manufactured an ingenious device by means of which they can exploit the possibilities of our contemporary situation, as described above. The heroes of their tale are neither crime-fighters nor global guardians, but, by some perfect stroke of inspiration, archaeologists. People digging down beneath the surface of the world to learn its past, its secrets and its marvels. In this instance, though, the world that's under excavation is not our immediate sphere, despite the fact that it is almost as familiar. Instead, we dig into a planet that is nothing less than the accumulated landscape of almost a hundred years of fantasy, of comic books.

We learn the secret histories of those gamma-saturated flats, those early space-probes, all those alien incursions. Working a broad canvas, the creators take us to a strange pop-culture echo of Japan, to radioactive boneyards of giant moths and saurians, to Hong Kong boulevards still haunted by their flickering, action-movie

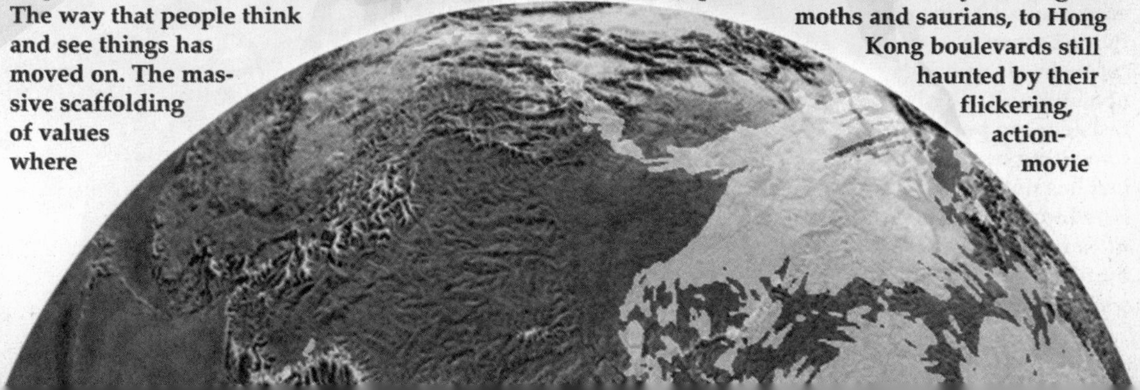

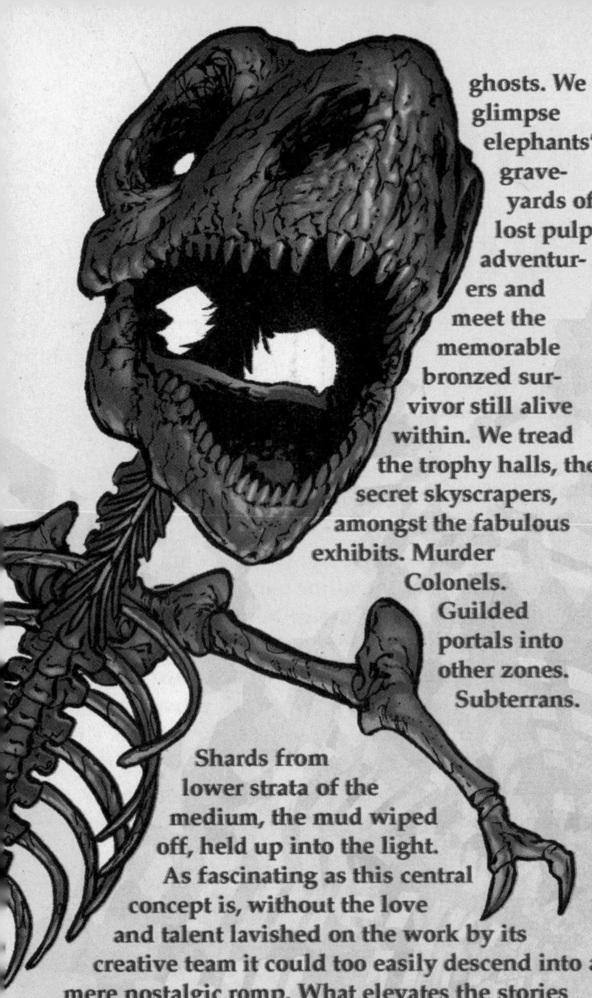

ghosts. We glimpse elephants' graveyards of lost pulp adventurers and meet the memorable bronzed survivor still alive within. We tread the trophy halls, the secret skyscrapers, amongst the fabulous exhibits. Murder Colonels. Guilded portals into other zones. Subterrans.

Shards from lower strata of the medium, the mud wiped off, held up into the light.

As fascinating as this central concept is, without the love and talent lavished on the work by its creative team it could too easily descend into a mere nostalgic romp. What elevates the stories here above the level of the simple rose-tinged retrospective is the sheer imaginative energy and craft involved, the impulse to accomplish something new in mainstream superhero comics that transcends the backward-looking and historical approach that any tale of archaeologists must obviously embrace. The tombs of the past are dismantled, stones taken to pave a way into whatever awaits in the comic field's future. The fuel of this enterprise is that sole asset that comics have always relied upon: the unique jolt of an imagination unbounded by cultural notions of fine art or taste, the breathless pulp rush of ideas in defiance of deadlines, or burnout, of fatigue.

Warren Ellis, as a writer, can be fierce about a multitude of things, yet one suspects that he is fiercest when it comes to his demands upon himself, on his insistence to push into something new, something that has not yet had time to bore him. With his work on *Planetary*, you can feel the burn, the struggle and the surge of invention, the desire to render each new concept sharper, more incendiary than the last, all this delivered with a fine ear for the nuances of dialogue and laguage, a fine eye for the dramatic situation and a sly and morbid sense of humour.

Luckily for Ellis, he's abetted by the opalescent talents of John Cassaday, an artist capable of stunningly imaginative vistas, costumes and constructions, all accomplished with a line combining strength and an almost ethereal delicacy. Cassaday seems almost to be in a both dynamic and productive rivalry with his writer, each one striving to outdo the other with some new outrageous notion, some delineation of an idea that will take it further, pushing it across the edge into the territory of that which has not previously been conceived. The end result is an extraordinary work of hard-edged science fiction, realized by a vision that the Pauls and Finlays, the acknowledged master illustrators of the genre, would not be ashamed of.

This is an exemplary turn-of-the-century mainstream comic book. During a period when many comics seem to have lapsed into an exhausted mire or else go blundering on ahead without the merest shred of a coherent plan, the work in *Planetary* has a glow and freshness that is all its own, a signature eruption of the neurons into novel, interesting patterns at the turn of each new page. It is at once concerned with everything that comics were and everything that comics could be, all condensed into a perfect jewelled and fractal snowflake. Read on and enjoy the remarkable comic book product of a remarkable comic book moment. And think *Planetary*.

— Alan Moore
Northampton
Dec. 14, 1999

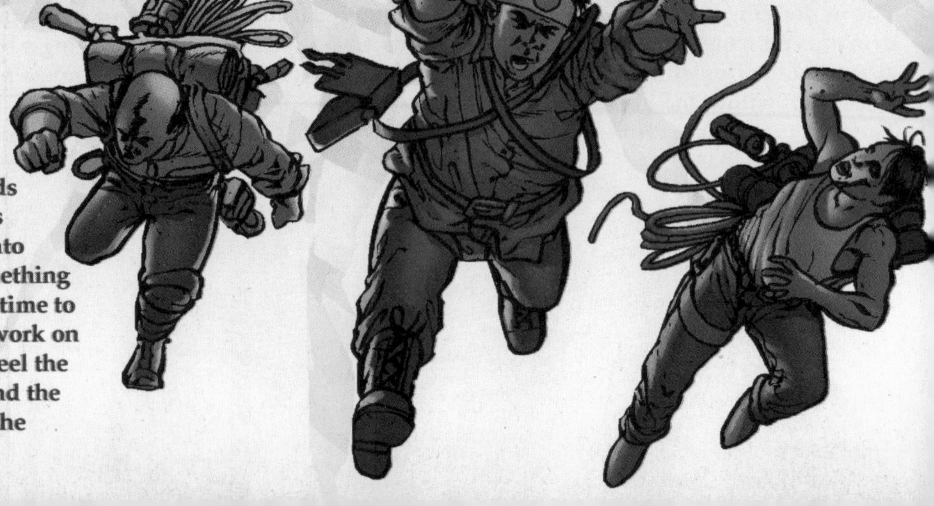

行っけ!!

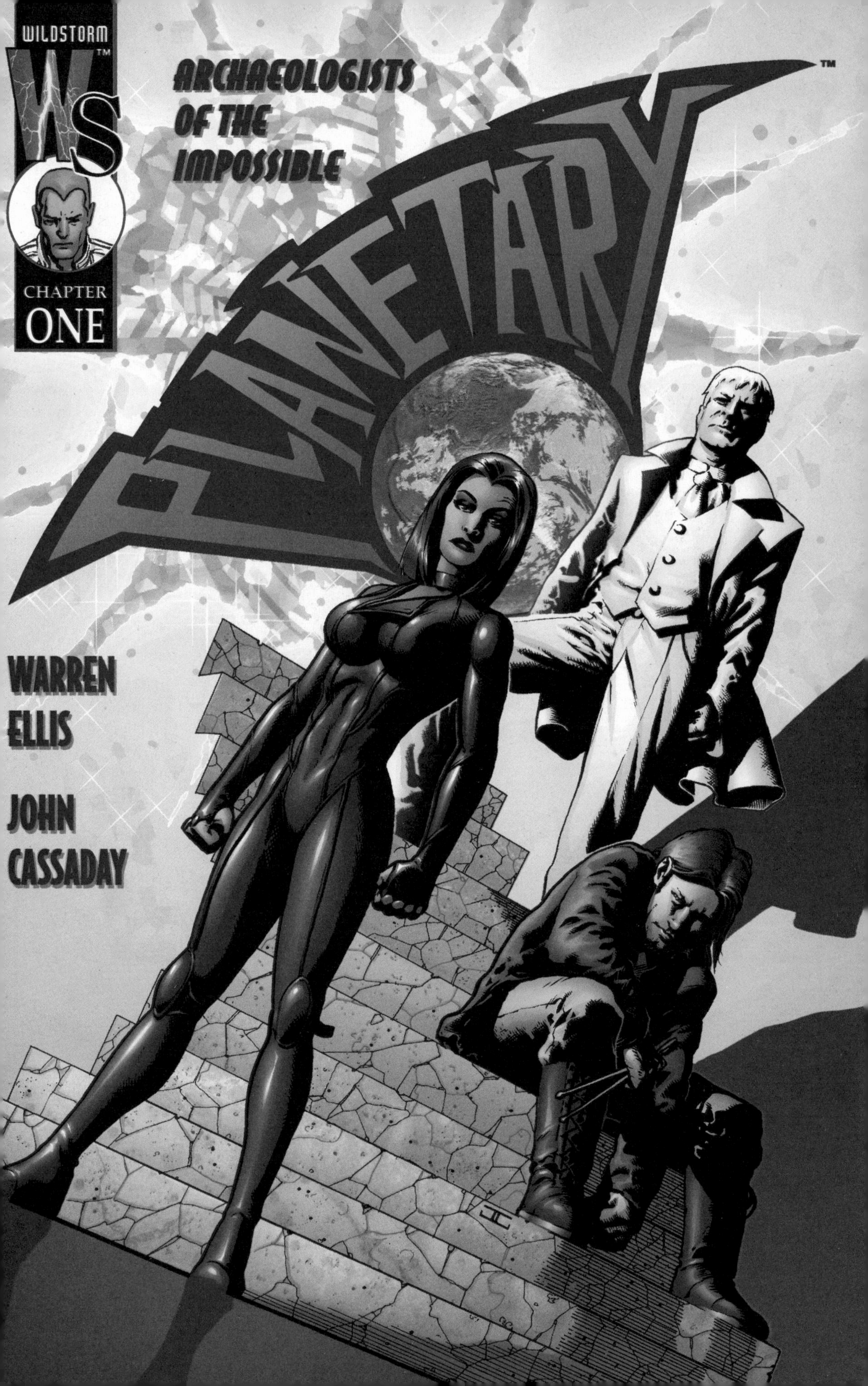
WILDSTORM
WS
CHAPTER ONE
ARCHAEOLOGISTS OF THE IMPOSSIBLE
PLANETARY
WARREN ELLIS
JOHN CASSADAY

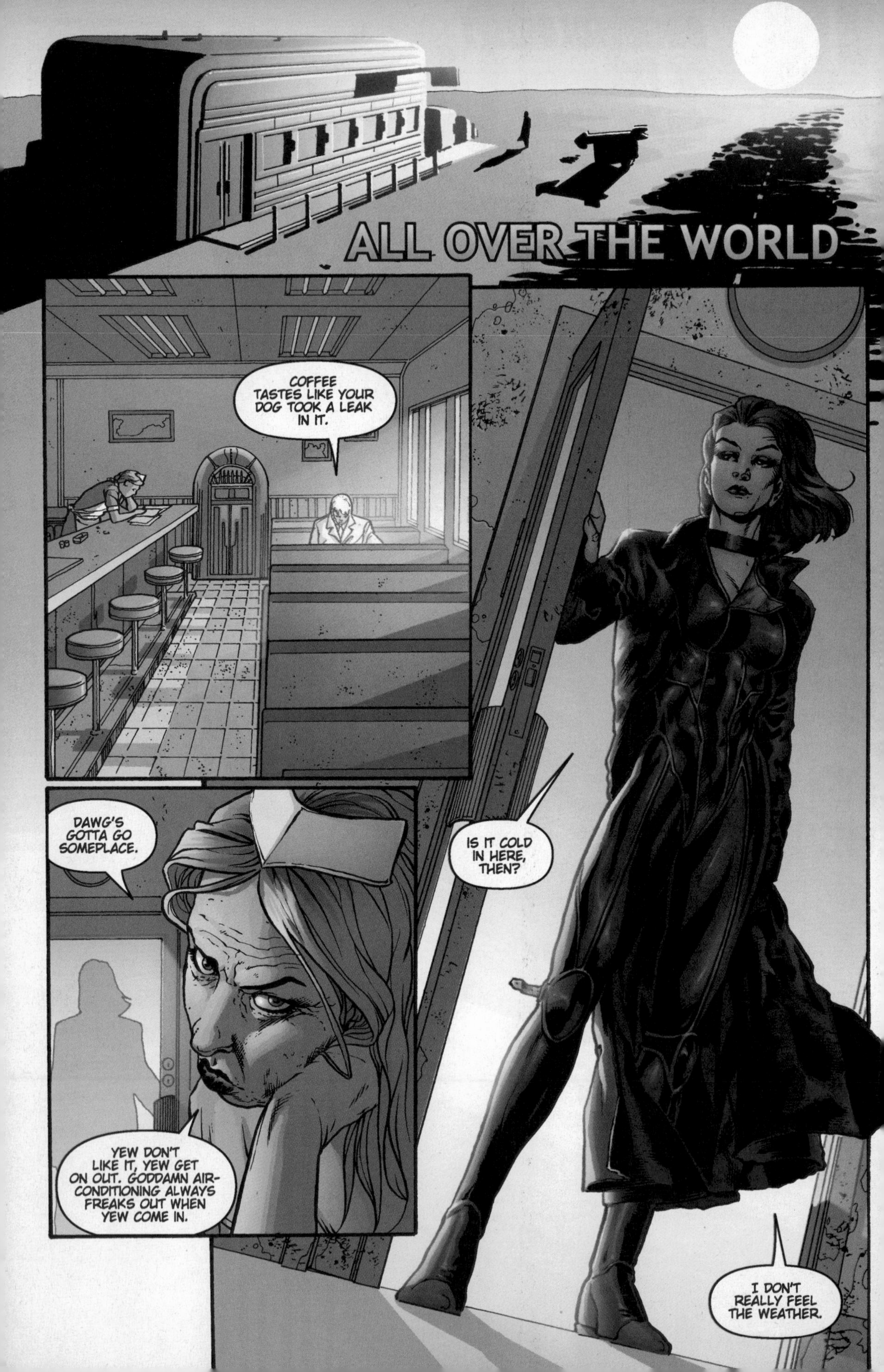
ALL OVER THE WORLD
COFFEE TASTES LIKE YOUR DOG TOOK A LEAK IN IT.
DAWG'S GOTTA GO SOMEPLACE.
YEW DON'T LIKE IT, YEW GET ON OUT. GODDAMN AIR-CONDITIONING ALWAYS FREAKS OUT WHEN YEW COME IN.
IS IT COLD IN HERE, THEN?
I DON'T REALLY FEEL THE WEATHER.

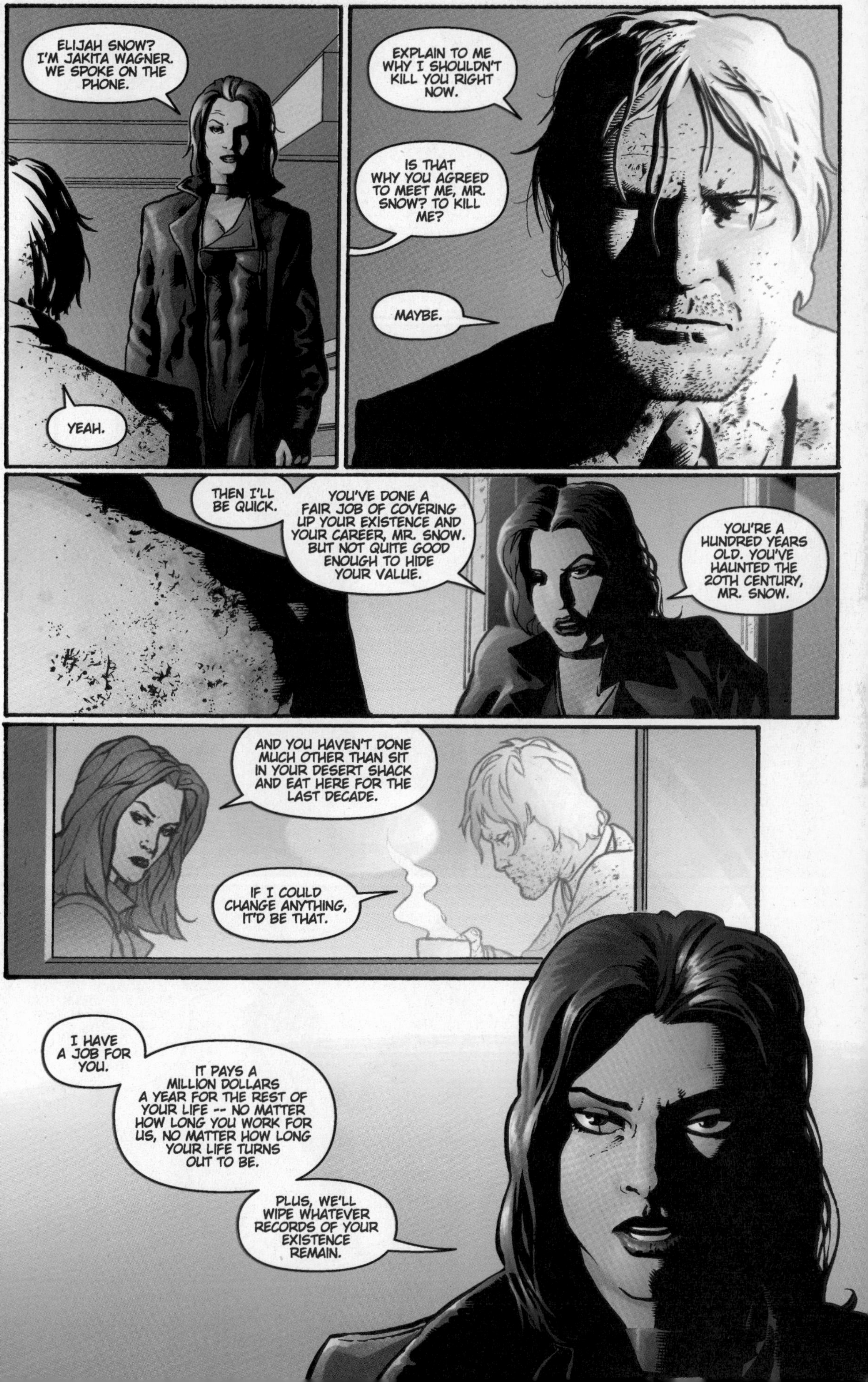
ELIJAH SNOW? I'M JAKITA WAGNER. WE SPOKE ON THE PHONE.
YEAH.
EXPLAIN TO ME WHY I SHOULDN'T KILL YOU RIGHT NOW.
IS THAT WHY YOU AGREED TO MEET ME, MR. SNOW? TO KILL ME?
MAYBE.
THEN I'LL BE QUICK.
YOU'VE DONE A FAIR JOB OF COVERING UP YOUR EXISTENCE AND YOUR CAREER, MR. SNOW. BUT NOT QUITE GOOD ENOUGH TO HIDE YOUR VALUE.
YOU'RE A HUNDRED YEARS OLD. YOU'VE HAUNTED THE 20TH CENTURY, MR. SNOW.
AND YOU HAVEN'T DONE MUCH OTHER THAN SIT IN YOUR DESERT SHACK AND EAT HERE FOR THE LAST DECADE.
IF I COULD CHANGE ANYTHING, IT'D BE THAT.
I HAVE A JOB FOR YOU.
IT PAYS A MILLION DOLLARS A YEAR FOR THE REST OF YOUR LIFE -- NO MATTER HOW LONG YOU WORK FOR US, NO MATTER HOW LONG YOUR LIFE TURNS OUT TO BE.
PLUS, WE'LL WIPE WHATEVER RECORDS OF YOUR EXISTENCE REMAIN.

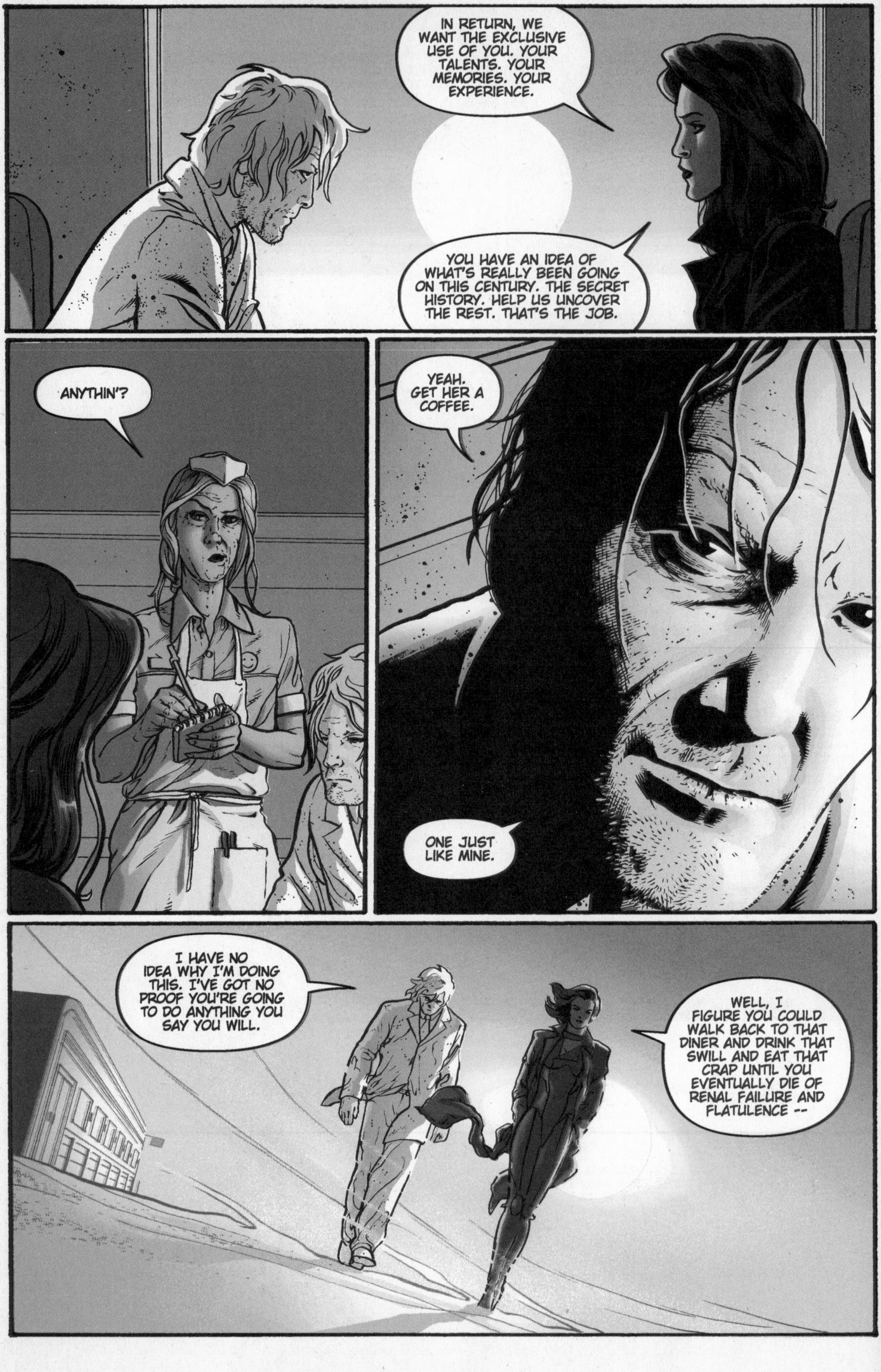
IN RETURN, WE WANT THE EXCLUSIVE USE OF YOU. YOUR TALENTS. YOUR MEMORIES. YOUR EXPERIENCE.
YOU HAVE AN IDEA OF WHAT'S REALLY BEEN GOING ON THIS CENTURY. THE SECRET HISTORY. HELP US UNCOVER THE REST. THAT'S THE JOB.
ANYTHIN'?
YEAH. GET HER A COFFEE.
ONE JUST LIKE MINE.
I HAVE NO IDEA WHY I'M DOING THIS. I'VE GOT NO PROOF YOU'RE GOING TO DO ANYTHING YOU SAY YOU WILL.
WELL, I FIGURE YOU COULD WALK BACK TO THAT DINER AND DRINK THAT SWILL AND EAT THAT CRAP UNTIL YOU EVENTUALLY DIE OF RENAL FAILURE AND FLATULENCE --

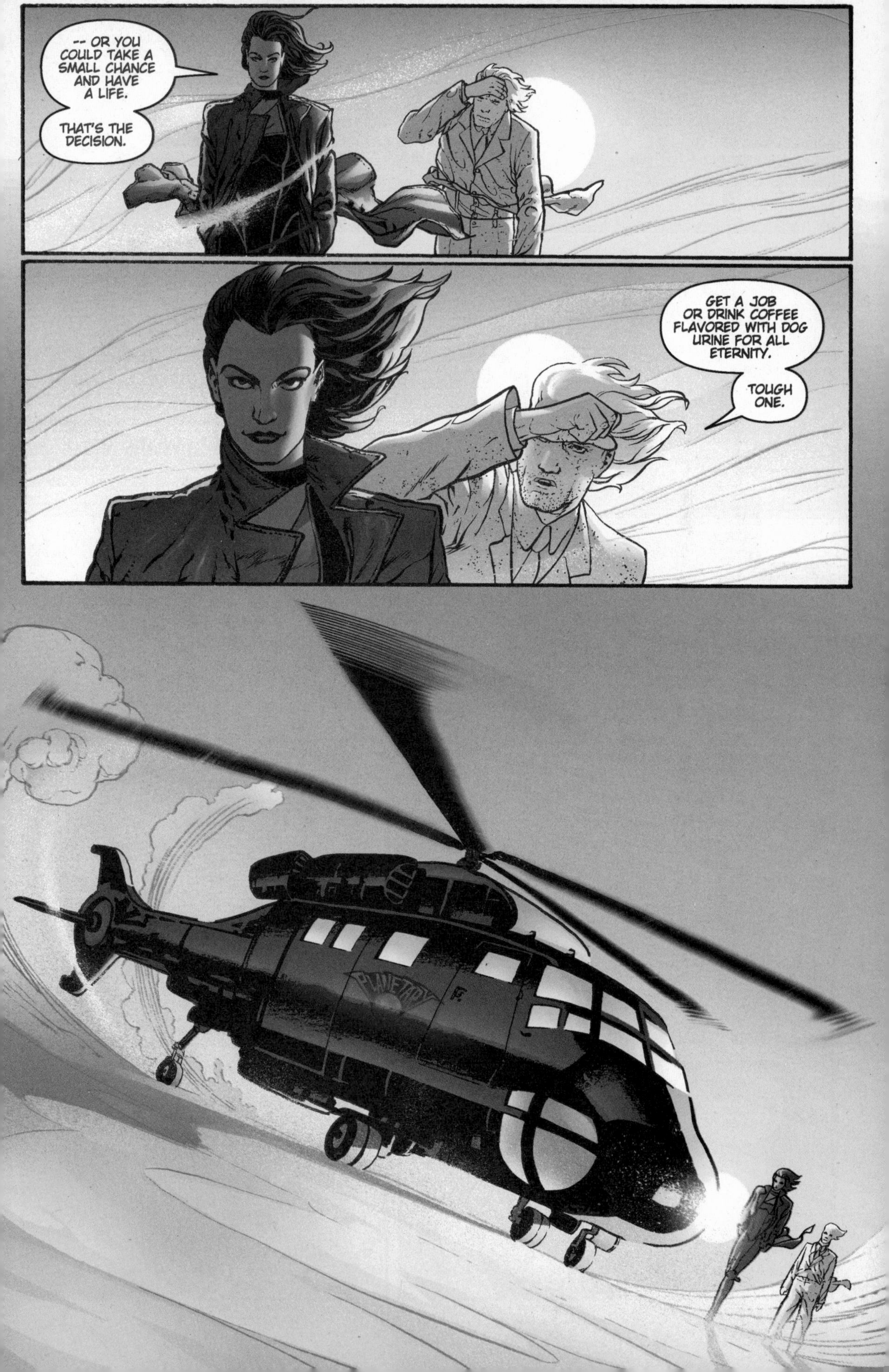
-- OR YOU COULD TAKE A SMALL CHANCE AND HAVE A LIFE.
THAT'S THE DECISION.
GET A JOB OR DRINK COFFEE FLAVORED WITH DOG URINE FOR ALL ETERNITY.
TOUGH ONE.

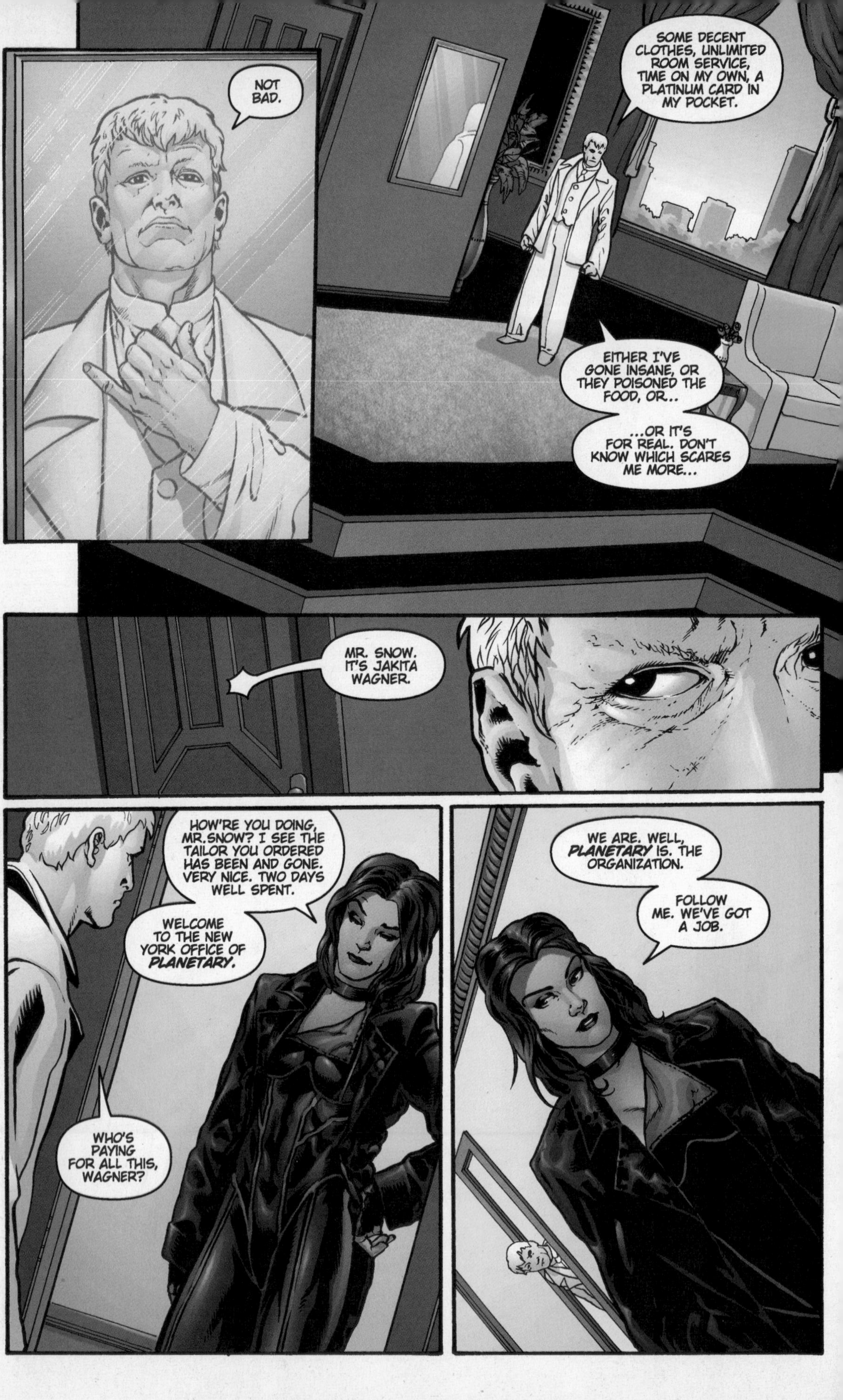
NOT BAD.
SOME DECENT CLOTHES, UNLIMITED ROOM SERVICE, TIME ON MY OWN, A PLATINUM CARD IN MY POCKET.
EITHER I'VE GONE INSANE, OR THEY POISONED THE FOOD, OR..
...OR IT'S FOR REAL. DON'T KNOW WHICH SCARES ME MORE...
MR. SNOW. IT'S JAKITA WAGNER.
HOW'RE YOU DOING, MR.SNOW? I SEE THE TAILOR YOU ORDERED HAS BEEN AND GONE. VERY NICE. TWO DAYS WELL SPENT.
WELCOME TO THE NEW YORK OFFICE OF *PLANETARY*.
WHO'S PAYING FOR ALL THIS, WAGNER?
WE ARE. WELL, *PLANETARY* IS. THE ORGANIZATION.
FOLLOW ME. WE'VE GOT A JOB.

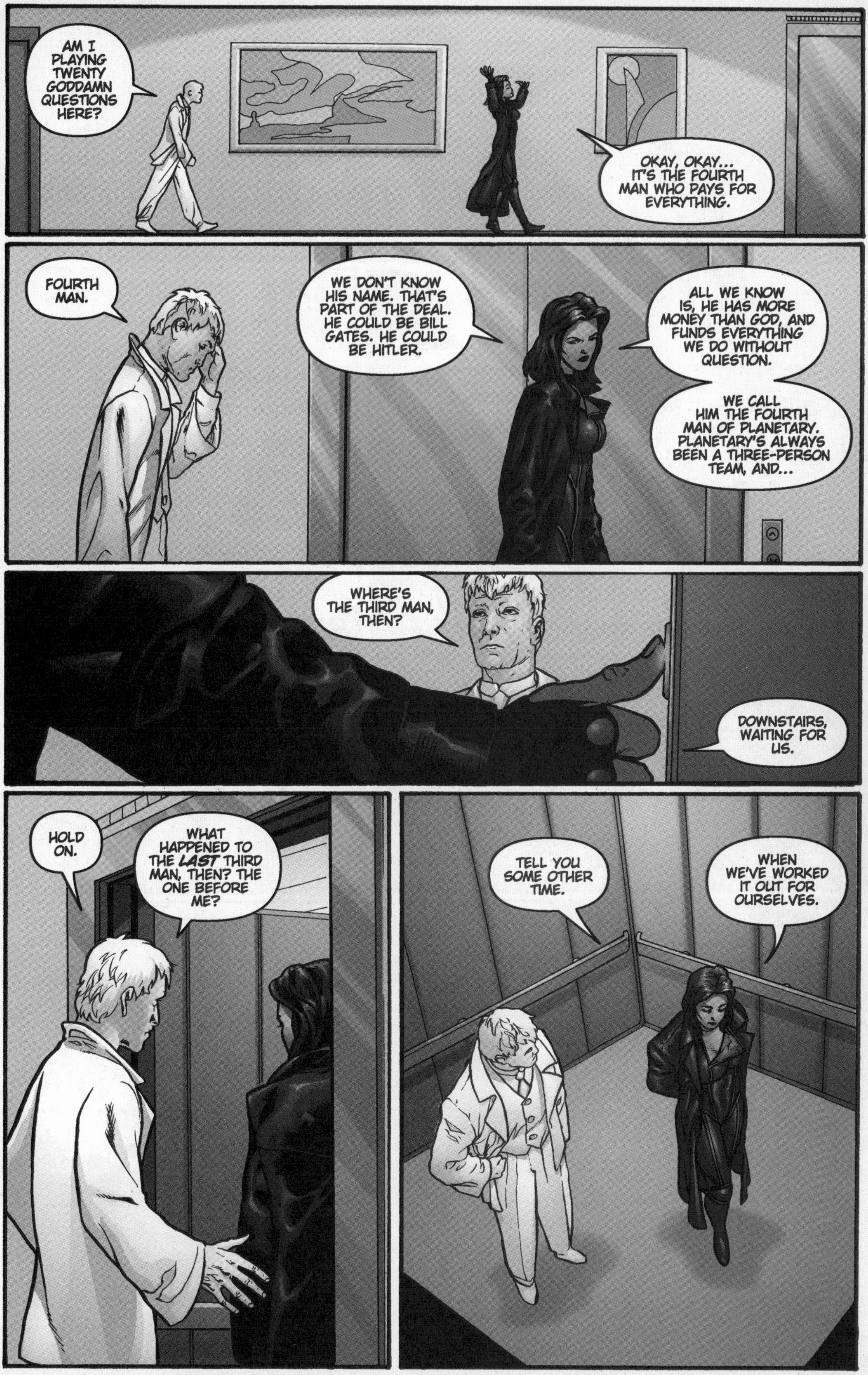
AM I PLAYING TWENTY GODDAMN QUESTIONS HERE?
OKAY, OKAY... IT'S THE FOURTH MAN WHO PAYS FOR EVERYTHING.
FOURTH MAN.
WE DON'T KNOW HIS NAME. THAT'S PART OF THE DEAL. HE COULD BE BILL GATES. HE COULD BE HITLER.
ALL WE KNOW IS, HE HAS MORE MONEY THAN GOD, AND FUNDS EVERYTHING WE DO WITHOUT QUESTION.
WE CALL HIM THE FOURTH MAN OF PLANETARY. PLANETARY'S ALWAYS BEEN A THREE-PERSON TEAM, AND...
WHERE'S THE THIRD MAN, THEN?
DOWNSTAIRS, WAITING FOR US.
HOLD ON.
WHAT HAPPENED TO THE *LAST* THIRD MAN, THEN? THE ONE BEFORE ME?
TELL YOU SOME OTHER TIME.
WHEN WE'VE WORKED IT OUT FOR OURSELVES.

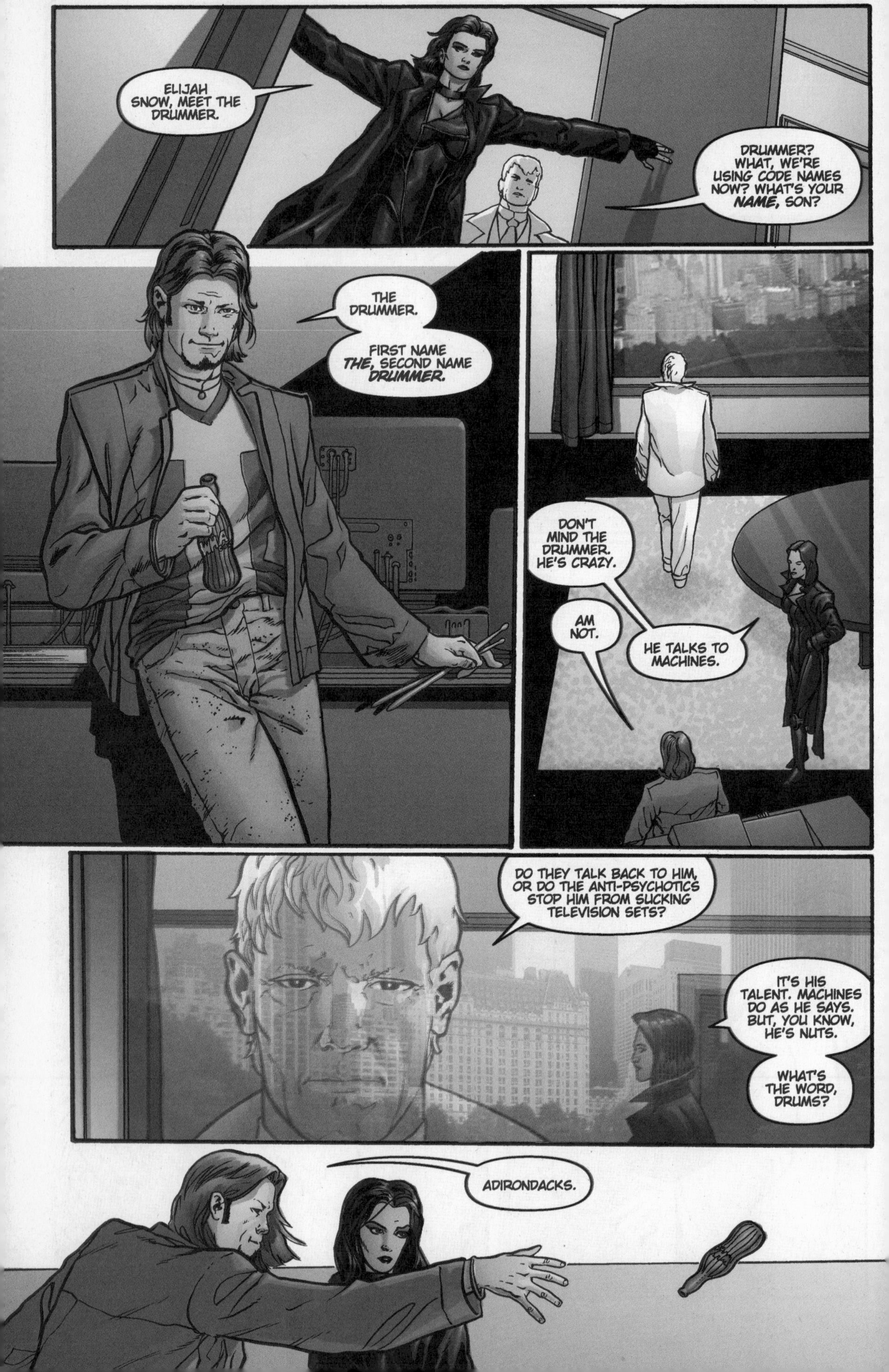
ELIJAH SNOW, MEET THE DRUMMER.
DRUMMER? WHAT, WE'RE USING CODE NAMES NOW? WHAT'S YOUR NAME, SON?
THE DRUMMER.
FIRST NAME THE, SECOND NAME DRUMMER.
DON'T MIND THE DRUMMER. HE'S CRAZY.
AM NOT.
HE TALKS TO MACHINES.
DO THEY TALK BACK TO HIM, OR DO THE ANTI-PSYCHOTICS STOP HIM FROM SUCKING TELEVISION SETS?
IT'S HIS TALENT. MACHINES DO AS HE SAYS. BUT, YOU KNOW, HE'S NUTS.
WHAT'S THE WORD, DRUMS?
ADIRONDACKS.

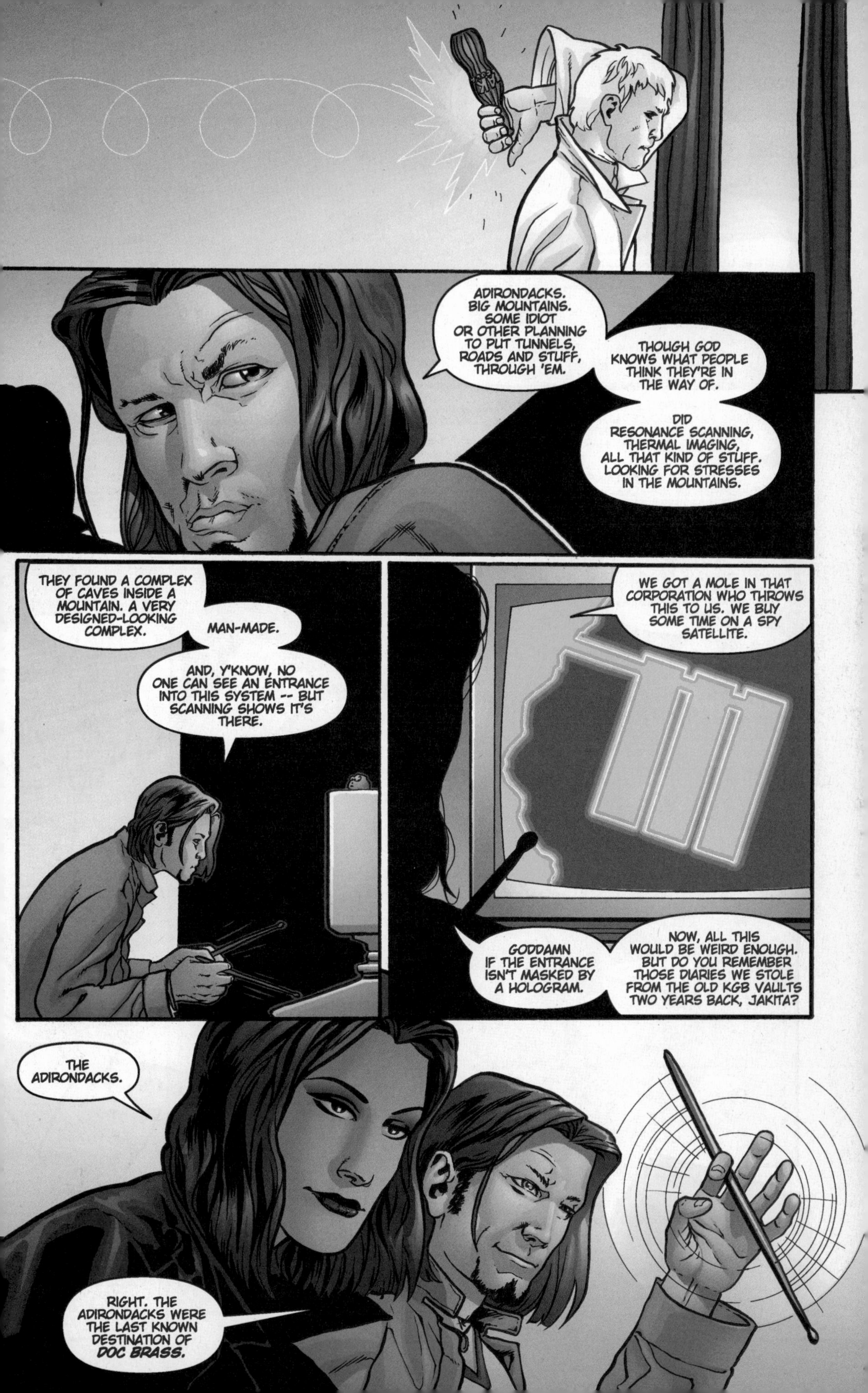
ADIRONDACKS. BIG MOUNTAINS. SOME IDIOT OR OTHER PLANNING TO PUT TUNNELS, ROADS AND STUFF, THROUGH 'EM.
THOUGH GOD KNOWS WHAT PEOPLE THINK THEY'RE IN THE WAY OF.
DID RESONANCE SCANNING, THERMAL IMAGING, ALL THAT KIND OF STUFF. LOOKING FOR STRESSES IN THE MOUNTAINS.
THEY FOUND A COMPLEX OF CAVES INSIDE A MOUNTAIN. A VERY DESIGNED-LOOKING COMPLEX.
MAN-MADE.
AND, Y'KNOW, NO ONE CAN SEE AN ENTRANCE INTO THIS SYSTEM -- BUT SCANNING SHOWS IT'S THERE.
WE GOT A MOLE IN THAT CORPORATION WHO THROWS THIS TO US. WE BUY SOME TIME ON A SPY SATELLITE.
GODDAMN IF THE ENTRANCE ISN'T MASKED BY A HOLOGRAM.
NOW, ALL THIS WOULD BE WEIRD ENOUGH. BUT DO YOU REMEMBER THOSE DIARIES WE STOLE FROM THE OLD KGB VAULTS TWO YEARS BACK, JAKITA?
THE ADIRONDACKS.
RIGHT. THE ADIRONDACKS WERE THE LAST KNOWN DESTINATION OF DOC BRASS.

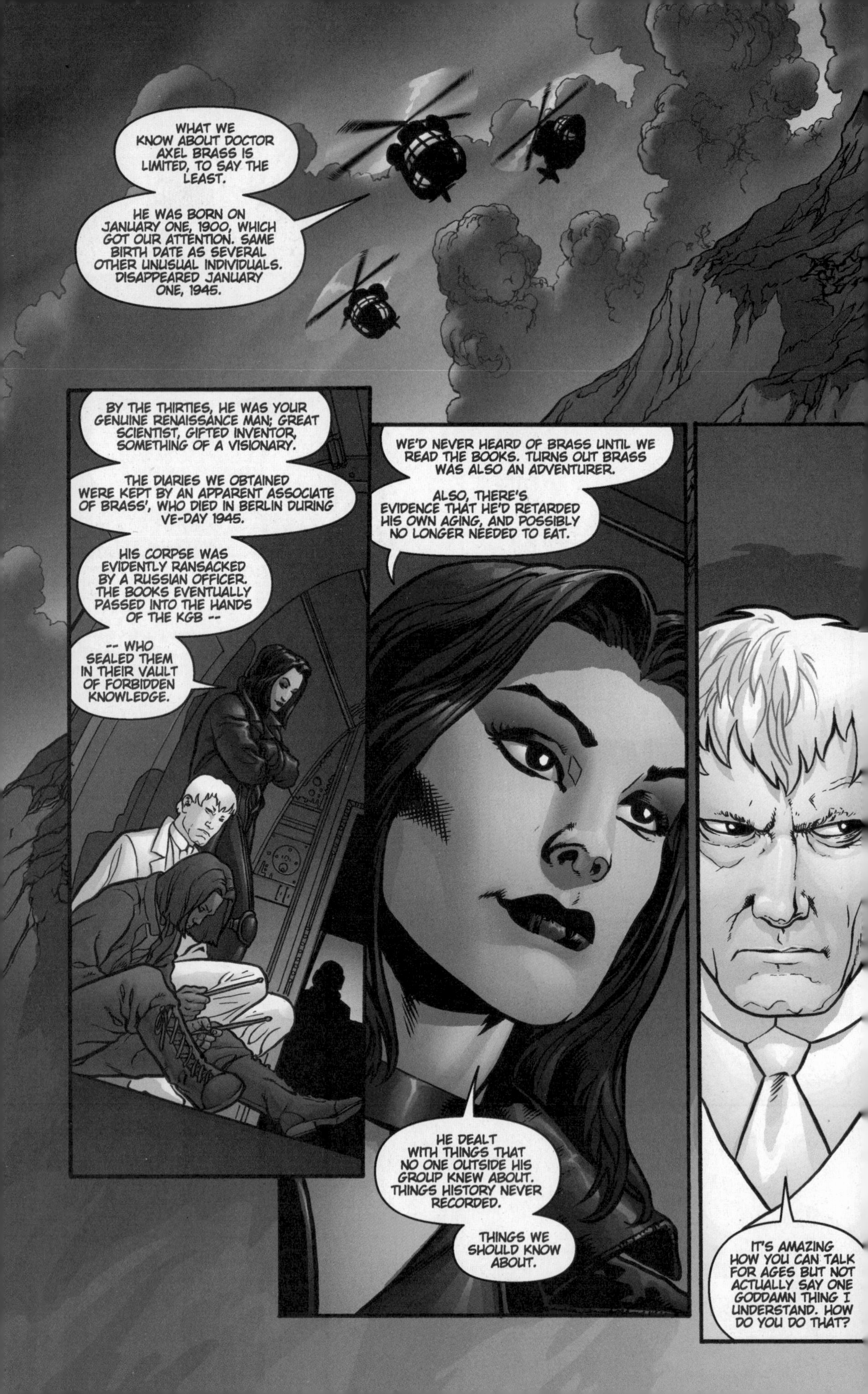

WHAT WE KNOW ABOUT DOCTOR AXEL BRASS IS LIMITED, TO SAY THE LEAST.
HE WAS BORN ON JANUARY ONE, 1900, WHICH GOT OUR ATTENTION. SAME BIRTH DATE AS SEVERAL OTHER UNUSUAL INDIVIDUALS. DISAPPEARED JANUARY ONE, 1945.
BY THE THIRTIES, HE WAS YOUR GENUINE RENAISSANCE MAN; GREAT SCIENTIST, GIFTED INVENTOR, SOMETHING OF A VISIONARY.
THE DIARIES WE OBTAINED WERE KEPT BY AN APPARENT ASSOCIATE OF BRASS', WHO DIED IN BERLIN DURING VE-DAY 1945.
HIS CORPSE WAS EVIDENTLY RANSACKED BY A RUSSIAN OFFICER. THE BOOKS EVENTUALLY PASSED INTO THE HANDS OF THE KGB --
-- WHO SEALED THEM IN THEIR VAULT OF FORBIDDEN KNOWLEDGE.
WE'D NEVER HEARD OF BRASS UNTIL WE READ THE BOOKS. TURNS OUT BRASS WAS ALSO AN ADVENTURER.
ALSO, THERE'S EVIDENCE THAT HE'D RETARDED HIS OWN AGING, AND POSSIBLY NO LONGER NEEDED TO EAT.
HE DEALT WITH THINGS THAT NO ONE OUTSIDE HIS GROUP KNEW ABOUT. THINGS HISTORY NEVER RECORDED.
THINGS WE SHOULD KNOW ABOUT.
IT'S AMAZING HOW YOU CAN TALK FOR AGES BUT NOT ACTUALLY SAY ONE GODDAMN THING I UNDERSTAND. HOW DO YOU DO THAT?

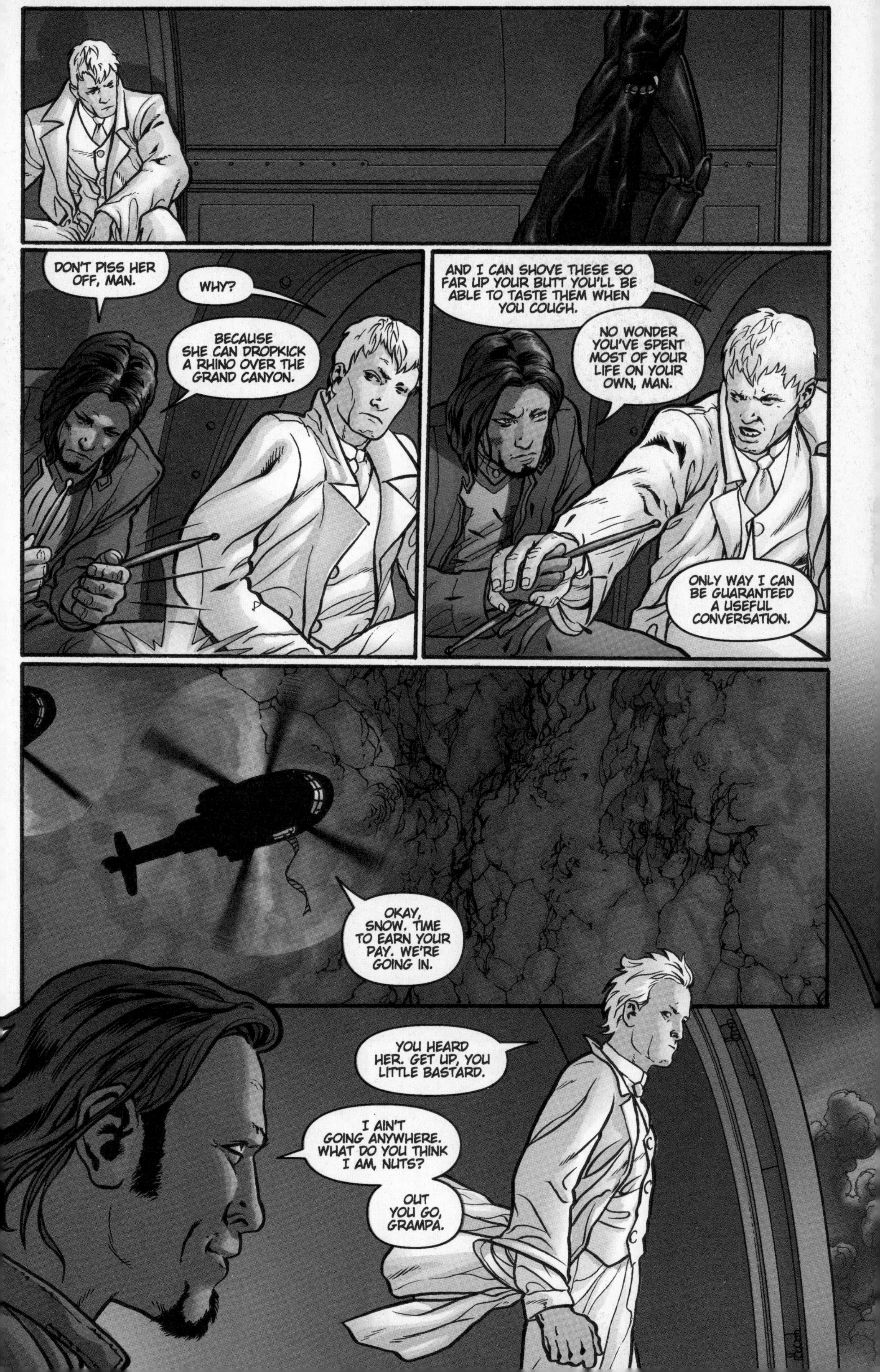
DON'T PISS HER OFF, MAN.
WHY?
BECAUSE SHE CAN DROPKICK A RHINO OVER THE GRAND CANYON.
AND I CAN SHOVE THESE SO FAR UP YOUR BUTT YOU'LL BE ABLE TO TASTE THEM WHEN YOU COUGH.
NO WONDER YOU'VE SPENT MOST OF YOUR LIFE ON YOUR OWN, MAN.
ONLY WAY I CAN BE GUARANTEED A USEFUL CONVERSATION.
OKAY, SNOW. TIME TO EARN YOUR PAY. WE'RE GOING IN.
YOU HEARD HER. GET UP, YOU LITTLE BASTARD.
I AIN'T GOING ANYWHERE. WHAT DO YOU THINK I AM, NUTS?
OUT YOU GO, GRAMPA.

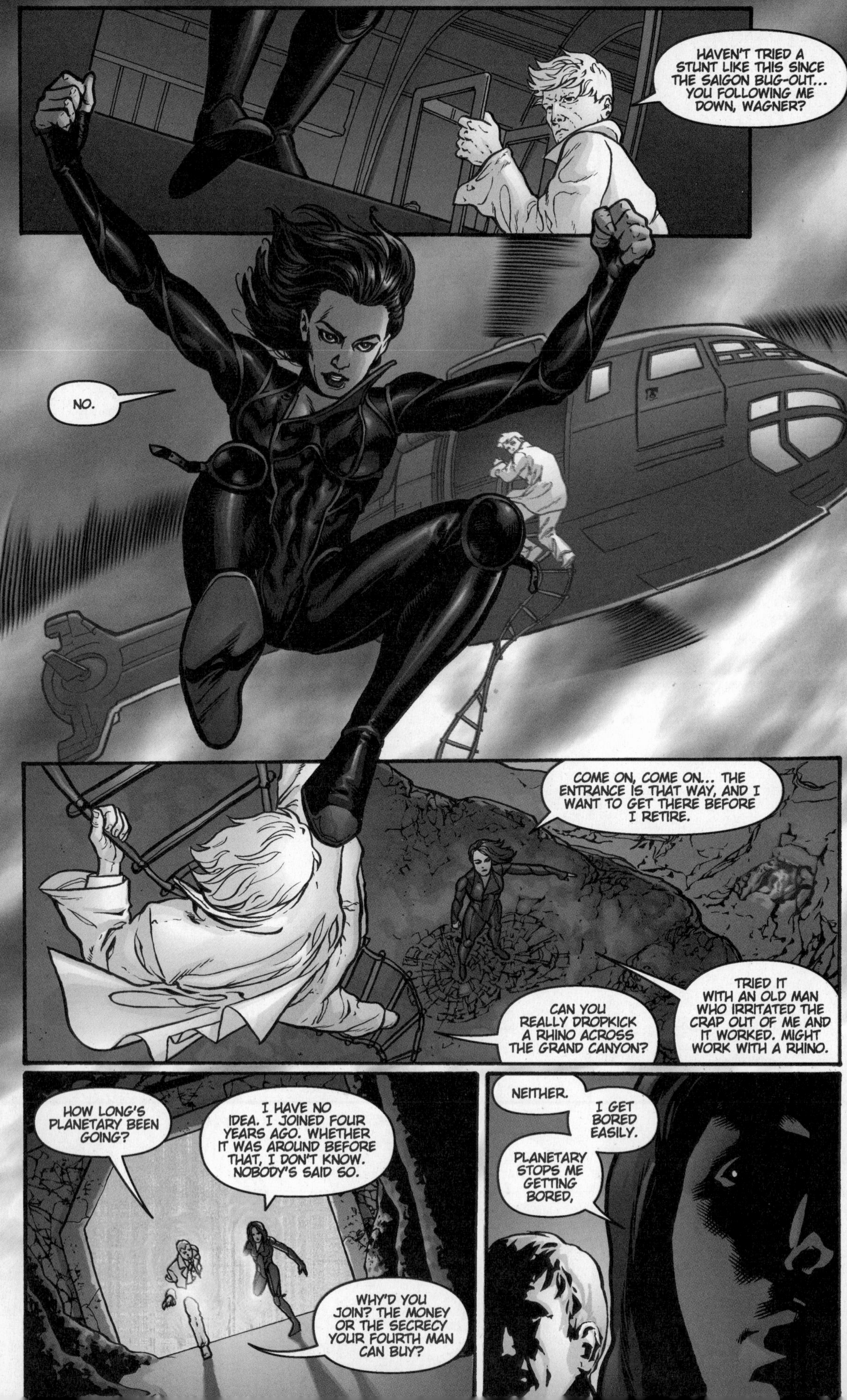
HAVEN'T TRIED A STUNT LIKE THIS SINCE THE SAIGON BUG-OUT... YOU FOLLOWING ME DOWN, WAGNER?
NO.
COME ON, COME ON... THE ENTRANCE IS THAT WAY, AND I WANT TO GET THERE BEFORE I RETIRE.
CAN YOU REALLY DROPKICK A RHINO ACROSS THE GRAND CANYON?
TRIED IT WITH AN OLD MAN WHO IRRITATED THE CRAP OUT OF ME AND IT WORKED. MIGHT WORK WITH A RHINO.
HOW LONG'S PLANETARY BEEN GOING?
I HAVE NO IDEA. I JOINED FOUR YEARS AGO. WHETHER IT WAS AROUND BEFORE THAT, I DON'T KNOW. NOBODY'S SAID SO.
WHY'D YOU JOIN? THE MONEY OR THE SECRECY YOUR FOURTH MAN CAN BUY?
NEITHER.
I GET BORED EASILY.
PLANETARY STOPS ME GETTING BORED,

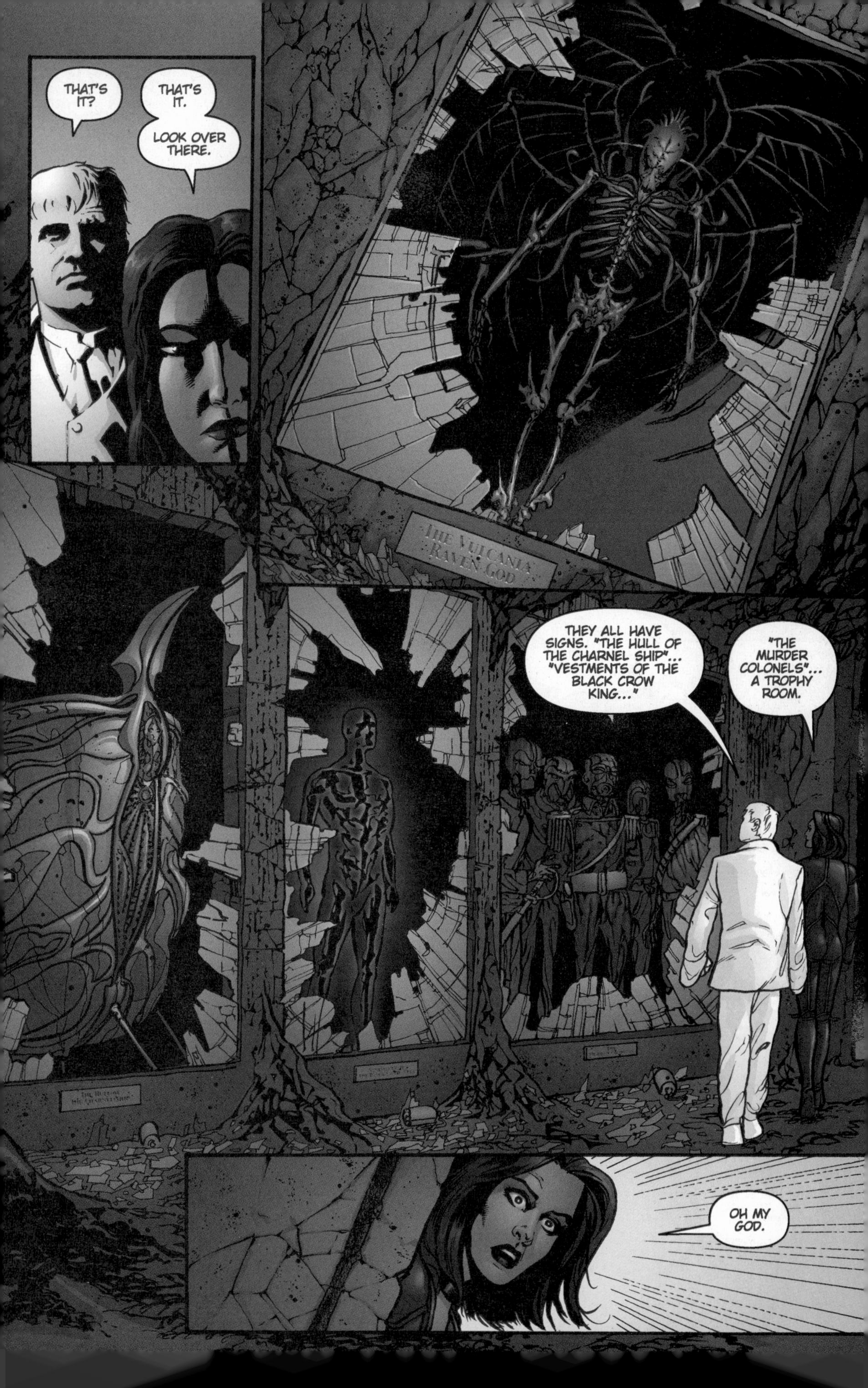
THAT'S IT?
THAT'S IT.
LOOK OVER THERE.
THE VULCANIA RAVEN GOD
THEY ALL HAVE SIGNS. "THE HULL OF THE CHARNEL SHIP"... "VESTMENTS OF THE BLACK CROW KING..."
"THE MURDER COLONELS"... A TROPHY ROOM.
OH MY GOD.

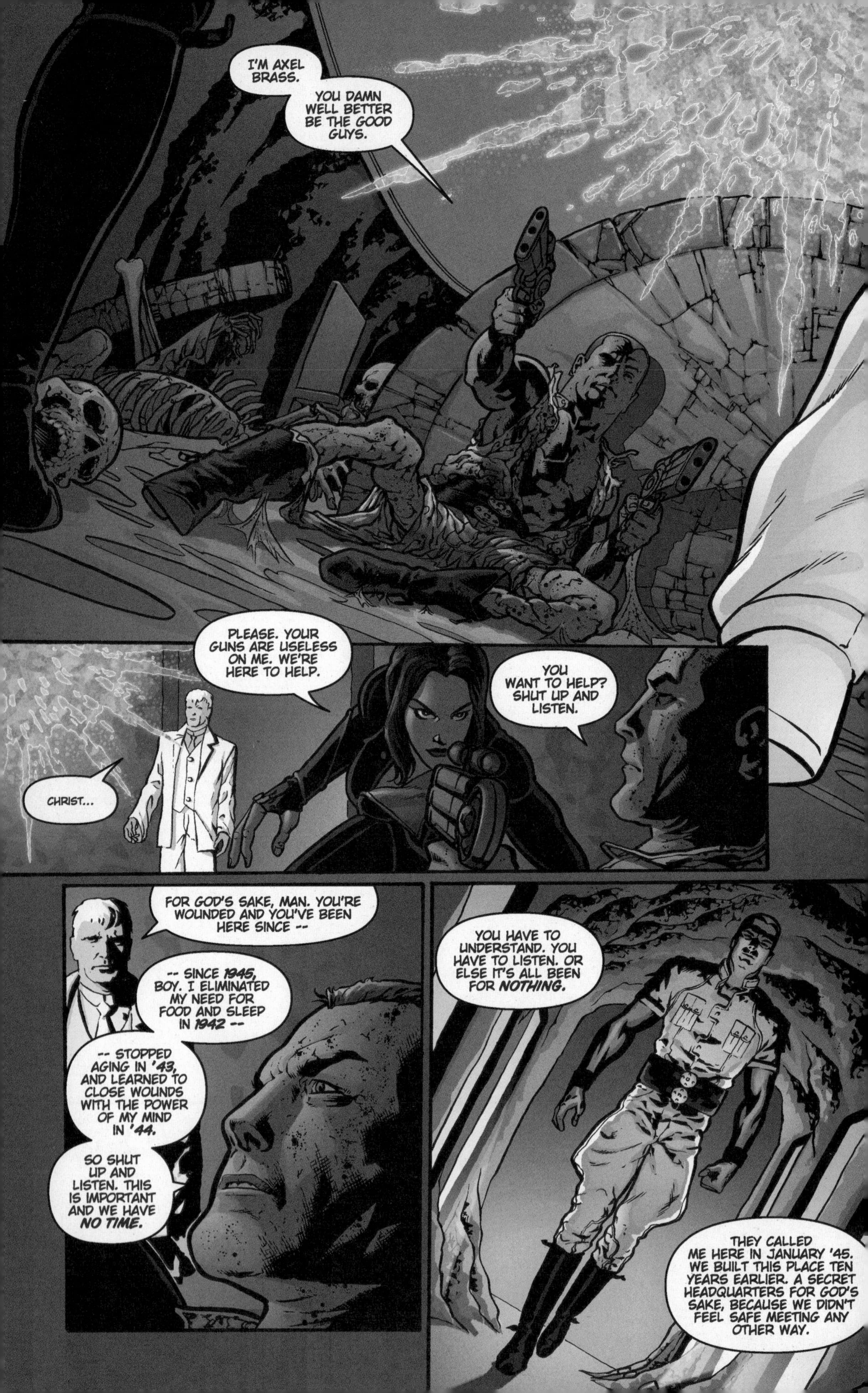
I'M AXEL BRASS.
YOU DAMN WELL BETTER BE THE GOOD GUYS.
PLEASE. YOUR GUNS ARE USELESS ON ME. WE'RE HERE TO HELP.
YOU WANT TO HELP? SHUT UP AND LISTEN.
CHRIST...
FOR GOD'S SAKE, MAN. YOU'RE WOUNDED AND YOU'VE BEEN HERE SINCE --
-- SINCE *1945*, BOY. I ELIMINATED MY NEED FOR FOOD AND SLEEP IN *1942* --
-- STOPPED AGING IN *'43*, AND LEARNED TO CLOSE WOUNDS WITH THE POWER OF MY MIND IN *'44*.
SO SHUT UP AND LISTEN. THIS IS IMPORTANT AND WE HAVE ***NO TIME***.
YOU HAVE TO UNDERSTAND. YOU HAVE TO LISTEN. OR ELSE IT'S ALL BEEN FOR ***NOTHING***.
THEY CALLED ME HERE IN JANUARY '45. WE BUILT THIS PLACE TEN YEARS EARLIER. A SECRET HEADQUARTERS FOR GOD'S SAKE, BECAUSE WE DIDN'T FEEL SAFE MEETING ANY OTHER WAY.

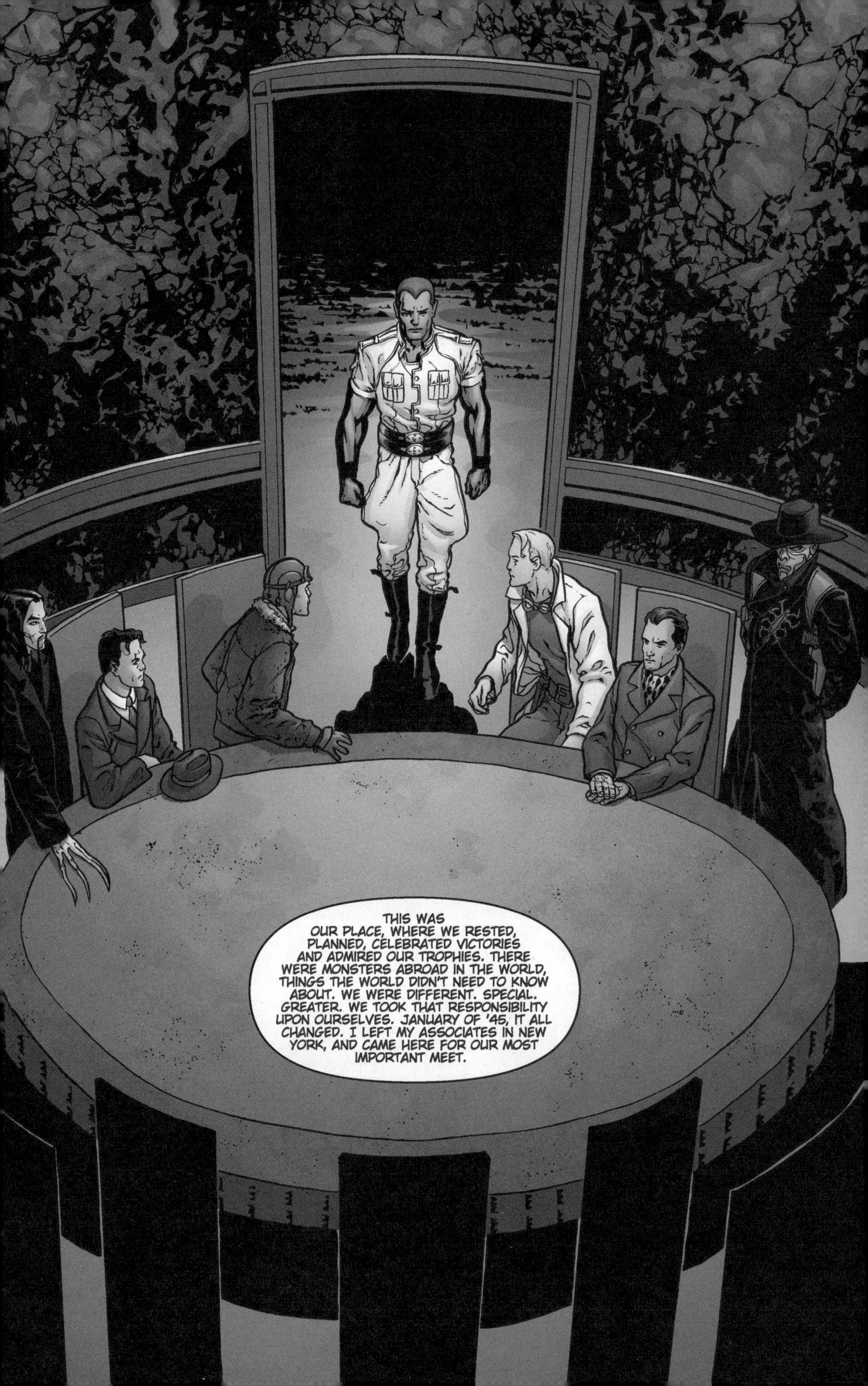
THIS WAS OUR PLACE, WHERE WE RESTED, PLANNED, CELEBRATED VICTORIES AND ADMIRED OUR TROPHIES. THERE WERE MONSTERS ABROAD IN THE WORLD, THINGS THE WORLD DIDN'T NEED TO KNOW ABOUT. WE WERE DIFFERENT. SPECIAL. GREATER. WE TOOK THAT RESPONSIBILITY UPON OURSELVES. JANUARY OF '45, IT ALL CHANGED. I LEFT MY ASSOCIATES IN NEW YORK, AND CAME HERE FOR OUR MOST IMPORTANT MEET.

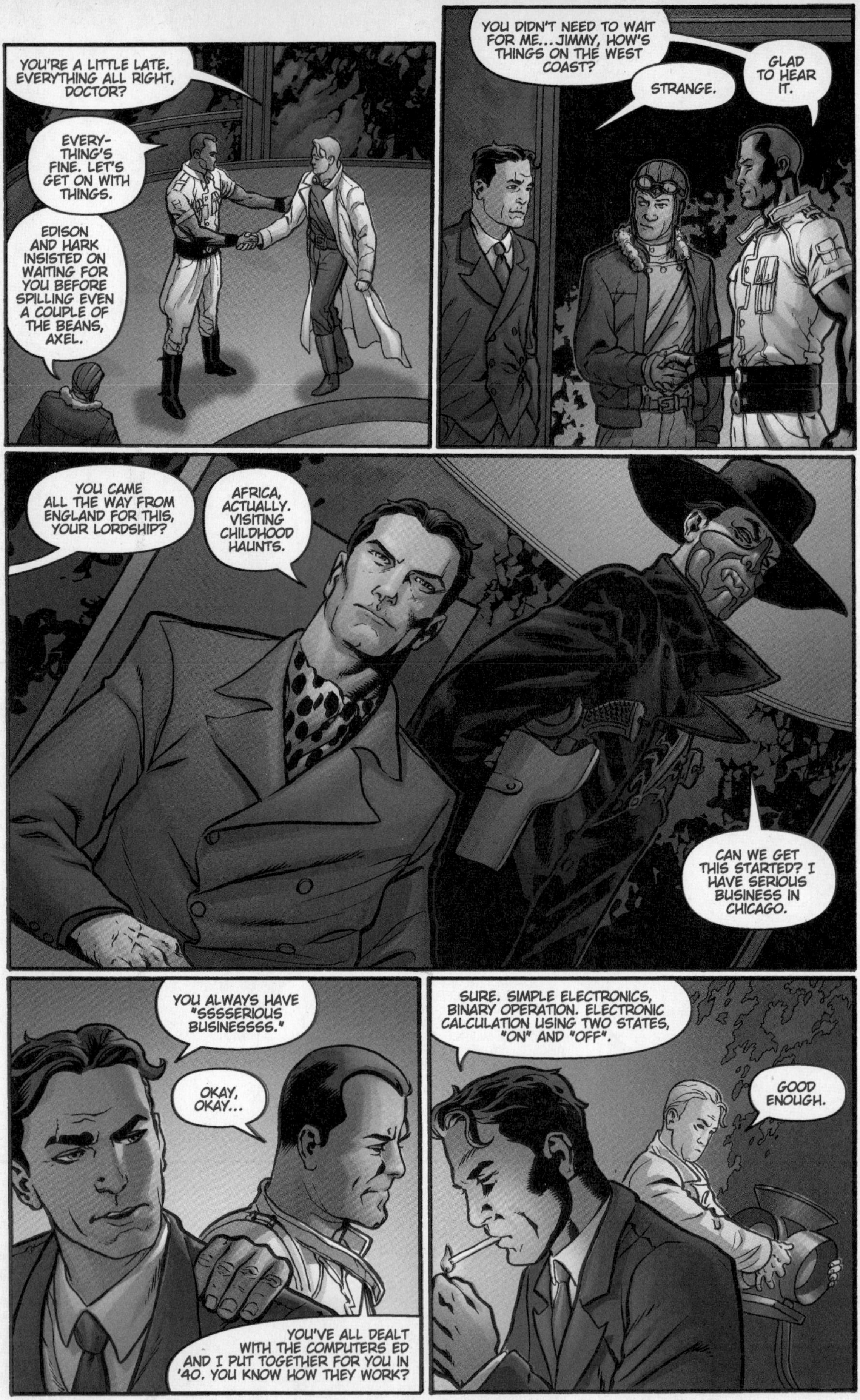
YOU'RE A LITTLE LATE. EVERYTHING ALL RIGHT, DOCTOR?
EVERY-THING'S FINE. LET'S GET ON WITH THINGS.
EDISON AND HARK INSISTED ON WAITING FOR YOU BEFORE SPILLING EVEN A COUPLE OF THE BEANS, AXEL.
YOU DIDN'T NEED TO WAIT FOR ME... JIMMY, HOW'S THINGS ON THE WEST COAST?
STRANGE.
GLAD TO HEAR IT.
YOU CAME ALL THE WAY FROM ENGLAND FOR THIS, YOUR LORDSHIP?
AFRICA, ACTUALLY. VISITING CHILDHOOD HAUNTS.
CAN WE GET THIS STARTED? I HAVE SERIOUS BUSINESS IN CHICAGO.
YOU ALWAYS HAVE "SSSSERIOUS BUSINESSSS."
OKAY, OKAY...
YOU'VE ALL DEALT WITH THE COMPUTERS ED AND I PUT TOGETHER FOR YOU IN '40. YOU KNOW HOW THEY WORK?
SURE. SIMPLE ELECTRONICS, BINARY OPERATION. ELECTRONIC CALCULATION USING TWO STATES, "ON" AND "OFF".
GOOD ENOUGH.

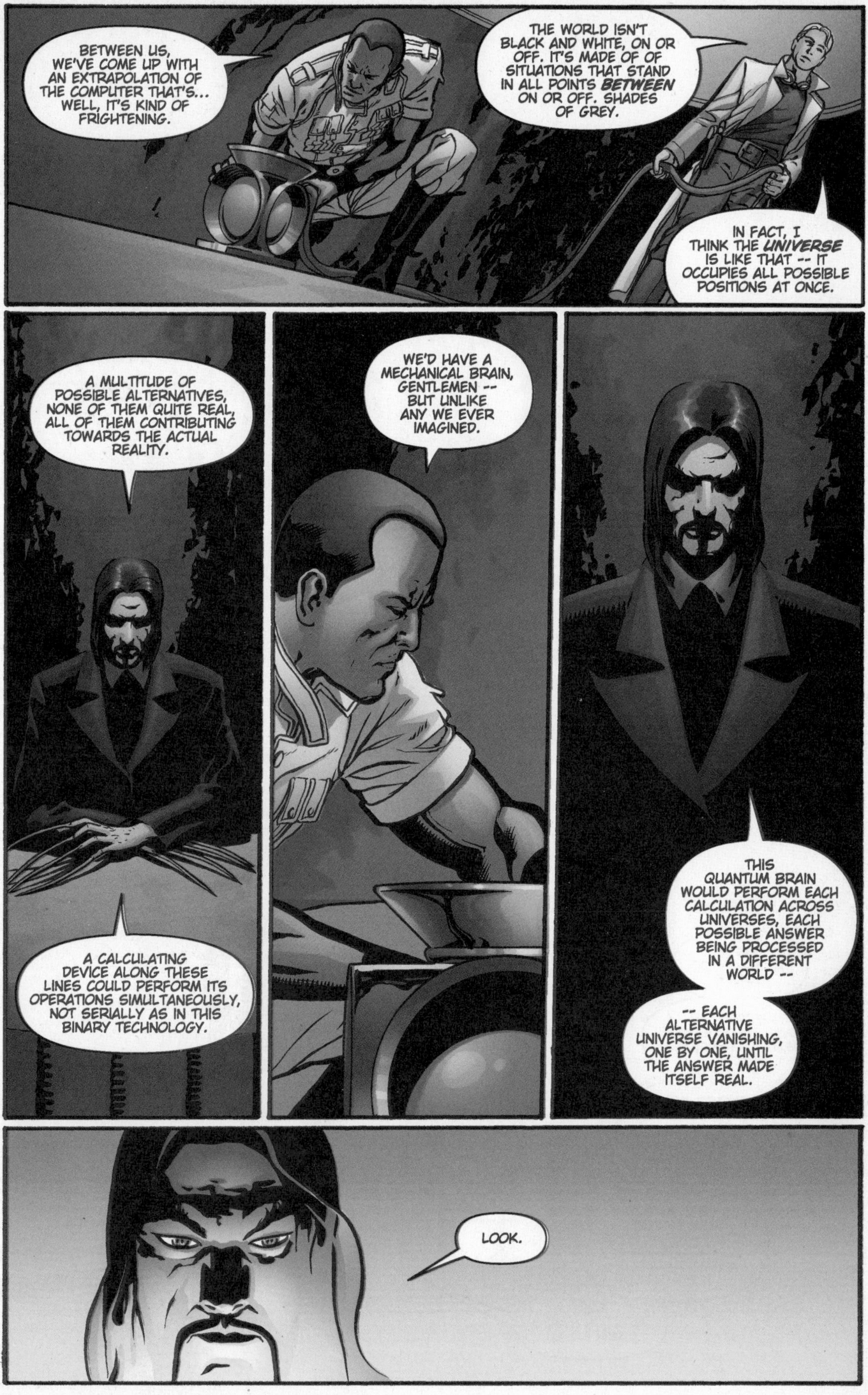
BETWEEN US, WE'VE COME UP WITH AN EXTRAPOLATION OF THE COMPUTER THAT'S... WELL, IT'S KIND OF FRIGHTENING.
THE WORLD ISN'T BLACK AND WHITE, ON OR OFF. IT'S MADE OF OF SITUATIONS THAT STAND IN ALL POINTS *BETWEEN* ON OR OFF. SHADES OF GREY.
IN FACT, I THINK THE *UNIVERSE* IS LIKE THAT -- IT OCCUPIES ALL POSSIBLE POSITIONS AT ONCE.
A MULTITUDE OF POSSIBLE ALTERNATIVES, NONE OF THEM QUITE REAL, ALL OF THEM CONTRIBUTING TOWARDS THE ACTUAL REALITY.
A CALCULATING DEVICE ALONG THESE LINES COULD PERFORM ITS OPERATIONS SIMULTANEOUSLY, NOT SERIALLY AS IN THIS BINARY TECHNOLOGY.
WE'D HAVE A MECHANICAL BRAIN, GENTLEMEN -- BUT UNLIKE ANY WE EVER IMAGINED.
THIS QUANTUM BRAIN WOULD PERFORM EACH CALCULATION ACROSS UNIVERSES, EACH POSSIBLE ANSWER BEING PROCESSED IN A DIFFERENT WORLD --
-- EACH ALTERNATIVE UNIVERSE VANISHING, ONE BY ONE, UNTIL THE ANSWER MADE ITSELF REAL.
LOOK.

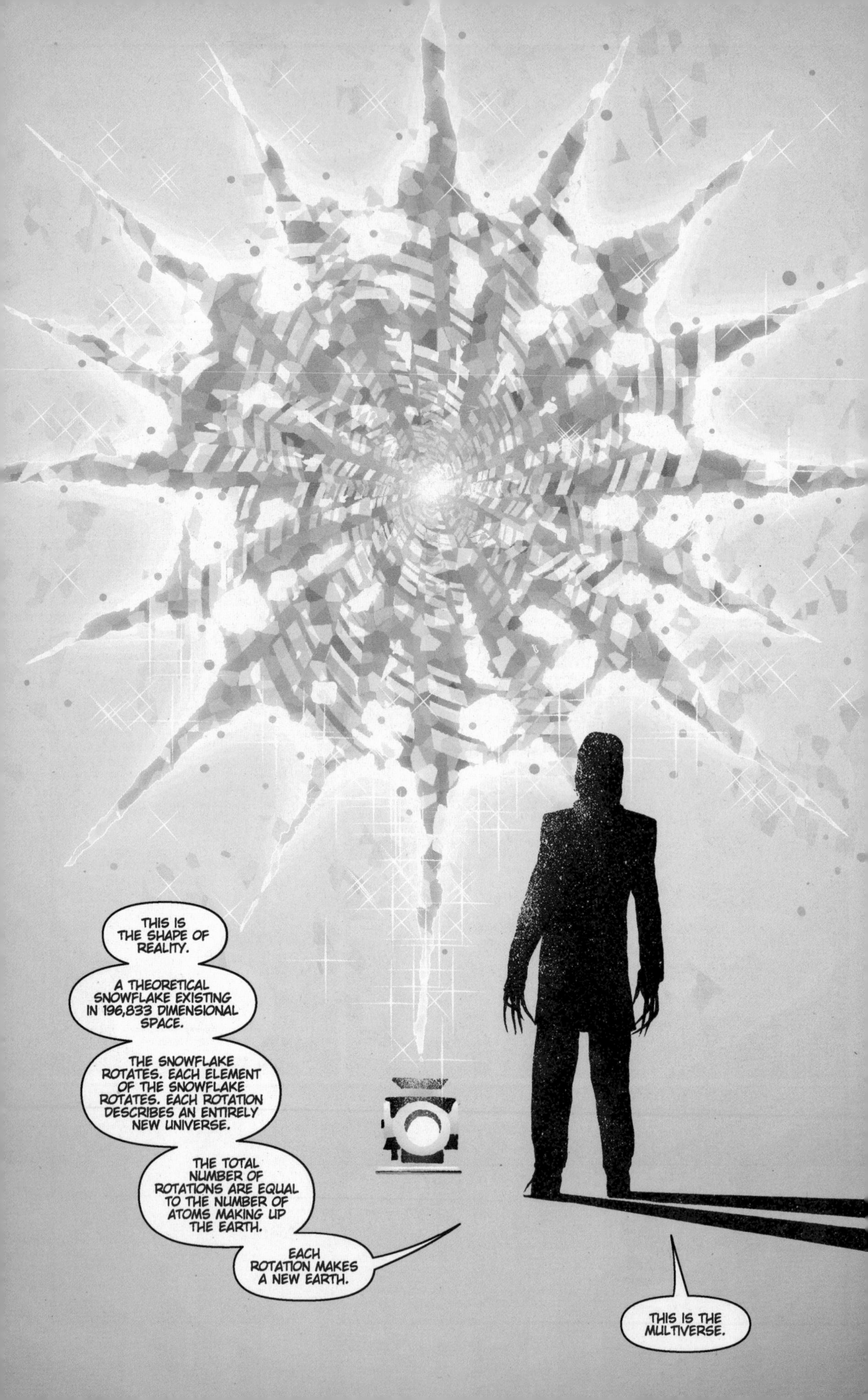
THIS IS THE SHAPE OF REALITY.
A THEORETICAL SNOWFLAKE EXISTING IN 196,833 DIMENSIONAL SPACE.
THE SNOWFLAKE ROTATES. EACH ELEMENT OF THE SNOWFLAKE ROTATES. EACH ROTATION DESCRIBES AN ENTIRELY NEW UNIVERSE.
THE TOTAL NUMBER OF ROTATIONS ARE EQUAL TO THE NUMBER OF ATOMS MAKING UP THE EARTH.
EACH ROTATION MAKES A NEW EARTH.
THIS IS THE MULTIVERSE.

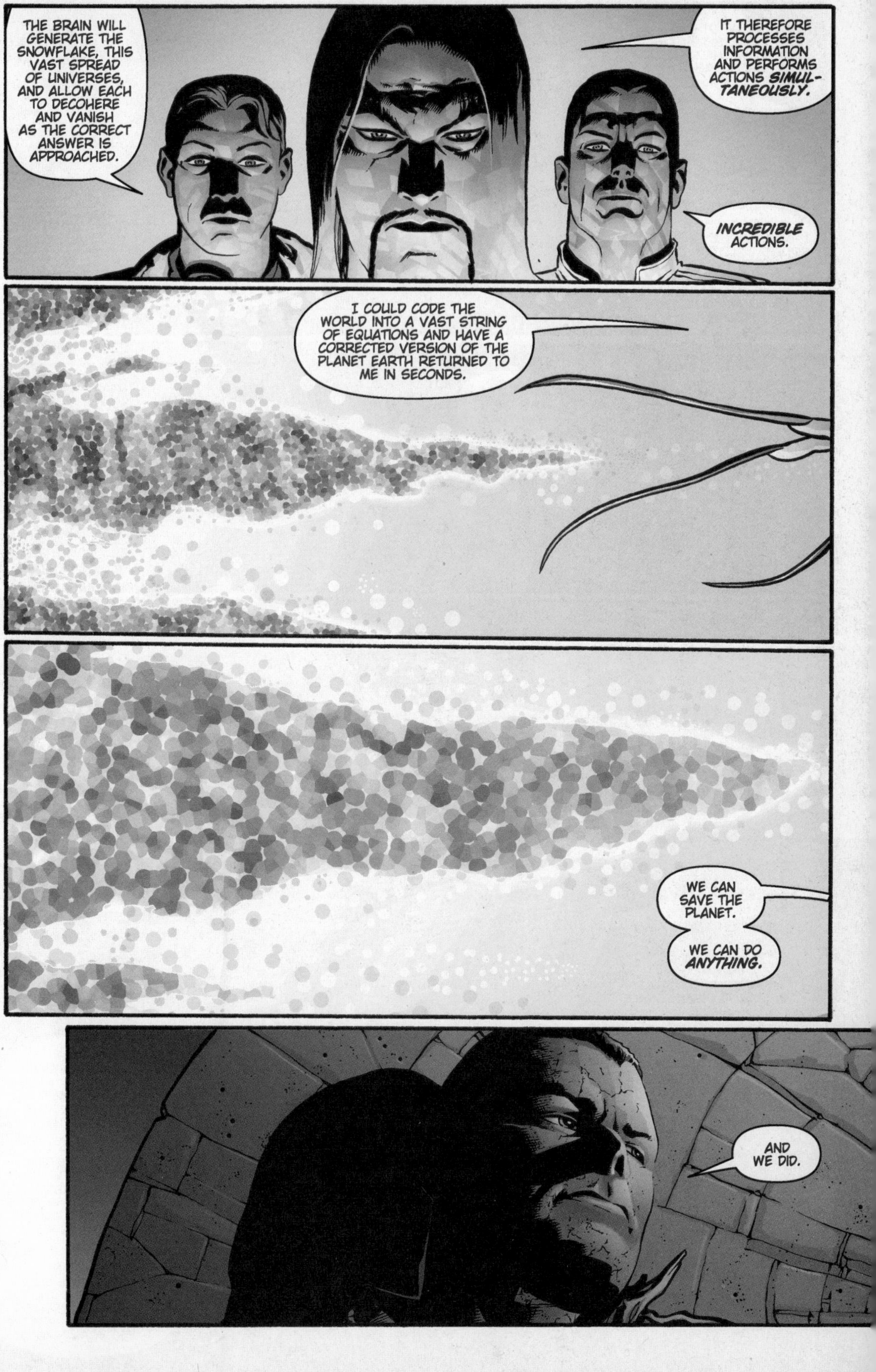
THE BRAIN WILL GENERATE THE SNOWFLAKE, THIS VAST SPREAD OF UNIVERSES, AND ALLOW EACH TO DECOHERE AND VANISH AS THE CORRECT ANSWER IS APPROACHED.
IT THEREFORE PROCESSES INFORMATION AND PERFORMS ACTIONS *SIMULTANEOUSLY.*
INCREDIBLE ACTIONS.
I COULD CODE THE WORLD INTO A VAST STRING OF EQUATIONS AND HAVE A CORRECTED VERSION OF THE PLANET EARTH RETURNED TO ME IN SECONDS.
WE CAN SAVE THE PLANET.
WE CAN DO *ANYTHING.*
AND WE DID.

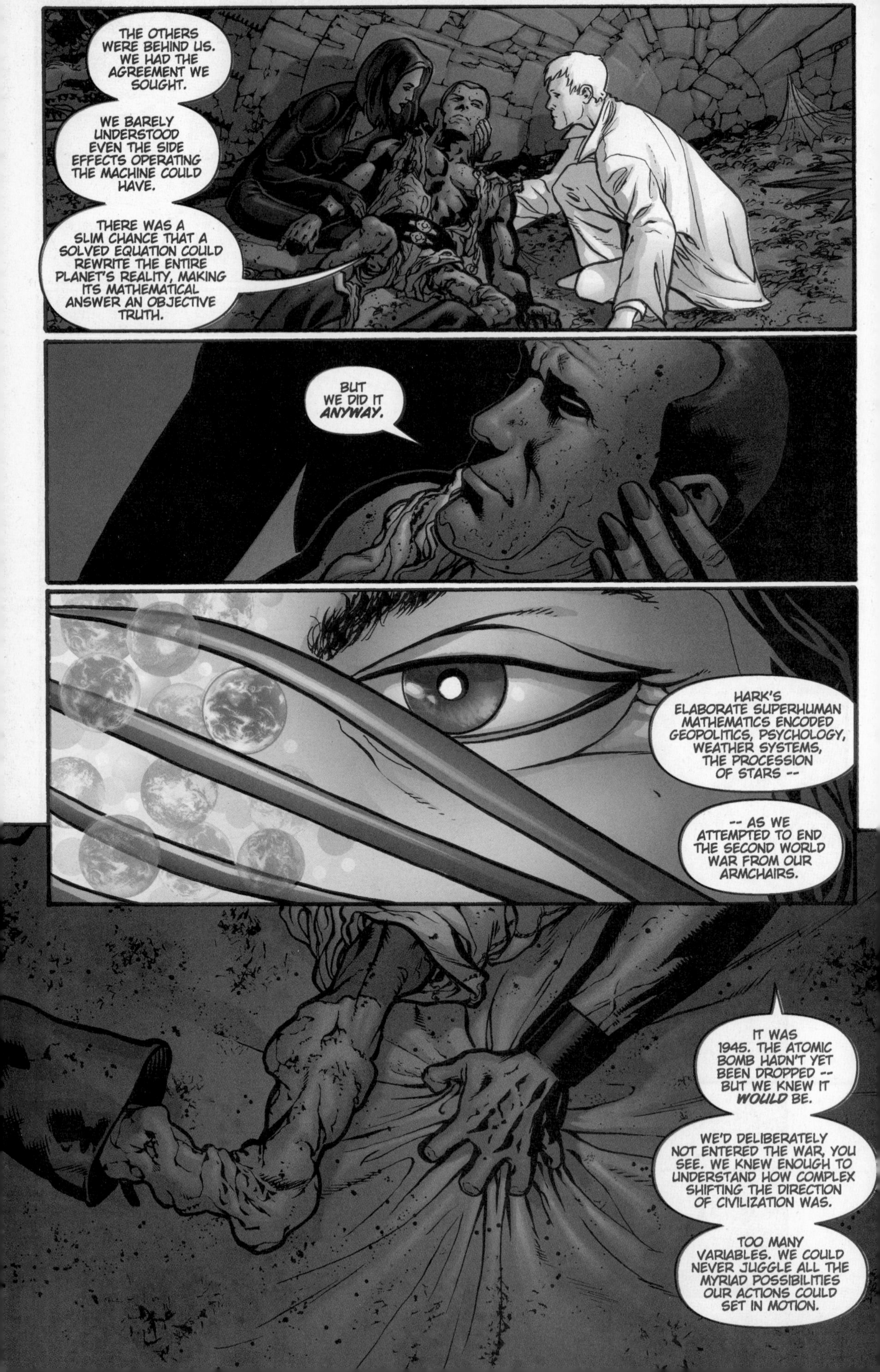
THE OTHERS WERE BEHIND US. WE HAD THE AGREEMENT WE SOUGHT.
WE BARELY UNDERSTOOD EVEN THE SIDE EFFECTS OPERATING THE MACHINE COULD HAVE.
THERE WAS A SLIM CHANCE THAT A SOLVED EQUATION COULD REWRITE THE ENTIRE PLANET'S REALITY, MAKING ITS MATHEMATICAL ANSWER AN OBJECTIVE TRUTH.
BUT WE DID IT *ANYWAY.*
HARK'S ELABORATE SUPERHUMAN MATHEMATICS ENCODED GEOPOLITICS, PSYCHOLOGY, WEATHER SYSTEMS, THE PROCESSION OF STARS --
-- AS WE ATTEMPTED TO END THE SECOND WORLD WAR FROM OUR ARMCHAIRS.
IT WAS 1945. THE ATOMIC BOMB HADN'T YET BEEN DROPPED -- BUT WE KNEW IT *WOULD* BE.
WE'D DELIBERATELY NOT ENTERED THE WAR, YOU SEE. WE KNEW ENOUGH TO UNDERSTAND HOW COMPLEX SHIFTING THE DIRECTION OF CIVILIZATION WAS.
TOO MANY VARIABLES. WE COULD NEVER JUGGLE ALL THE MYRIAD POSSIBILITIES OUR ACTIONS COULD SET IN MOTION.

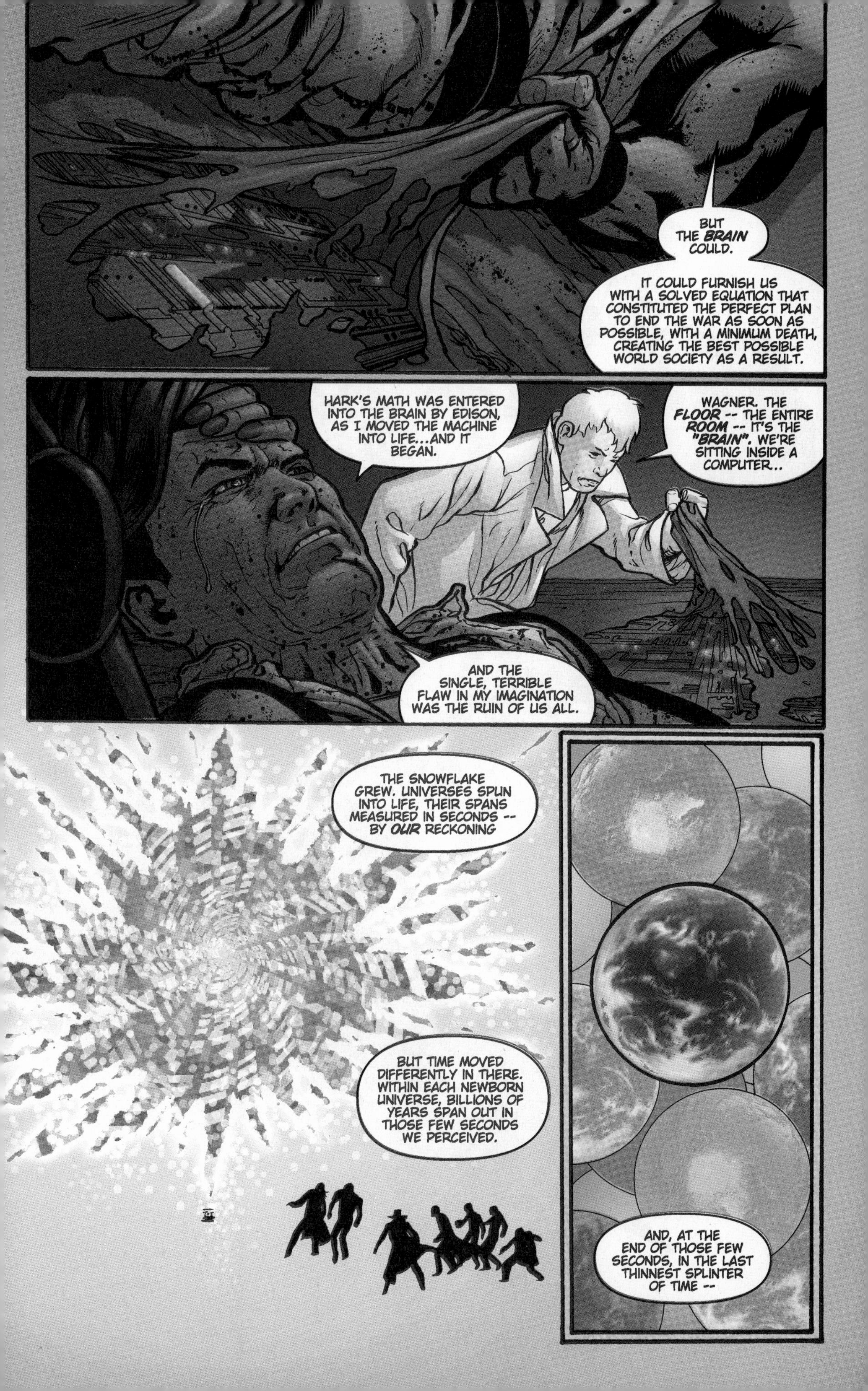
BUT THE BRAIN COULD.
IT COULD FURNISH US WITH A SOLVED EQUATION THAT CONSTITUTED THE PERFECT PLAN TO END THE WAR AS SOON AS POSSIBLE, WITH A MINIMUM DEATH, CREATING THE BEST POSSIBLE WORLD SOCIETY AS A RESULT.
HARK'S MATH WAS ENTERED INTO THE BRAIN BY EDISON, AS I MOVED THE MACHINE INTO LIFE...AND IT BEGAN.
WAGNER. THE FLOOR -- THE ENTIRE ROOM -- IT'S THE "BRAIN". WE'RE SITTING INSIDE A COMPUTER..
AND THE SINGLE, TERRIBLE FLAW IN MY IMAGINATION WAS THE RUIN OF US ALL.
THE SNOWFLAKE GREW. UNIVERSES SPUN INTO LIFE, THEIR SPANS MEASURED IN SECONDS -- BY OUR RECKONING
BUT TIME MOVED DIFFERENTLY IN THERE. WITHIN EACH NEWBORN UNIVERSE, BILLIONS OF YEARS SPAN OUT IN THOSE FEW SECONDS WE PERCEIVED.
AND, AT THE END OF THOSE FEW SECONDS, IN THE LAST THINNEST SPLINTER OF TIME --

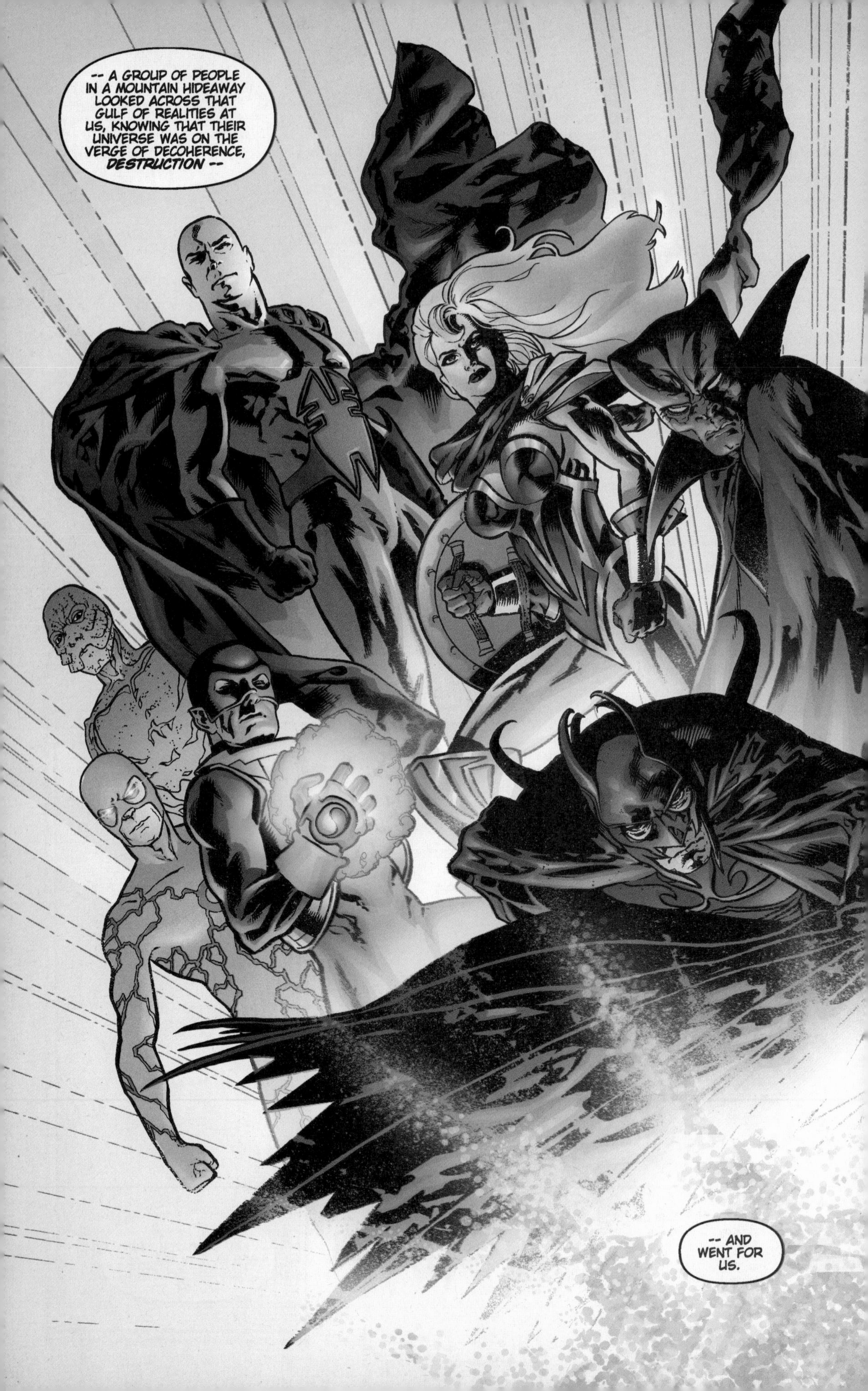
-- A GROUP OF PEOPLE IN A MOUNTAIN HIDEAWAY LOOKED ACROSS THAT GULF OF REALITIES AT US, KNOWING THAT THEIR UNIVERSE WAS ON THE VERGE OF DECOHERENCE, DESTRUCTION --
-- AND WENT FOR US.

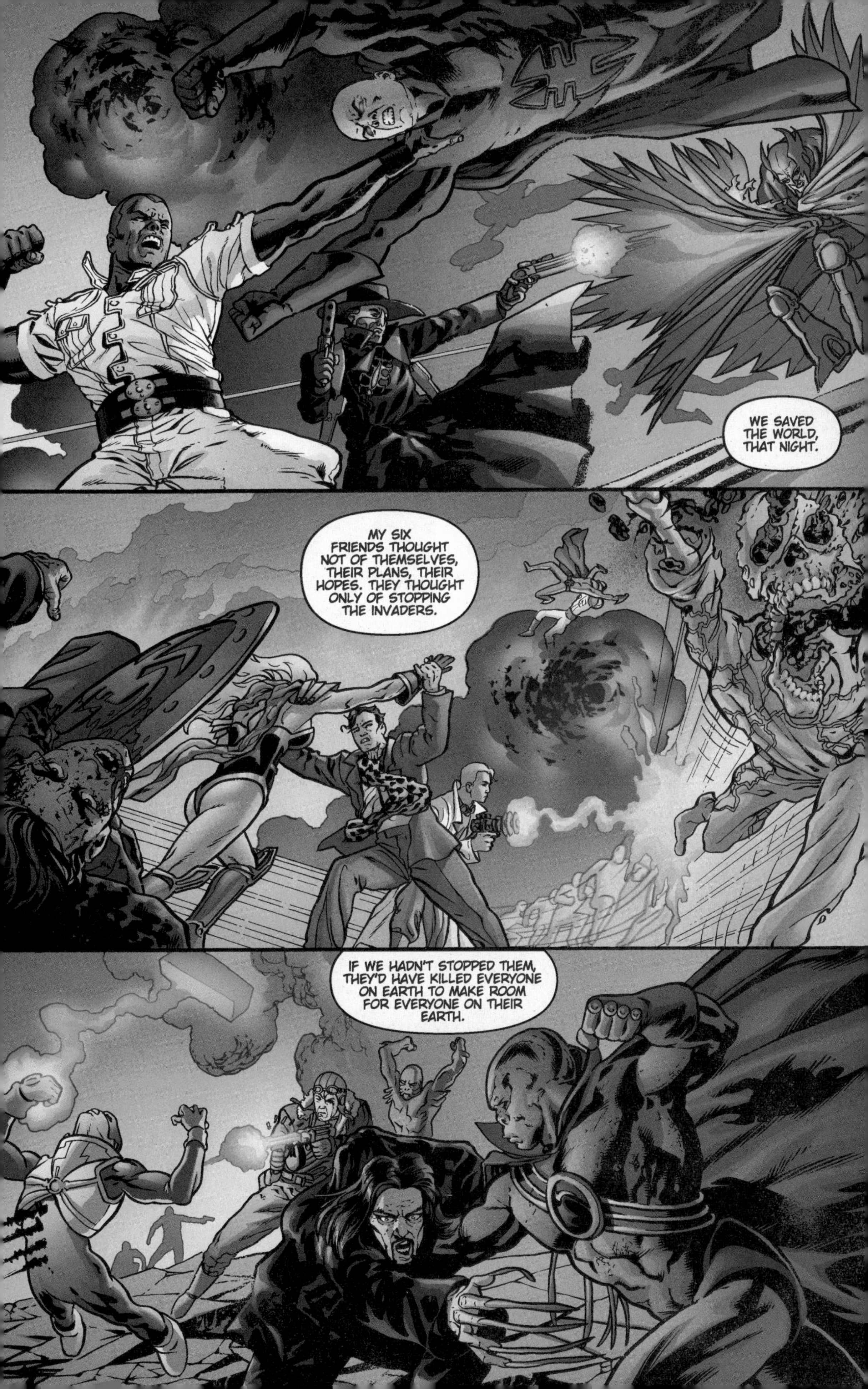
WE SAVED THE WORLD, THAT NIGHT.
MY SIX FRIENDS THOUGHT NOT OF THEMSELVES, THEIR PLANS, THEIR HOPES. THEY THOUGHT ONLY OF STOPPING THE INVADERS.
IF WE HADN'T STOPPED THEM, THEY'D HAVE KILLED EVERYONE ON EARTH TO MAKE ROOM FOR EVERYONE ON THEIR EARTH.

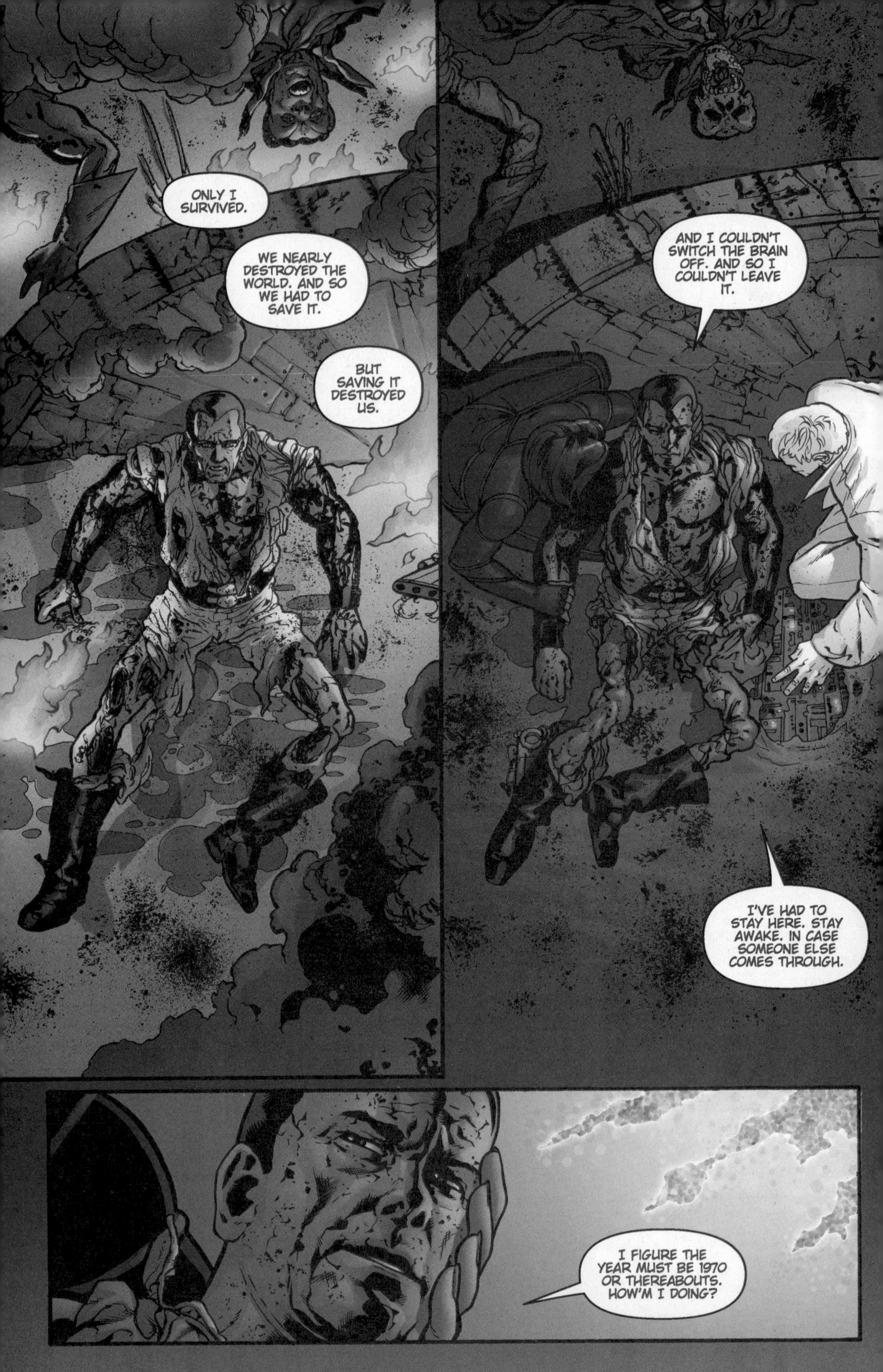
ONLY I SURVIVED.
WE NEARLY DESTROYED THE WORLD. AND SO WE HAD TO SAVE IT.
BUT SAVING IT DESTROYED US.
AND I COULDN'T SWITCH THE BRAIN OFF. AND SO I COULDN'T LEAVE IT.
I'VE HAD TO STAY HERE. STAY AWAKE. IN CASE SOMEONE ELSE COMES THROUGH.
I FIGURE THE YEAR MUST BE 1970 OR THEREABOUTS. HOW'M I DOING?

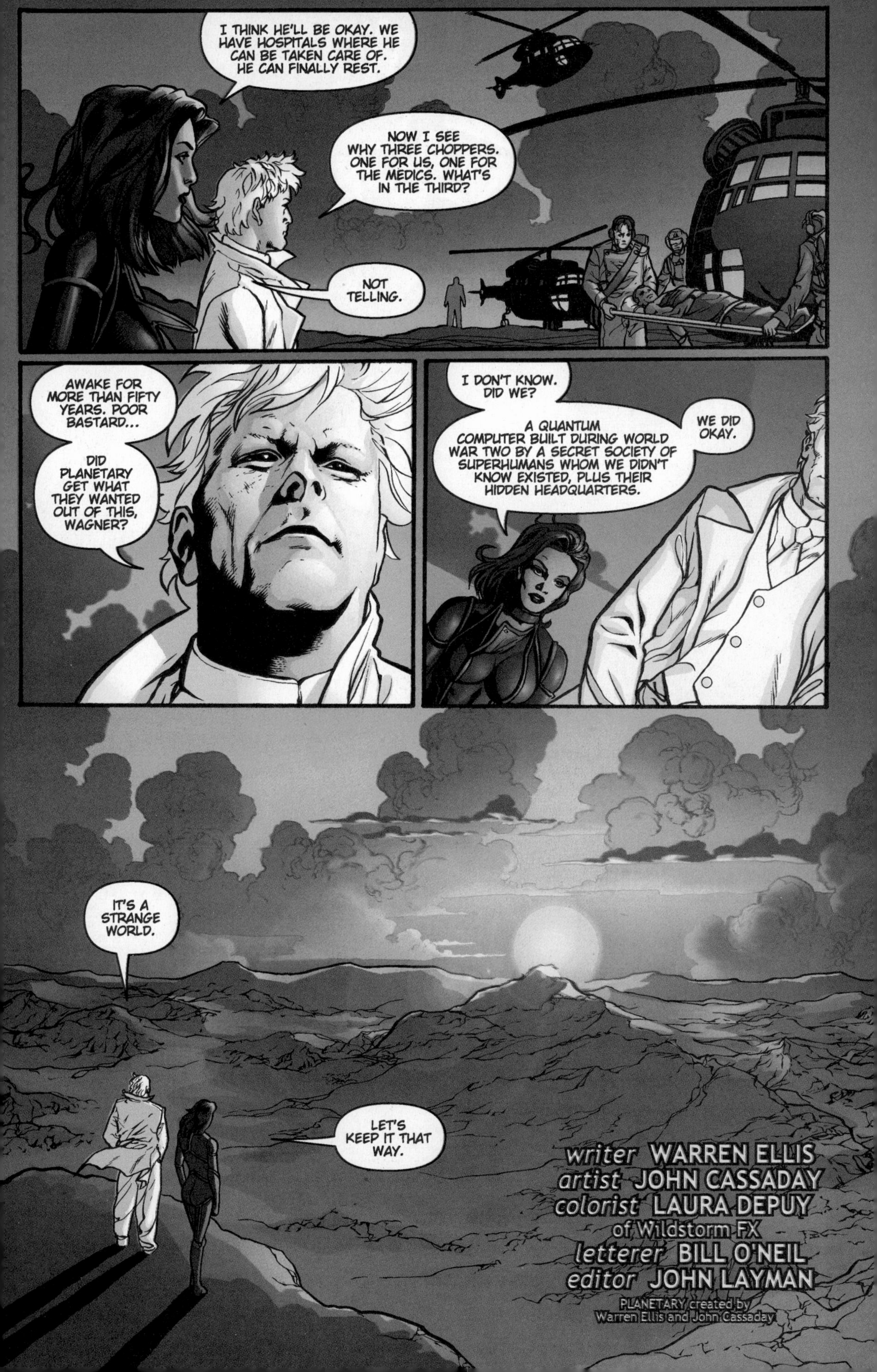
I THINK HE'LL BE OKAY. WE HAVE HOSPITALS WHERE HE CAN BE TAKEN CARE OF. HE CAN FINALLY REST.
NOW I SEE WHY THREE CHOPPERS. ONE FOR US, ONE FOR THE MEDICS. WHAT'S IN THE THIRD?
NOT TELLING.
AWAKE FOR MORE THAN FIFTY YEARS. POOR BASTARD...
DID PLANETARY GET WHAT THEY WANTED OUT OF THIS, WAGNER?
I DON'T KNOW. DID WE?
WE DID OKAY.
A QUANTUM COMPUTER BUILT DURING WORLD WAR TWO BY A SECRET SOCIETY OF SUPERHUMANS WHOM WE DIDN'T KNOW EXISTED, PLUS THEIR HIDDEN HEADQUARTERS.
IT'S A STRANGE WORLD.
LET'S KEEP IT THAT WAY.
writer WARREN ELLIS
artist JOHN CASSADAY
colorist LAURA DEPUY
of Wildstorm FX
letterer BILL O'NEIL
editor JOHN LAYMAN
PLANETARY created by
Warren Ellis and John Cassaday

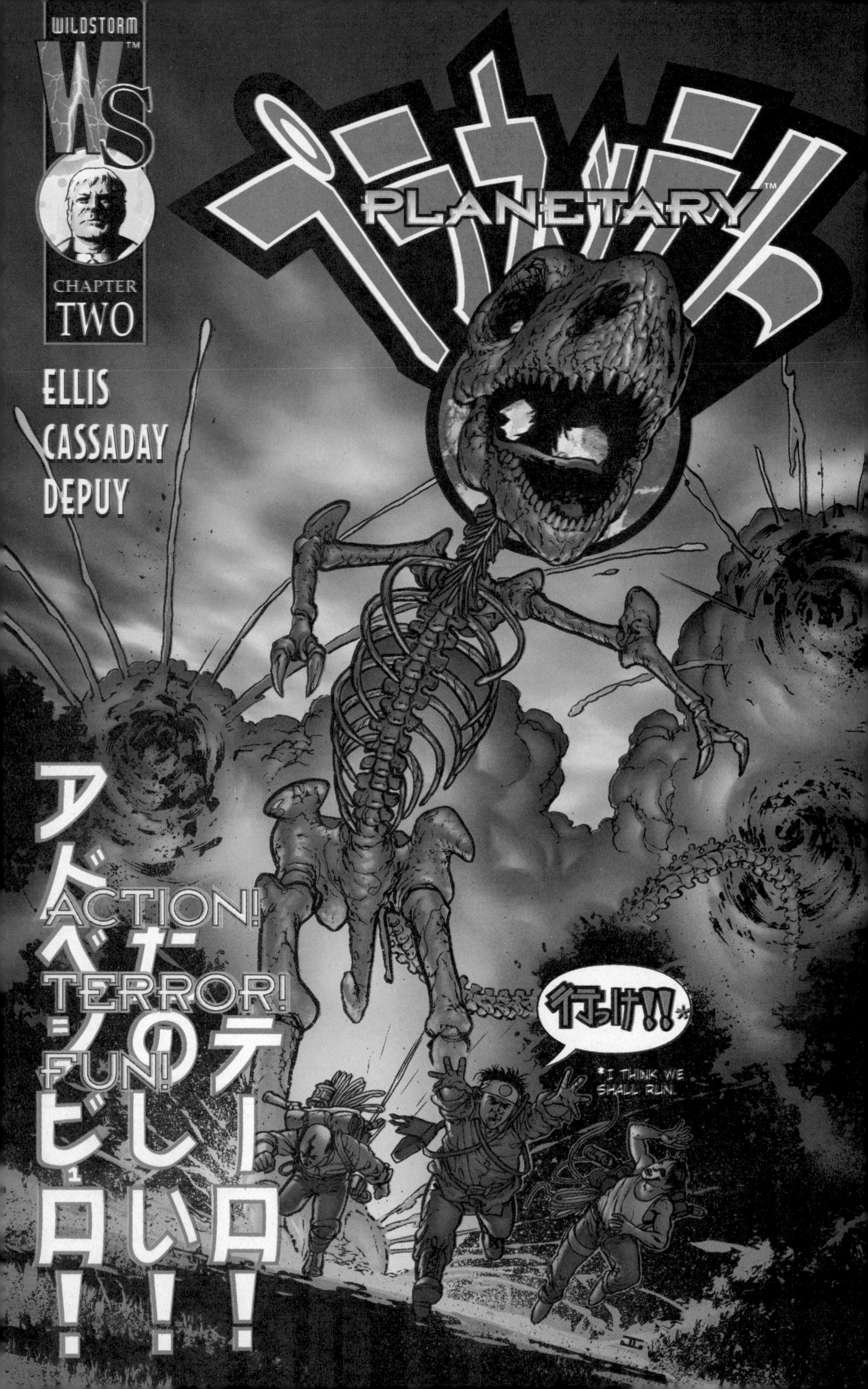
WILDSTORM
WS
CHAPTER TWO
PLANETARY
ELLIS
CASSADAY
DEPUY
ACTION!
TERROR!
FUN!
行け!!*
*I THINK WE SHALL RUN.

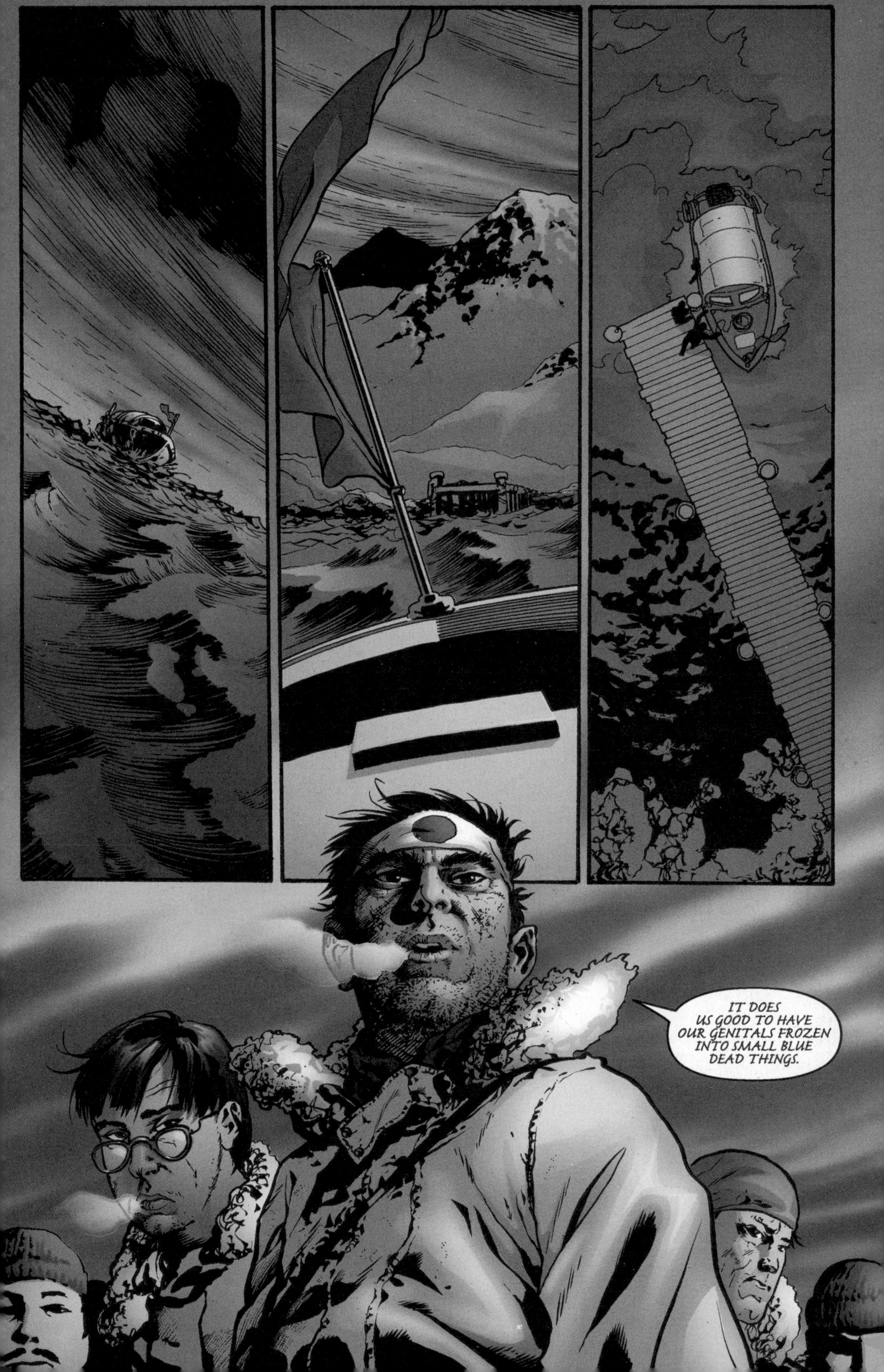
IT DOES US GOOD TO HAVE OUR GENITALS FROZEN INTO SMALL BLUE DEAD THINGS.

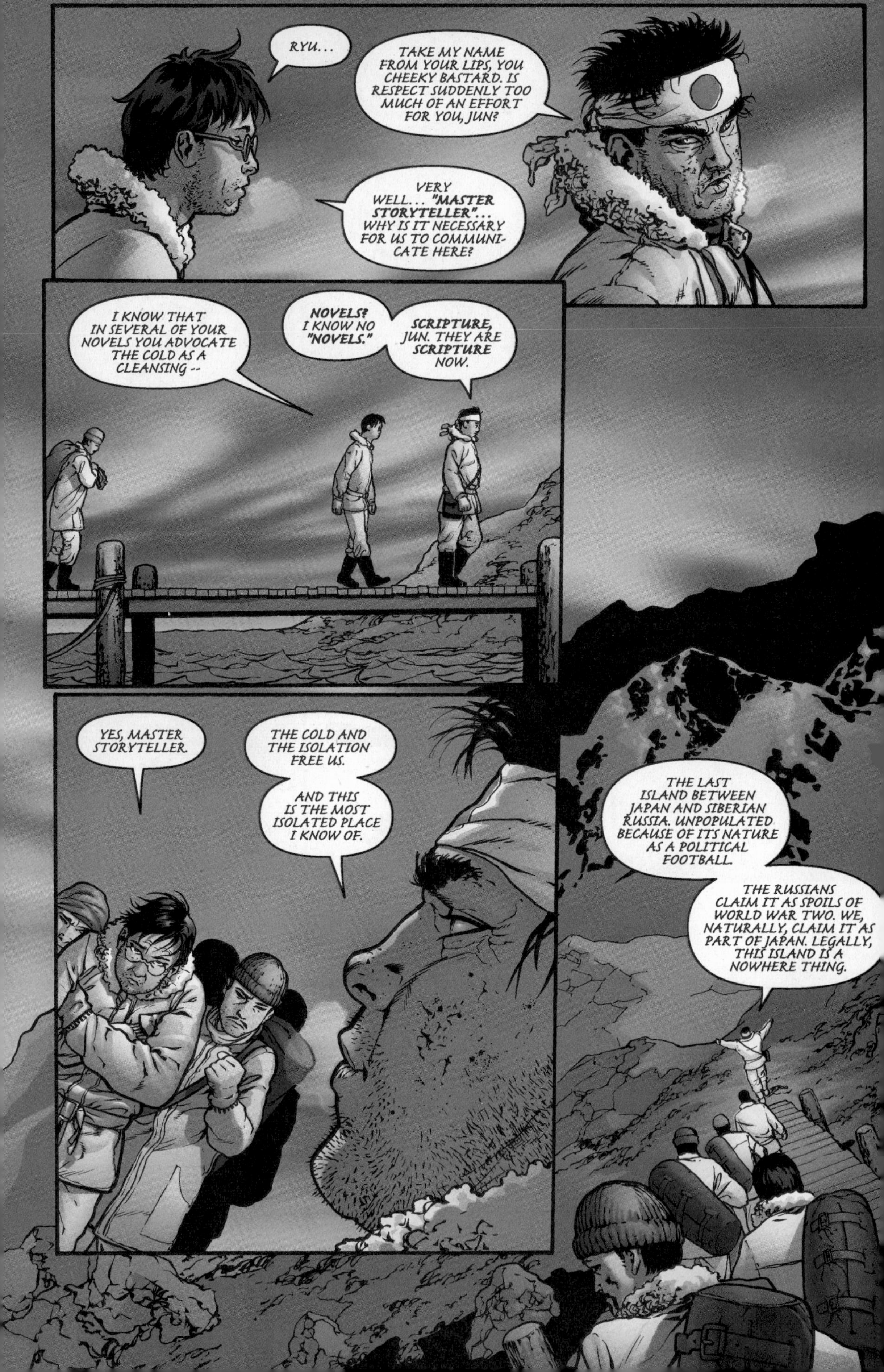
RYU...
TAKE MY NAME FROM YOUR LIPS, YOU CHEEKY BASTARD. IS RESPECT SUDDENLY TOO MUCH OF AN EFFORT FOR YOU, JUN?
VERY WELL... "MASTER STORYTELLER"... WHY IS IT NECESSARY FOR US TO COMMUNICATE HERE?
I KNOW THAT IN SEVERAL OF YOUR NOVELS YOU ADVOCATE THE COLD AS A CLEANSING --
NOVELS? I KNOW NO "NOVELS."
SCRIPTURE, JUN. THEY ARE SCRIPTURE NOW.
YES, MASTER STORYTELLER.
THE COLD AND THE ISOLATION FREE US.
AND THIS IS THE MOST ISOLATED PLACE I KNOW OF.
THE LAST ISLAND BETWEEN JAPAN AND SIBERIAN RUSSIA. UNPOPULATED BECAUSE OF ITS NATURE AS A POLITICAL FOOTBALL.
THE RUSSIANS CLAIM IT AS SPOILS OF WORLD WAR TWO. WE, NATURALLY, CLAIM IT AS PART OF JAPAN. LEGALLY, THIS ISLAND IS A NOWHERE THING.

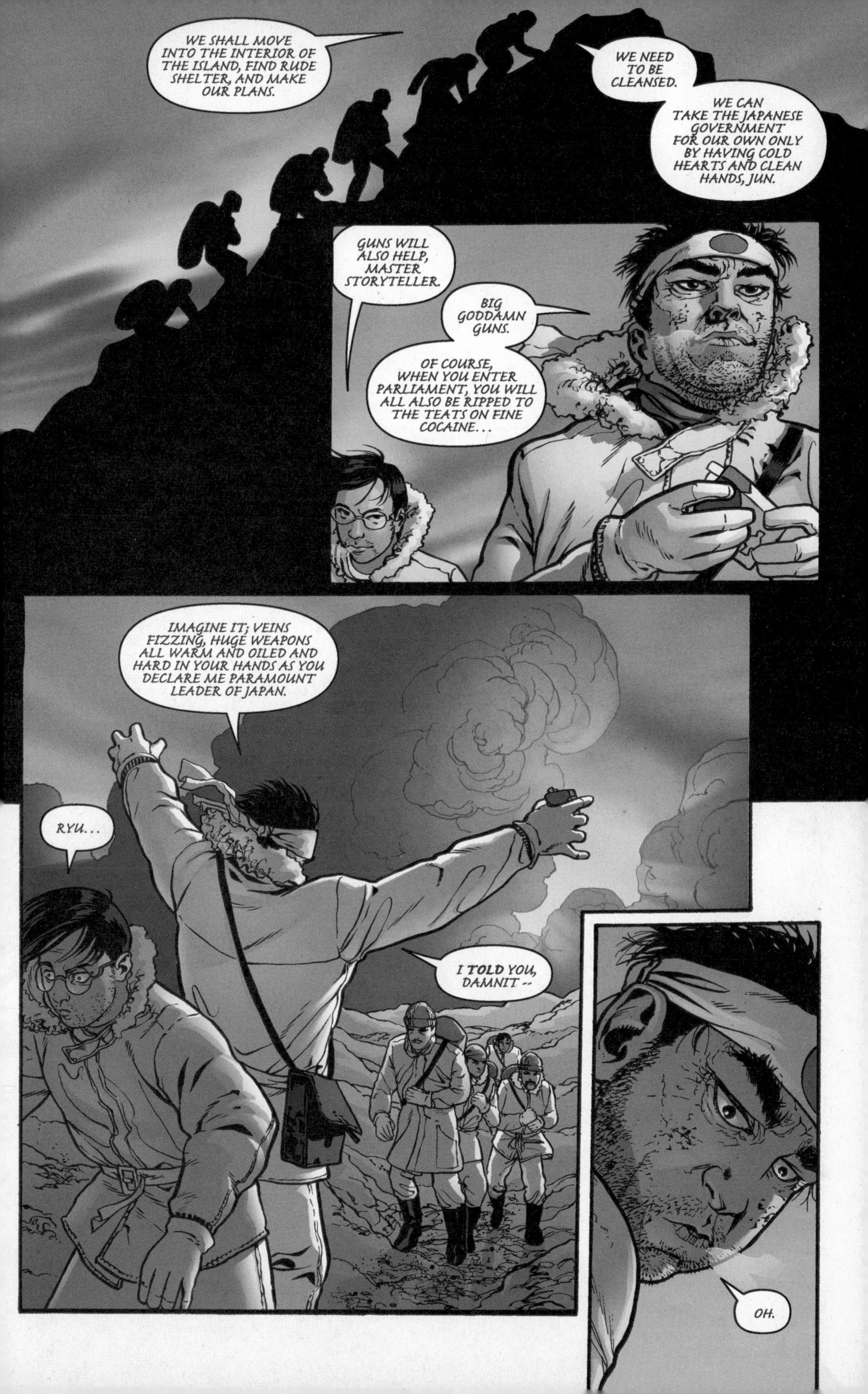
WE SHALL MOVE INTO THE INTERIOR OF THE ISLAND, FIND RUDE SHELTER, AND MAKE OUR PLANS.
WE NEED TO BE CLEANSED.
WE CAN TAKE THE JAPANESE GOVERNMENT FOR OUR OWN ONLY BY HAVING COLD HEARTS AND CLEAN HANDS, JUN.
GUNS WILL ALSO HELP, MASTER STORYTELLER.
BIG GODDAMN GUNS.
OF COURSE, WHEN YOU ENTER PARLIAMENT, YOU WILL ALL ALSO BE RIPPED TO THE TEATS ON FINE COCAINE...
IMAGINE IT; VEINS FIZZING, HUGE WEAPONS ALL WARM AND OILED AND HARD IN YOUR HANDS AS YOU DECLARE ME PARAMOUNT LEADER OF JAPAN.
RYU...
I **TOLD** YOU, DAMNIT --
OH.

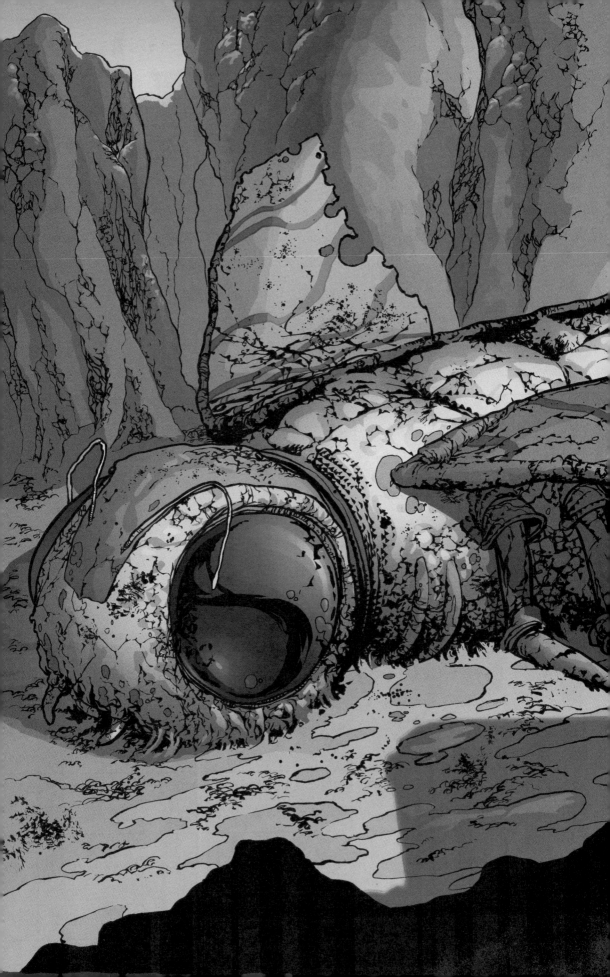

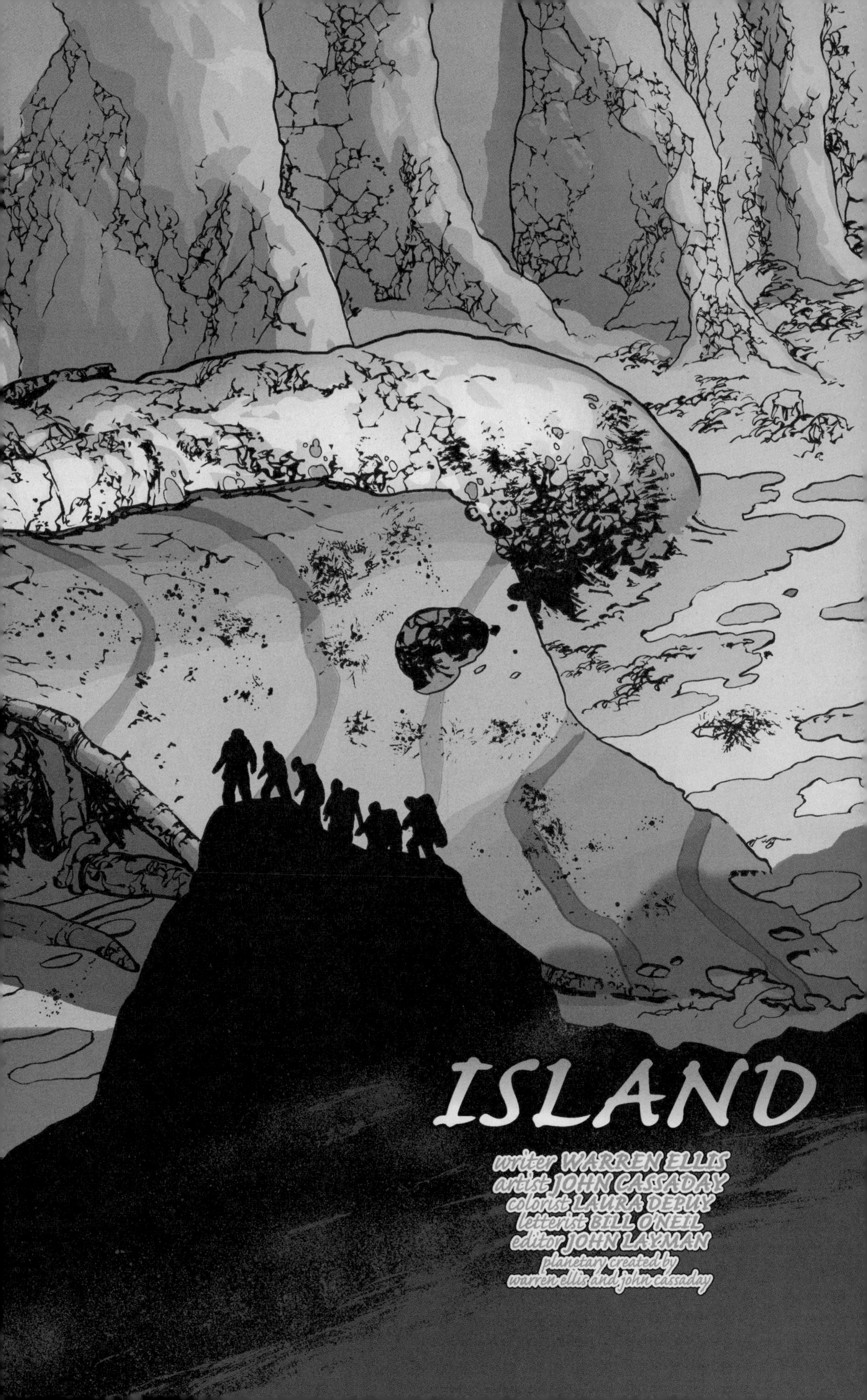
ISLAND
writer WARREN ELLIS
artist JOHN CASSADAY
colorist LAURA DEPUY
letterist BILL O'NEIL
editor JOHN LAYMAN
planetary created by
warren ellis and john cassaday

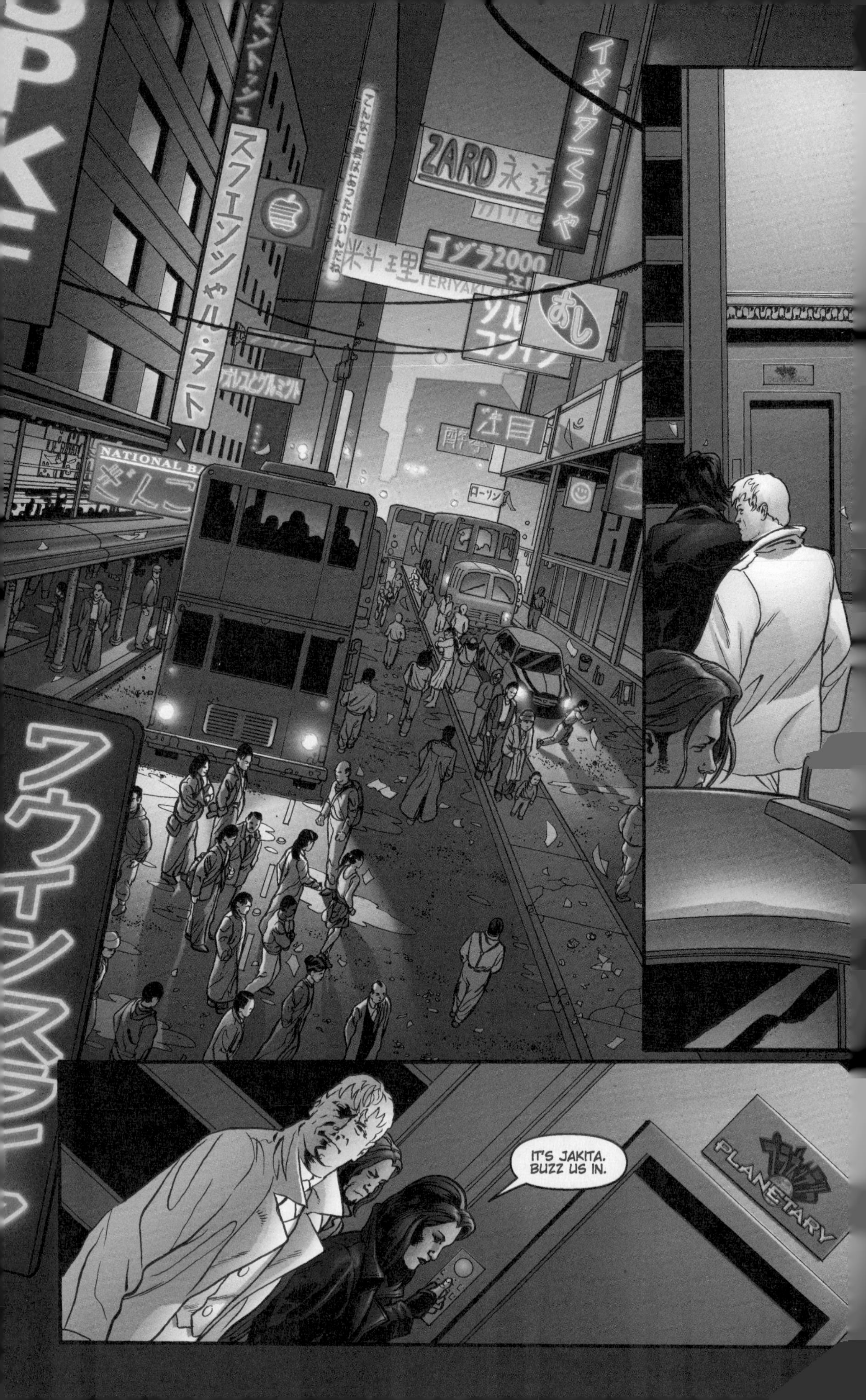
ZARD
ゴジラ2000
IT'S JAKITA.
BUZZ US IN.
PLANETARY

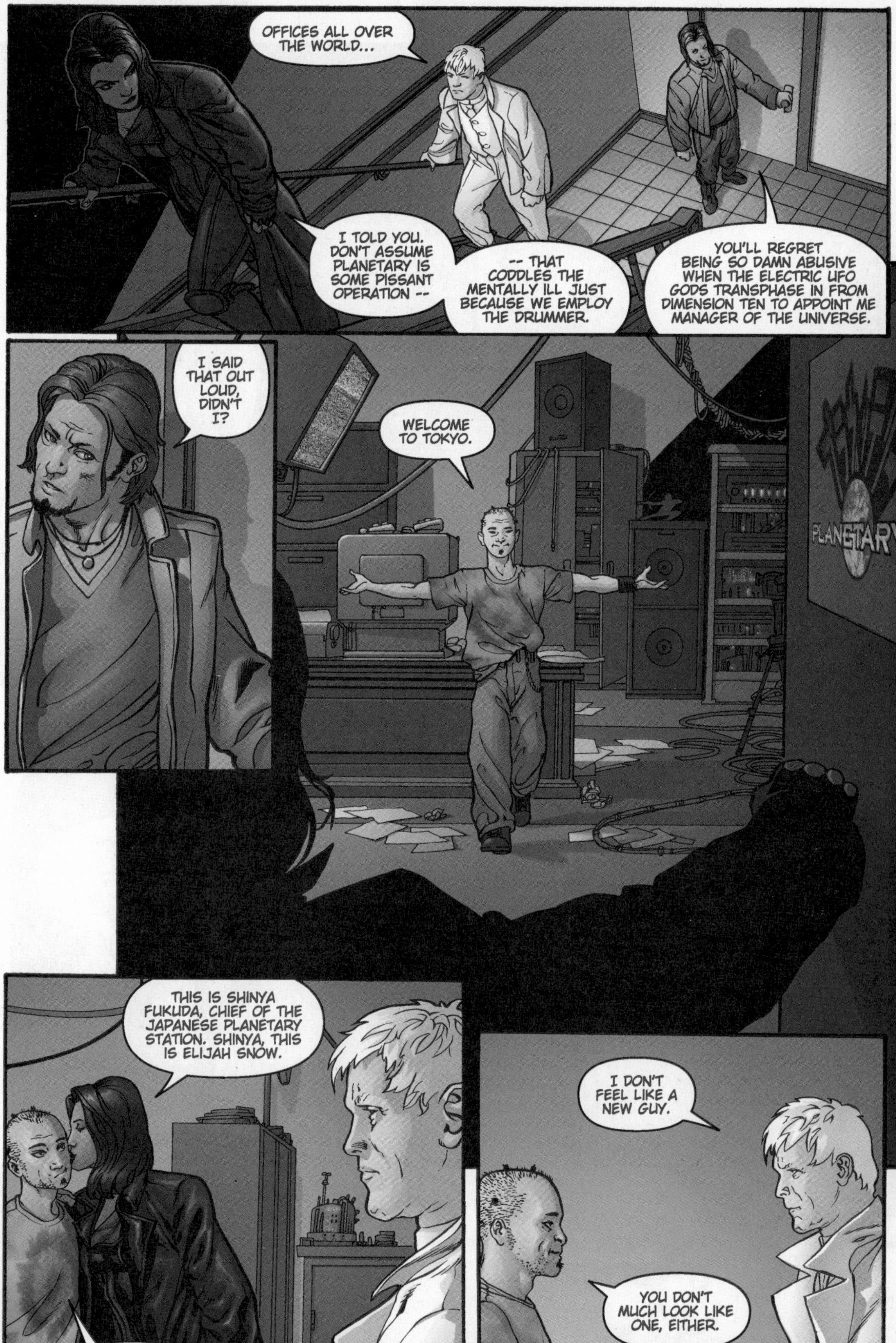
OFFICES ALL OVER THE WORLD...
I TOLD YOU. DON'T ASSUME PLANETARY IS SOME PISSANT OPERATION --
-- THAT CODDLES THE MENTALLY ILL JUST BECAUSE WE EMPLOY THE DRUMMER.
YOU'LL REGRET BEING SO DAMN ABUSIVE WHEN THE ELECTRIC UFO GODS TRANSPHASE IN FROM DIMENSION TEN TO APPOINT ME MANAGER OF THE UNIVERSE.
I SAID THAT OUT LOUD, DIDN'T I?
WELCOME TO TOKYO.
PLANETARY
THIS IS SHINYA FUKUDA, CHIEF OF THE JAPANESE PLANETARY STATION. SHINYA, THIS IS ELIJAH SNOW.
THE NEW GUY. PLEASED TO MEET YOU.
I DON'T FEEL LIKE A NEW GUY.
YOU DON'T MUCH LOOK LIKE ONE, EITHER.

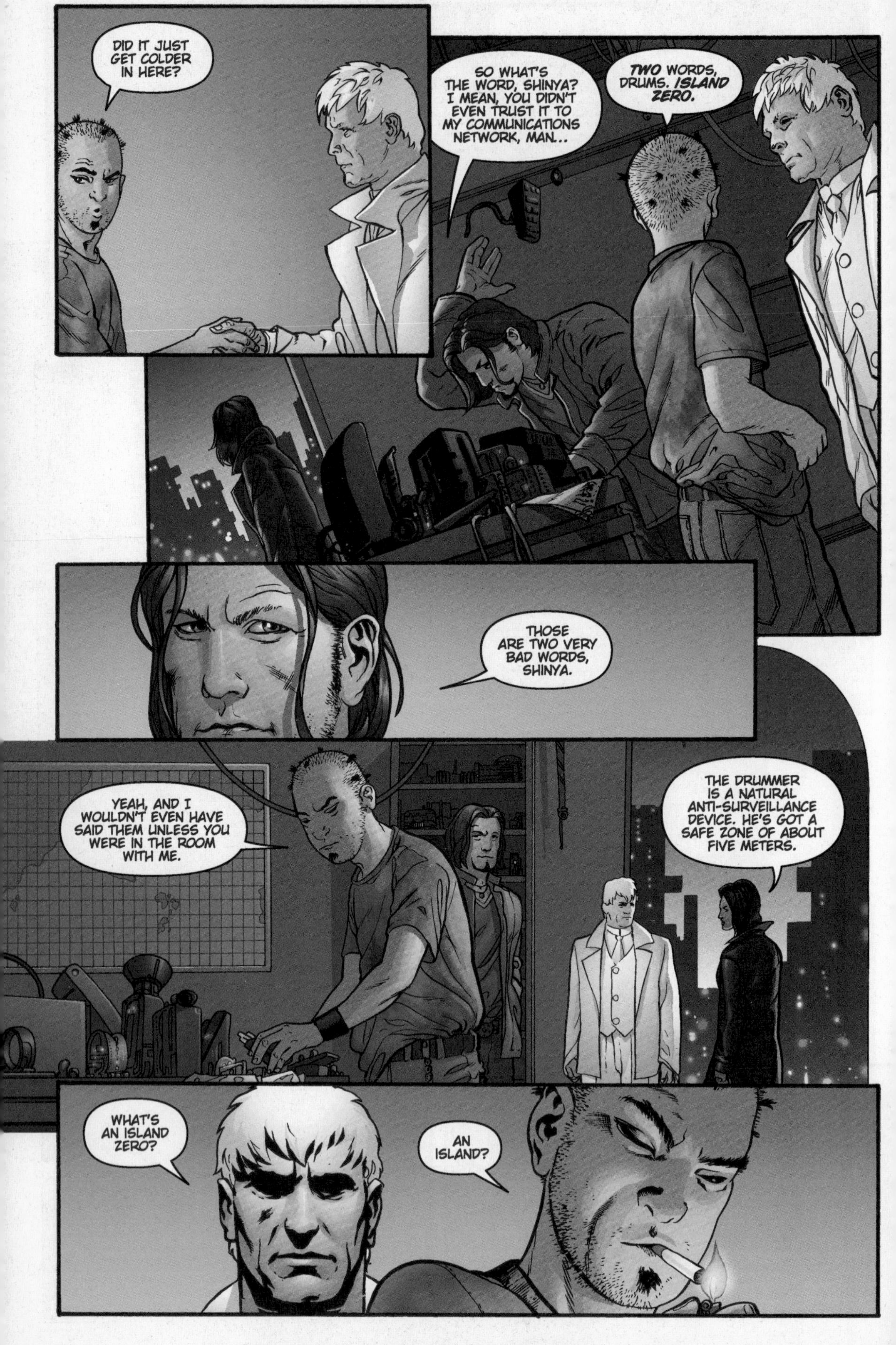
DID IT JUST GET COLDER IN HERE?
SO WHAT'S THE WORD, SHINYA? I MEAN, YOU DIDN'T EVEN TRUST IT TO MY COMMUNICATIONS NETWORK, MAN...
TWO WORDS, DRUMS. ISLAND ZERO.
THOSE ARE TWO VERY BAD WORDS, SHINYA.
YEAH, AND I WOULDN'T EVEN HAVE SAID THEM UNLESS YOU WERE IN THE ROOM WITH ME.
THE DRUMMER IS A NATURAL ANTI-SURVEILLANCE DEVICE. HE'S GOT A SAFE ZONE OF ABOUT FIVE METERS.
WHAT'S AN ISLAND ZERO?
AN ISLAND?

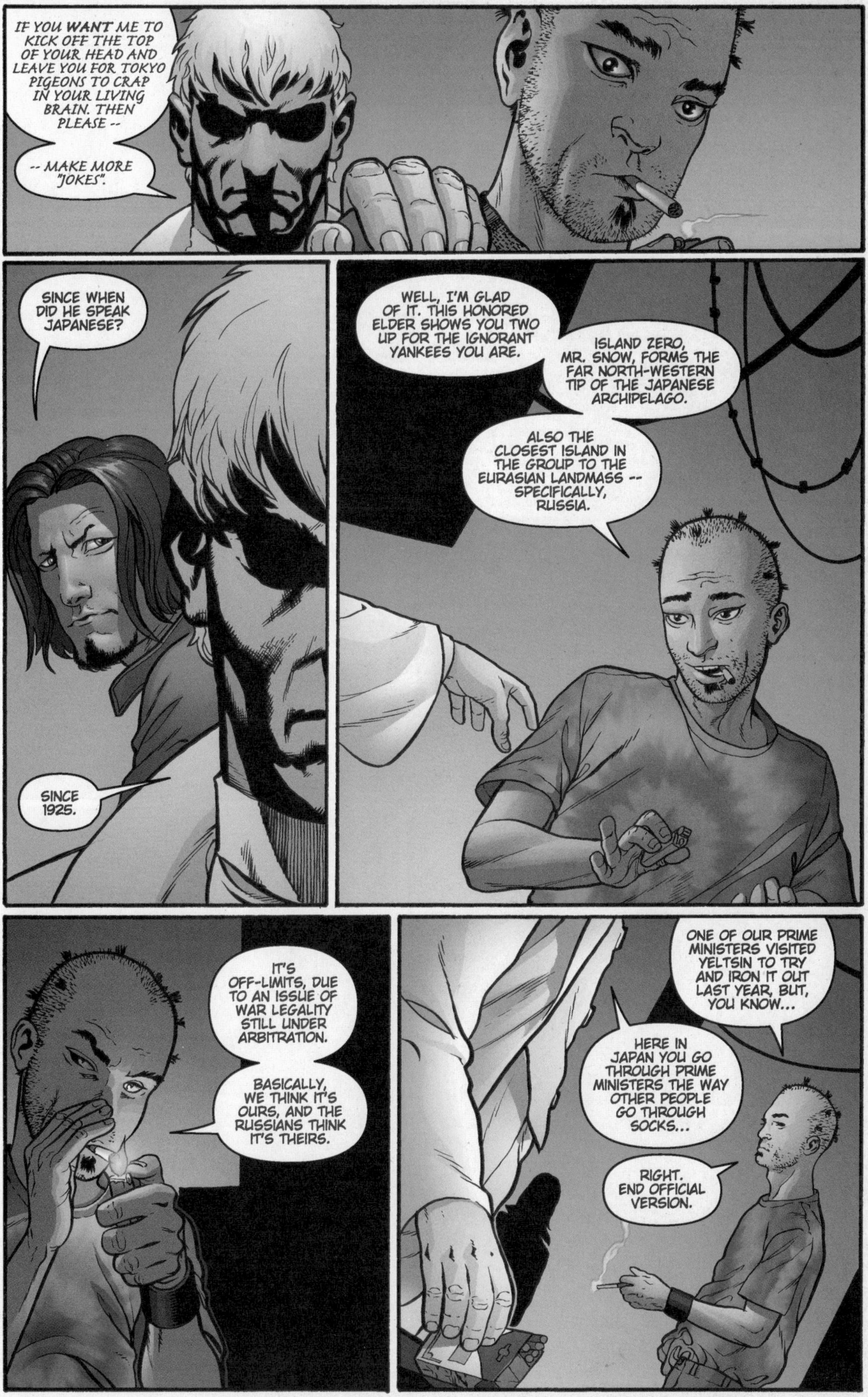
IF YOU WANT ME TO KICK OFF THE TOP OF YOUR HEAD AND LEAVE YOU FOR TOKYO PIGEONS TO CRAP IN YOUR LIVING BRAIN. THEN PLEASE --
-- MAKE MORE "JOKES".
SINCE WHEN DID HE SPEAK JAPANESE?
SINCE 1925.
WELL, I'M GLAD OF IT. THIS HONORED ELDER SHOWS YOU TWO UP FOR THE IGNORANT YANKEES YOU ARE.
ISLAND ZERO, MR. SNOW, FORMS THE FAR NORTH-WESTERN TIP OF THE JAPANESE ARCHIPELAGO.
ALSO THE CLOSEST ISLAND IN THE GROUP TO THE EURASIAN LANDMASS -- SPECIFICALLY, RUSSIA.
IT'S OFF-LIMITS, DUE TO AN ISSUE OF WAR LEGALITY STILL UNDER ARBITRATION.
BASICALLY, WE THINK IT'S OURS, AND THE RUSSIANS THINK IT'S THEIRS.
ONE OF OUR PRIME MINISTERS VISITED YELTSIN TO TRY AND IRON IT OUT LAST YEAR, BUT, YOU KNOW...
HERE IN JAPAN YOU GO THROUGH PRIME MINISTERS THE WAY OTHER PEOPLE GO THROUGH SOCKS...
RIGHT. END OFFICIAL VERSION.

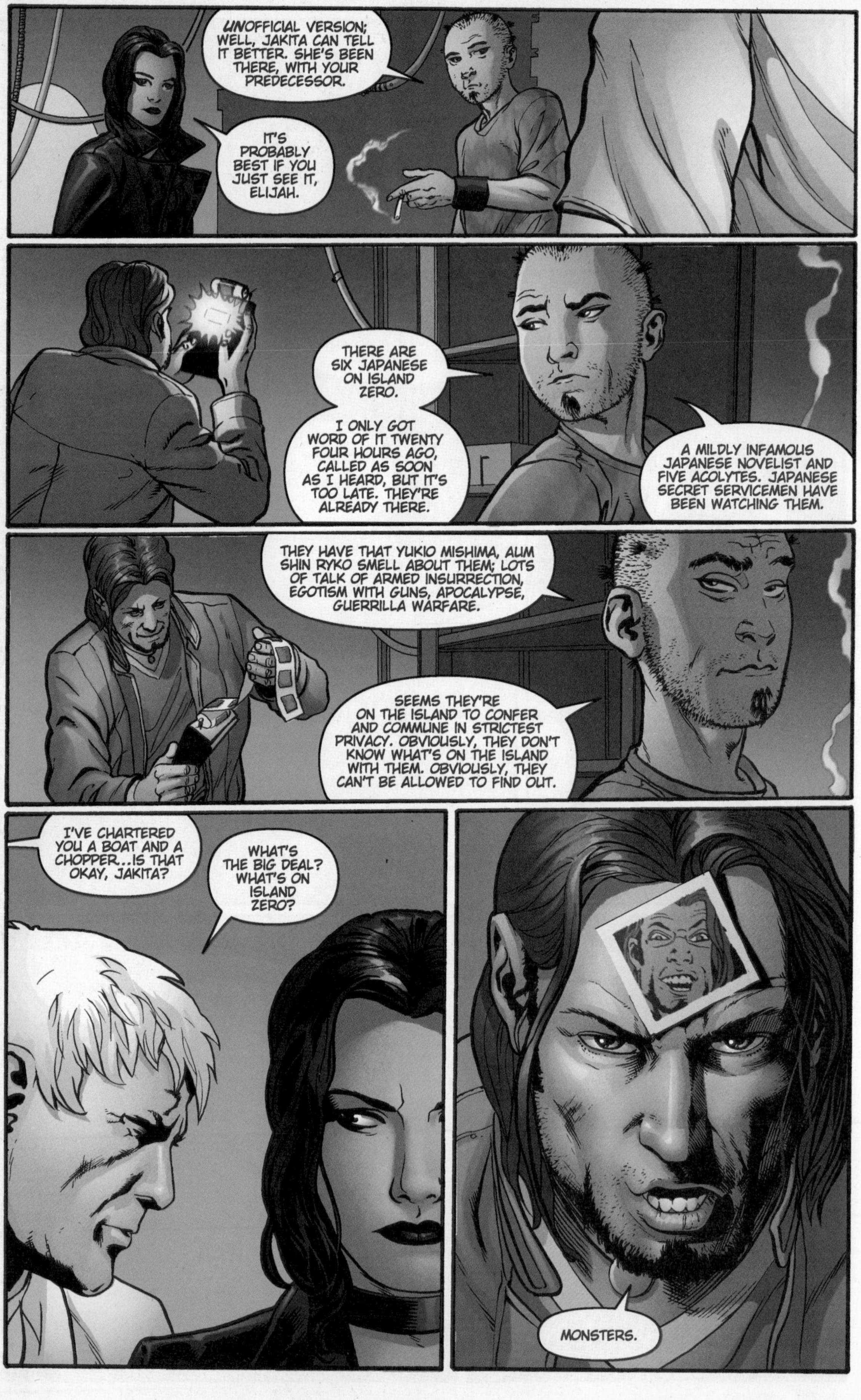
UNOFFICIAL VERSION; WELL, JAKITA CAN TELL IT BETTER. SHE'S BEEN THERE, WITH YOUR PREDECESSOR.
IT'S PROBABLY BEST IF YOU JUST SEE IT, ELIJAH.
THERE ARE SIX JAPANESE ON ISLAND ZERO.
I ONLY GOT WORD OF IT TWENTY FOUR HOURS AGO, CALLED AS SOON AS I HEARD, BUT IT'S TOO LATE. THEY'RE ALREADY THERE.
A MILDLY INFAMOUS JAPANESE NOVELIST AND FIVE ACOLYTES. JAPANESE SECRET SERVICEMEN HAVE BEEN WATCHING THEM.
THEY HAVE THAT YUKIO MISHIMA, AUM SHIN RYKO SMELL ABOUT THEM; LOTS OF TALK OF ARMED INSURRECTION, EGOTISM WITH GUNS, APOCALYPSE, GUERRILLA WARFARE.
SEEMS THEY'RE ON THE ISLAND TO CONFER AND COMMUNE IN STRICTEST PRIVACY. OBVIOUSLY, THEY DON'T KNOW WHAT'S ON THE ISLAND WITH THEM. OBVIOUSLY, THEY CAN'T BE ALLOWED TO FIND OUT.
I'VE CHARTERED YOU A BOAT AND A CHOPPER...IS THAT OKAY, JAKITA?
WHAT'S THE BIG DEAL? WHAT'S ON ISLAND ZERO?
MONSTERS.

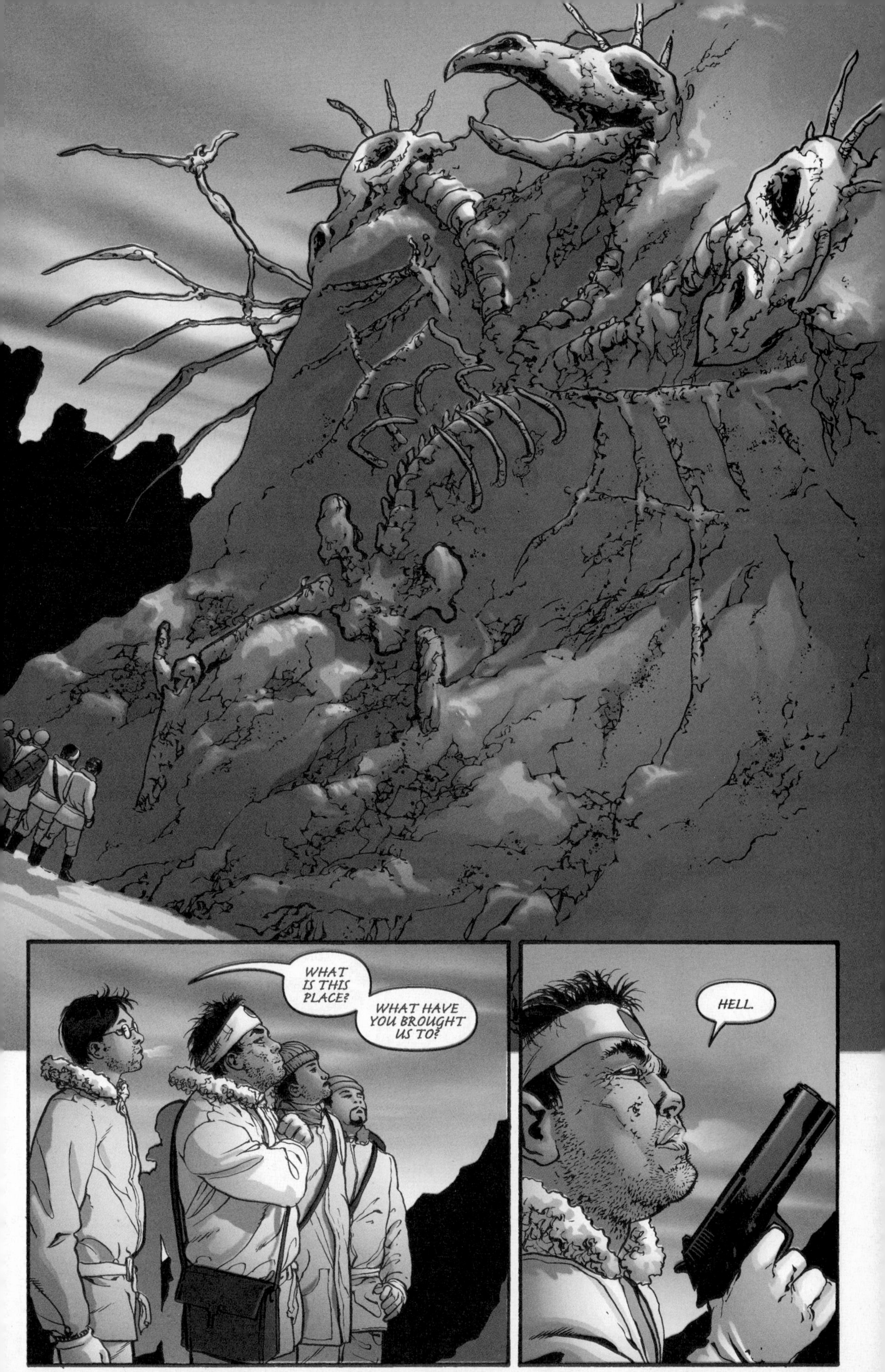
WHAT IS THIS PLACE?
WHAT HAVE YOU BROUGHT US TO?
HELL.

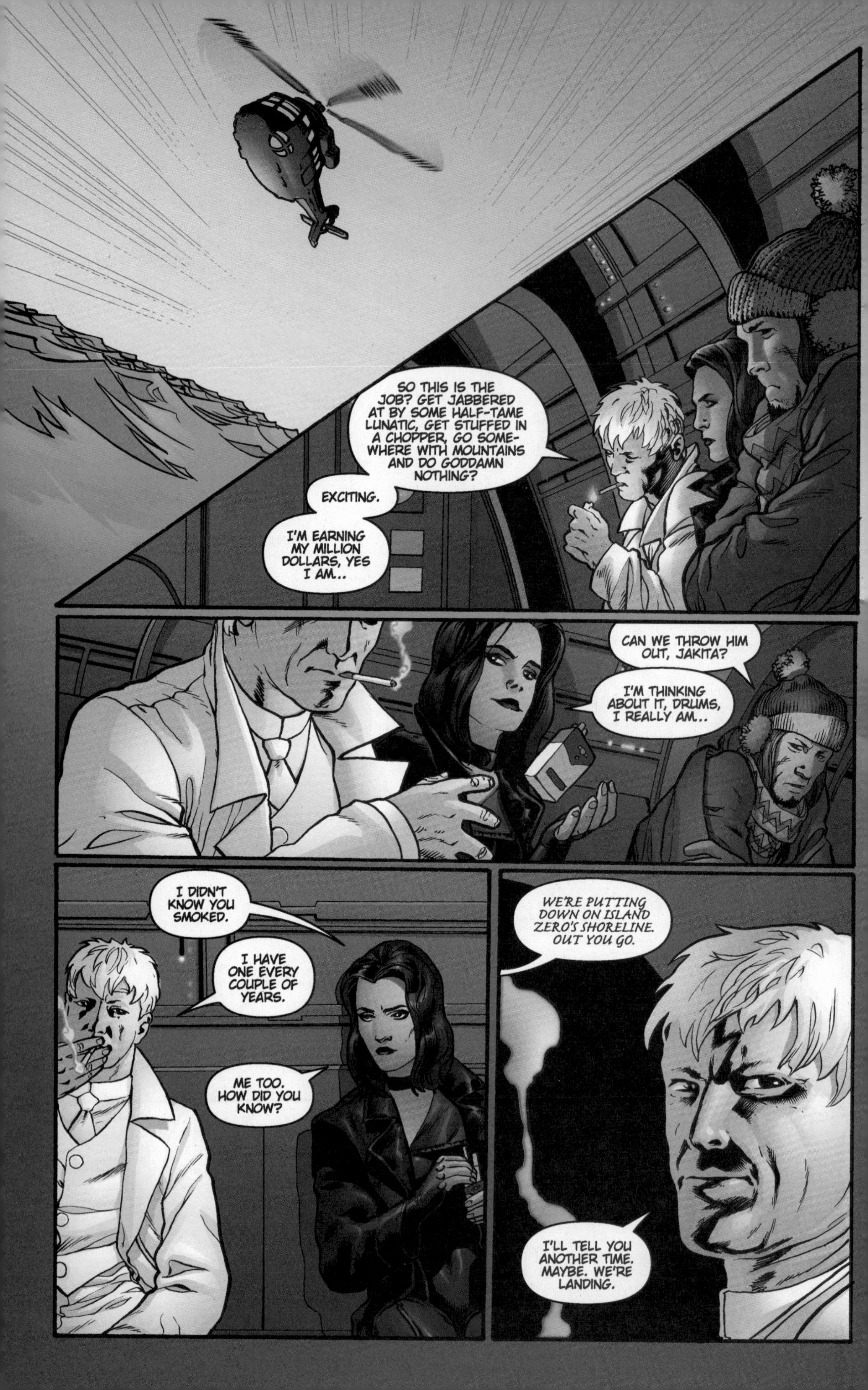
SO THIS IS THE JOB? GET JABBERED AT BY SOME HALF-TAME LUNATIC, GET STUFFED IN A CHOPPER, GO SOMEWHERE WITH MOUNTAINS AND DO GODDAMN NOTHING?
EXCITING.
I'M EARNING MY MILLION DOLLARS, YES I AM...
CAN WE THROW HIM OUT, JAKITA?
I'M THINKING ABOUT IT, DRUMS, I REALLY AM...
I DIDN'T KNOW YOU SMOKED.
I HAVE ONE EVERY COUPLE OF YEARS.
ME TOO. HOW DID YOU KNOW?
WE'RE PUTTING DOWN ON ISLAND ZERO'S SHORELINE. OUT YOU GO.
I'LL TELL YOU ANOTHER TIME. MAYBE. WE'RE LANDING.

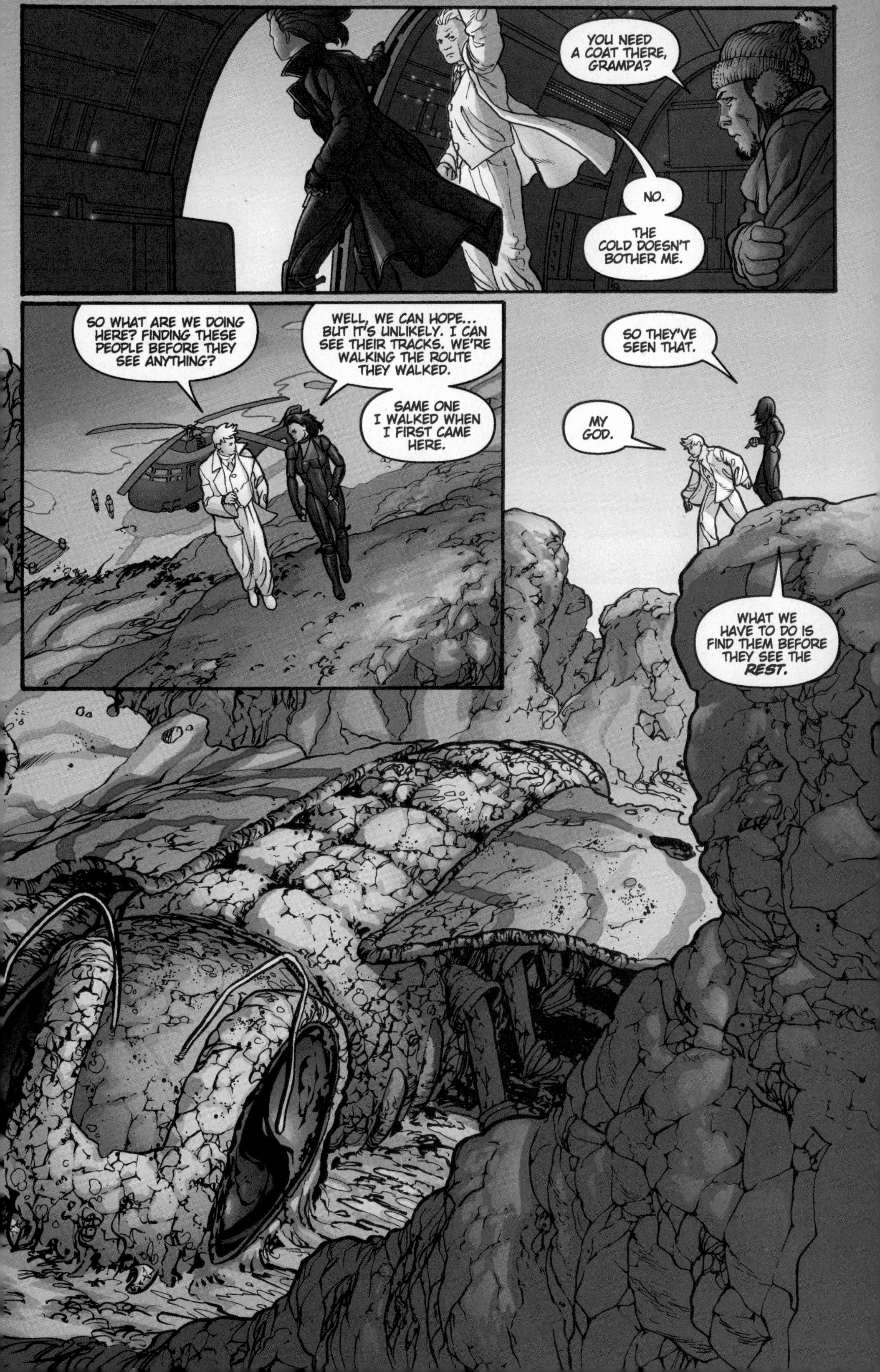
YOU NEED A COAT THERE, GRAMPA?
NO.
THE COLD DOESN'T BOTHER ME.
SO WHAT ARE WE DOING HERE? FINDING THESE PEOPLE BEFORE THEY SEE ANYTHING?
WELL, WE CAN HOPE... BUT IT'S UNLIKELY. I CAN SEE THEIR TRACKS. WE'RE WALKING THE ROUTE THEY WALKED.
SAME ONE I WALKED WHEN I FIRST CAME HERE.
SO THEY'VE SEEN THAT.
MY GOD.
WHAT WE HAVE TO DO IS FIND THEM BEFORE THEY SEE THE ***REST***.

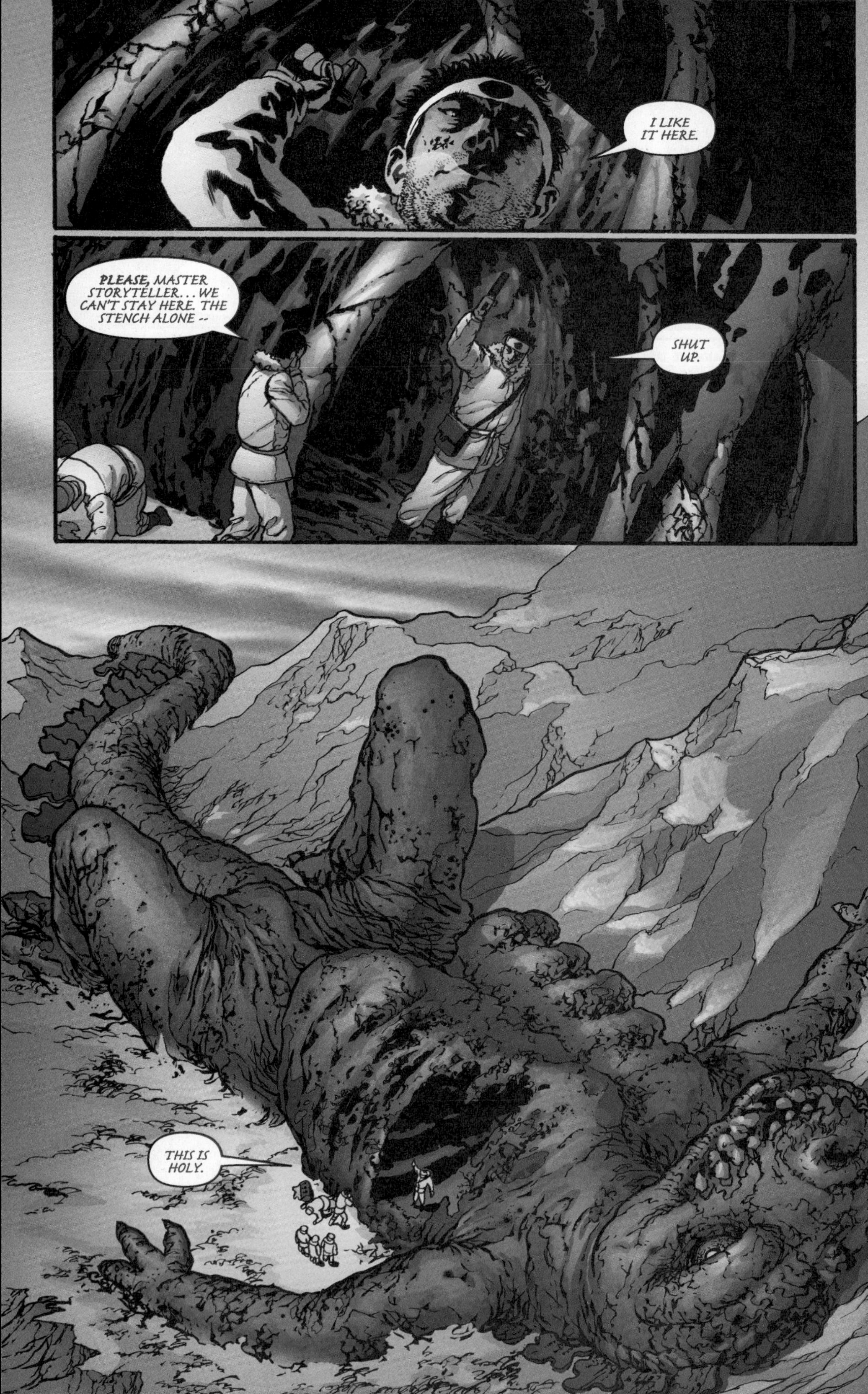
I LIKE IT HERE.
PLEASE, MASTER STORYTELLER... WE CAN'T STAY HERE. THE STENCH ALONE --
SHUT UP.
THIS IS HOLY.

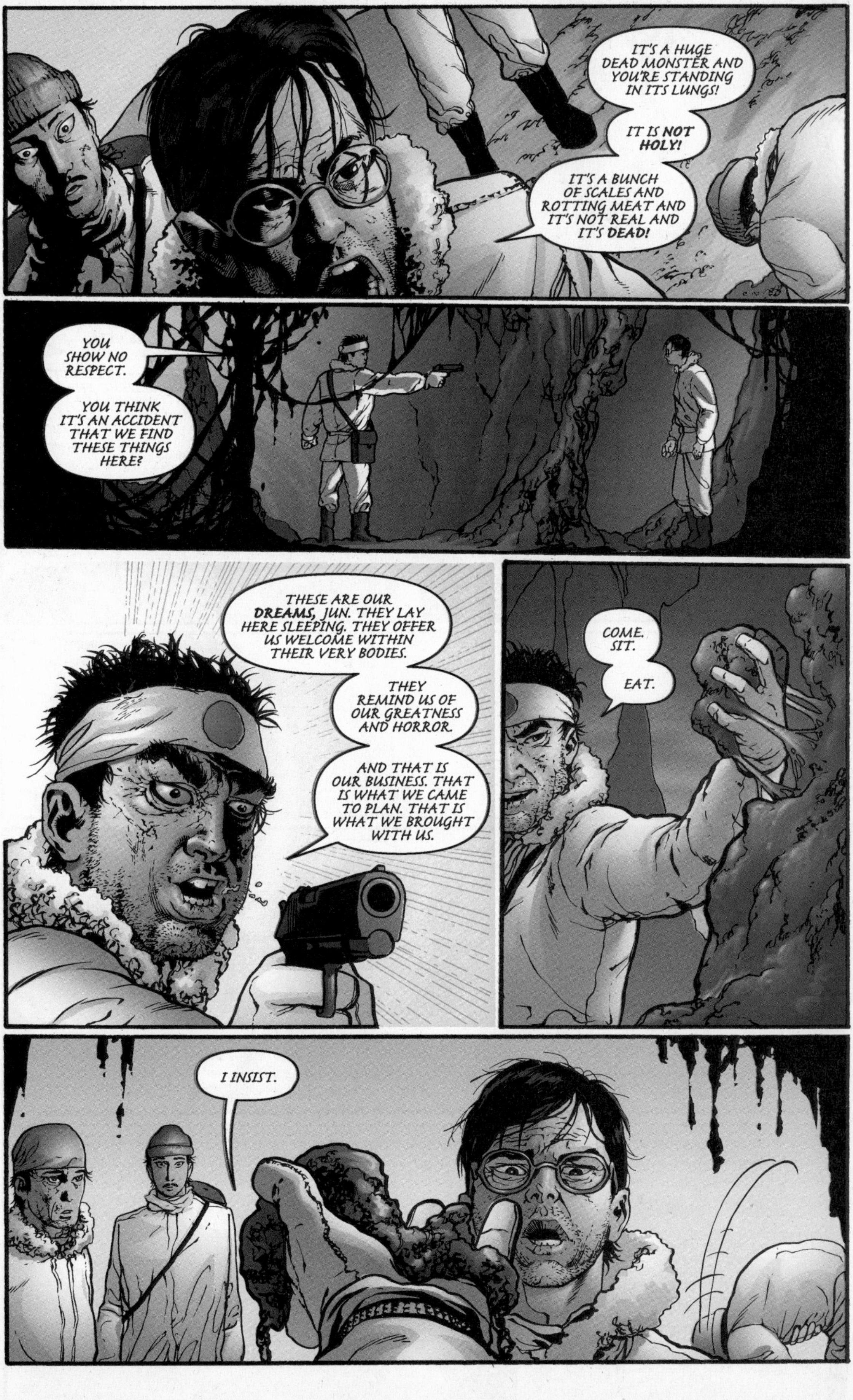
IT'S A HUGE DEAD MONSTER AND YOU'RE STANDING IN ITS LUNGS!
IT IS **NOT HOLY!**
IT'S A BUNCH OF SCALES AND ROTTING MEAT AND IT'S NOT REAL AND IT'S **DEAD!**
YOU SHOW NO RESPECT.
YOU THINK IT'S AN ACCIDENT THAT WE FIND THESE THINGS HERE?
THESE ARE OUR **DREAMS,** JUN. THEY LAY HERE SLEEPING. THEY OFFER US WELCOME WITHIN THEIR VERY BODIES.
THEY REMIND US OF OUR GREATNESS AND HORROR.
AND THAT IS OUR BUSINESS. THAT IS WHAT WE CAME TO PLAN. THAT IS WHAT WE BROUGHT WITH US.
COME. SIT.
EAT.
I INSIST.

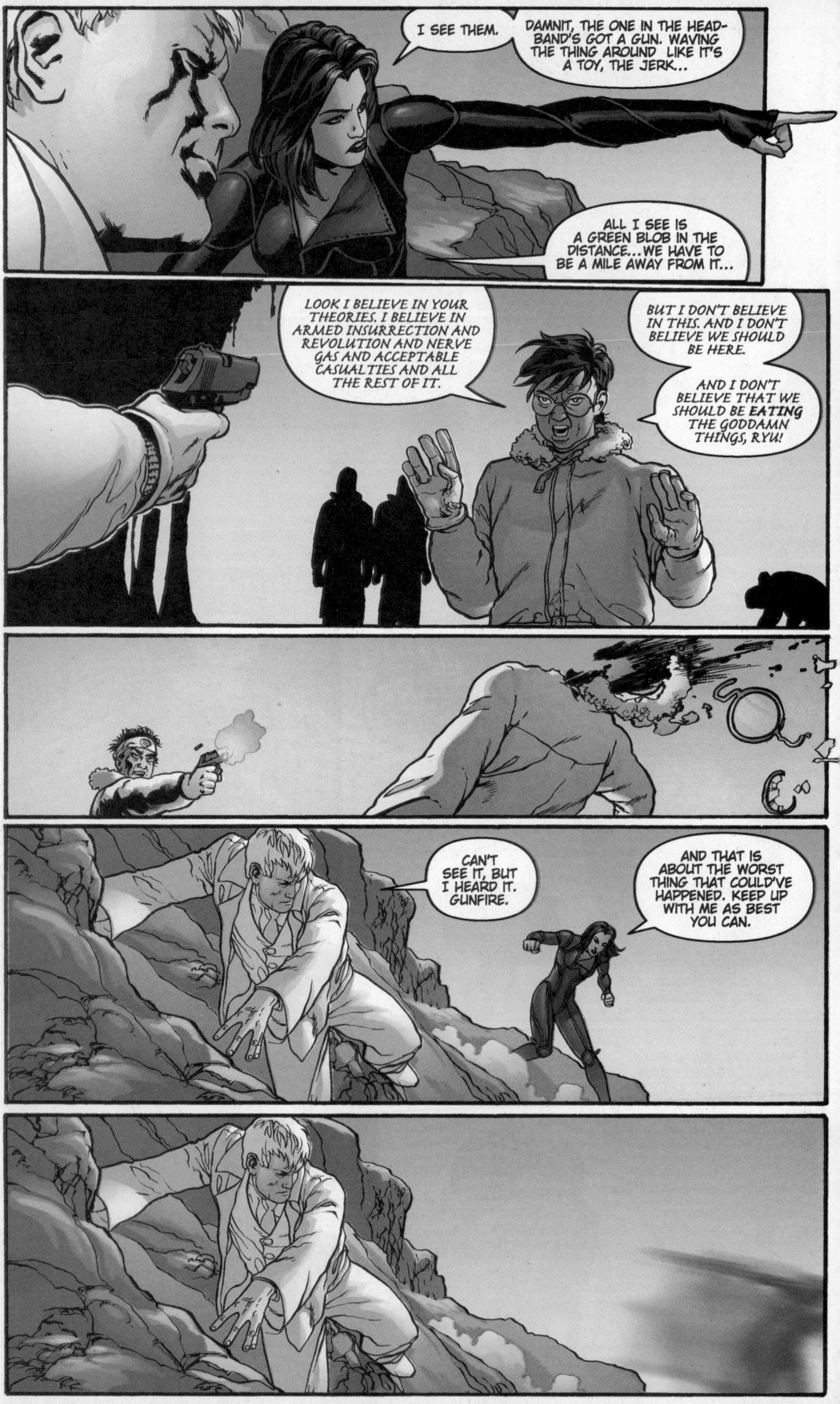
I SEE THEM.
DAMNIT, THE ONE IN THE HEAD-BAND'S GOT A GUN. WAVING THE THING AROUND LIKE IT'S A TOY, THE JERK...
ALL I SEE IS A GREEN BLOB IN THE DISTANCE...WE HAVE TO BE A MILE AWAY FROM IT...
LOOK I BELIEVE IN YOUR THEORIES. I BELIEVE IN ARMED INSURRECTION AND REVOLUTION AND NERVE GAS AND ACCEPTABLE CASUALTIES AND ALL THE REST OF IT.
BUT I DON'T BELIEVE IN THIS. AND I DON'T BELIEVE WE SHOULD BE HERE.
AND I DON'T BELIEVE THAT WE SHOULD BE EATING THE GODDAMN THINGS, RYU!
CAN'T SEE IT, BUT I HEARD IT. GUNFIRE.
AND THAT IS ABOUT THE WORST THING THAT COULD'VE HAPPENED. KEEP UP WITH ME AS BEST YOU CAN.

ARE THERE ANY MORE QUESTIONS ABOUT TONIGHT'S DINNER?

BRING ME THE KITBAGS. LET'S GET STARTED.

MAYBE WE SHOULD COOK JUN FIRST. AN APPETIZER.

I ATE HUMAN FLESH IN A SEX CLUB IN OSAKA IN 1989. BUT IT WASN'T COOKED. THEY SAID IT WOULD BE BAD TO DO THAT TO A GIRLFRIEND.

TURN AROUND.

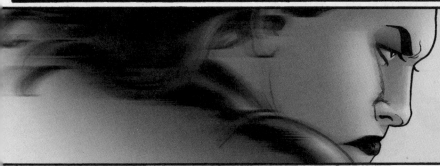

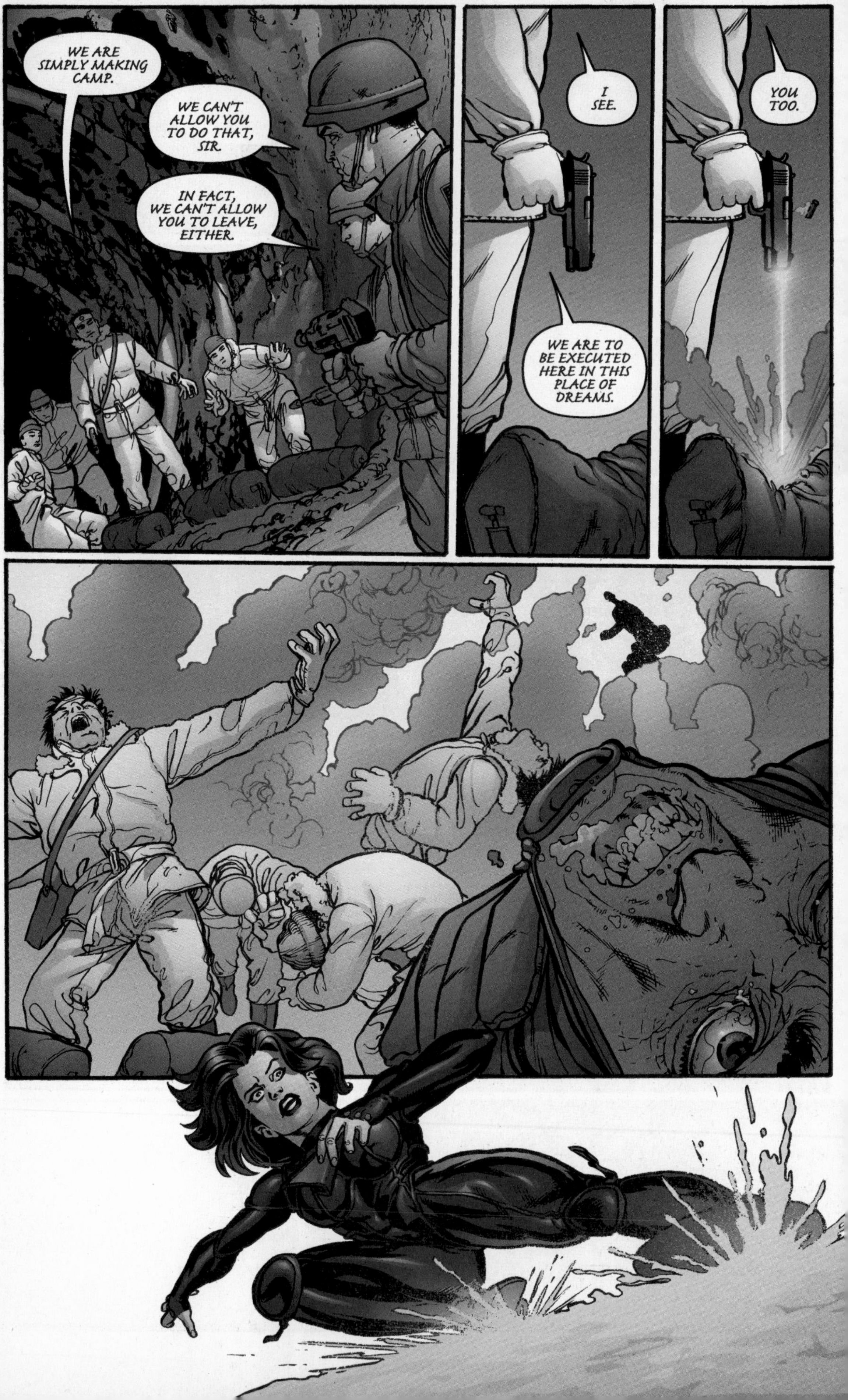
WE ARE SIMPLY MAKING CAMP.
WE CAN'T ALLOW YOU TO DO THAT, SIR.
IN FACT, WE CAN'T ALLOW YOU TO LEAVE, EITHER.
I SEE.
WE ARE TO BE EXECUTED HERE IN THIS PLACE OF DREAMS.
YOU TOO.

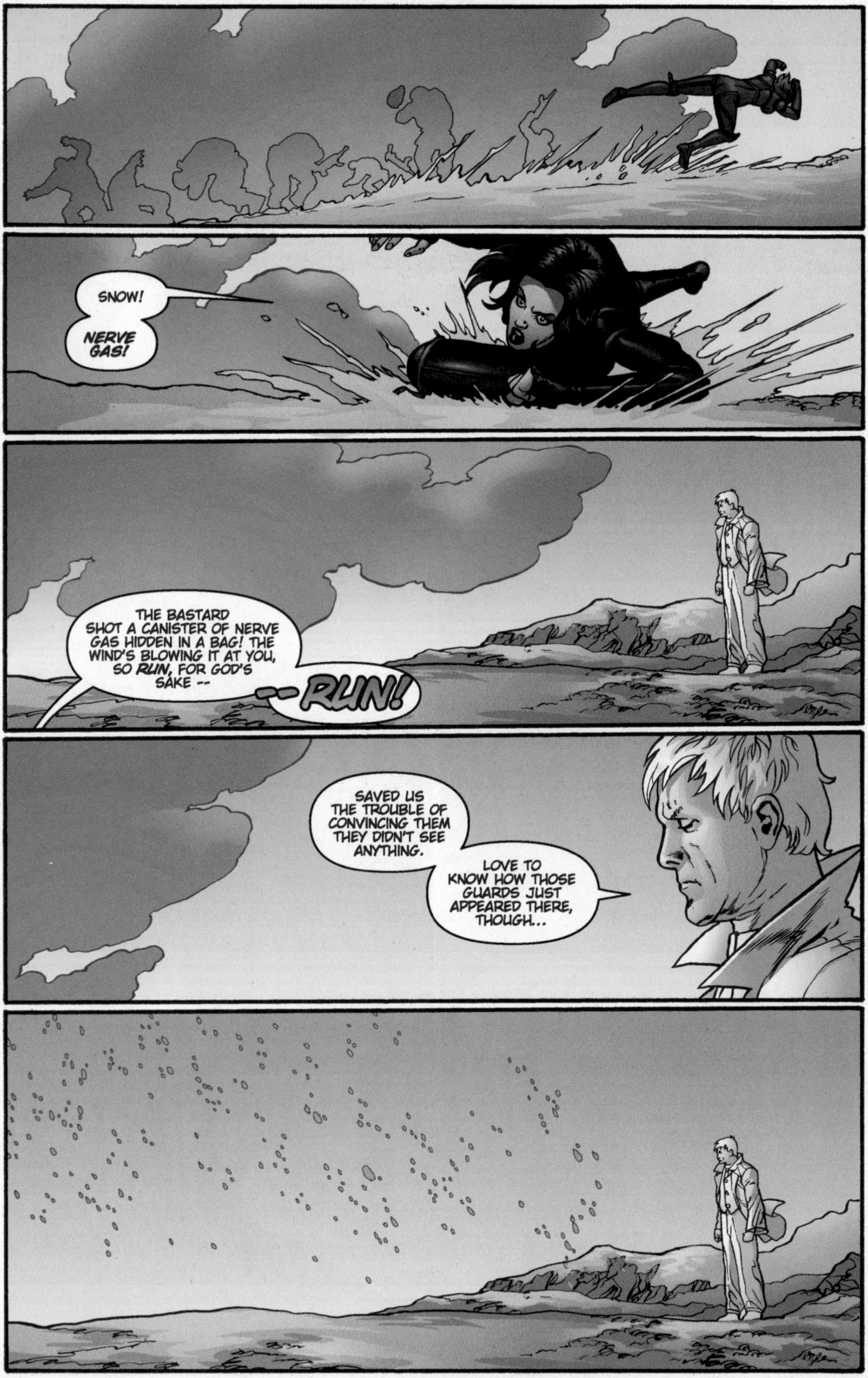

SNOW!
NERVE GAS!
THE BASTARD SHOT A CANISTER OF NERVE GAS HIDDEN IN A BAG! THE WIND'S BLOWING IT AT YOU, SO RUN, FOR GOD'S SAKE --
--RUN!
SAVED US THE TROUBLE OF CONVINCING THEM THEY DIDN'T SEE ANYTHING.
LOVE TO KNOW HOW THOSE GUARDS JUST APPEARED THERE, THOUGH...

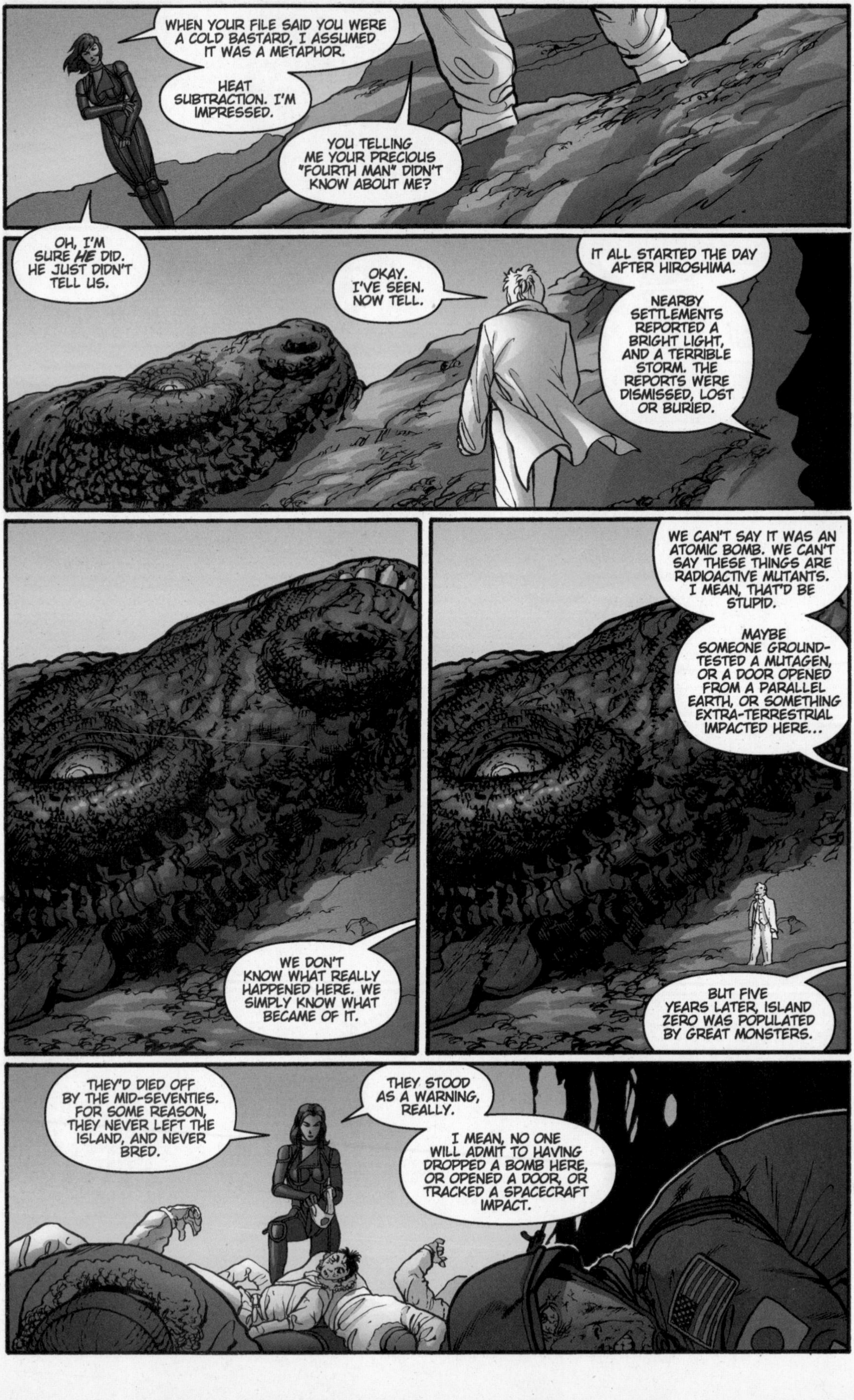
WHEN YOUR FILE SAID YOU WERE A COLD BASTARD, I ASSUMED IT WAS A METAPHOR.
HEAT SUBTRACTION. I'M IMPRESSED.
YOU TELLING ME YOUR PRECIOUS "FOURTH MAN" DIDN'T KNOW ABOUT ME?
OH, I'M SURE HE DID. HE JUST DIDN'T TELL US.
OKAY. I'VE SEEN. NOW TELL.
IT ALL STARTED THE DAY AFTER HIROSHIMA.
NEARBY SETTLEMENTS REPORTED A BRIGHT LIGHT, AND A TERRIBLE STORM. THE REPORTS WERE DISMISSED, LOST OR BURIED.
WE DON'T KNOW WHAT REALLY HAPPENED HERE. WE SIMPLY KNOW WHAT BECAME OF IT.
WE CAN'T SAY IT WAS AN ATOMIC BOMB. WE CAN'T SAY THESE THINGS ARE RADIOACTIVE MUTANTS. I MEAN, THAT'D BE STUPID.
MAYBE SOMEONE GROUND-TESTED A MUTAGEN, OR A DOOR OPENED FROM A PARALLEL EARTH, OR SOMETHING EXTRA-TERRESTRIAL IMPACTED HERE...
BUT FIVE YEARS LATER, ISLAND ZERO WAS POPULATED BY GREAT MONSTERS.
THEY'D DIED OFF BY THE MID-SEVENTIES. FOR SOME REASON, THEY NEVER LEFT THE ISLAND, AND NEVER BRED.
THEY STOOD AS A WARNING, REALLY.
I MEAN, NO ONE WILL ADMIT TO HAVING DROPPED A BOMB HERE, OR OPENED A DOOR, OR TRACKED A SPACECRAFT IMPACT.

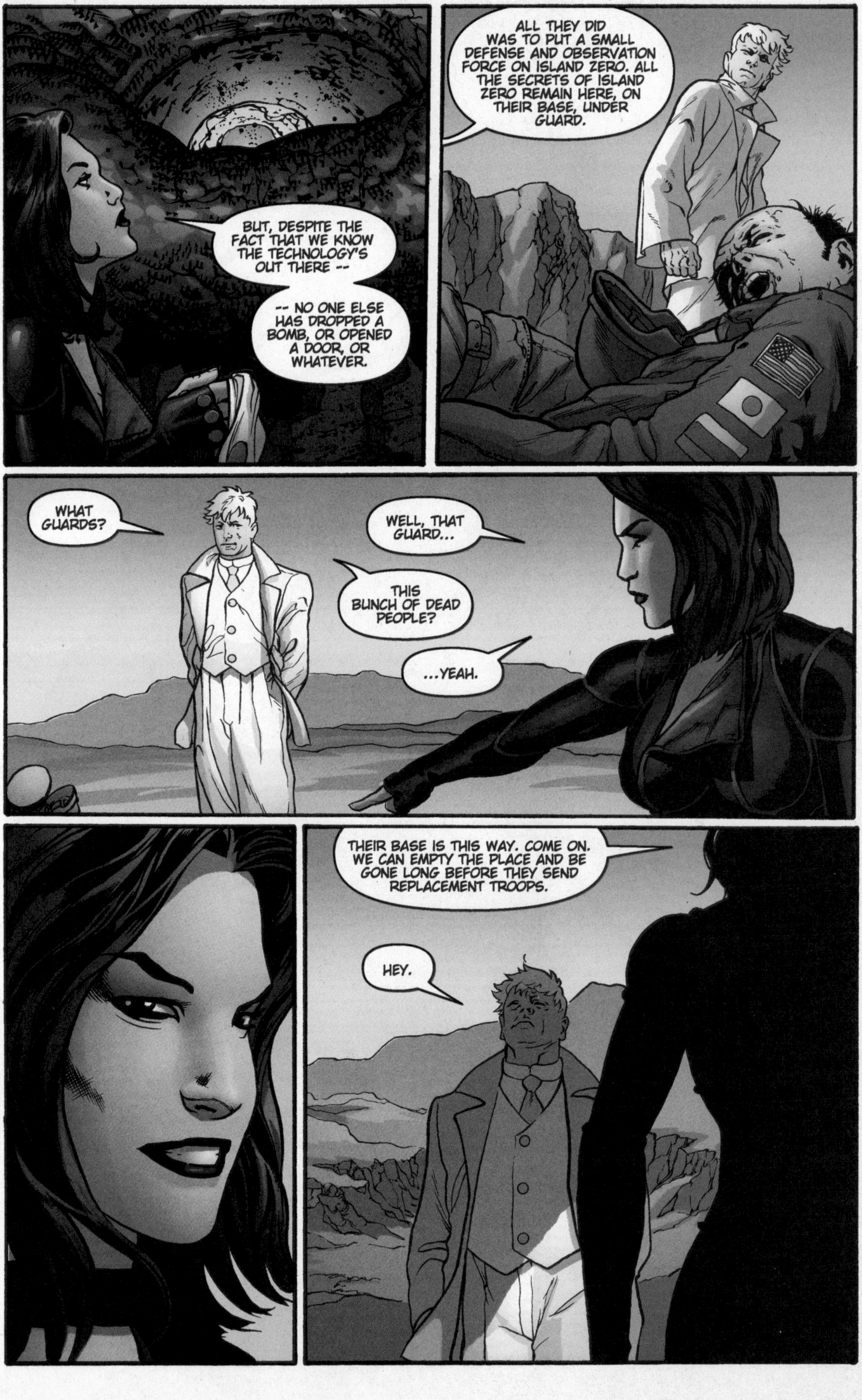
BUT, DESPITE THE FACT THAT WE KNOW THE TECHNOLOGY'S OUT THERE --
-- NO ONE ELSE HAS DROPPED A BOMB, OR OPENED A DOOR, OR WHATEVER.
ALL THEY DID WAS TO PUT A SMALL DEFENSE AND OBSERVATION FORCE ON ISLAND ZERO. ALL THE SECRETS OF ISLAND ZERO REMAIN HERE, ON THEIR BASE, UNDER GUARD.
WHAT GUARDS?
WELL, THAT GUARD...
THIS BUNCH OF DEAD PEOPLE?
...YEAH.
THEIR BASE IS THIS WAY. COME ON. WE CAN EMPTY THE PLACE AND BE GONE LONG BEFORE THEY SEND REPLACEMENT TROOPS.
HEY.

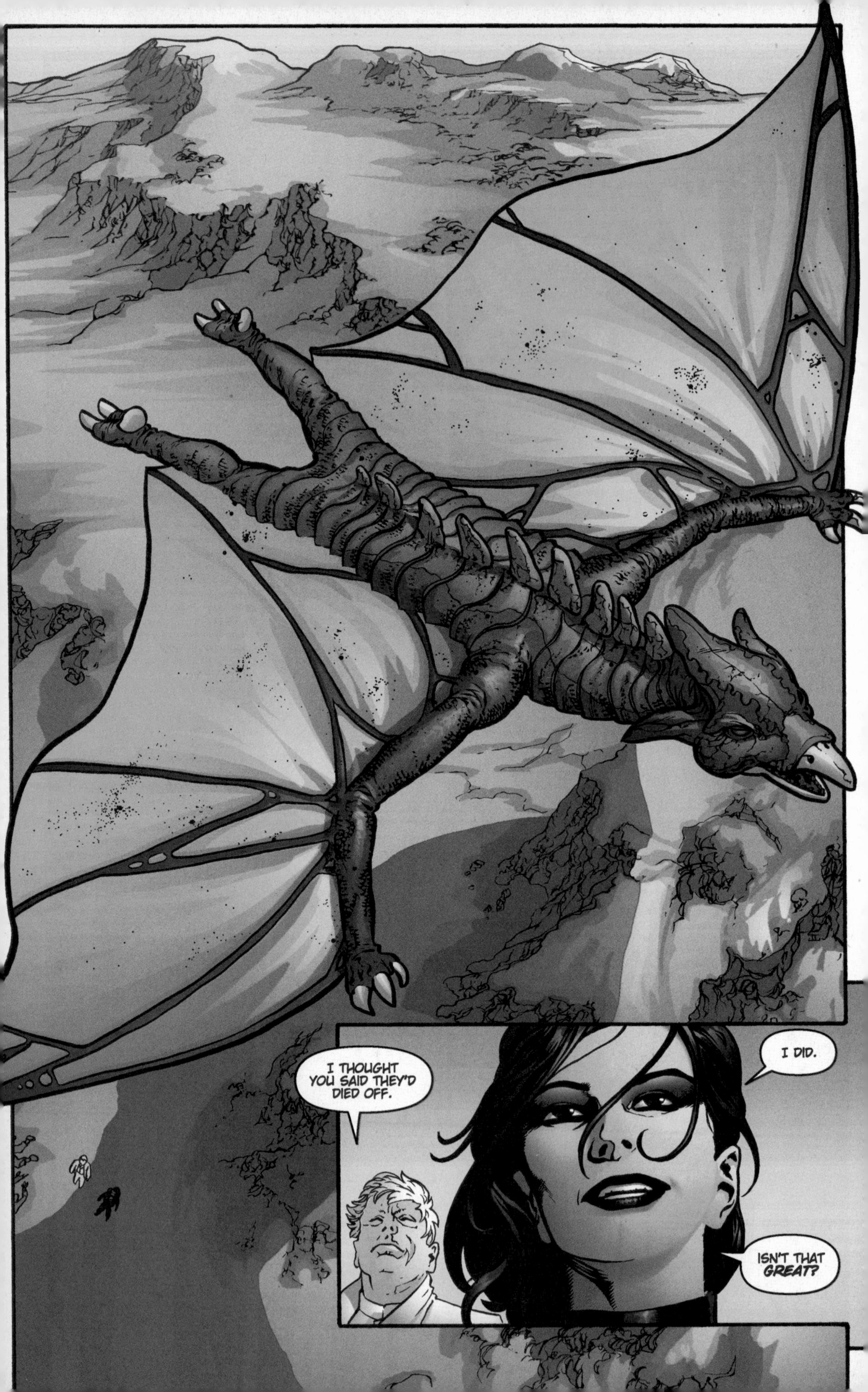
I THOUGHT YOU SAID THEY'D DIED OFF.
I DID.
ISN'T THAT *GREAT?*

CHAPTER
THREE

PLANETARY™

ELLIS · CASSADAY · DEPUY

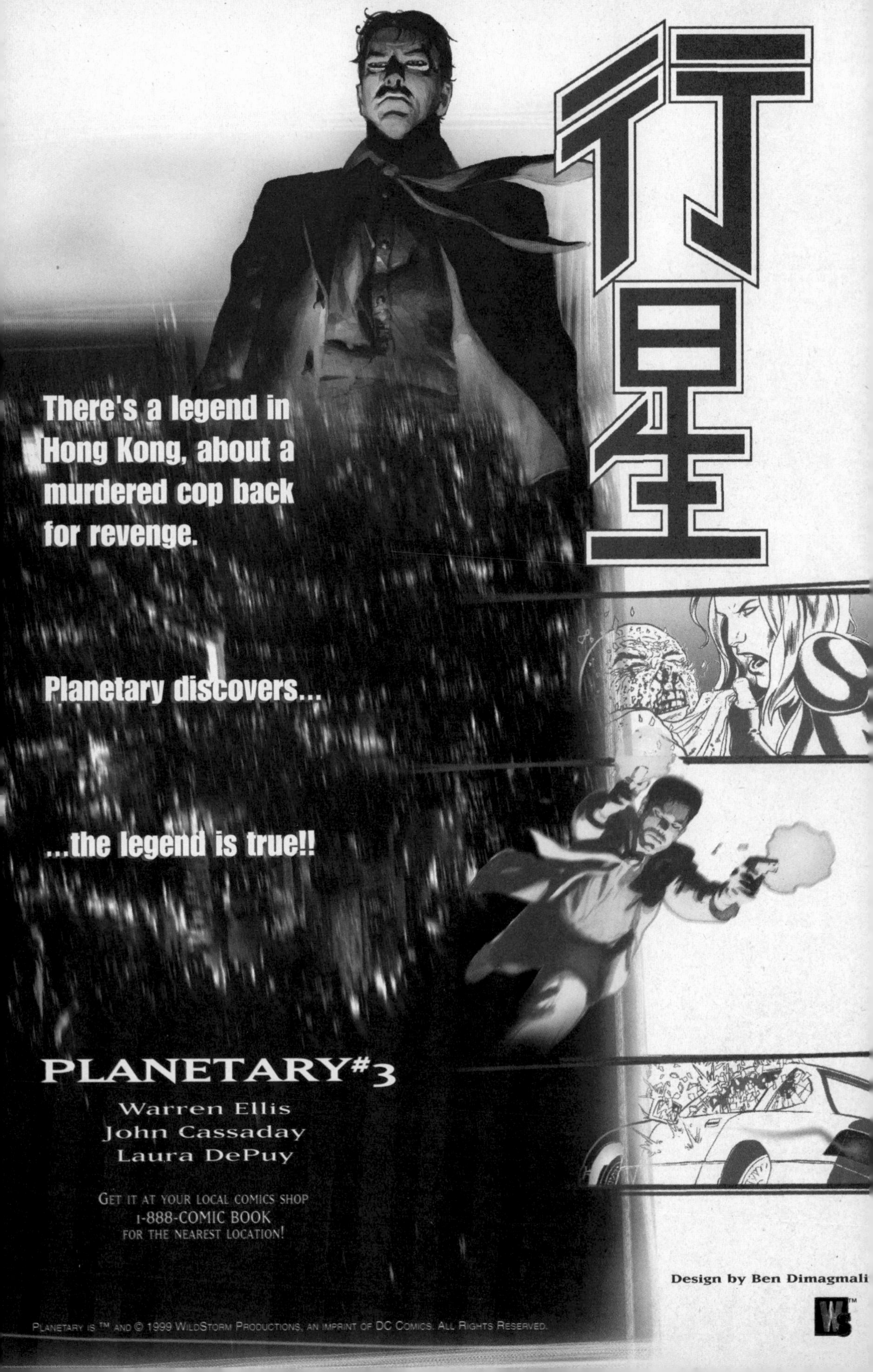
There's a legend in Hong Kong, about a murdered cop back for revenge.
Planetary discovers...
...the legend is true!!
PLANETARY#3
Warren Ellis
John Cassaday
Laura DePuy
GET IT AT YOUR LOCAL COMICS SHOP
1-888-COMIC BOOK
FOR THE NEAREST LOCATION!
Design by Ben Dimagmali
PLANETARY IS ™ AND © 1999 WILDSTORM PRODUCTIONS, AN IMPRINT OF DC COMICS. ALL RIGHTS RESERVED.

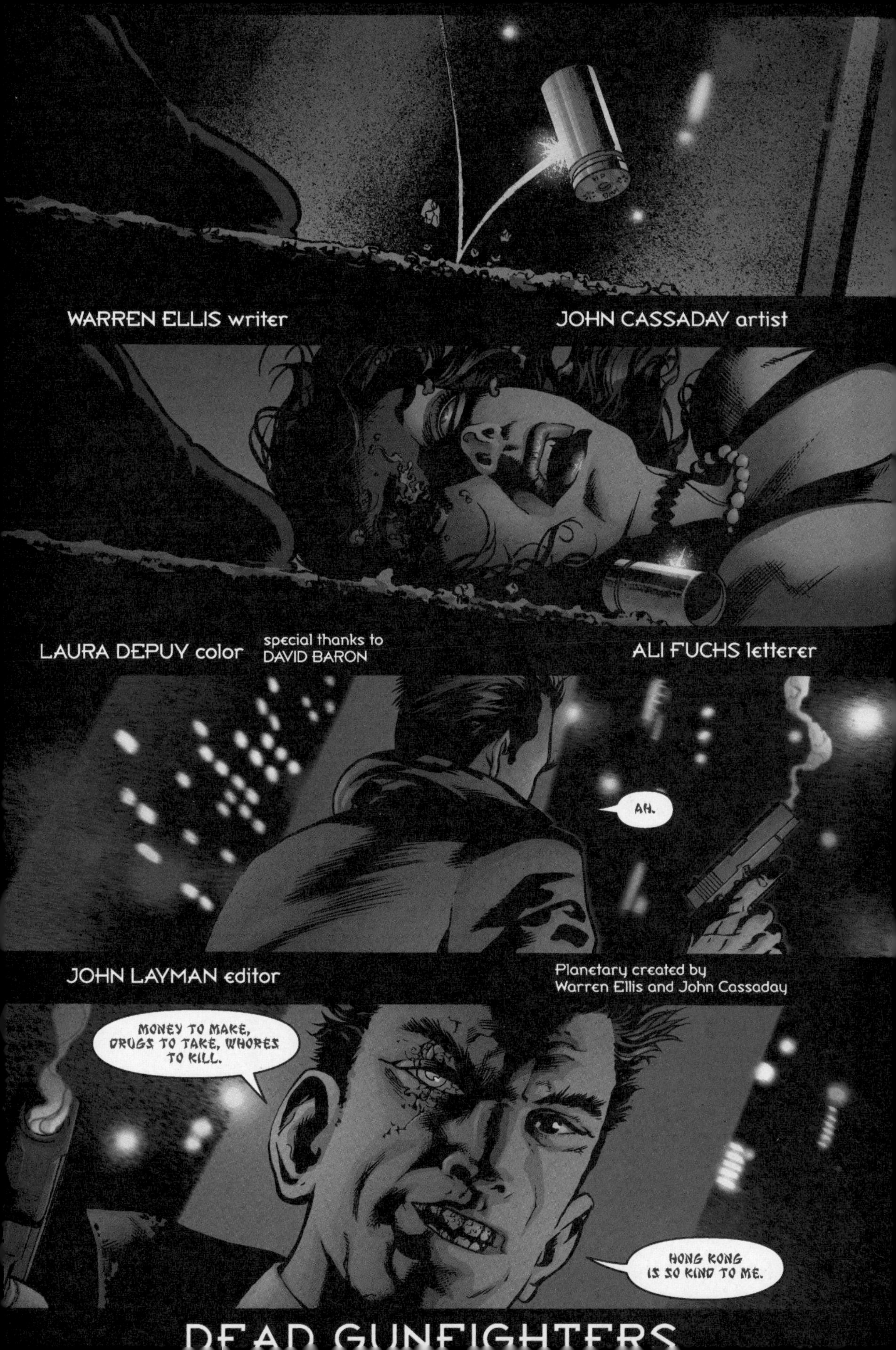
WARREN ELLIS writer
JOHN CASSADAY artist
LAURA DEPUY color
special thanks to DAVID BARON
ALI FUCHS letterer
AH.
JOHN LAYMAN editor
Planetary created by Warren Ellis and John Cassaday
MONEY TO MAKE, DRUGS TO TAKE, WHORES TO KILL.
HONG KONG IS SO KIND TO ME.
DEAD GUNFIGHTERS

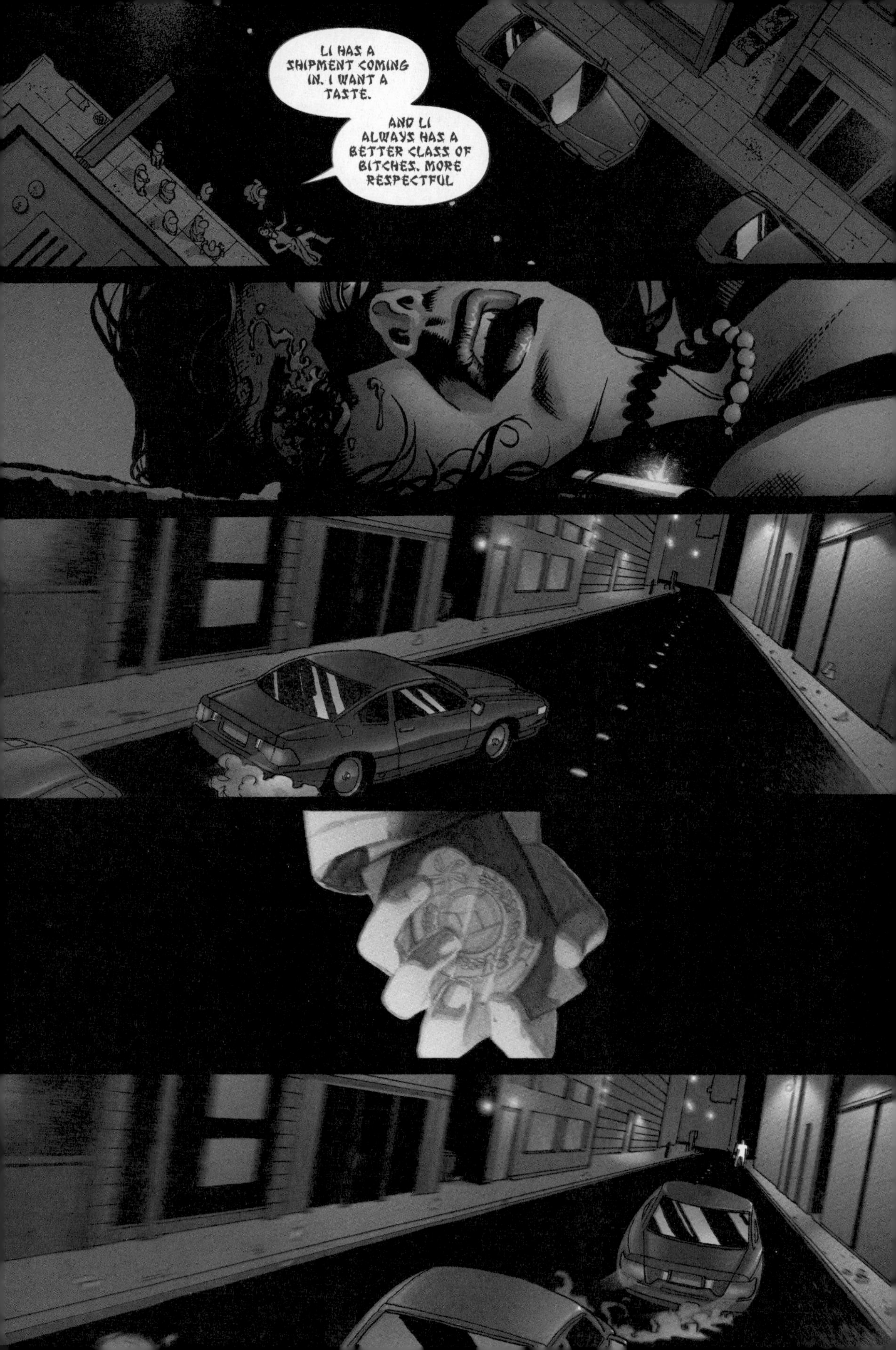
LI HAS A SHIPMENT COMING IN. I WANT A TASTE.
AND LI ALWAYS HAS A BETTER CLASS OF BITCHES. MORE RESPECTFUL

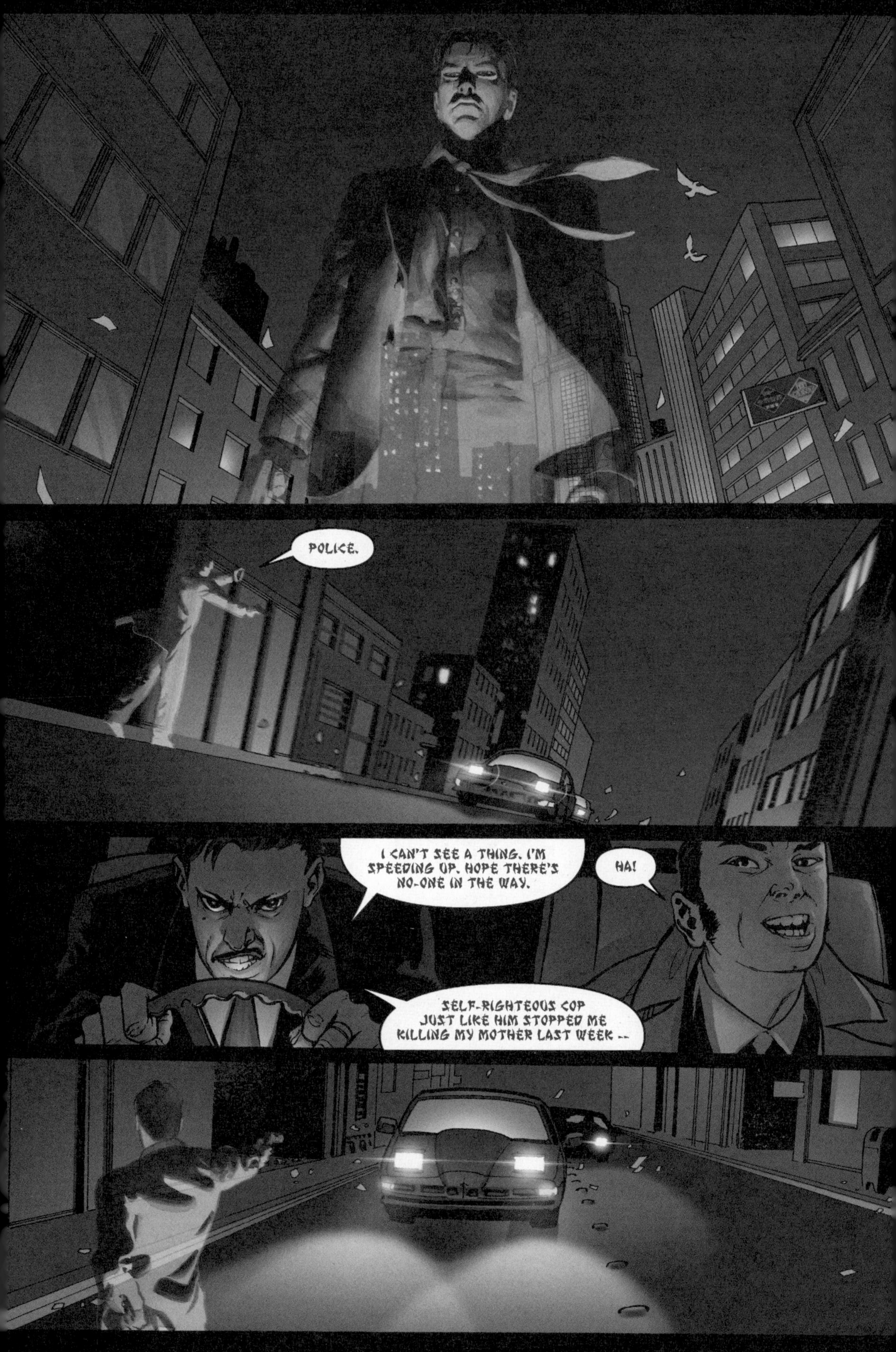
POLICE.
I CAN'T SEE A THING. I'M SPEEDING UP. HOPE THERE'S NO-ONE IN THE WAY.
HA!
SELF-RIGHTEOUS COP JUST LIKE HIM STOPPED ME KILLING MY MOTHER LAST WEEK --

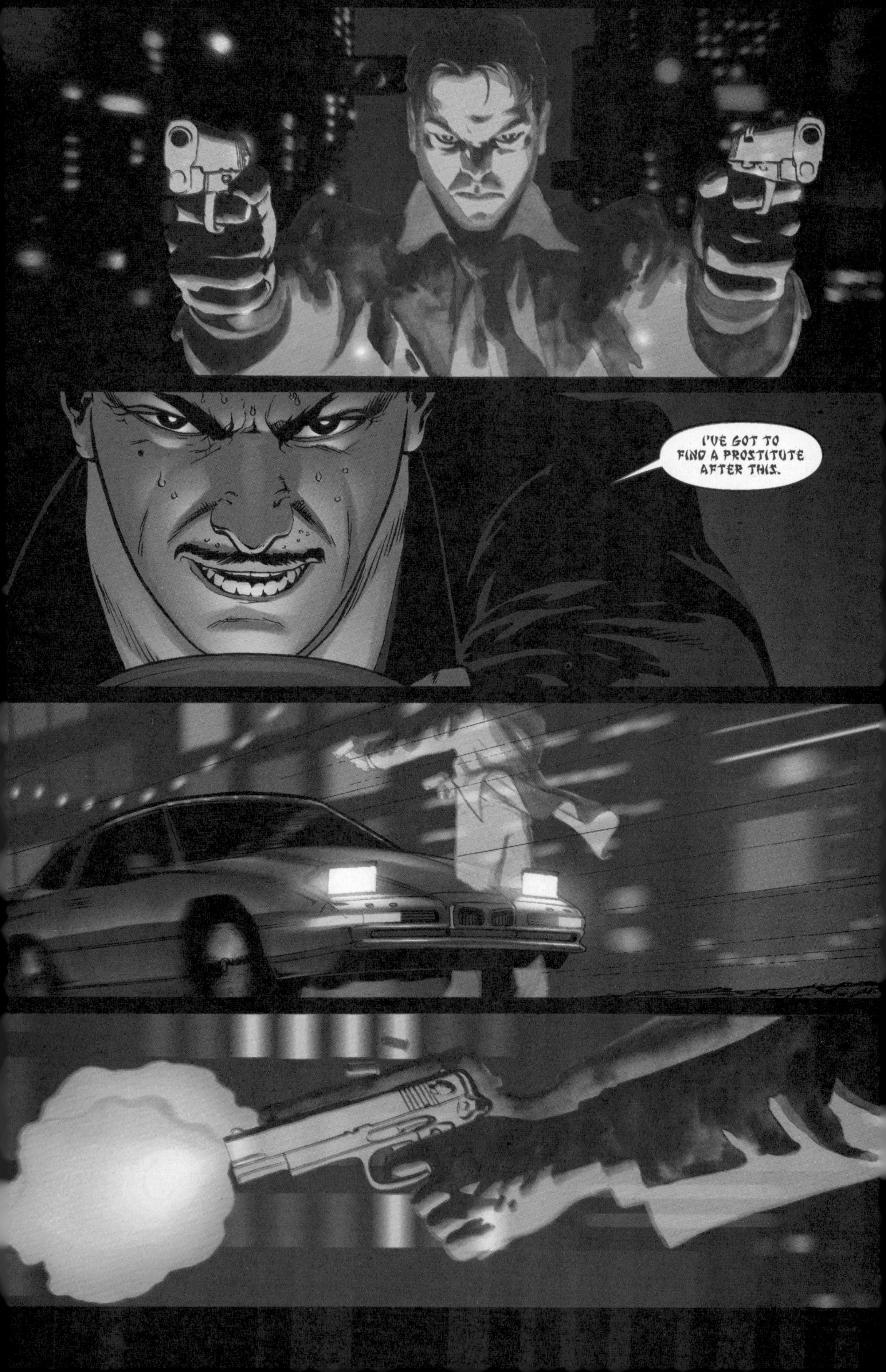
I'VE GOT TO FIND A PROSTITUTE AFTER THIS.

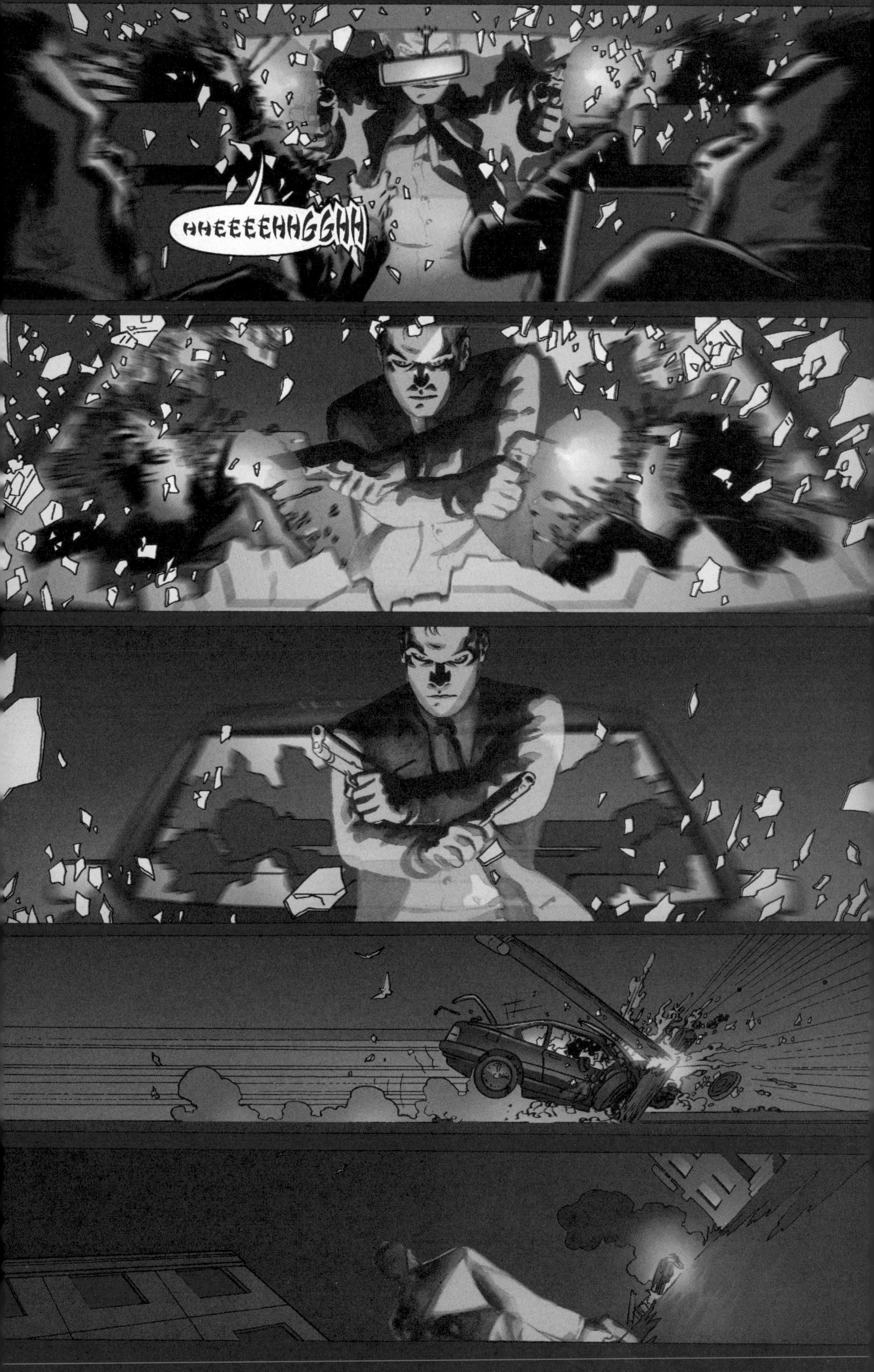
HHEEEEEHHGGHH

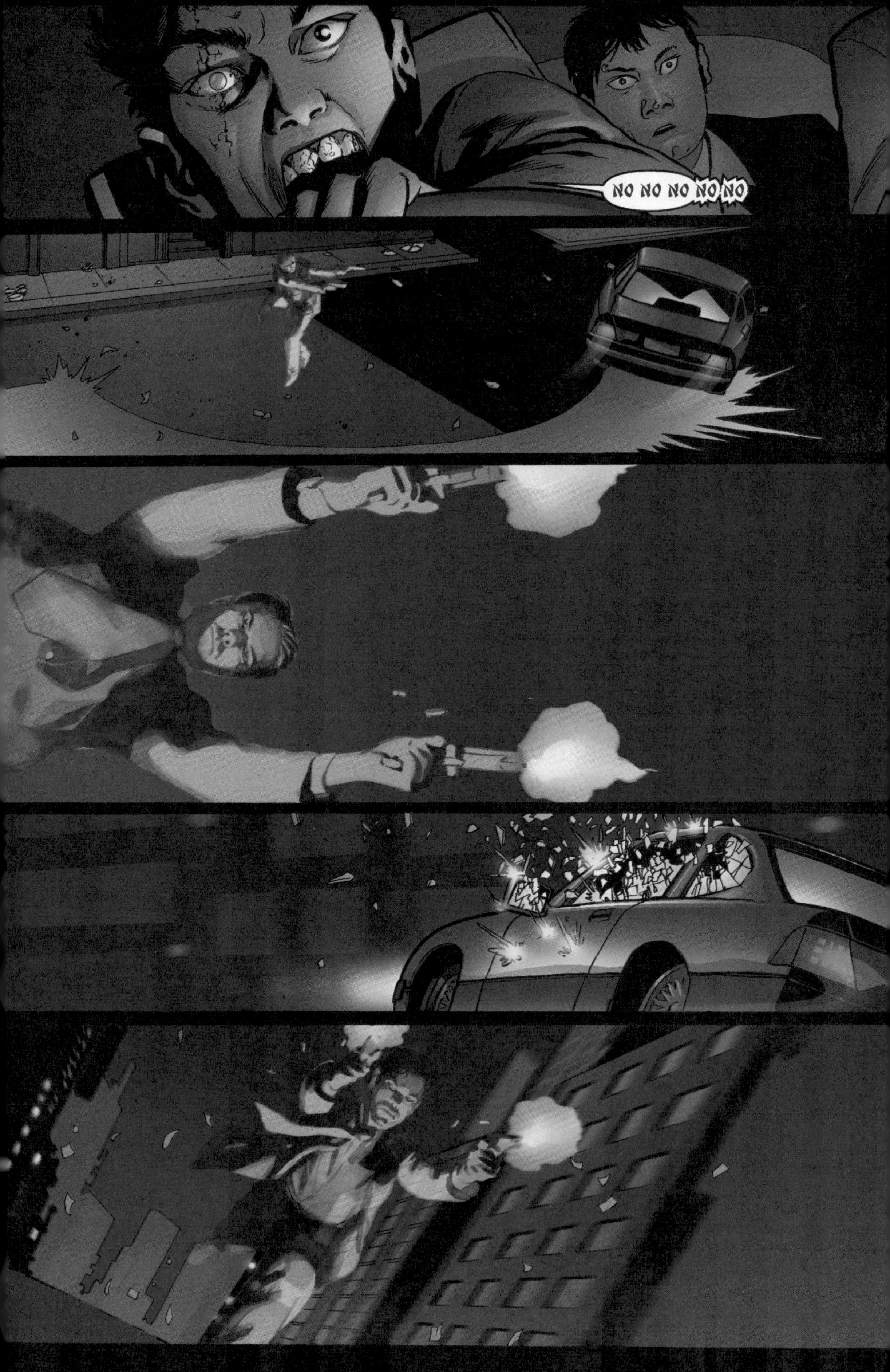
NO NO NO NO NO

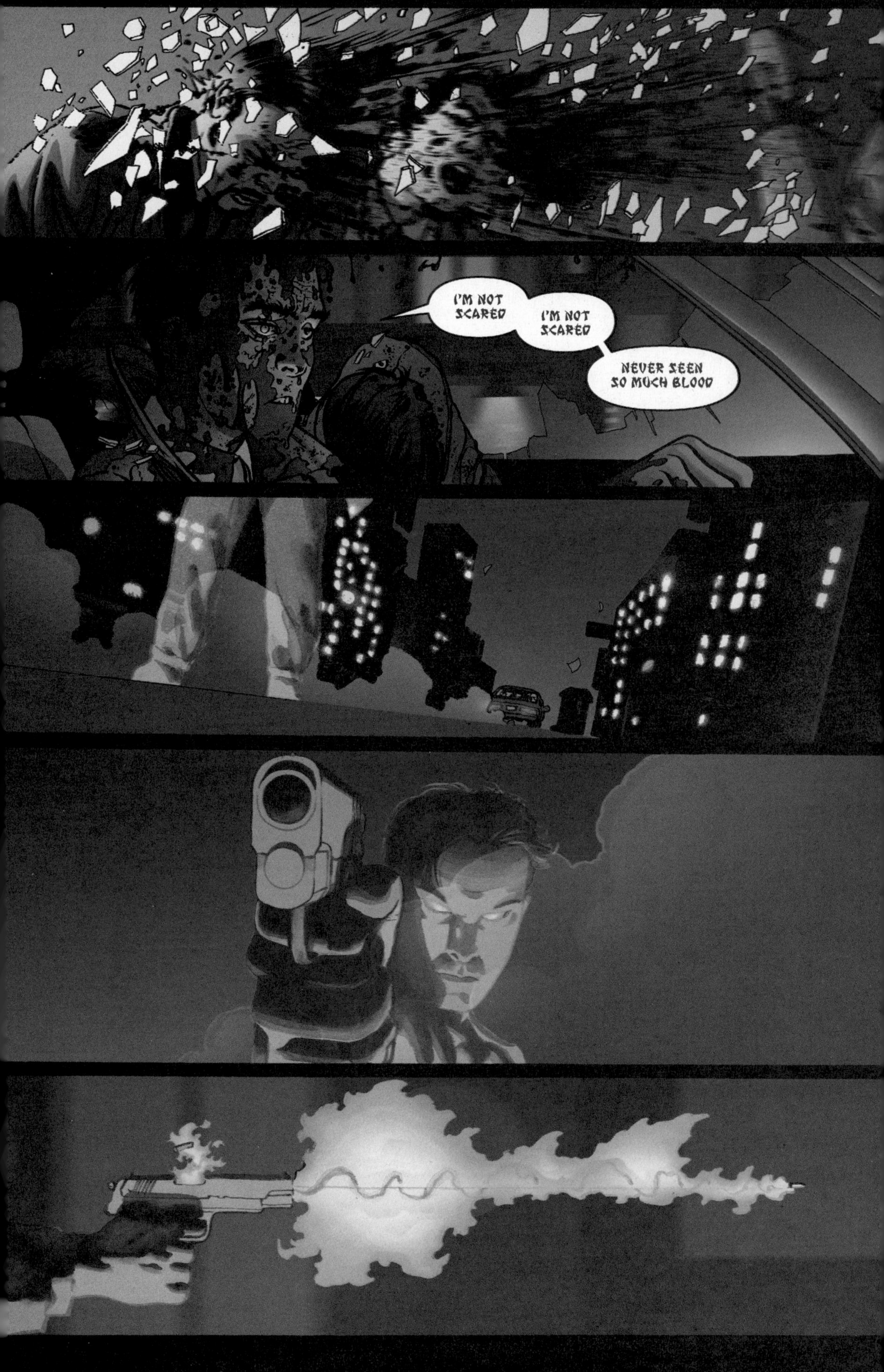
I'M NOT SCARED
I'M NOT SCARED
NEVER SEEN SO MUCH BLOOD

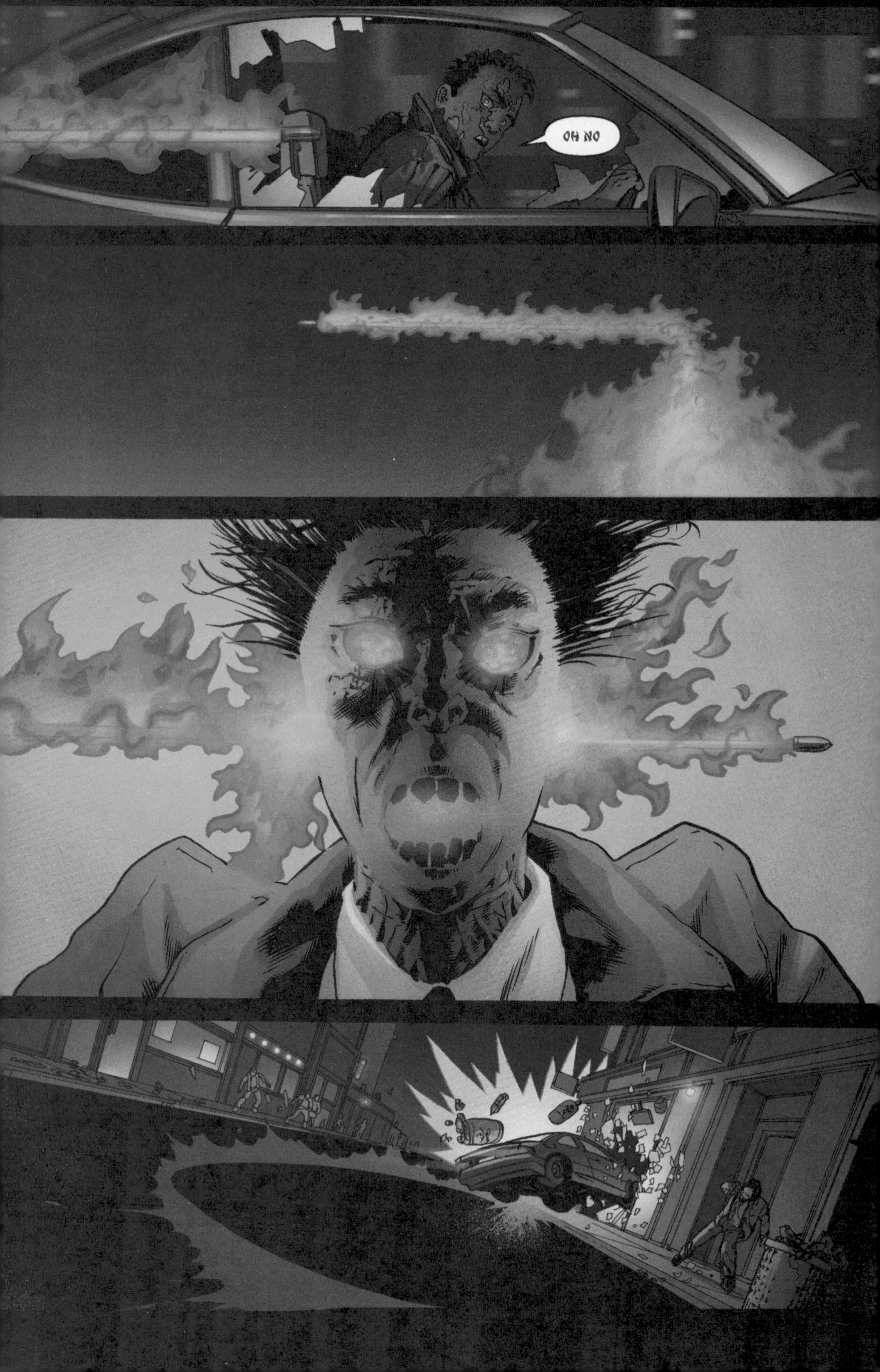
OH NO

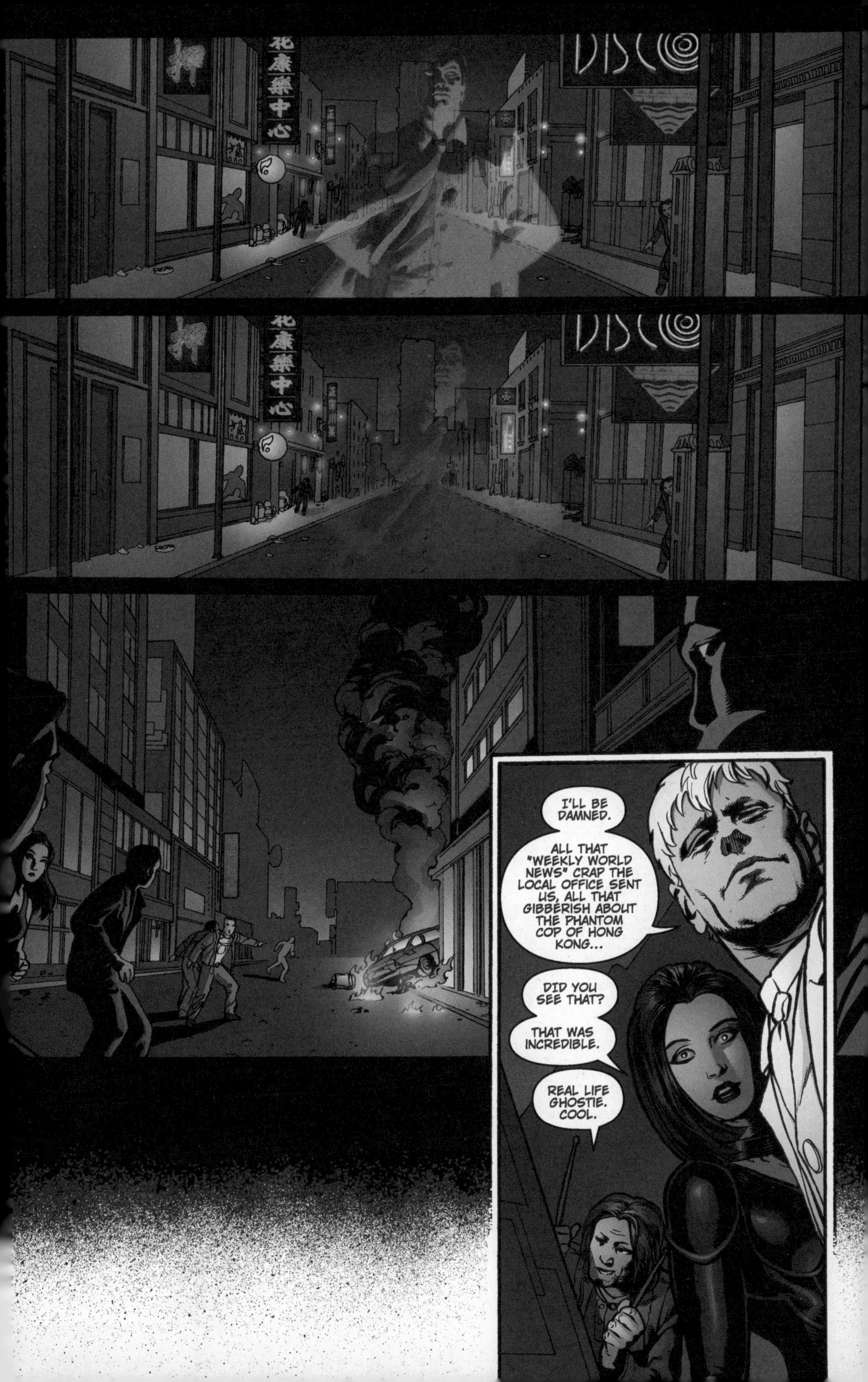
DISCO
I'LL BE DAMNED.
ALL THAT "WEEKLY WORLD NEWS" CRAP THE LOCAL OFFICE SENT US, ALL THAT GIBBERISH ABOUT THE PHANTOM COP OF HONG KONG...
DID YOU SEE THAT?
THAT WAS INCREDIBLE.
REAL LIFE GHOSTIE. COOL.

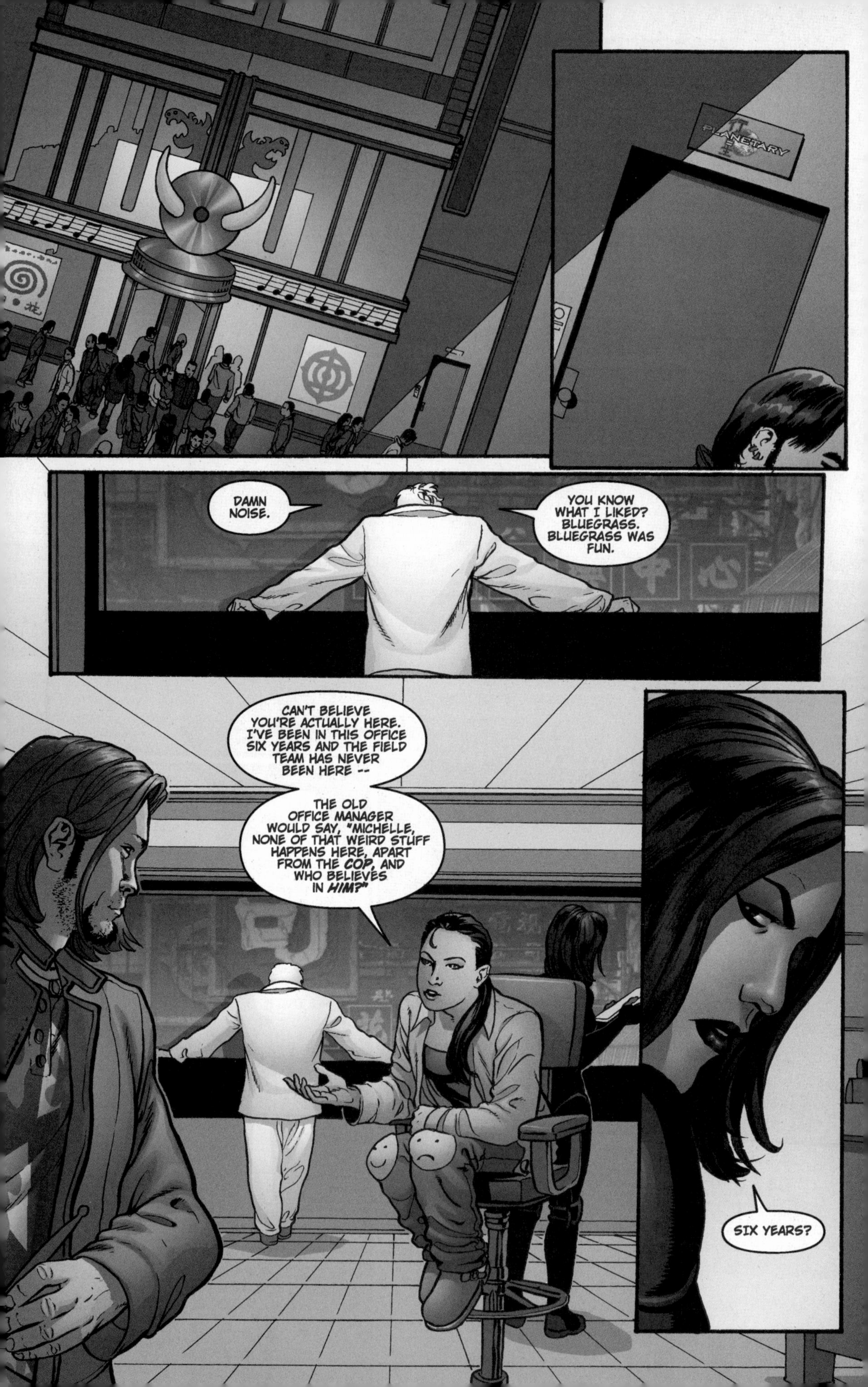
PLANETARY
DAMN NOISE.
YOU KNOW WHAT I LIKED? BLUEGRASS. BLUEGRASS WAS FUN.
CAN'T BELIEVE YOU'RE ACTUALLY HERE. I'VE BEEN IN THIS OFFICE SIX YEARS AND THE FIELD TEAM HAS NEVER BEEN HERE --
THE OLD OFFICE MANAGER WOULD SAY, "MICHELLE, NONE OF THAT WEIRD STUFF HAPPENS HERE, APART FROM THE COP, AND WHO BELIEVES IN HIM?"
SIX YEARS?

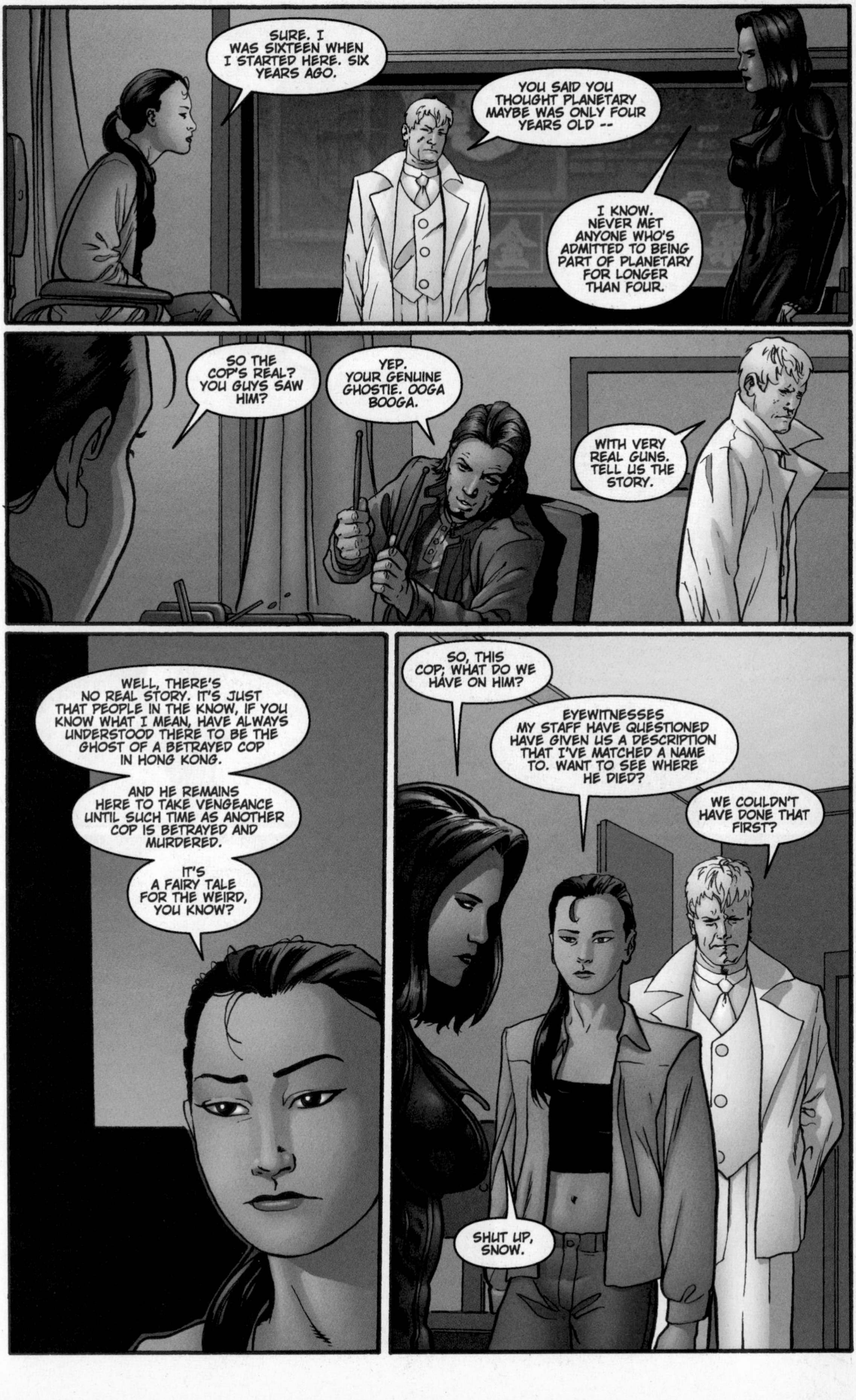
SURE. I WAS SIXTEEN WHEN I STARTED HERE. SIX YEARS AGO.
YOU SAID YOU THOUGHT PLANETARY MAYBE WAS ONLY FOUR YEARS OLD --
I KNOW. NEVER MET ANYONE WHO'S ADMITTED TO BEING PART OF PLANETARY FOR LONGER THAN FOUR.
SO THE COP'S REAL? YOU GUYS SAW HIM?
YEP. YOUR GENUINE GHOSTIE. OOGA BOOGA.
WITH VERY REAL GUNS. TELL US THE STORY.
WELL, THERE'S NO REAL STORY. IT'S JUST THAT PEOPLE IN THE KNOW, IF YOU KNOW WHAT I MEAN, HAVE ALWAYS UNDERSTOOD THERE TO BE THE GHOST OF A BETRAYED COP IN HONG KONG.
AND HE REMAINS HERE TO TAKE VENGEANCE UNTIL SUCH TIME AS ANOTHER COP IS BETRAYED AND MURDERED.
IT'S A FAIRY TALE FOR THE WEIRD, YOU KNOW?
SO, THIS COP; WHAT DO WE HAVE ON HIM?
EYEWITNESSES MY STAFF HAVE QUESTIONED HAVE GIVEN US A DESCRIPTION THAT I'VE MATCHED A NAME TO. WANT TO SEE WHERE HE DIED?
WE COULDN'T HAVE DONE THAT FIRST?
SHUT UP, SNOW.

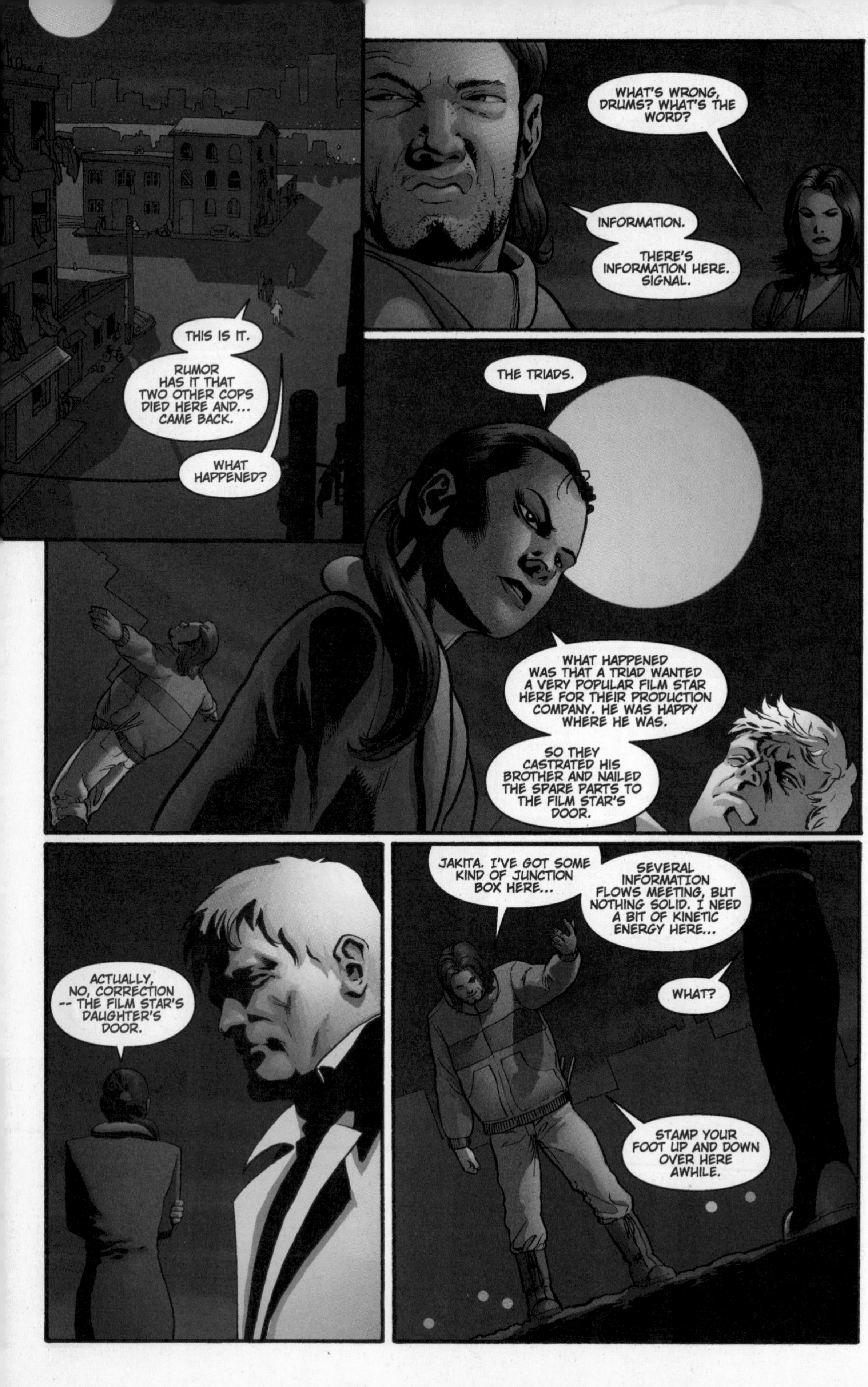
WHAT'S WRONG, DRUMS? WHAT'S THE WORD?
INFORMATION.
THERE'S INFORMATION HERE. SIGNAL.
THIS IS IT.
RUMOR HAS IT THAT TWO OTHER COPS DIED HERE AND... CAME BACK.
WHAT HAPPENED?
THE TRIADS.
WHAT HAPPENED WAS THAT A TRIAD WANTED A VERY POPULAR FILM STAR HERE FOR THEIR PRODUCTION COMPANY. HE WAS HAPPY WHERE HE WAS.
SO THEY CASTRATED HIS BROTHER AND NAILED THE SPARE PARTS TO THE FILM STAR'S DOOR.
ACTUALLY, NO, CORRECTION -- THE FILM STAR'S DAUGHTER'S DOOR.
JAKITA. I'VE GOT SOME KIND OF JUNCTION BOX HERE...
SEVERAL INFORMATION FLOWS MEETING, BUT NOTHING SOLID. I NEED A BIT OF KINETIC ENERGY HERE...
WHAT?
STAMP YOUR FOOT UP AND DOWN OVER HERE AWHILE.

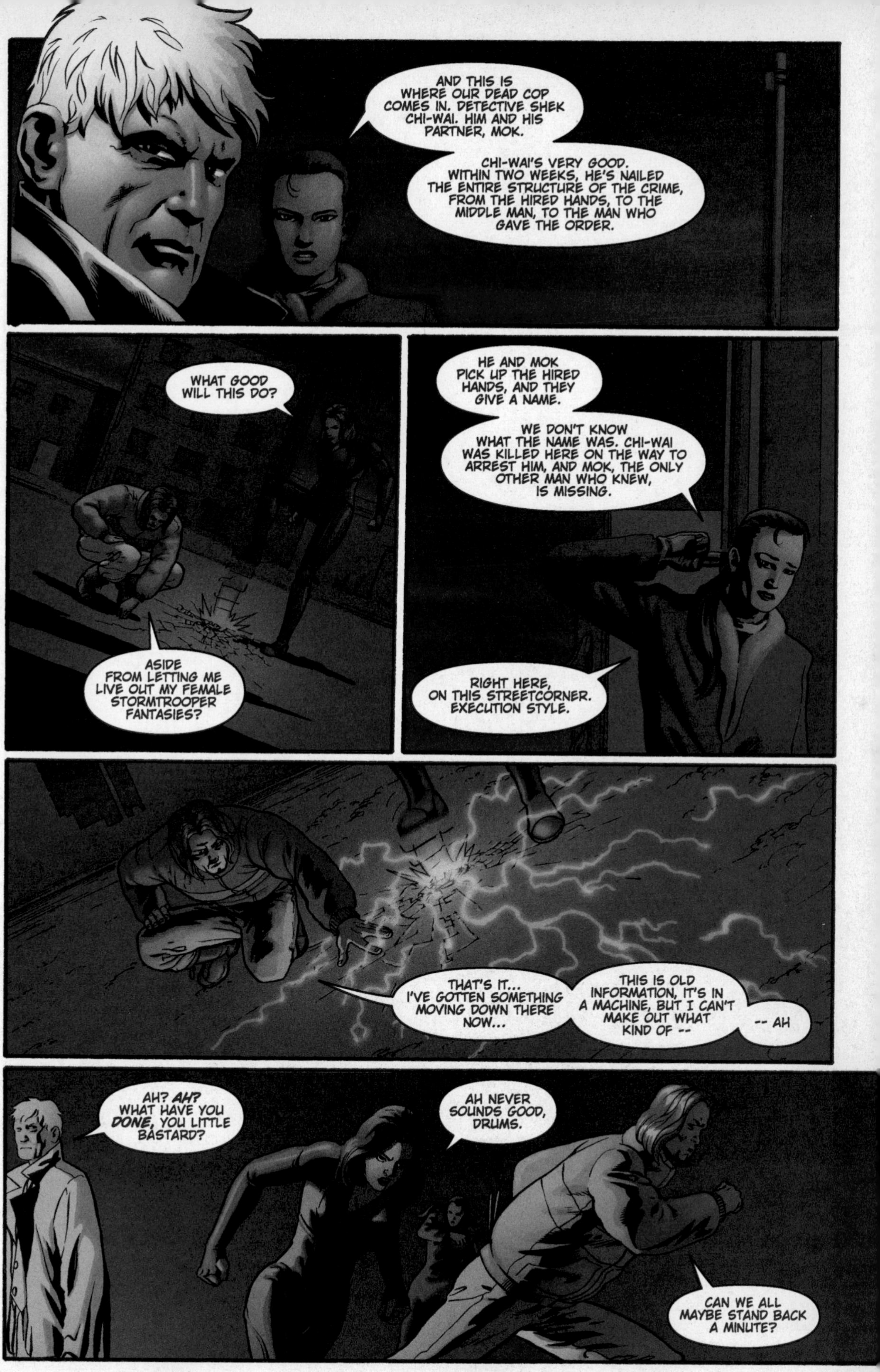
AND THIS IS WHERE OUR DEAD COP COMES IN. DETECTIVE SHEK CHI-WAI. HIM AND HIS PARTNER, MOK.
CHI-WAI'S VERY GOOD. WITHIN TWO WEEKS, HE'S NAILED THE ENTIRE STRUCTURE OF THE CRIME, FROM THE HIRED HANDS, TO THE MIDDLE MAN, TO THE MAN WHO GAVE THE ORDER.
WHAT GOOD WILL THIS DO?
ASIDE FROM LETTING ME LIVE OUT MY FEMALE STORMTROOPER FANTASIES?
HE AND MOK PICK UP THE HIRED HANDS, AND THEY GIVE A NAME.
WE DON'T KNOW WHAT THE NAME WAS. CHI-WAI WAS KILLED HERE ON THE WAY TO ARREST HIM, AND MOK, THE ONLY OTHER MAN WHO KNEW, IS MISSING.
RIGHT HERE, ON THIS STREETCORNER. EXECUTION STYLE.
THAT'S IT... I'VE GOTTEN SOMETHING MOVING DOWN THERE NOW...
THIS IS OLD INFORMATION, IT'S IN A MACHINE, BUT I CAN'T MAKE OUT WHAT KIND OF --
-- AH
AH? AH? WHAT HAVE YOU DONE, YOU LITTLE BASTARD?
AH NEVER SOUNDS GOOD, DRUMS.
CAN WE ALL MAYBE STAND BACK A MINUTE?

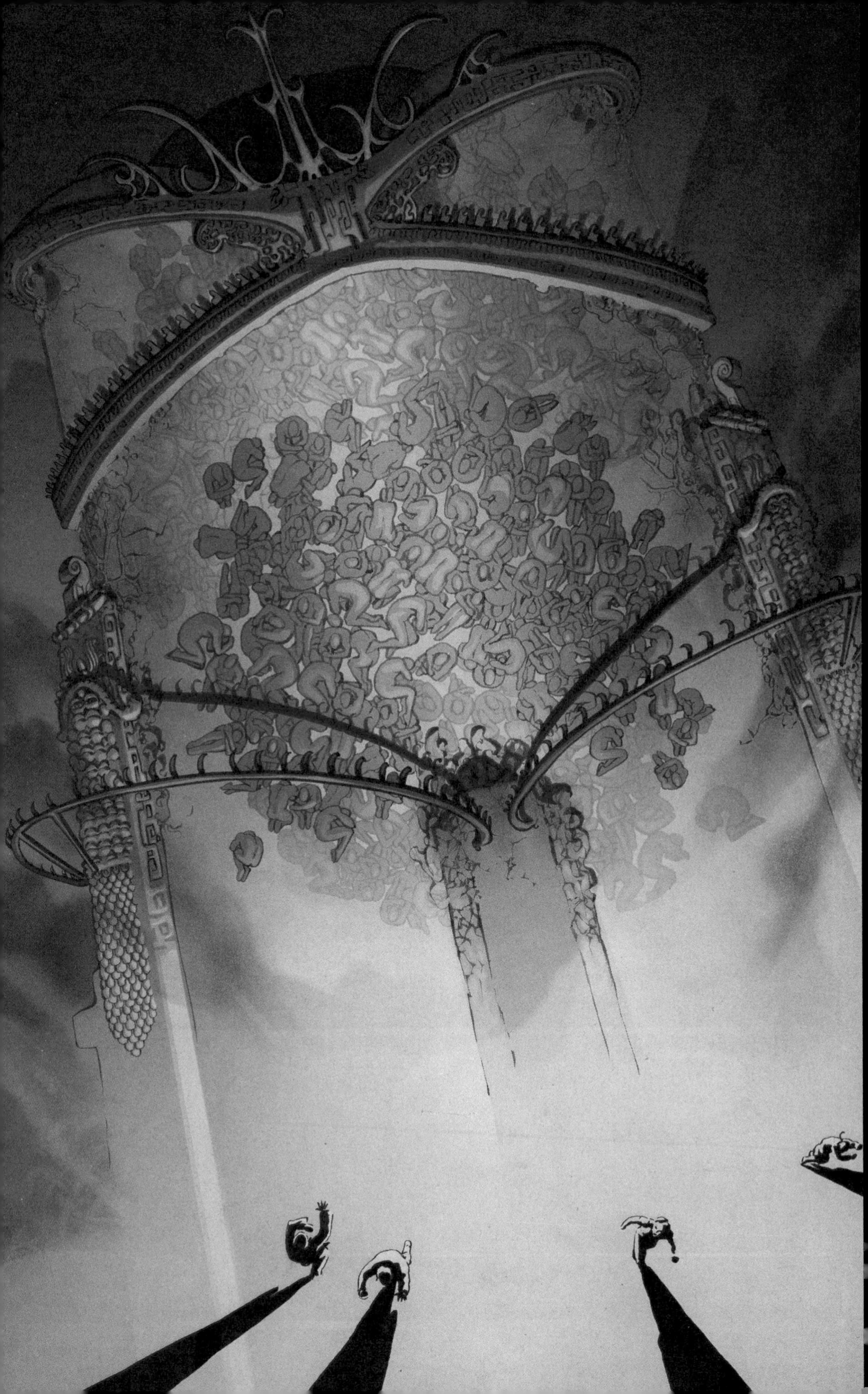

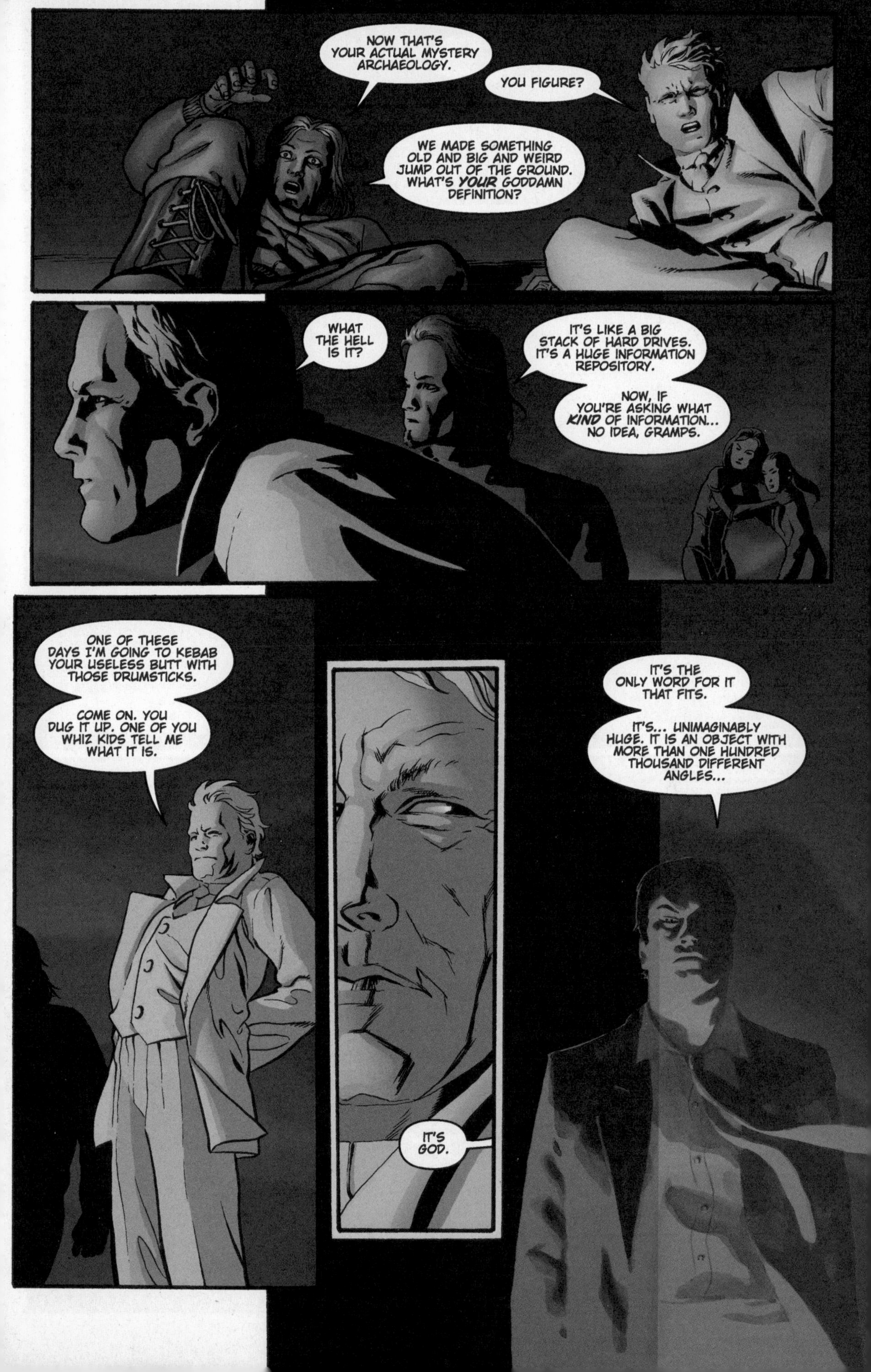
NOW THAT'S YOUR ACTUAL MYSTERY ARCHAEOLOGY.
YOU FIGURE?
WE MADE SOMETHING OLD AND BIG AND WEIRD JUMP OUT OF THE GROUND. WHAT'S YOUR GODDAMN DEFINITION?
WHAT THE HELL IS IT?
IT'S LIKE A BIG STACK OF HARD DRIVES. IT'S A HUGE INFORMATION REPOSITORY.
NOW, IF YOU'RE ASKING WHAT KIND OF INFORMATION... NO IDEA, GRAMPS.
ONE OF THESE DAYS I'M GOING TO KEBAB YOUR USELESS BUTT WITH THOSE DRUMSTICKS.
COME ON. YOU DUG IT UP. ONE OF YOU WHIZ KIDS TELL ME WHAT IT IS.
IT'S GOD.
IT'S THE ONLY WORD FOR IT THAT FITS.
IT'S... UNIMAGINABLY HUGE. IT IS AN OBJECT WITH MORE THAN ONE HUNDRED THOUSAND DIFFERENT ANGLES...

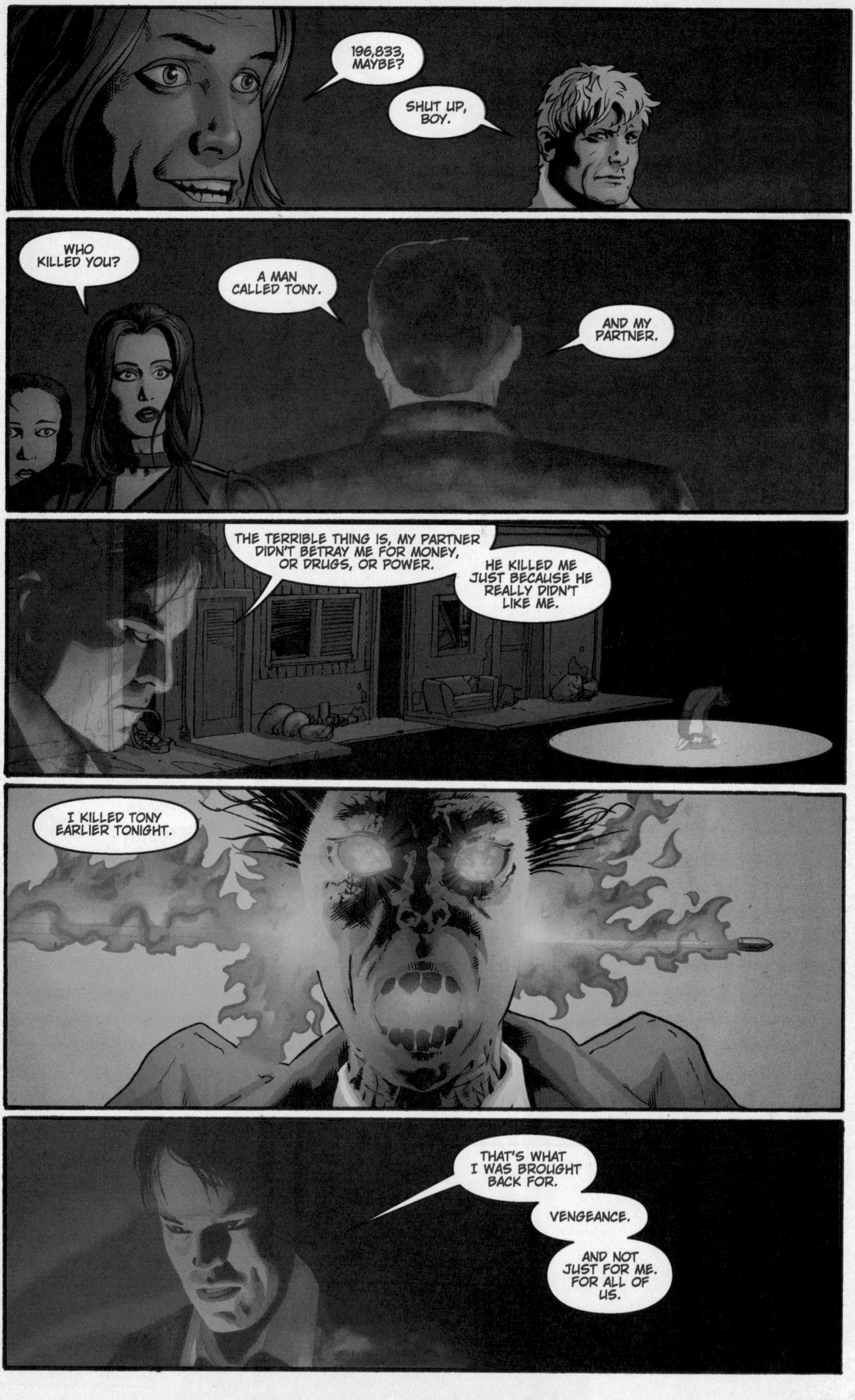
196,833, MAYBE?
SHUT UP, BOY.
WHO KILLED YOU?
A MAN CALLED TONY.
AND MY PARTNER.
THE TERRIBLE THING IS, MY PARTNER DIDN'T BETRAY ME FOR MONEY, OR DRUGS, OR POWER.
HE KILLED ME JUST BECAUSE HE REALLY DIDN'T LIKE ME.
I KILLED TONY EARLIER TONIGHT.
THAT'S WHAT I WAS BROUGHT BACK FOR.
VENGEANCE.
AND NOT JUST FOR ME. FOR ALL OF US.

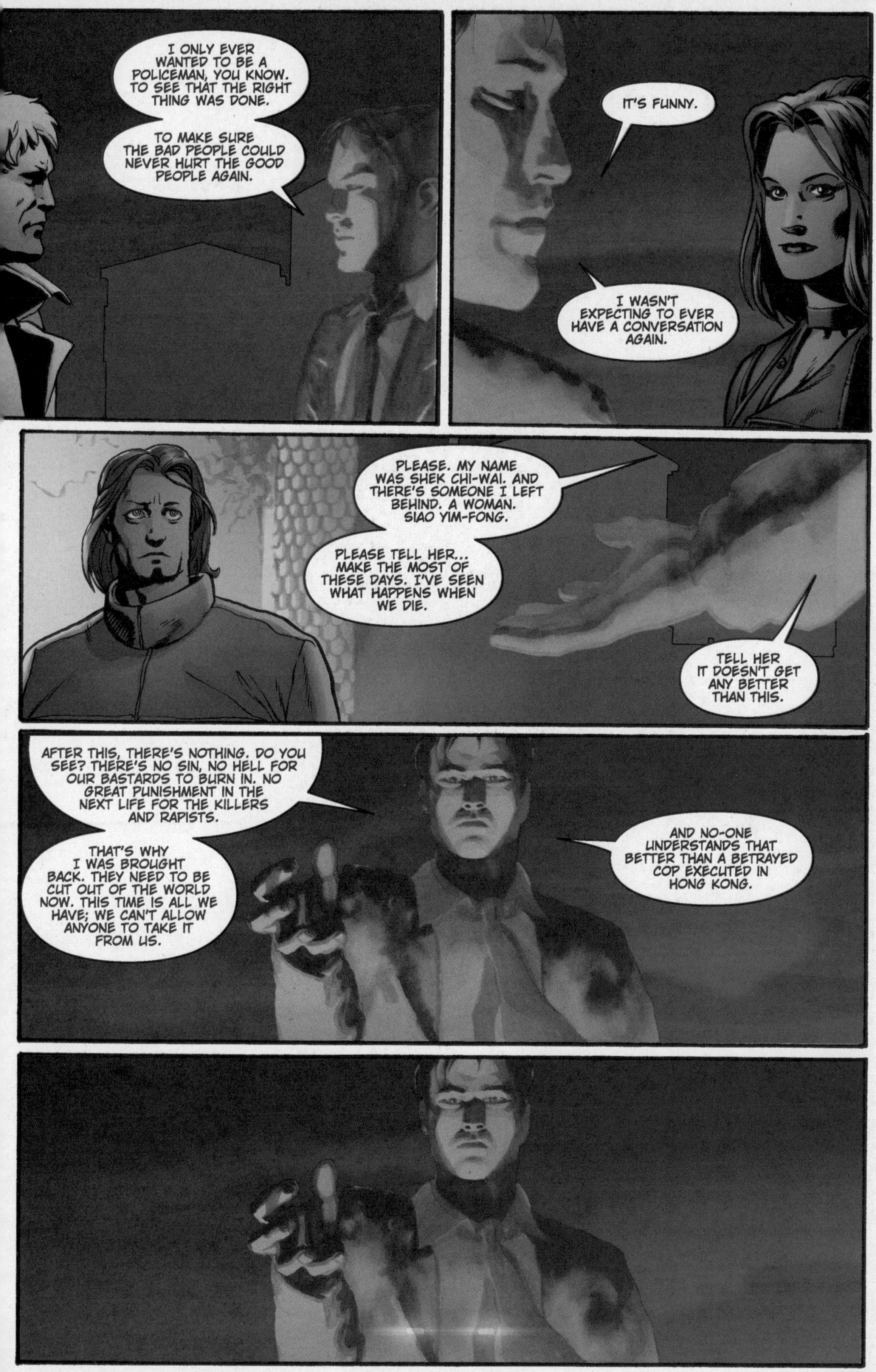
I ONLY EVER WANTED TO BE A POLICEMAN, YOU KNOW. TO SEE THAT THE RIGHT THING WAS DONE.
TO MAKE SURE THE BAD PEOPLE COULD NEVER HURT THE GOOD PEOPLE AGAIN.
IT'S FUNNY.
I WASN'T EXPECTING TO EVER HAVE A CONVERSATION AGAIN.
PLEASE. MY NAME WAS SHEK CHI-WAI. AND THERE'S SOMEONE I LEFT BEHIND. A WOMAN. SIAO YIM-FONG.
PLEASE TELL HER... MAKE THE MOST OF THESE DAYS. I'VE SEEN WHAT HAPPENS WHEN WE DIE.
TELL HER IT DOESN'T GET ANY BETTER THAN THIS.
AFTER THIS, THERE'S NOTHING. DO YOU SEE? THERE'S NO SIN, NO HELL FOR OUR BASTARDS TO BURN IN. NO GREAT PUNISHMENT IN THE NEXT LIFE FOR THE KILLERS AND RAPISTS.
THAT'S WHY I WAS BROUGHT BACK. THEY NEED TO BE CUT OUT OF THE WORLD NOW. THIS TIME IS ALL WE HAVE; WE CAN'T ALLOW ANYONE TO TAKE IT FROM US.
AND NO-ONE UNDERSTANDS THAT BETTER THAN A BETRAYED COP EXECUTED IN HONG KONG.

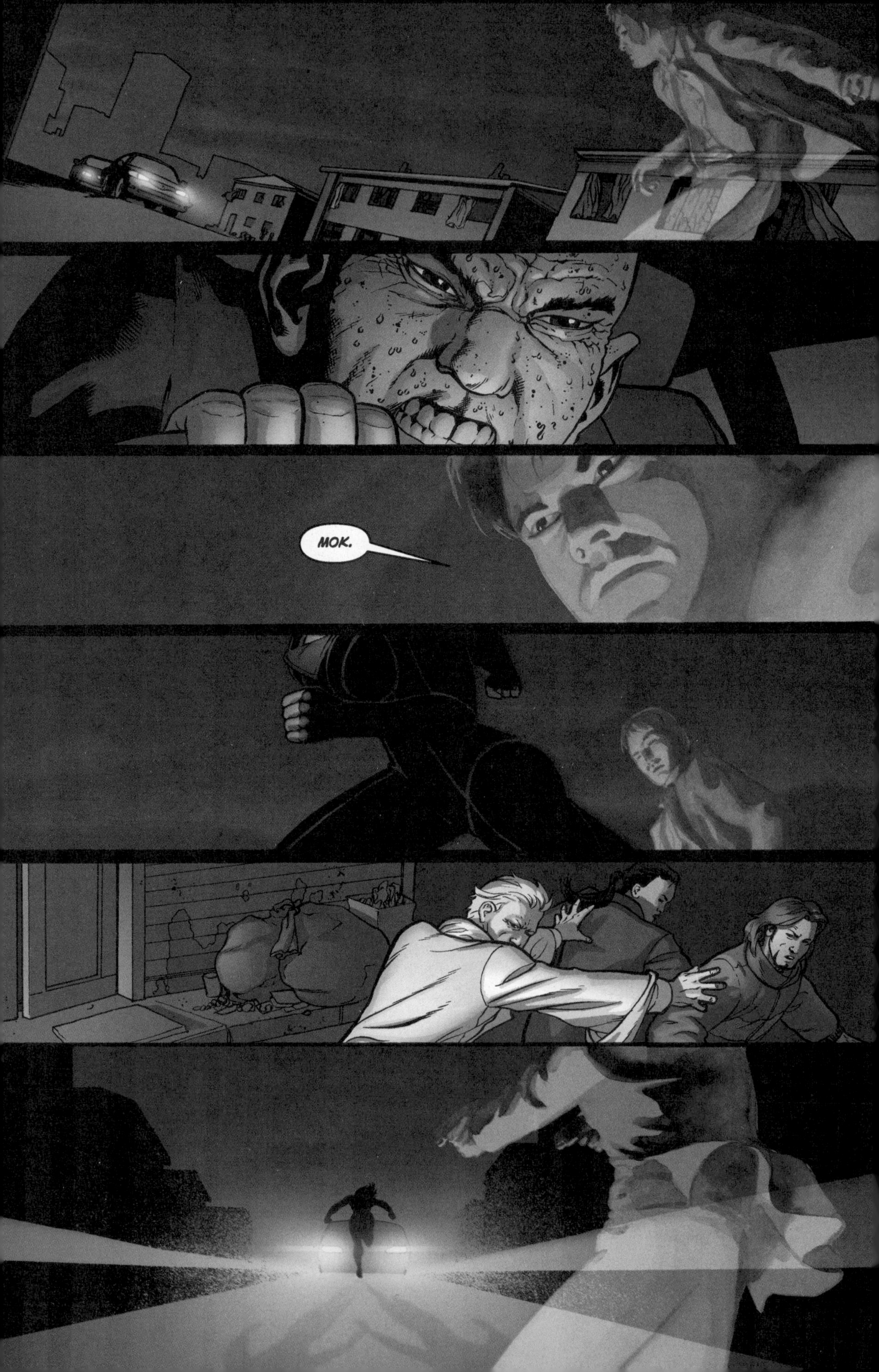
MOK.

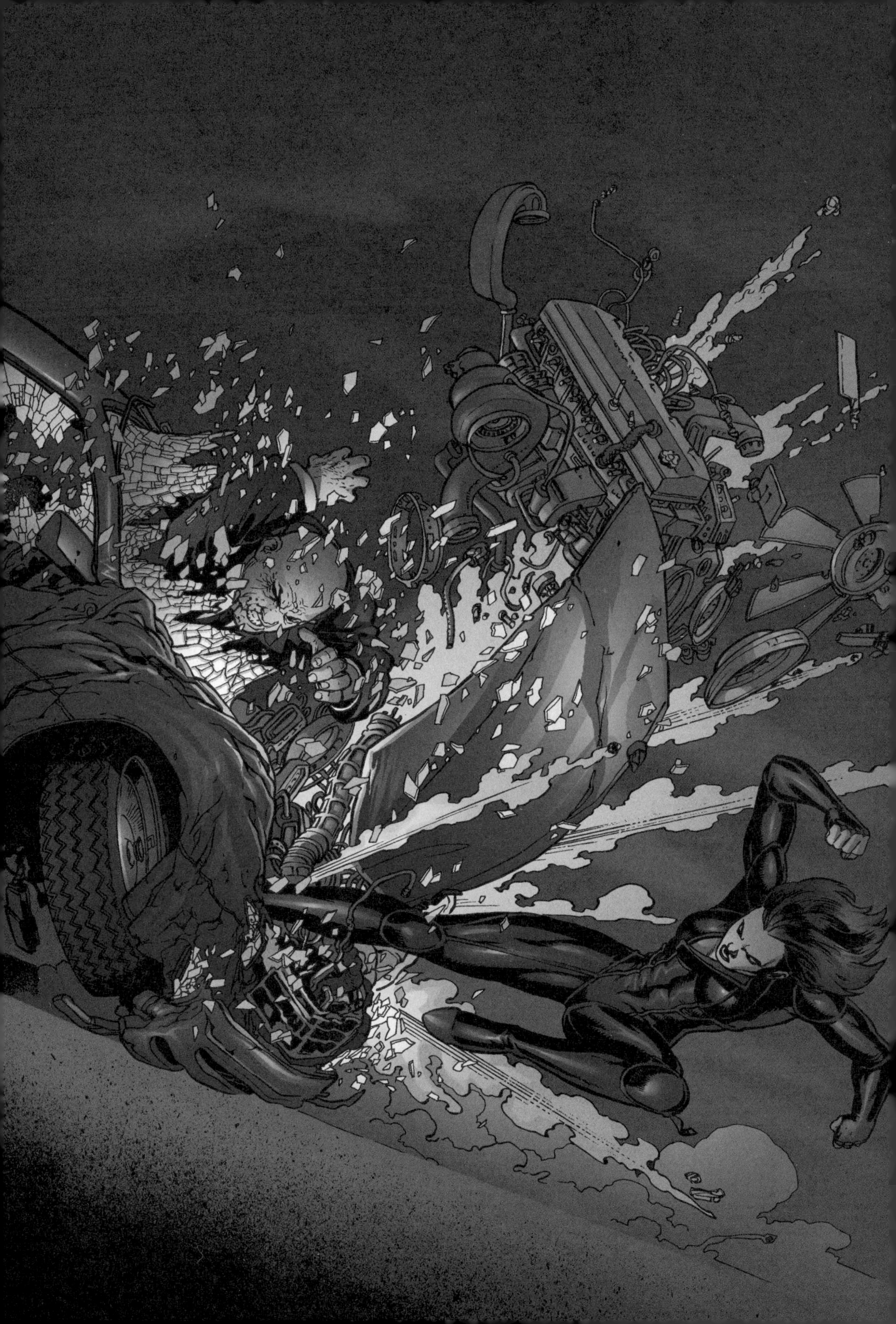

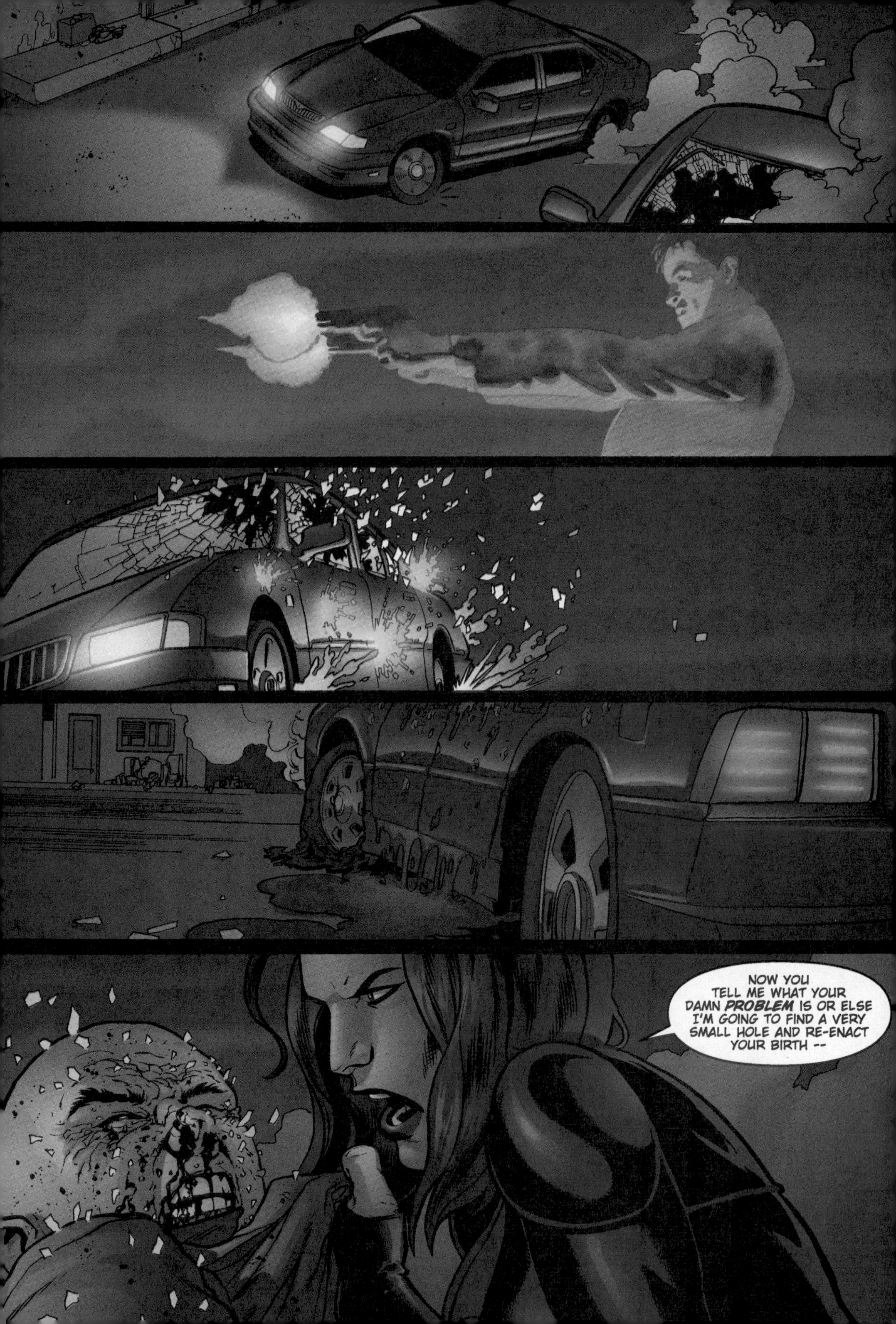
NOW YOU TELL ME WHAT YOUR DAMN PROBLEM IS OR ELSE I'M GOING TO FIND A VERY SMALL HOLE AND RE-ENACT YOUR BIRTH --

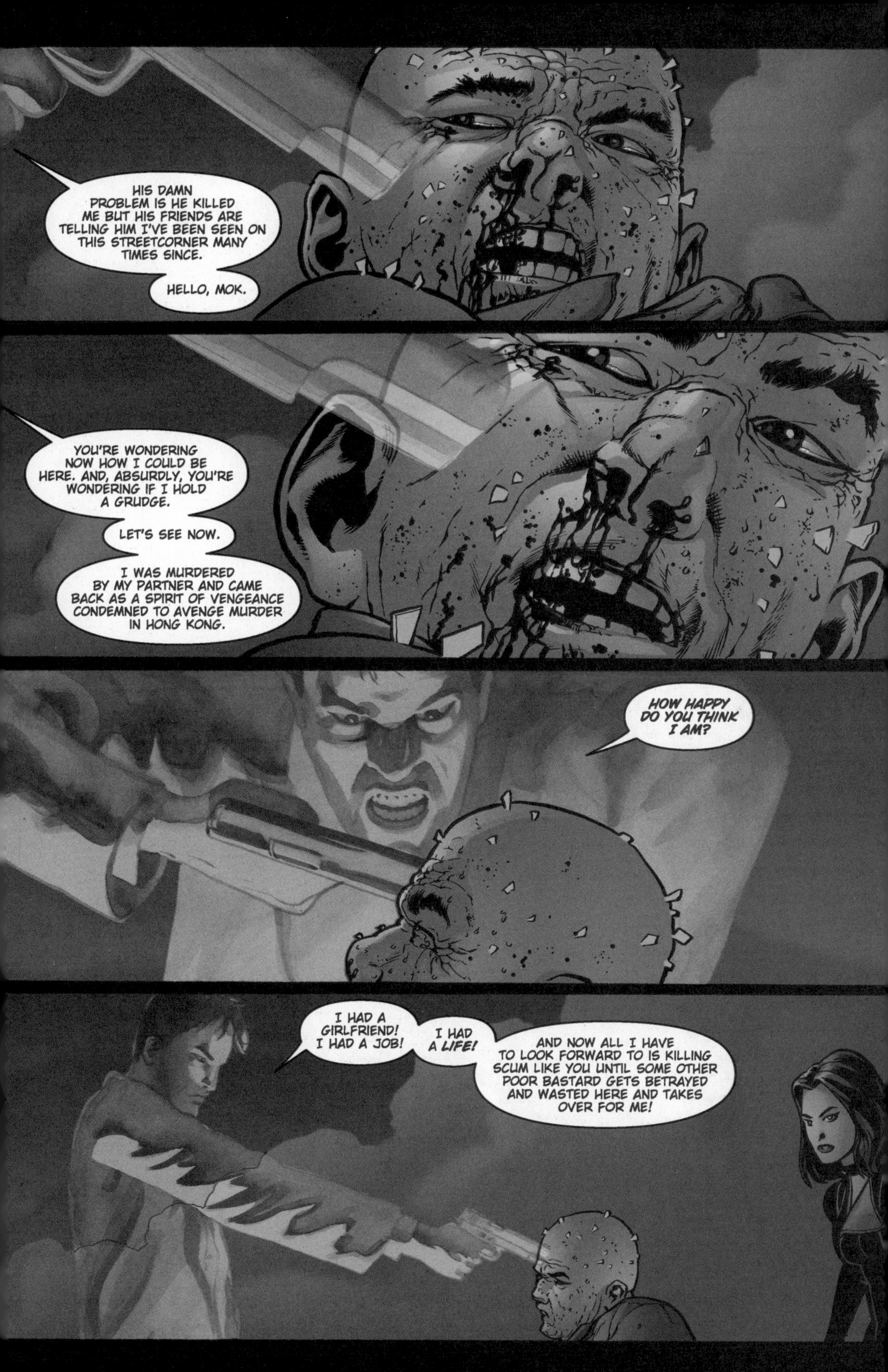
HIS DAMN PROBLEM IS HE KILLED ME BUT HIS FRIENDS ARE TELLING HIM I'VE BEEN SEEN ON THIS STREETCORNER MANY TIMES SINCE.
HELLO, MOK.
YOU'RE WONDERING NOW HOW I COULD BE HERE. AND, ABSURDLY, YOU'RE WONDERING IF I HOLD A GRUDGE.
LET'S SEE NOW.
I WAS MURDERED BY MY PARTNER AND CAME BACK AS A SPIRIT OF VENGEANCE CONDEMNED TO AVENGE MURDER IN HONG KONG.
HOW HAPPY DO YOU THINK I AM?
I HAD A GIRLFRIEND! I HAD A JOB!
I HAD A LIFE!
AND NOW ALL I HAVE TO LOOK FORWARD TO IS KILLING SCUM LIKE YOU UNTIL SOME OTHER POOR BASTARD GETS BETRAYED AND WASTED HERE AND TAKES OVER FOR ME!

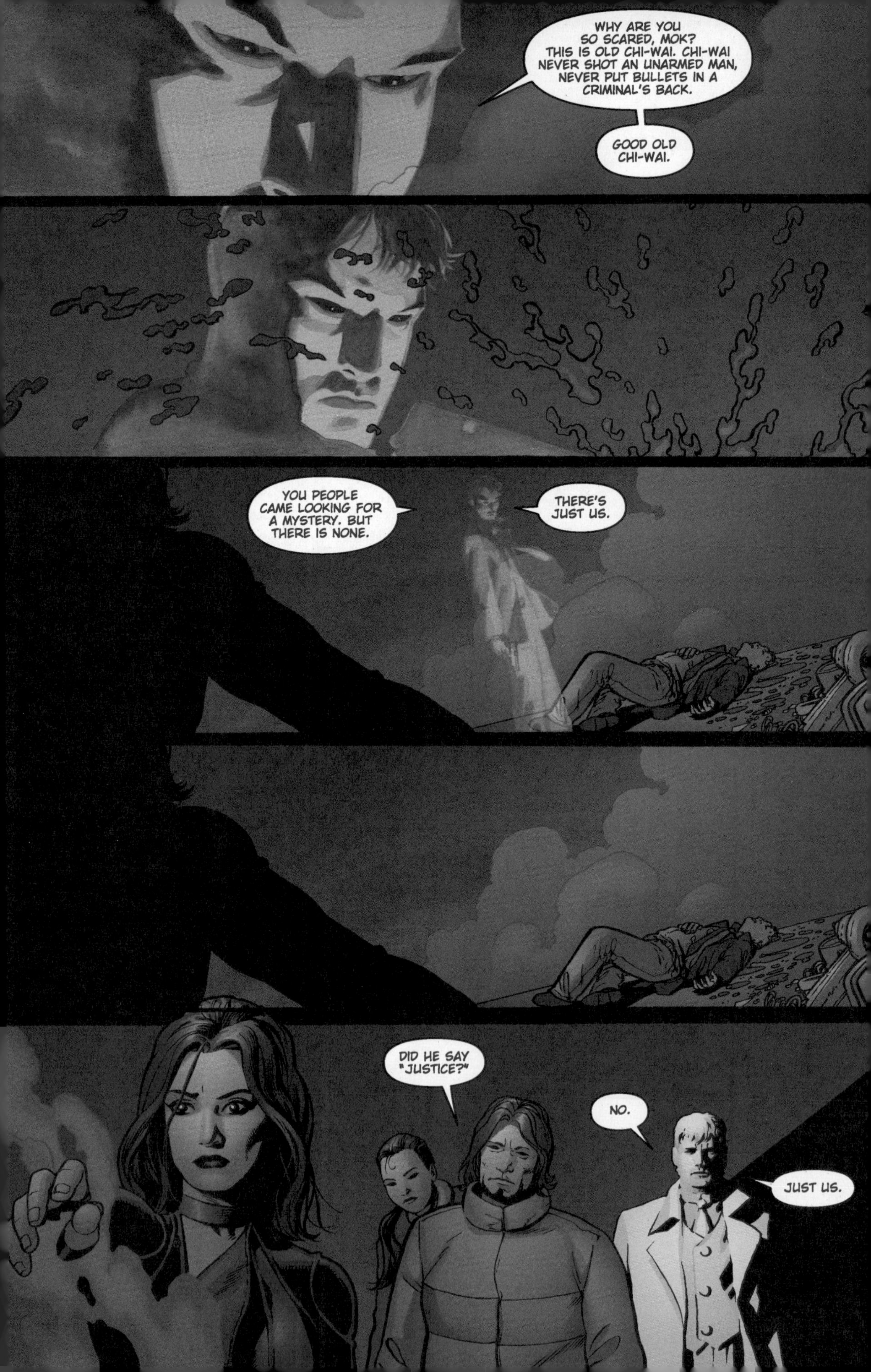
WHY ARE YOU SO SCARED, MOK? THIS IS OLD CHI-WAI. CHI-WAI NEVER SHOT AN UNARMED MAN, NEVER PUT BULLETS IN A CRIMINAL'S BACK.
GOOD OLD CHI-WAI.
YOU PEOPLE CAME LOOKING FOR A MYSTERY. BUT THERE IS NONE.
THERE'S JUST US.
DID HE SAY "JUSTICE?"
NO.
JUST US.

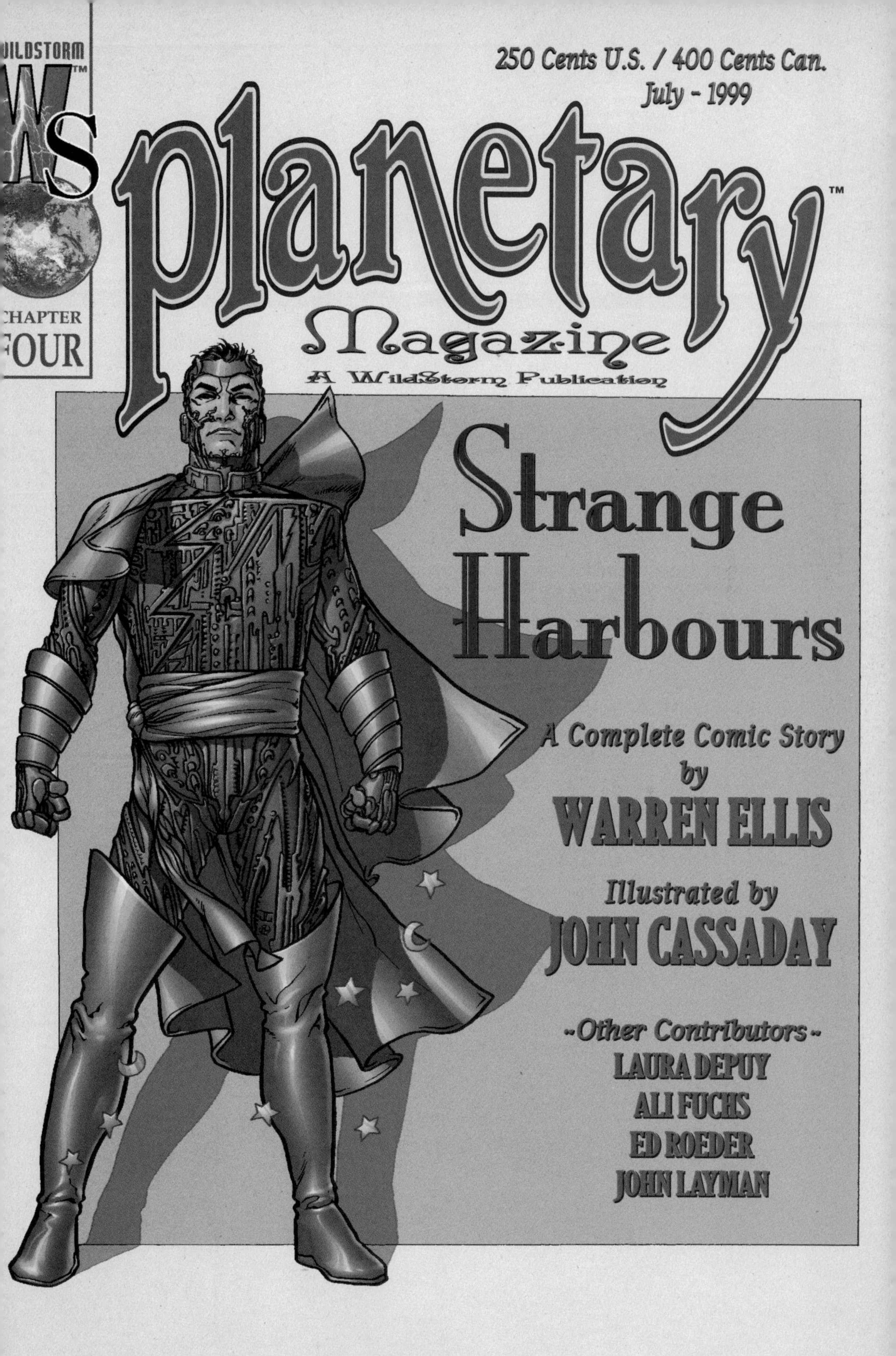
WILDSTORM
WS
CHAPTER
FOUR
250 Cents U.S. / 400 Cents Can.
July - 1999
planetary™
Magazine
A WildStorm Publication
Strange Harbours
A Complete Comic Story
by
WARREN ELLIS
Illustrated by
JOHN CASSADAY
~Other Contributors~
LAURA DEPUY
ALI FUCHS
ED ROEDER
JOHN LAYMAN

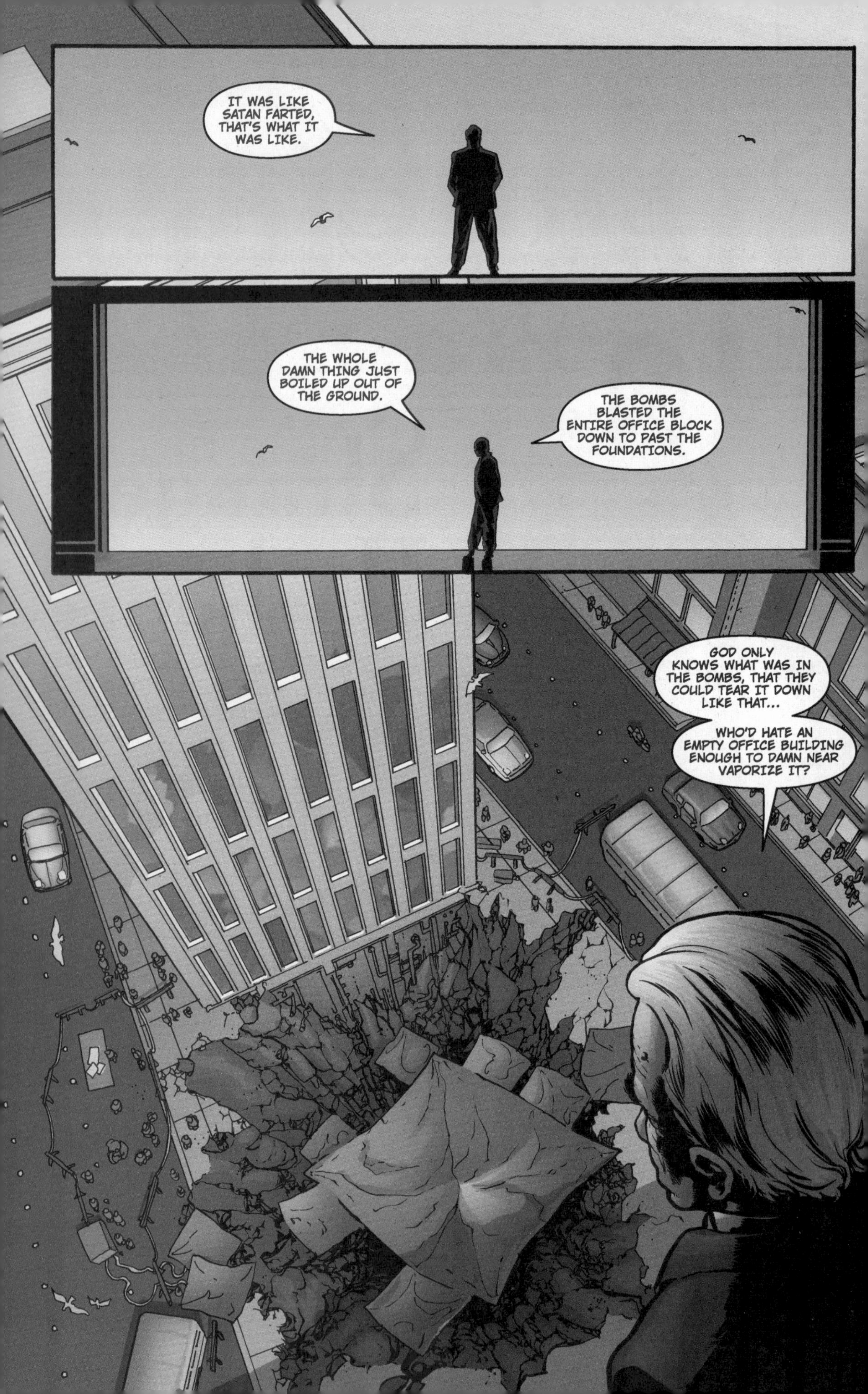
IT WAS LIKE SATAN FARTED, THAT'S WHAT IT WAS LIKE.
THE WHOLE DAMN THING JUST BOILED UP OUT OF THE GROUND.
THE BOMBS BLASTED THE ENTIRE OFFICE BLOCK DOWN TO PAST THE FOUNDATIONS.
GOD ONLY KNOWS WHAT WAS IN THE BOMBS, THAT THEY COULD TEAR IT DOWN LIKE THAT...
WHO'D HATE AN EMPTY OFFICE BUILDING ENOUGH TO DAMN NEAR VAPORIZE IT?

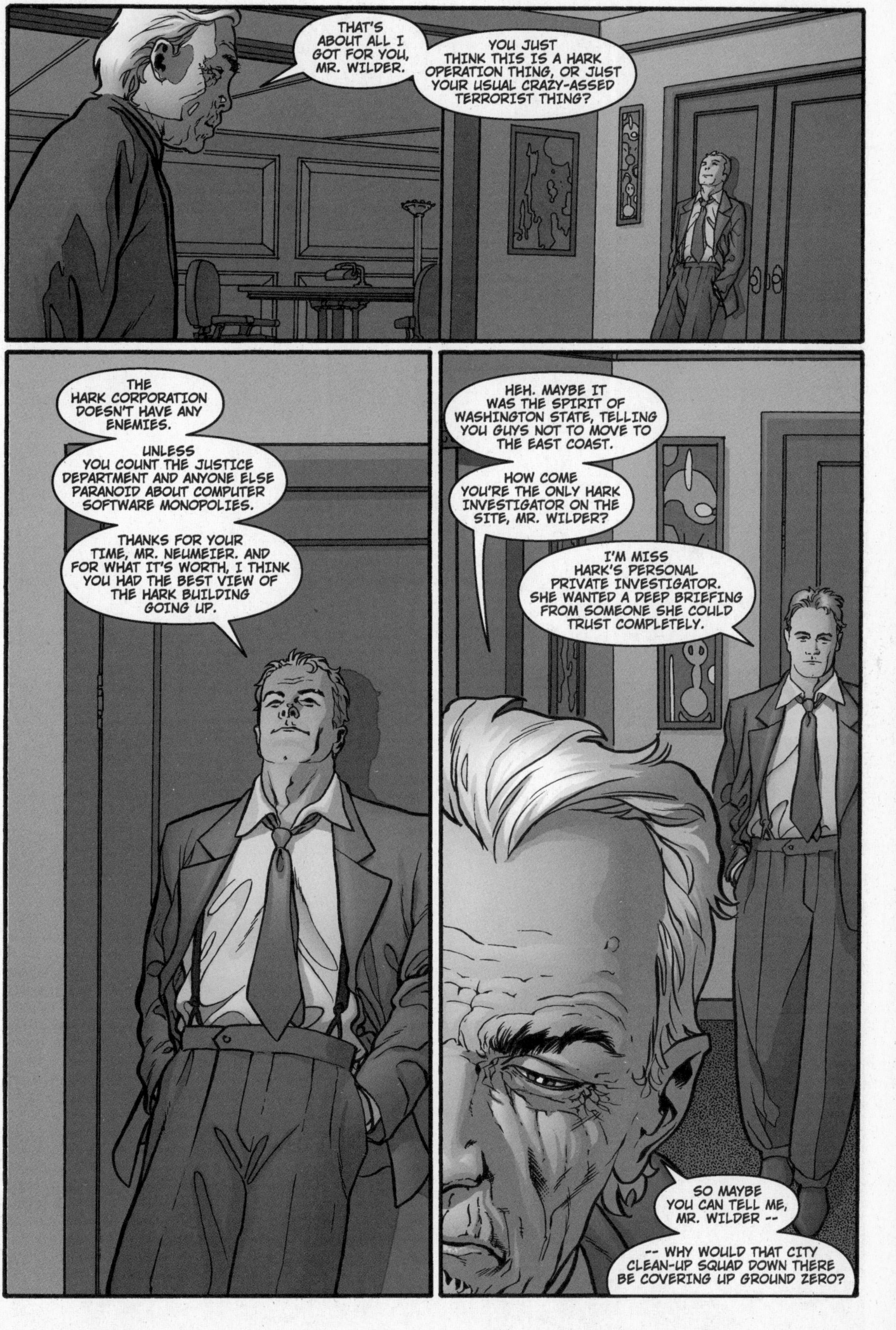
THAT'S ABOUT ALL I GOT FOR YOU, MR. WILDER.
YOU JUST THINK THIS IS A HARK OPERATION THING, OR JUST YOUR USUAL CRAZY-ASSED TERRORIST THING?
THE HARK CORPORATION DOESN'T HAVE ANY ENEMIES.
UNLESS YOU COUNT THE JUSTICE DEPARTMENT AND ANYONE ELSE PARANOID ABOUT COMPUTER SOFTWARE MONOPOLIES.
THANKS FOR YOUR TIME, MR. NEUMEIER. AND FOR WHAT IT'S WORTH, I THINK YOU HAD THE BEST VIEW OF THE HARK BUILDING GOING UP.
HEH. MAYBE IT WAS THE SPIRIT OF WASHINGTON STATE, TELLING YOU GUYS NOT TO MOVE TO THE EAST COAST.
HOW COME YOU'RE THE ONLY HARK INVESTIGATOR ON THE SITE, MR. WILDER?
I'M MISS HARK'S PERSONAL PRIVATE INVESTIGATOR. SHE WANTED A DEEP BRIEFING FROM SOMEONE SHE COULD TRUST COMPLETELY.
SO MAYBE YOU CAN TELL ME, MR. WILDER --
-- WHY WOULD THAT CITY CLEAN-UP SQUAD DOWN THERE BE COVERING UP GROUND ZERO?

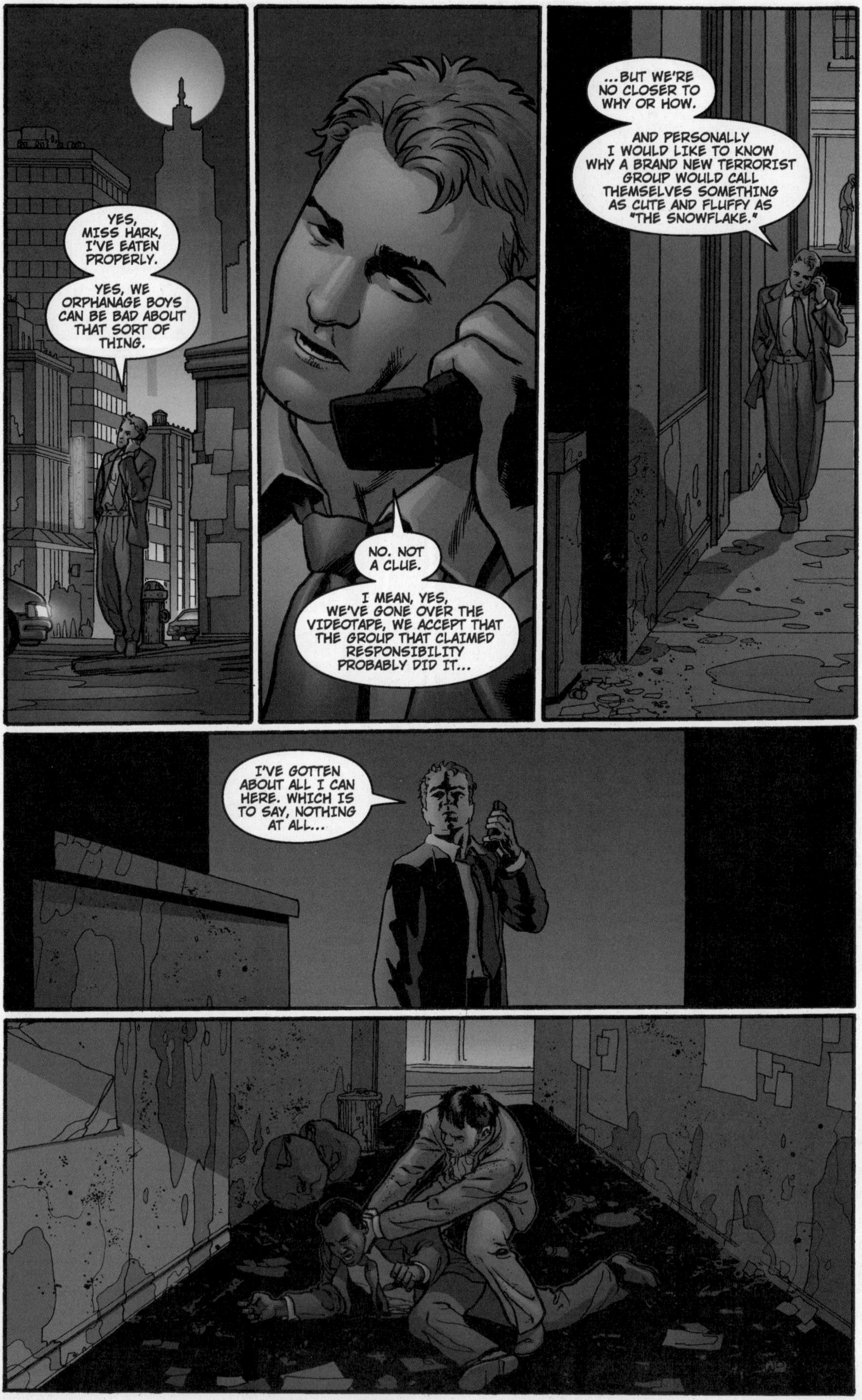
YES, MISS HARK, I'VE EATEN PROPERLY.
YES, WE ORPHANAGE BOYS CAN BE BAD ABOUT THAT SORT OF THING.
NO. NOT A CLUE.
I MEAN, YES, WE'VE GONE OVER THE VIDEOTAPE, WE ACCEPT THAT THE GROUP THAT CLAIMED RESPONSIBILITY PROBABLY DID IT...
...BUT WE'RE NO CLOSER TO WHY OR HOW.
AND PERSONALLY I WOULD LIKE TO KNOW WHY A BRAND NEW TERRORIST GROUP WOULD CALL THEMSELVES SOMETHING AS CUTE AND FLUFFY AS "THE SNOWFLAKE."
I'VE GOTTEN ABOUT ALL I CAN HERE. WHICH IS TO SAY, NOTHING AT ALL...

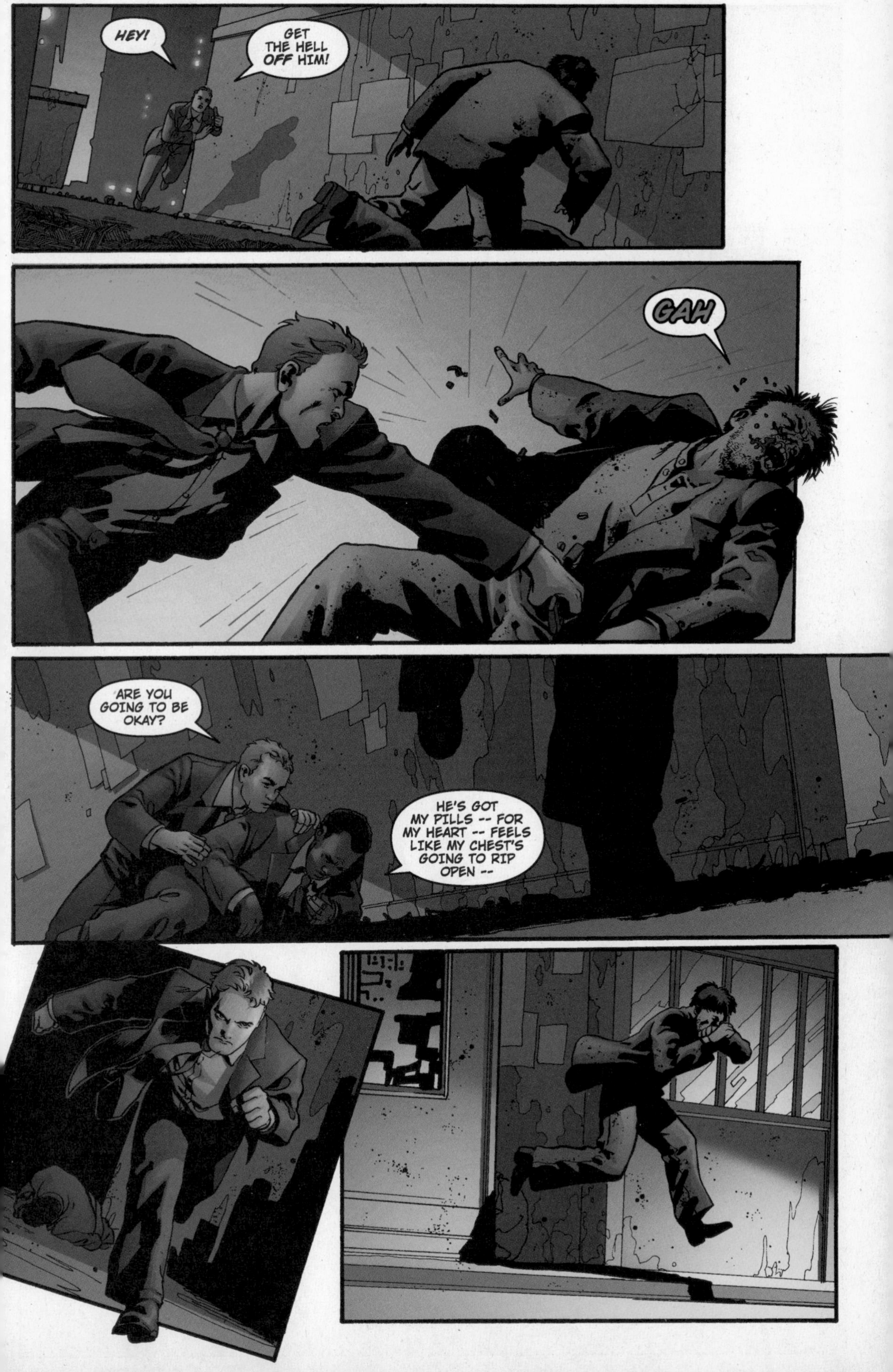
HEY!
GET THE HELL OFF HIM!
GAH
ARE YOU GOING TO BE OKAY?
HE'S GOT MY PILLS -- FOR MY HEART -- FEELS LIKE MY CHEST'S GOING TO RIP OPEN --

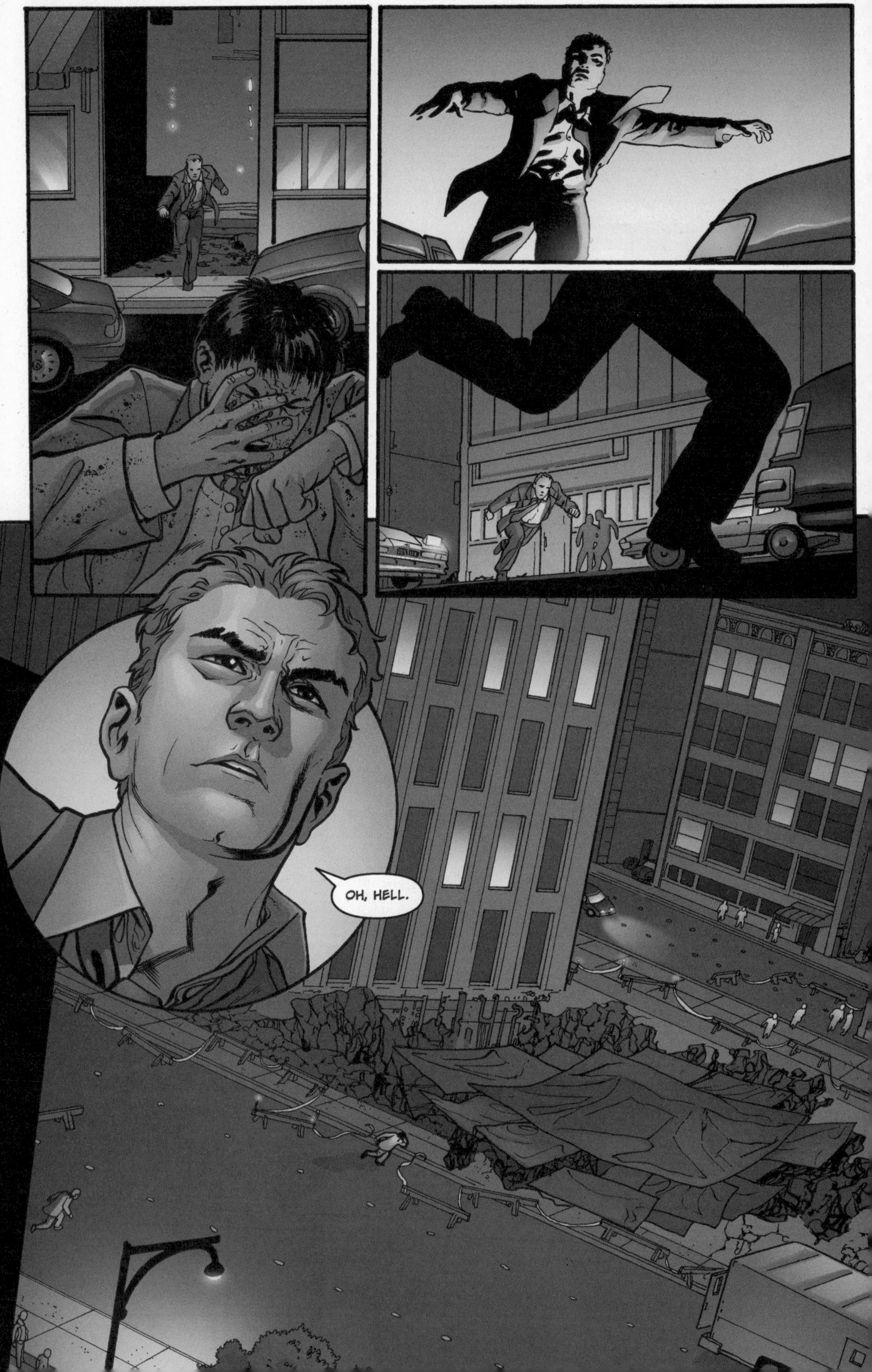
OH, HELL.

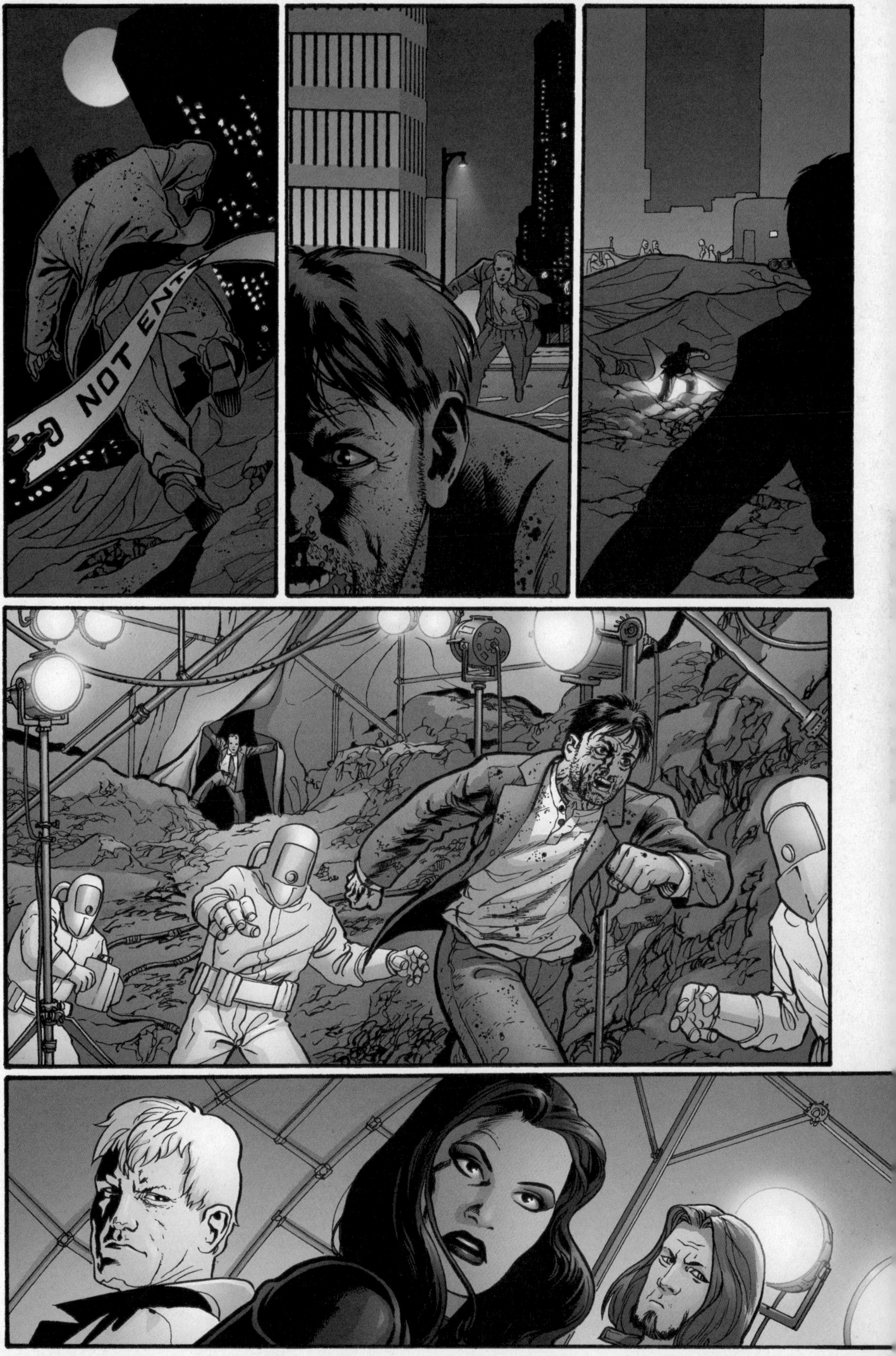
NOT ENT

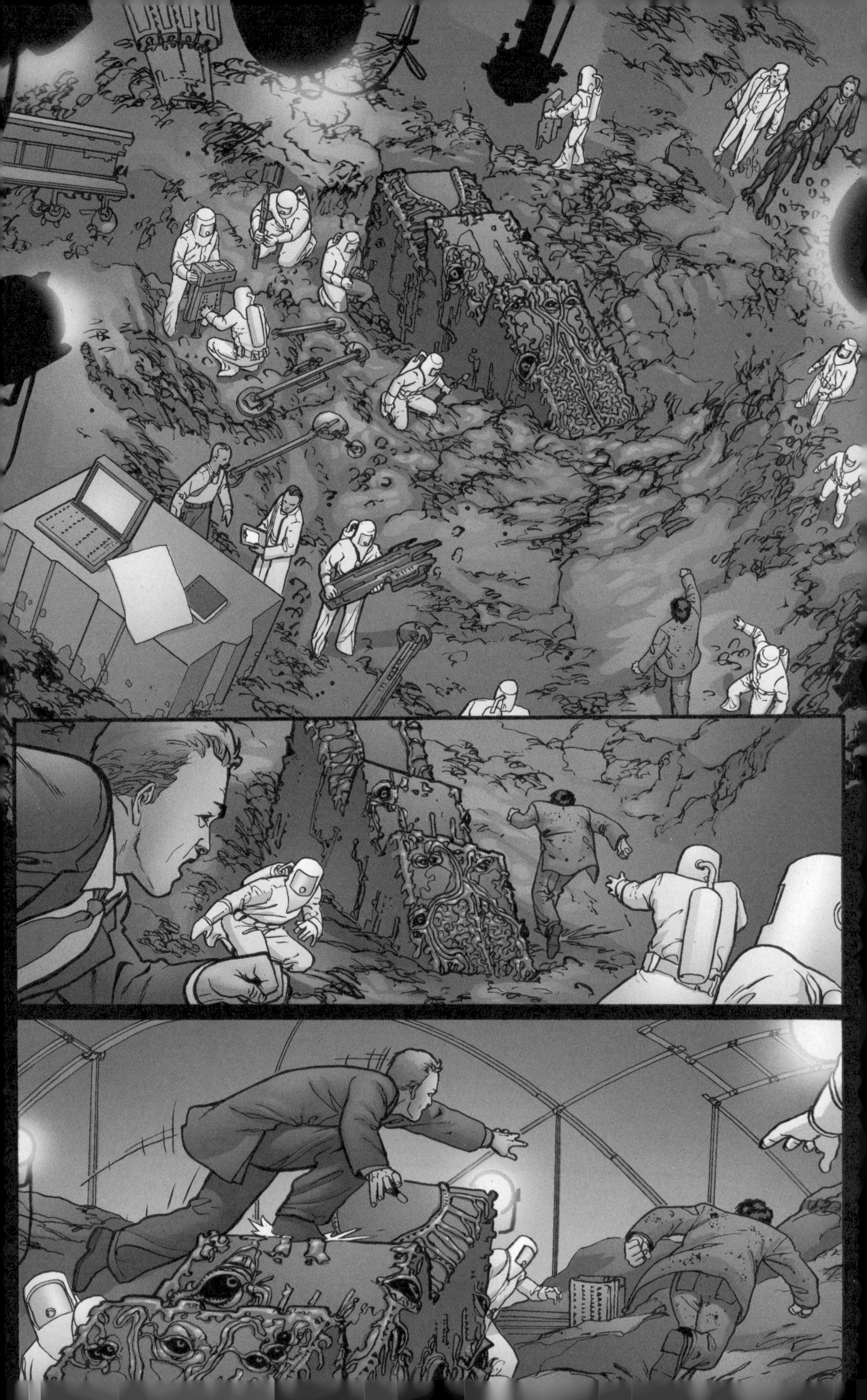

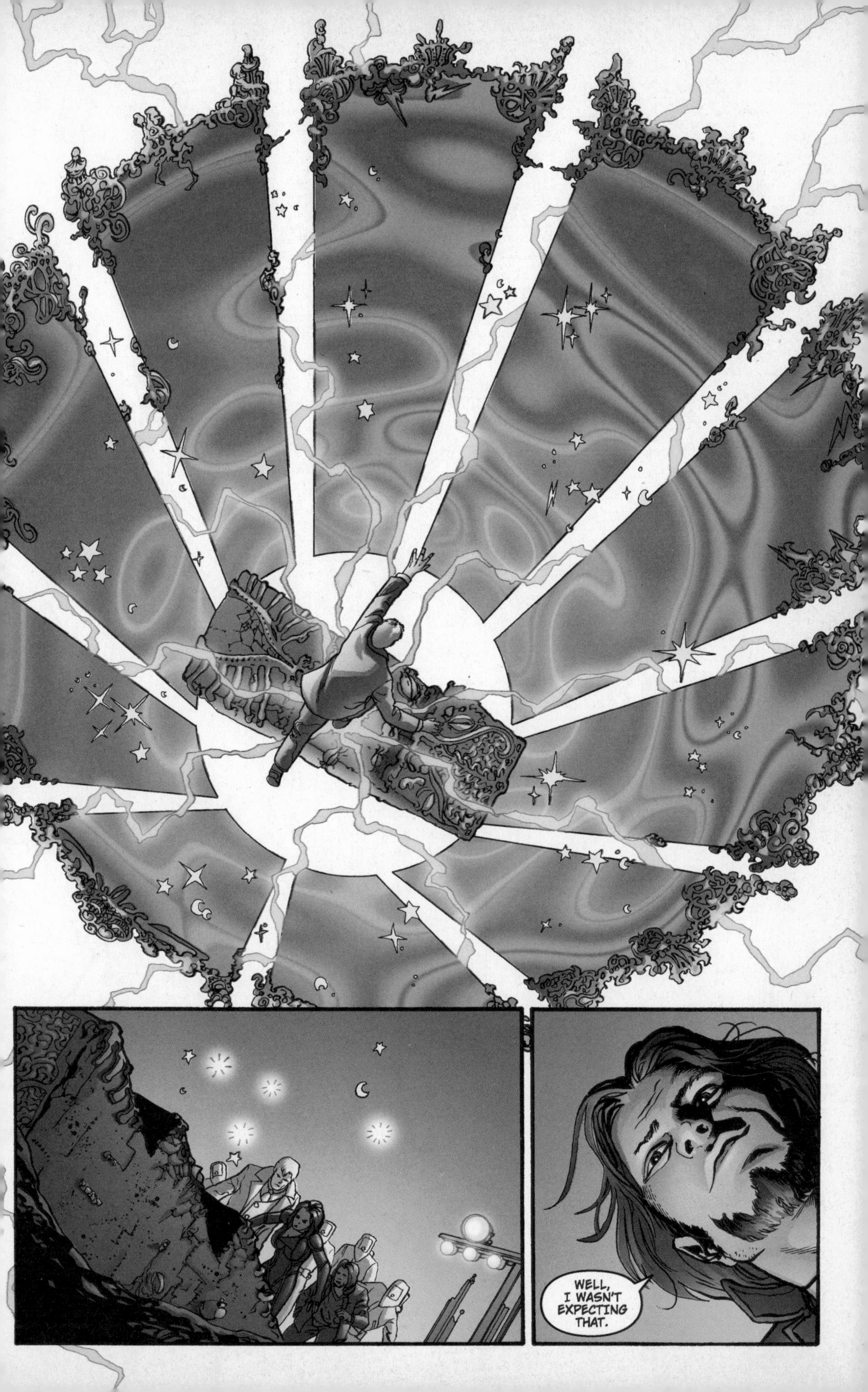
WELL, I WASN'T EXPECTING THAT.

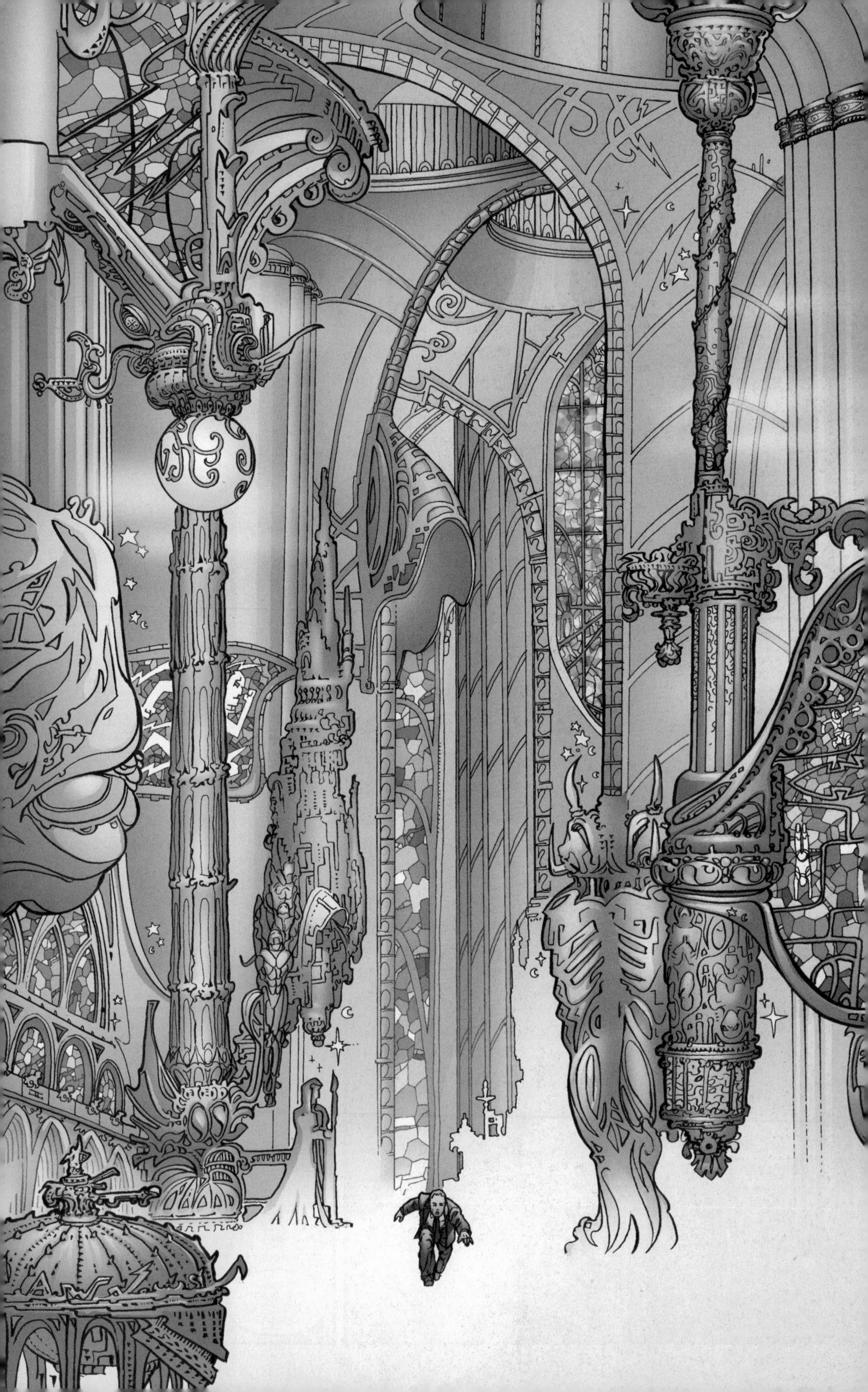

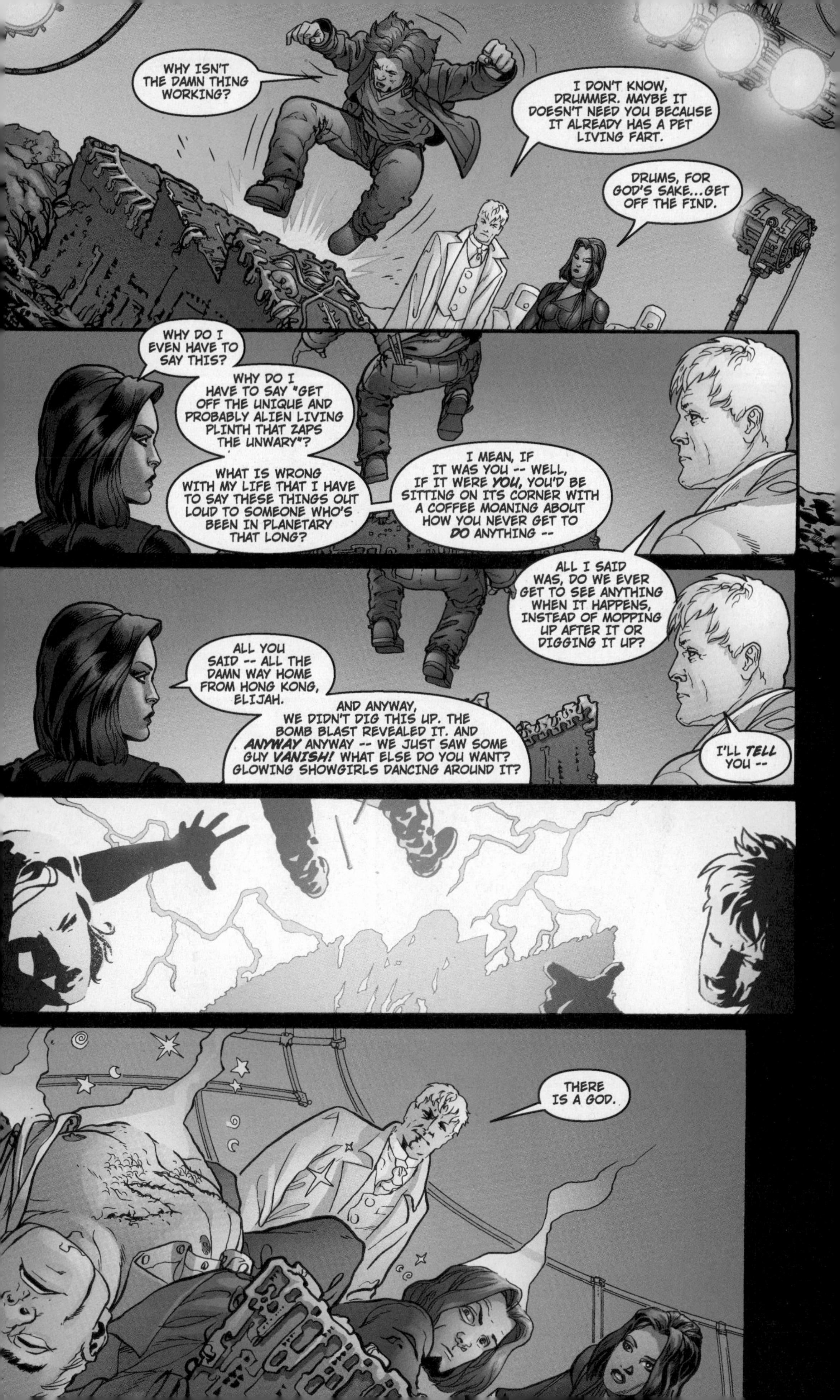
WHY ISN'T THE DAMN THING WORKING?
I DON'T KNOW, DRUMMER. MAYBE IT DOESN'T NEED YOU BECAUSE IT ALREADY HAS A PET LIVING FART.
DRUMS, FOR GOD'S SAKE...GET OFF THE FIND.
WHY DO I EVEN HAVE TO SAY THIS?
WHY DO I HAVE TO SAY "GET OFF THE UNIQUE AND PROBABLY ALIEN LIVING PLINTH THAT ZAPS THE UNWARY"?
WHAT IS WRONG WITH MY LIFE THAT I HAVE TO SAY THESE THINGS OUT LOUD TO SOMEONE WHO'S BEEN IN PLANETARY THAT LONG?
I MEAN, IF IT WAS YOU -- WELL, IF IT WERE *YOU*, YOU'D BE SITTING ON ITS CORNER WITH A COFFEE MOANING ABOUT HOW YOU NEVER GET TO *DO* ANYTHING --
ALL I SAID WAS, DO WE EVER GET TO SEE ANYTHING WHEN IT HAPPENS, INSTEAD OF MOPPING UP AFTER IT OR DIGGING IT UP?
ALL YOU SAID -- ALL THE DAMN WAY HOME FROM HONG KONG, ELIJAH.
AND ANYWAY, WE DIDN'T DIG THIS UP. THE BOMB BLAST REVEALED IT. AND *ANYWAY* ANYWAY -- WE JUST SAW SOME GUY *VANISH!* WHAT ELSE DO YOU WANT? GLOWING SHOWGIRLS DANCING AROUND IT?
I'LL *TELL* YOU --
THERE IS A GOD.

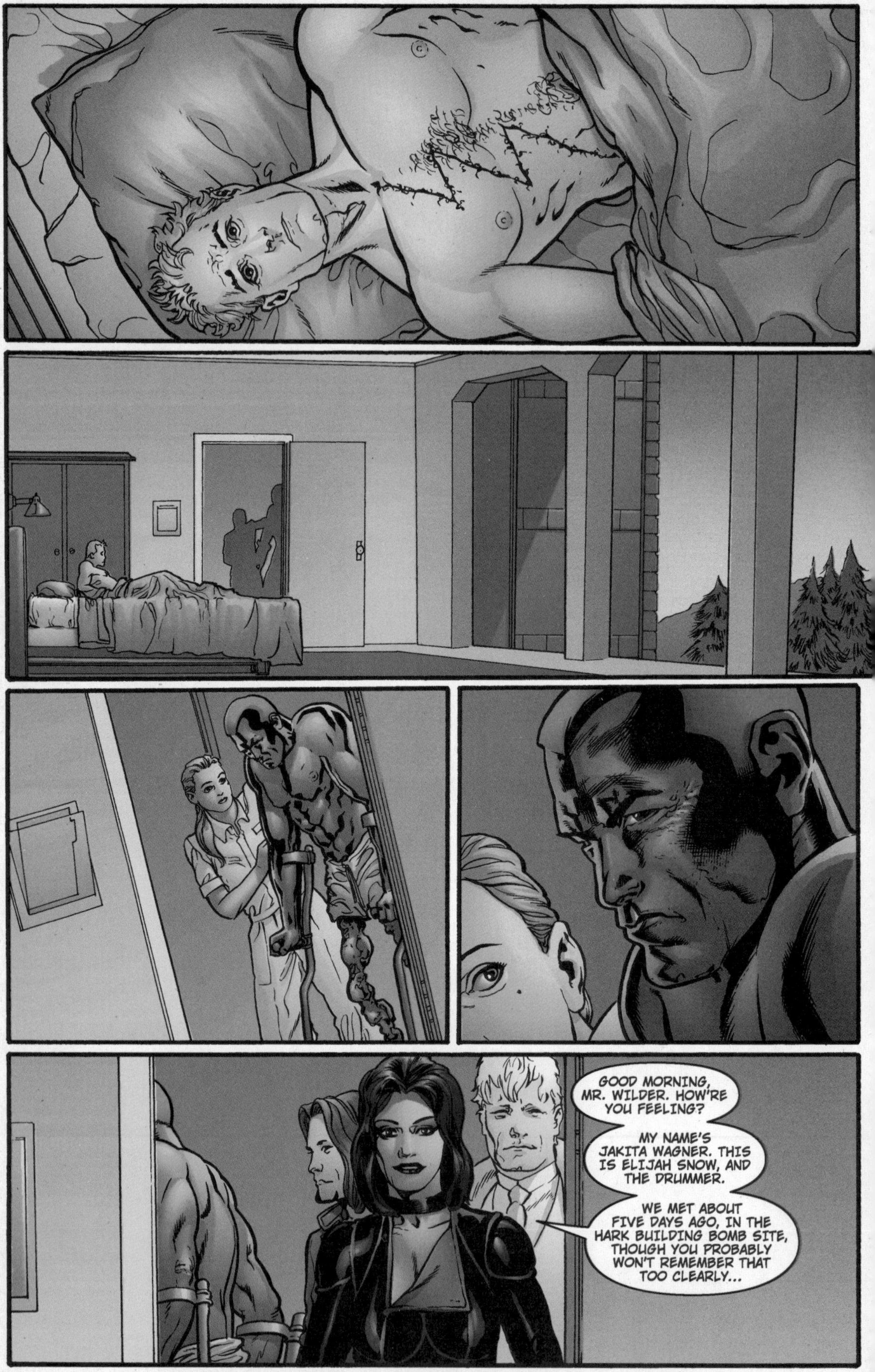
GOOD MORNING, MR. WILDER. HOW'RE YOU FEELING?
MY NAME'S JAKITA WAGNER. THIS IS ELIJAH SNOW, AND THE DRUMMER.
WE MET ABOUT FIVE DAYS AGO, IN THE HARK BUILDING BOMB SITE, THOUGH YOU PROBABLY WON'T REMEMBER THAT TOO CLEARLY...

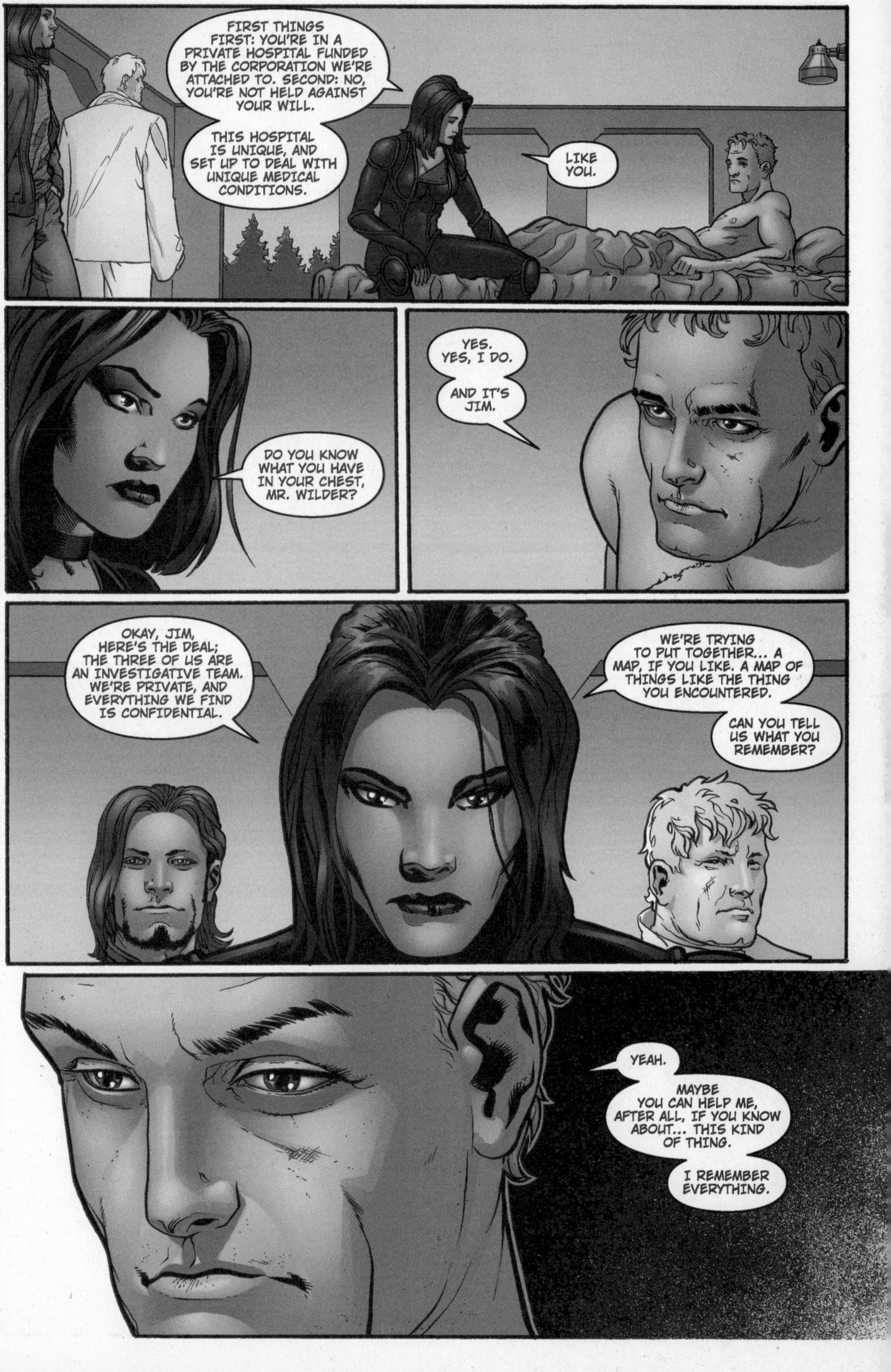
FIRST THINGS FIRST: YOU'RE IN A PRIVATE HOSPITAL FUNDED BY THE CORPORATION WE'RE ATTACHED TO. SECOND: NO, YOU'RE NOT HELD AGAINST YOUR WILL.
THIS HOSPITAL IS UNIQUE, AND SET UP TO DEAL WITH UNIQUE MEDICAL CONDITIONS.
LIKE YOU.
DO YOU KNOW WHAT YOU HAVE IN YOUR CHEST, MR. WILDER?
YES. YES, I DO.
AND IT'S JIM.
OKAY, JIM, HERE'S THE DEAL; THE THREE OF US ARE AN INVESTIGATIVE TEAM. WE'RE PRIVATE, AND EVERYTHING WE FIND IS CONFIDENTIAL.
WE'RE TRYING TO PUT TOGETHER... A MAP, IF YOU LIKE. A MAP OF THINGS LIKE THE THING YOU ENCOUNTERED.
CAN YOU TELL US WHAT YOU REMEMBER?
YEAH.
MAYBE YOU CAN HELP ME, AFTER ALL, IF YOU KNOW ABOUT... THIS KIND OF THING.
I REMEMBER EVERYTHING.

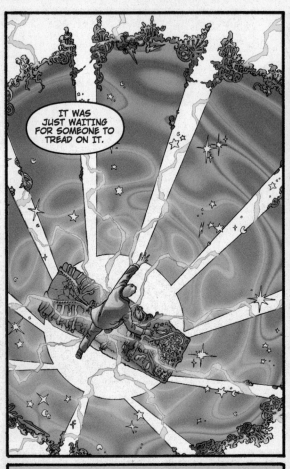

IT WAS JUST WAITING FOR SOMEONE TO TREAD ON IT.

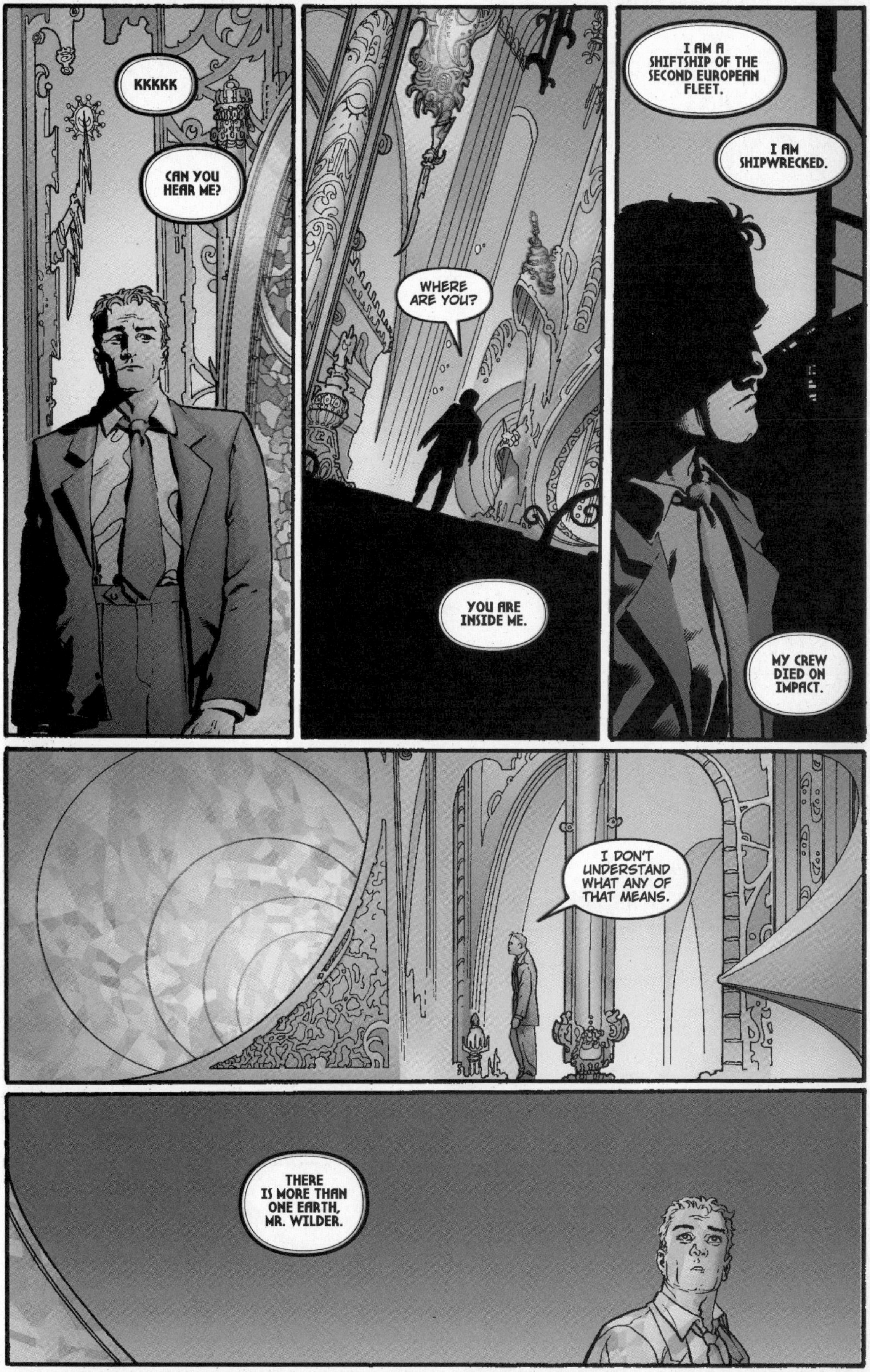
KKKKK
CAN YOU HEAR ME?
WHERE ARE YOU?
YOU ARE INSIDE ME.
I AM A SHIFTSHIP OF THE SECOND EUROPEAN FLEET.
I AM SHIPWRECKED.
MY CREW DIED ON IMPACT.
I DON'T UNDERSTAND WHAT ANY OF THAT MEANS.
THERE IS MORE THAN ONE EARTH, MR. WILDER.

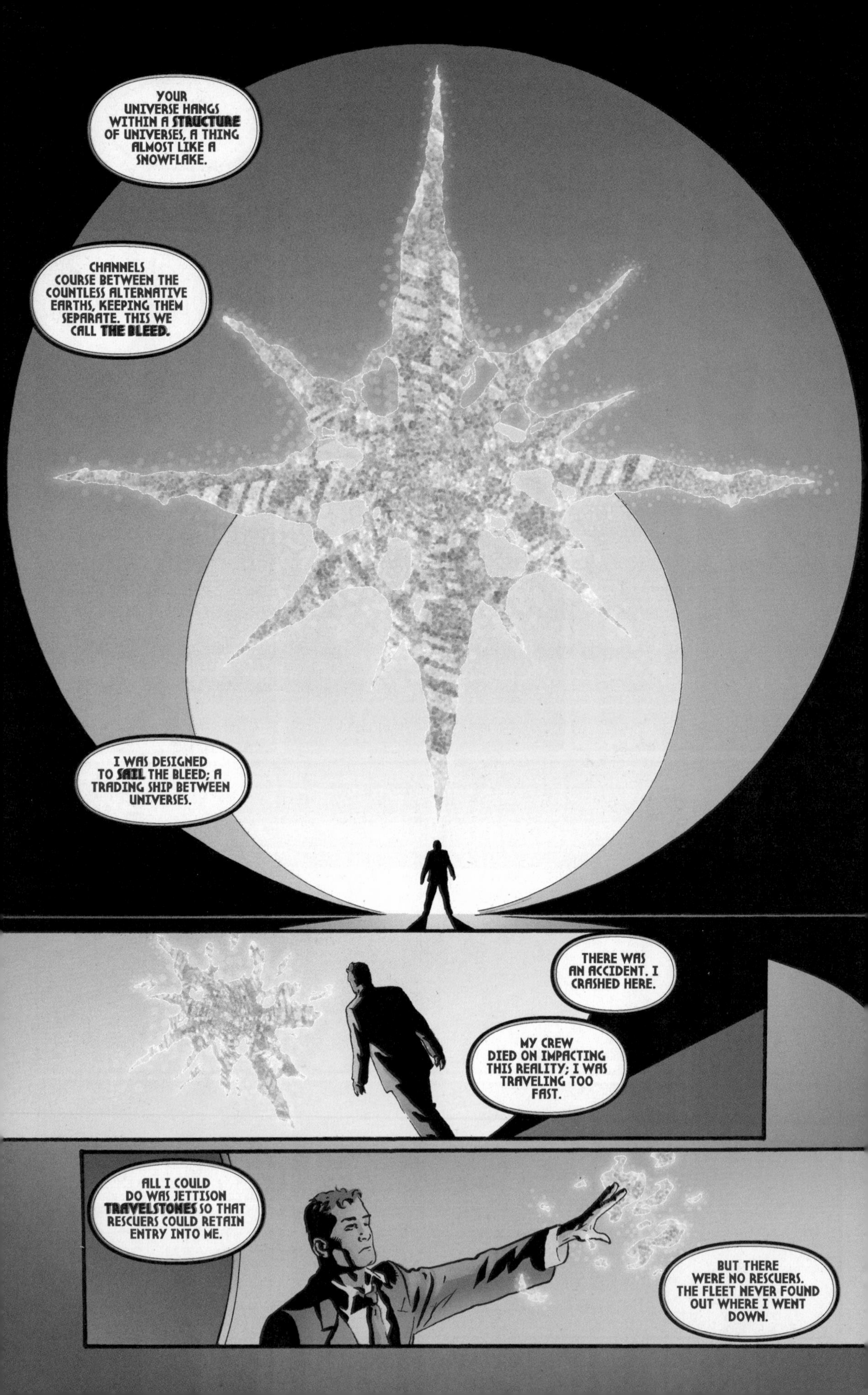
YOUR UNIVERSE HANGS WITHIN A STRUCTURE OF UNIVERSES, A THING ALMOST LIKE A SNOWFLAKE.
CHANNELS COURSE BETWEEN THE COUNTLESS ALTERNATIVE EARTHS, KEEPING THEM SEPARATE. THIS WE CALL THE BLEED.
I WAS DESIGNED TO SAIL THE BLEED; A TRADING SHIP BETWEEN UNIVERSES.
THERE WAS AN ACCIDENT. I CRASHED HERE.
MY CREW DIED ON IMPACTING THIS REALITY; I WAS TRAVELING TOO FAST.
ALL I COULD DO WAS JETTISON TRAVELSTONES SO THAT RESCUERS COULD RETAIN ENTRY INTO ME.
BUT THERE WERE NO RESCUERS. THE FLEET NEVER FOUND OUT WHERE I WENT DOWN.

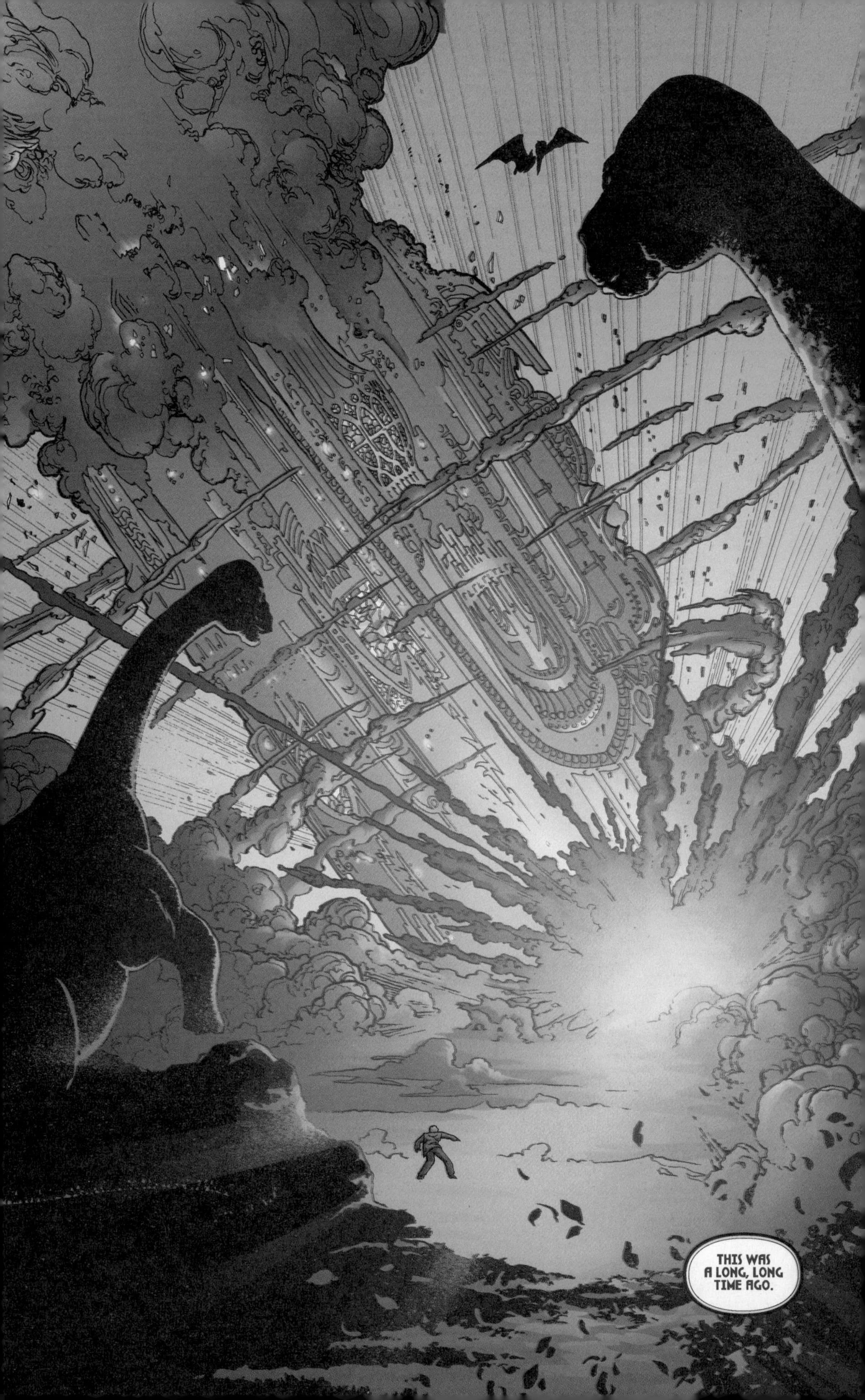
THIS WAS A LONG, LONG TIME AGO.

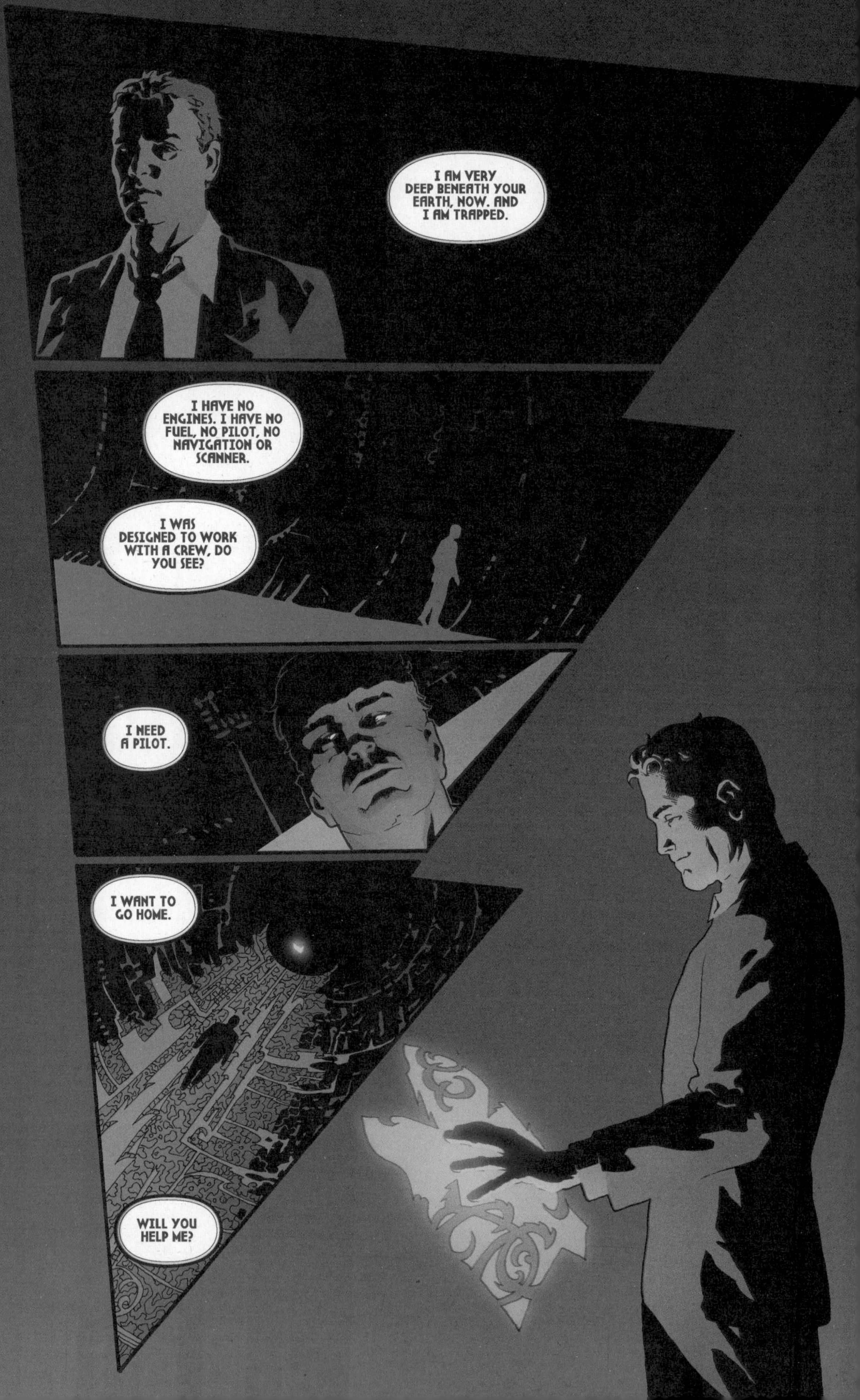
I AM VERY DEEP BENEATH YOUR EARTH, NOW. AND I AM TRAPPED.
I HAVE NO ENGINES. I HAVE NO FUEL, NO PILOT, NO NAVIGATION OR SCANNER.
I WAS DESIGNED TO WORK WITH A CREW, DO YOU SEE?
I NEED A PILOT.
I WANT TO GO HOME.
WILL YOU HELP ME?

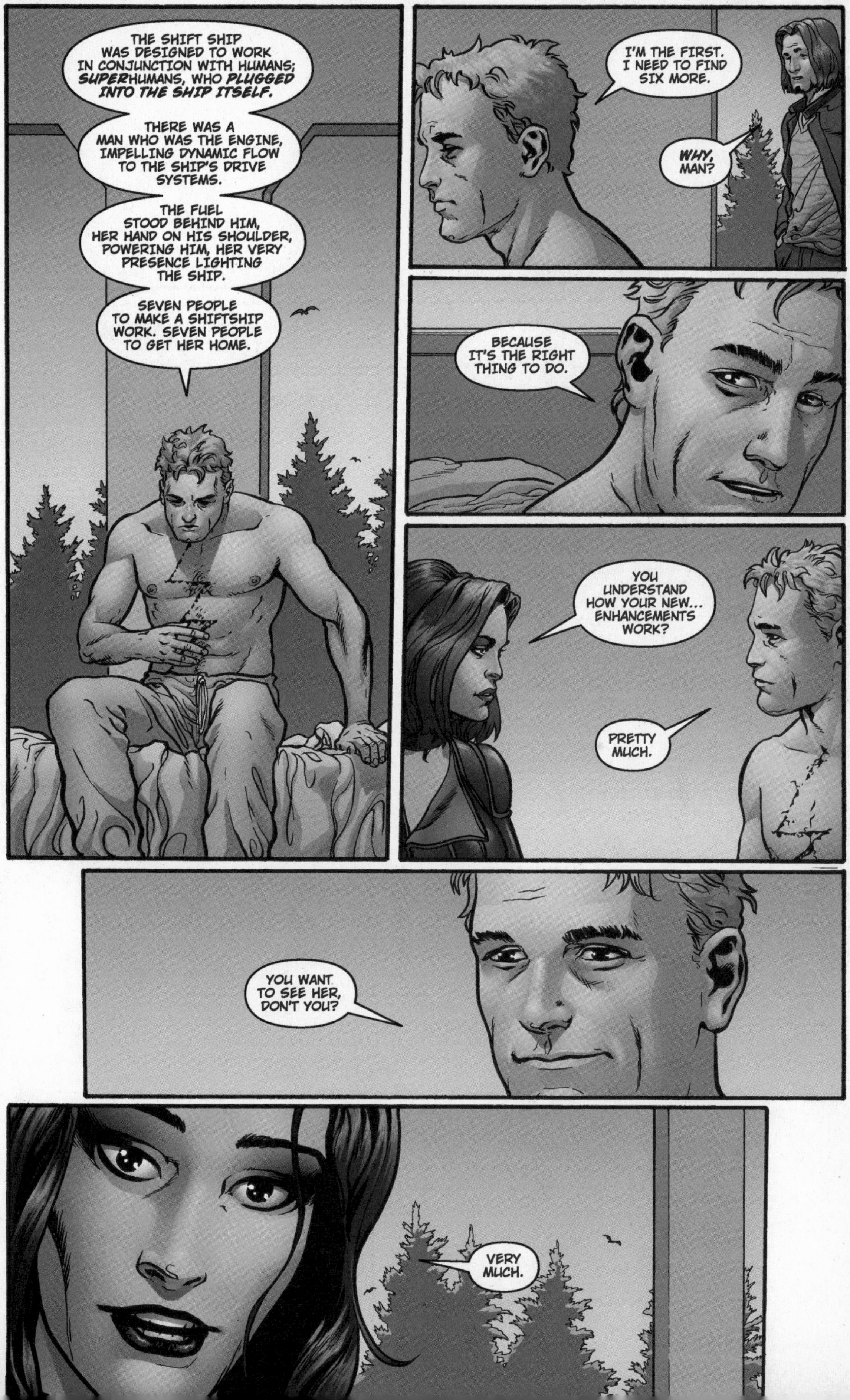
THE SHIFT SHIP WAS DESIGNED TO WORK IN CONJUNCTION WITH HUMANS; *SUPER*HUMANS, WHO *PLUGGED INTO THE SHIP ITSELF.*
THERE WAS A MAN WHO WAS THE ENGINE, IMPELLING DYNAMIC FLOW TO THE SHIP'S DRIVE SYSTEMS.
THE FUEL STOOD BEHIND HIM, HER HAND ON HIS SHOULDER, POWERING HIM, HER VERY PRESENCE LIGHTING THE SHIP.
SEVEN PEOPLE TO MAKE A SHIFTSHIP WORK. SEVEN PEOPLE TO GET HER HOME.
I'M THE FIRST. I NEED TO FIND SIX MORE.
WHY, MAN?
BECAUSE IT'S THE RIGHT THING TO DO.
YOU UNDERSTAND HOW YOUR NEW... ENHANCEMENTS WORK?
PRETTY MUCH.
YOU WANT TO SEE HER, DON'T YOU?
VERY MUCH.

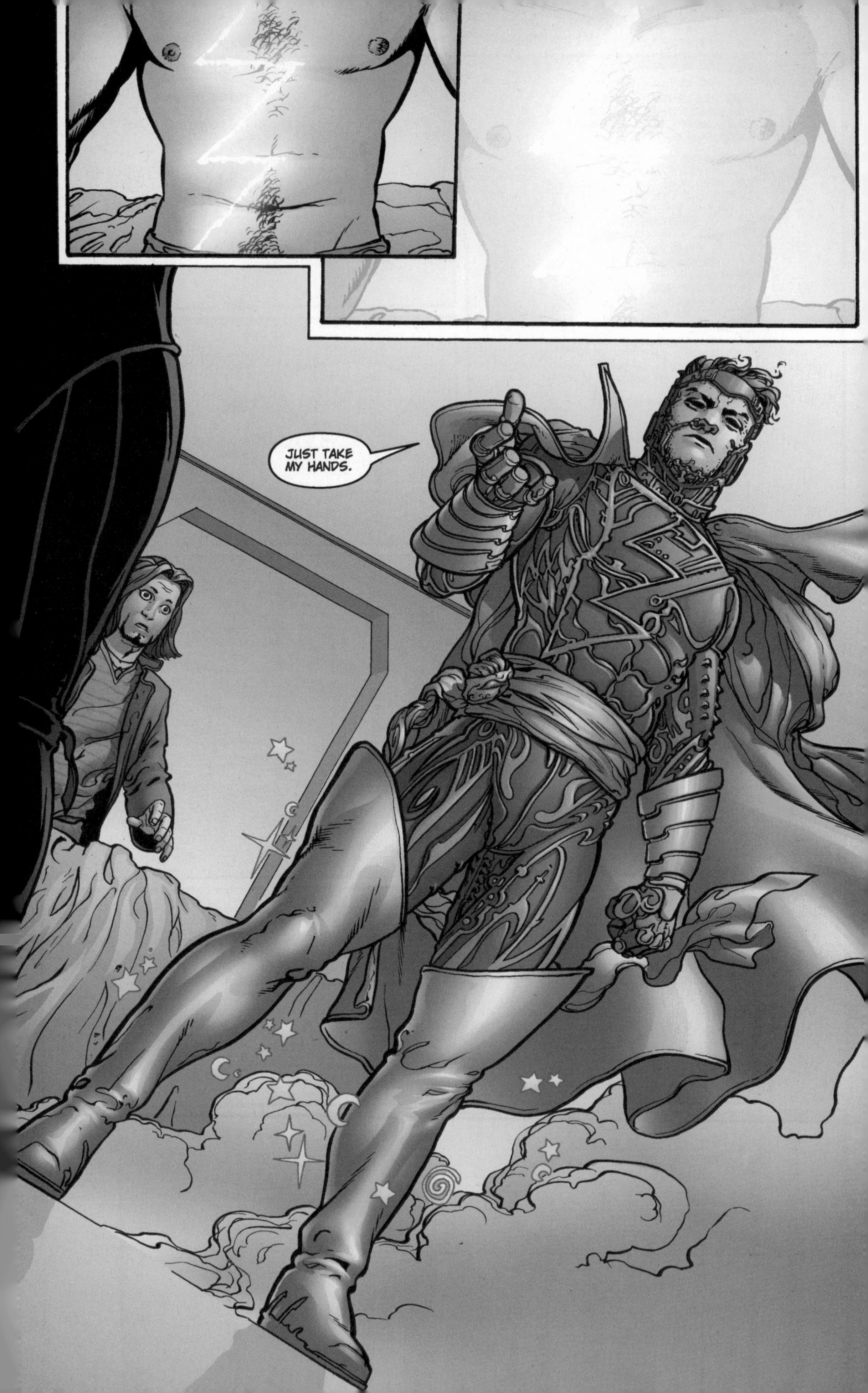
JUST TAKE MY HANDS.

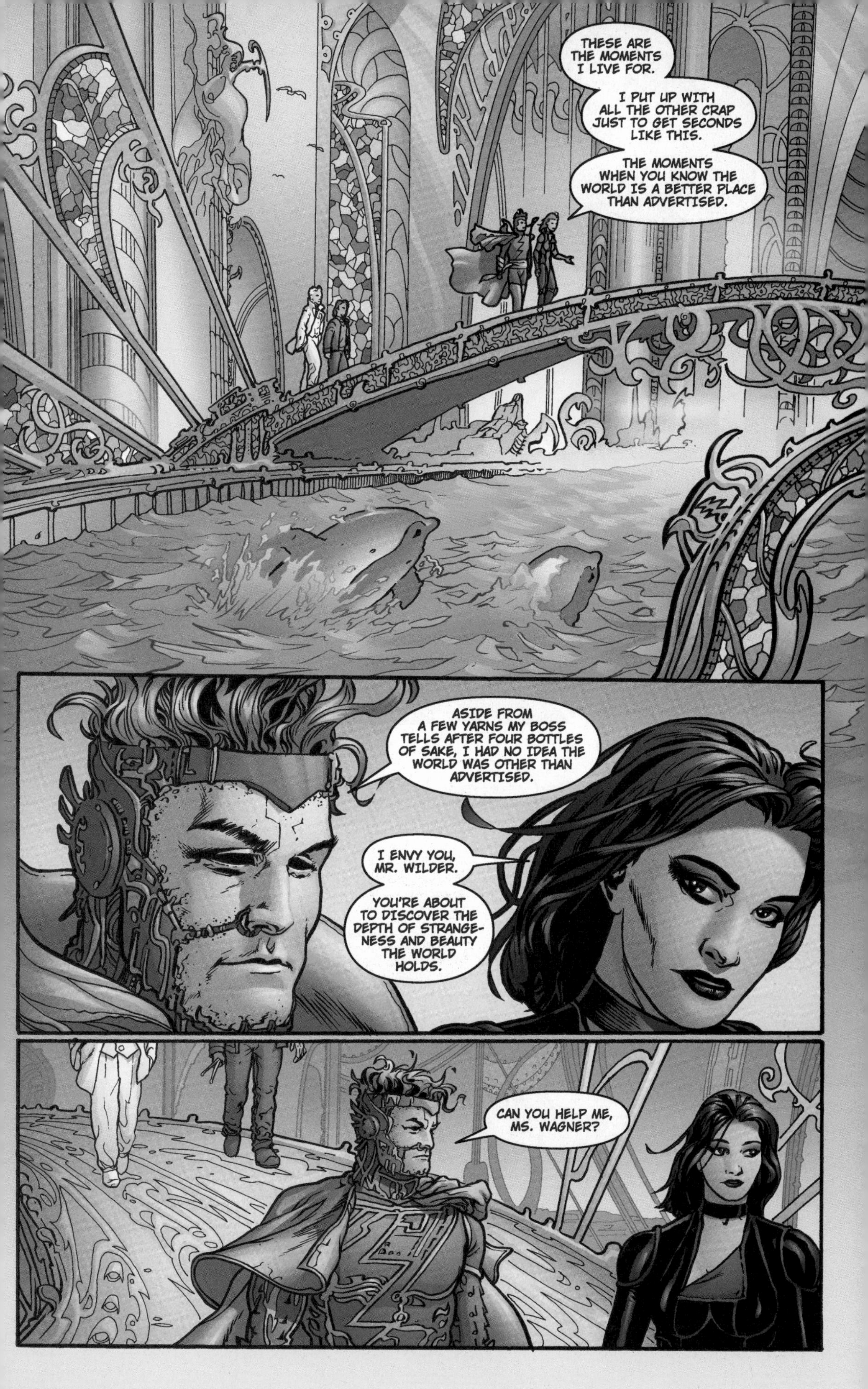
THESE ARE THE MOMENTS I LIVE FOR.
I PUT UP WITH ALL THE OTHER CRAP JUST TO GET SECONDS LIKE THIS.
THE MOMENTS WHEN YOU KNOW THE WORLD IS A BETTER PLACE THAN ADVERTISED.
ASIDE FROM A FEW YARNS MY BOSS TELLS AFTER FOUR BOTTLES OF SAKE, I HAD NO IDEA THE WORLD WAS OTHER THAN ADVERTISED.
I ENVY YOU, MR. WILDER.
YOU'RE ABOUT TO DISCOVER THE DEPTH OF STRANGE-NESS AND BEAUTY THE WORLD HOLDS.
CAN YOU HELP ME, MS. WAGNER?

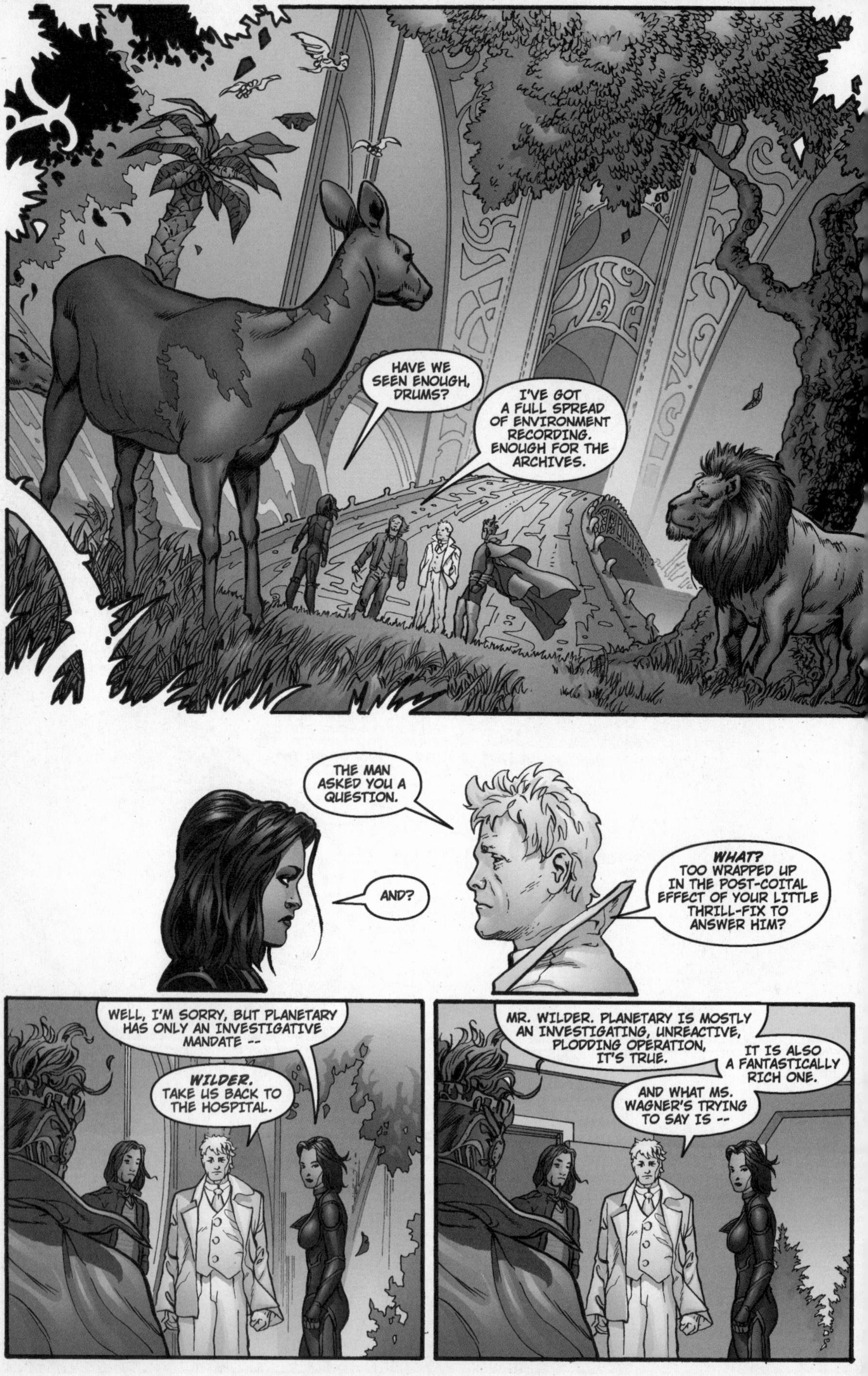
HAVE WE SEEN ENOUGH, DRUMS?
I'VE GOT A FULL SPREAD OF ENVIRONMENT RECORDING. ENOUGH FOR THE ARCHIVES.
THE MAN ASKED YOU A QUESTION.
AND?
WHAT? TOO WRAPPED UP IN THE POST-COITAL EFFECT OF YOUR LITTLE THRILL-FIX TO ANSWER HIM?
WELL, I'M SORRY, BUT PLANETARY HAS ONLY AN INVESTIGATIVE MANDATE --
WILDER. TAKE US BACK TO THE HOSPITAL.
MR. WILDER. PLANETARY IS MOSTLY AN INVESTIGATING, UNREACTIVE, PLODDING OPERATION, IT'S TRUE.
IT IS ALSO A FANTASTICALLY RICH ONE.
AND WHAT MS. WAGNER'S TRYING TO SAY IS --

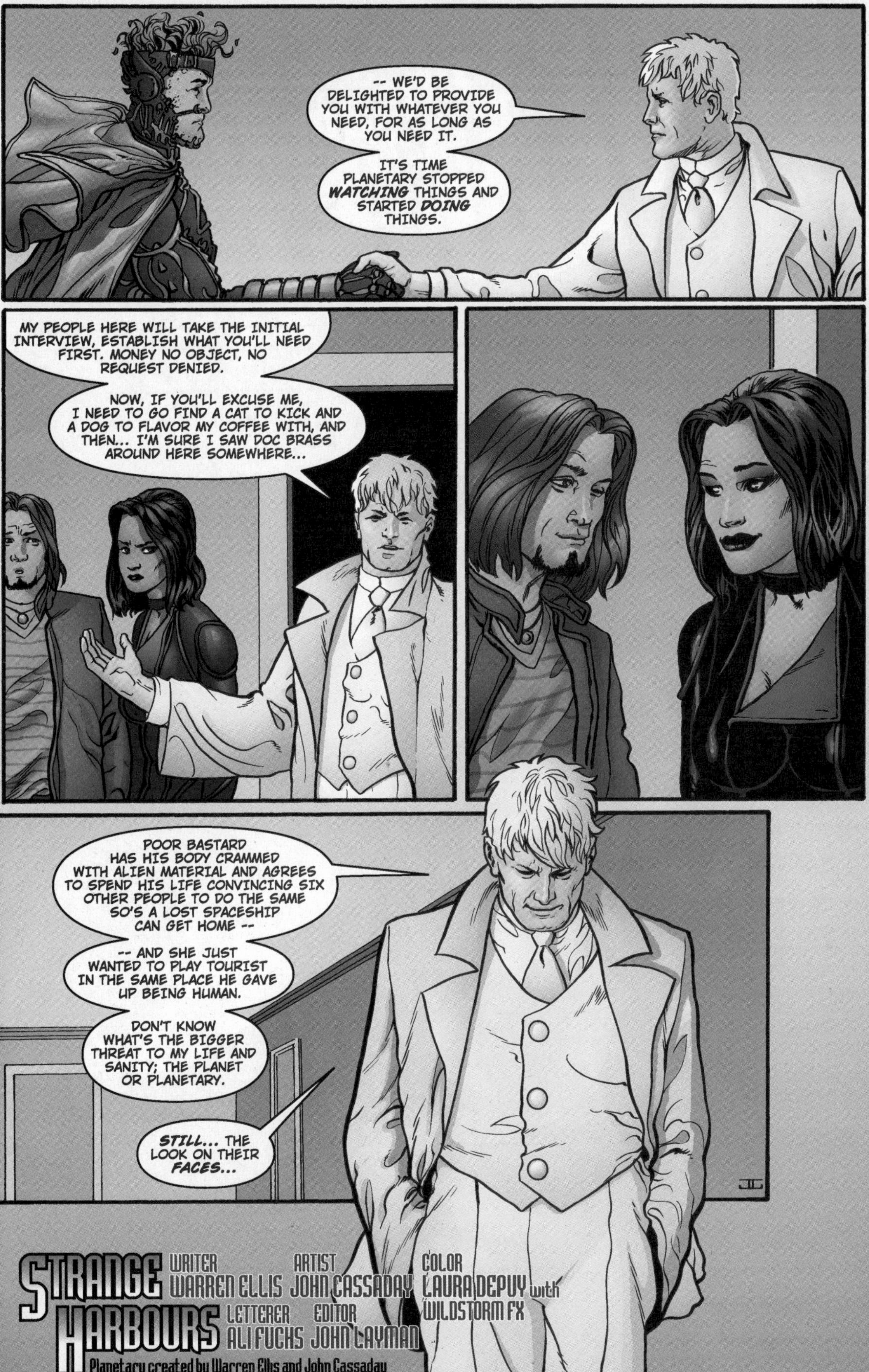
-- WE'D BE DELIGHTED TO PROVIDE YOU WITH WHATEVER YOU NEED, FOR AS LONG AS YOU NEED IT.
IT'S TIME PLANETARY STOPPED WATCHING THINGS AND STARTED DOING THINGS.
MY PEOPLE HERE WILL TAKE THE INITIAL INTERVIEW, ESTABLISH WHAT YOU'LL NEED FIRST. MONEY NO OBJECT, NO REQUEST DENIED.
NOW, IF YOU'LL EXCUSE ME, I NEED TO GO FIND A CAT TO KICK AND A DOG TO FLAVOR MY COFFEE WITH, AND THEN... I'M SURE I SAW DOC BRASS AROUND HERE SOMEWHERE...
POOR BASTARD HAS HIS BODY CRAMMED WITH ALIEN MATERIAL AND AGREES TO SPEND HIS LIFE CONVINCING SIX OTHER PEOPLE TO DO THE SAME SO'S A LOST SPACESHIP CAN GET HOME --
-- AND SHE JUST WANTED TO PLAY TOURIST IN THE SAME PLACE HE GAVE UP BEING HUMAN.
DON'T KNOW WHAT'S THE BIGGER THREAT TO MY LIFE AND SANITY; THE PLANET OR PLANETARY.
STILL... THE LOOK ON THEIR FACES...
JC
STRANGE HARBOURS
WRITER WARREN ELLIS
ARTIST JOHN CASSADAY
COLOR LAURA DEPUY with WILDSTORM FX
LETTERER ALI FUCHS
EDITOR JOHN LAYMAN
Planetary created by Warren Ellis and John Cassaday

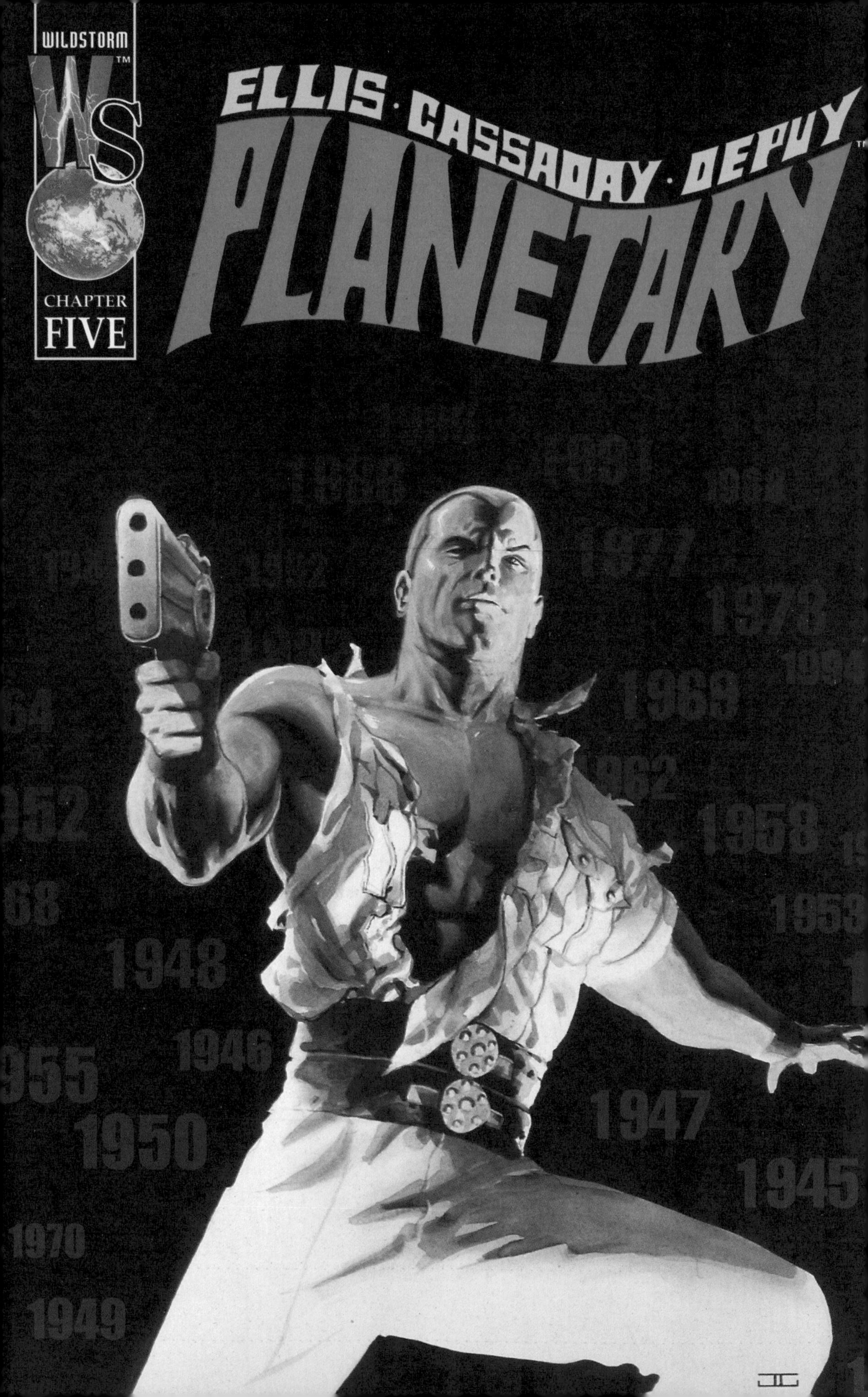
WILDSTORM
CHAPTER
FIVE
ELLIS · CASSADAY · DEPUY
PLANETARY
1977
1978
1969
1962
1958
1948
1946
1950
1947
1945
1970
1949

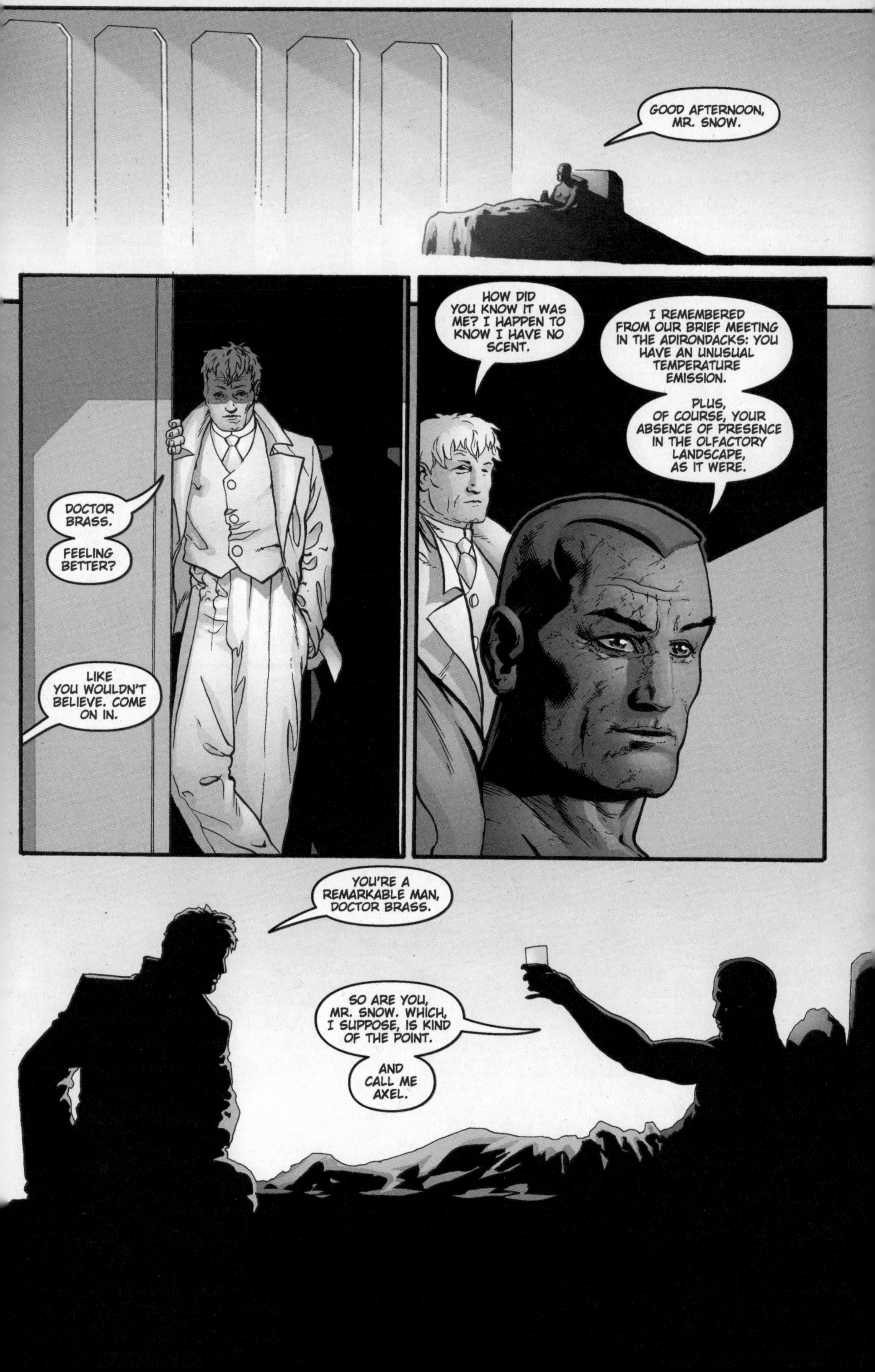
GOOD AFTERNOON, MR. SNOW.
DOCTOR BRASS.
FEELING BETTER?
LIKE YOU WOULDN'T BELIEVE. COME ON IN.
HOW DID YOU KNOW IT WAS ME? I HAPPEN TO KNOW I HAVE NO SCENT.
I REMEMBERED FROM OUR BRIEF MEETING IN THE ADIRONDACKS: YOU HAVE AN UNUSUAL TEMPERATURE EMISSION.
PLUS, OF COURSE, YOUR ABSENCE OF PRESENCE IN THE OLFACTORY LANDSCAPE, AS IT WERE.
YOU'RE A REMARKABLE MAN, DOCTOR BRASS.
SO ARE YOU, MR. SNOW. WHICH, I SUPPOSE, IS KIND OF THE POINT.
AND CALL ME AXEL.

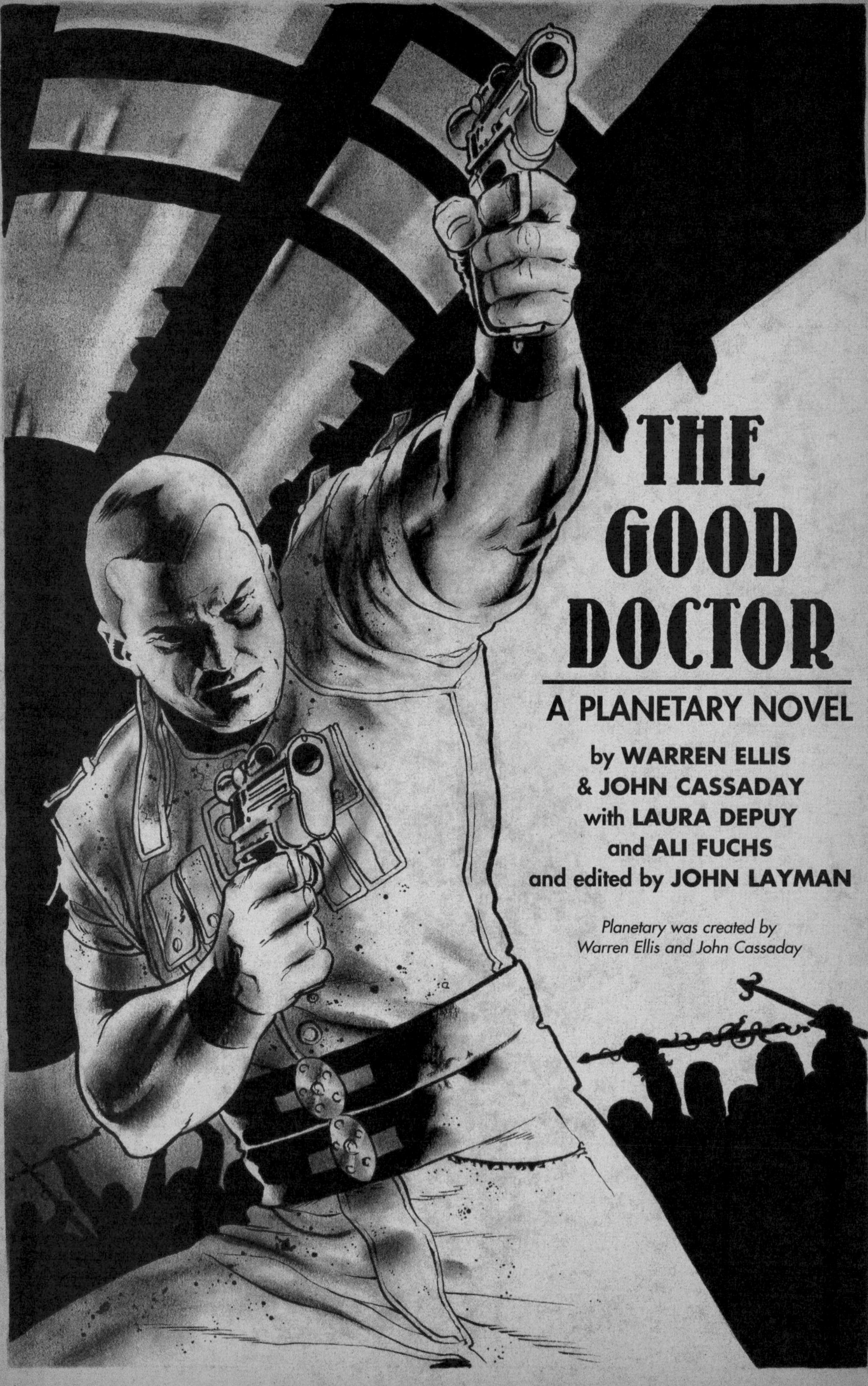
THE GOOD DOCTOR
A PLANETARY NOVEL
by WARREN ELLIS
& JOHN CASSADAY
with LAURA DEPUY
and ALI FUCHS
and edited by JOHN LAYMAN
Planetary was created by Warren Ellis and John Cassaday

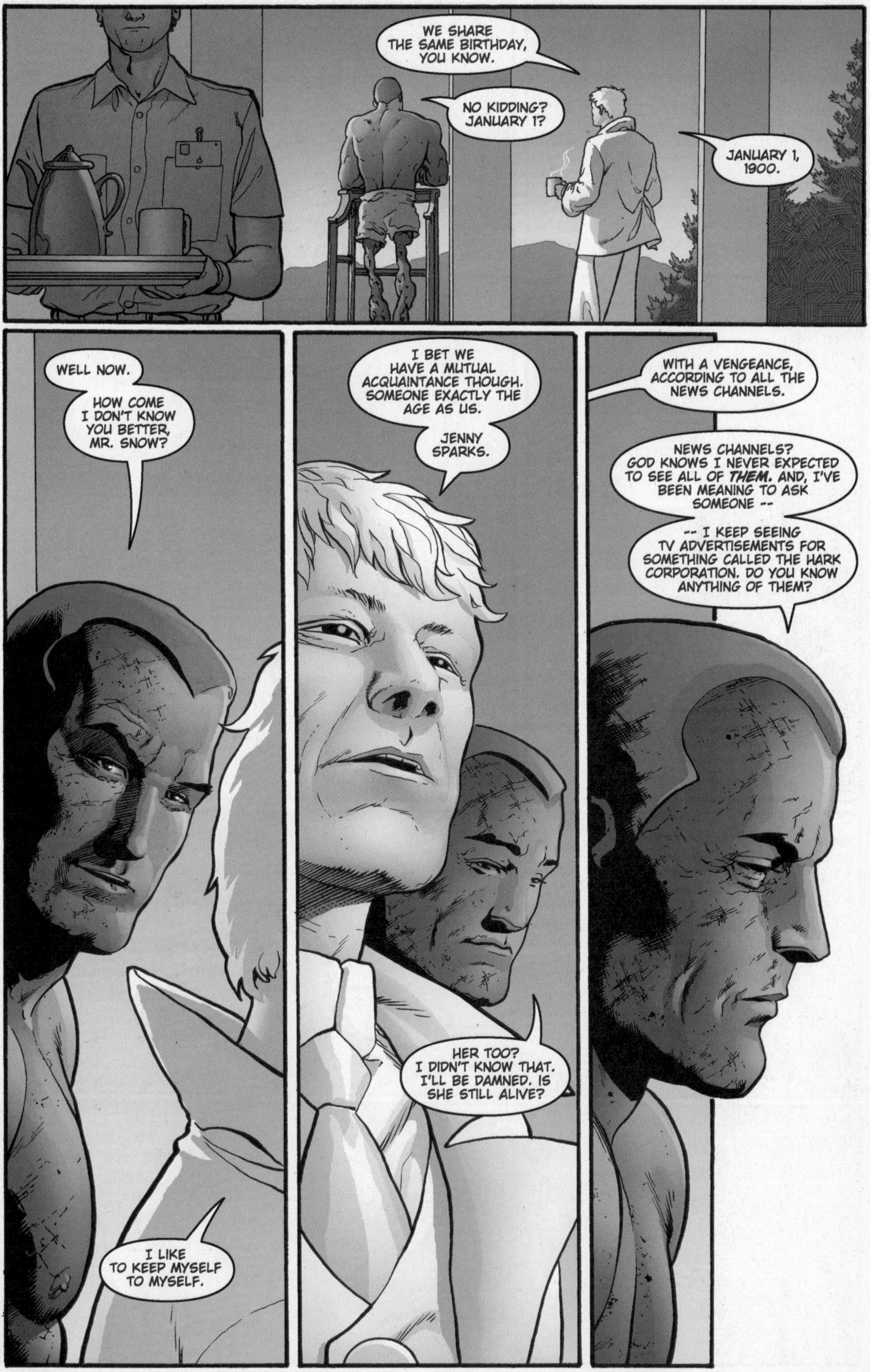
WE SHARE THE SAME BIRTHDAY, YOU KNOW.
NO KIDDING? JANUARY 1?
JANUARY 1, 1900.
WELL NOW.
HOW COME I DON'T KNOW YOU BETTER, MR. SNOW?
I LIKE TO KEEP MYSELF TO MYSELF.
I BET WE HAVE A MUTUAL ACQUAINTANCE THOUGH. SOMEONE EXACTLY THE AGE AS US.
JENNY SPARKS.
HER TOO? I DIDN'T KNOW THAT. I'LL BE DAMNED. IS SHE STILL ALIVE?
WITH A VENGEANCE, ACCORDING TO ALL THE NEWS CHANNELS.
NEWS CHANNELS? GOD KNOWS I NEVER EXPECTED TO SEE ALL OF *THEM.* AND, I'VE BEEN MEANING TO ASK SOMEONE --
-- I KEEP SEEING TV ADVERTISEMENTS FOR SOMETHING CALLED THE HARK CORPORATION. DO YOU KNOW ANYTHING OF THEM?

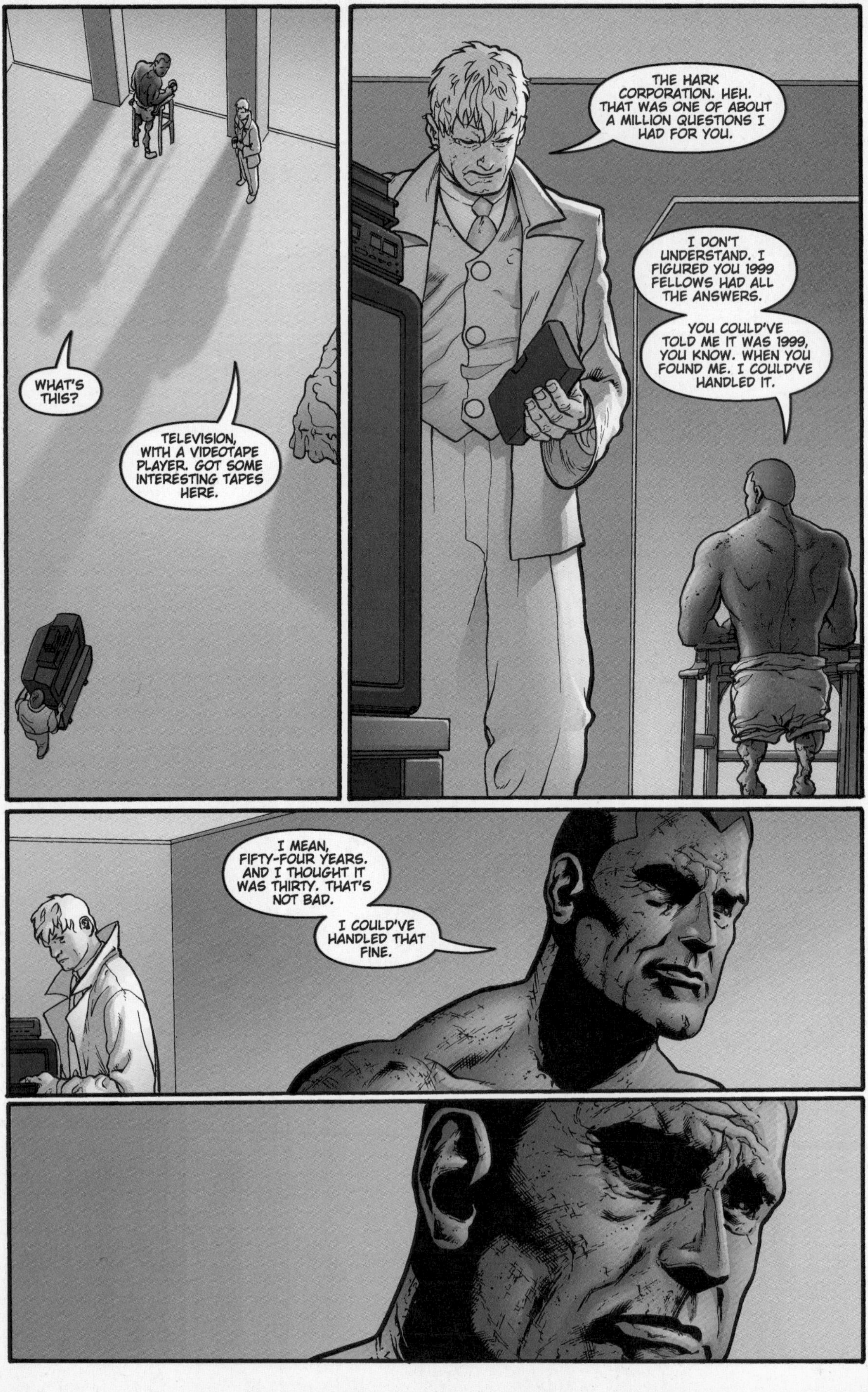
WHAT'S THIS?
TELEVISION, WITH A VIDEOTAPE PLAYER. GOT SOME INTERESTING TAPES HERE.
THE HARK CORPORATION. HEH. THAT WAS ONE OF ABOUT A MILLION QUESTIONS I HAD FOR YOU.
I DON'T UNDERSTAND. I FIGURED YOU 1999 FELLOWS HAD ALL THE ANSWERS.
YOU COULD'VE TOLD ME IT WAS 1999, YOU KNOW. WHEN YOU FOUND ME. I COULD'VE HANDLED IT.
I MEAN, FIFTY-FOUR YEARS. AND I THOUGHT IT WAS THIRTY. THAT'S NOT BAD.
I COULD'VE HANDLED THAT FINE.

"Doc Brass began to pace the
office like a caged tiger..."

D oc Brass' strange eyes glittered in the
dark. "You want to know how I ended
up in this dodge?"

Doc Brass began to pace the office like a caged
tiger. "I was born for it. Trained for it. Trained
for anything.

"My parents came from a society stretching back
to the French Revolution. There was a need, they
felt, to develop people worthy of a revolutionary
society. These were the greatest minds of intellec-
tual Europe, come together to write a plan for the
Superman.

"They created a new kind of diet, a new learning
system, a radically original exercise regime, and
began to apply it to their own children. Each new
generation was stronger, and stranger, than the
last.

"I'm the last of them, the end of the revolutionary
line. I've been bred, born and trained to deal with
anything.

"Except the unspeakable evil of my own parents,
warped brother and sister that they were."

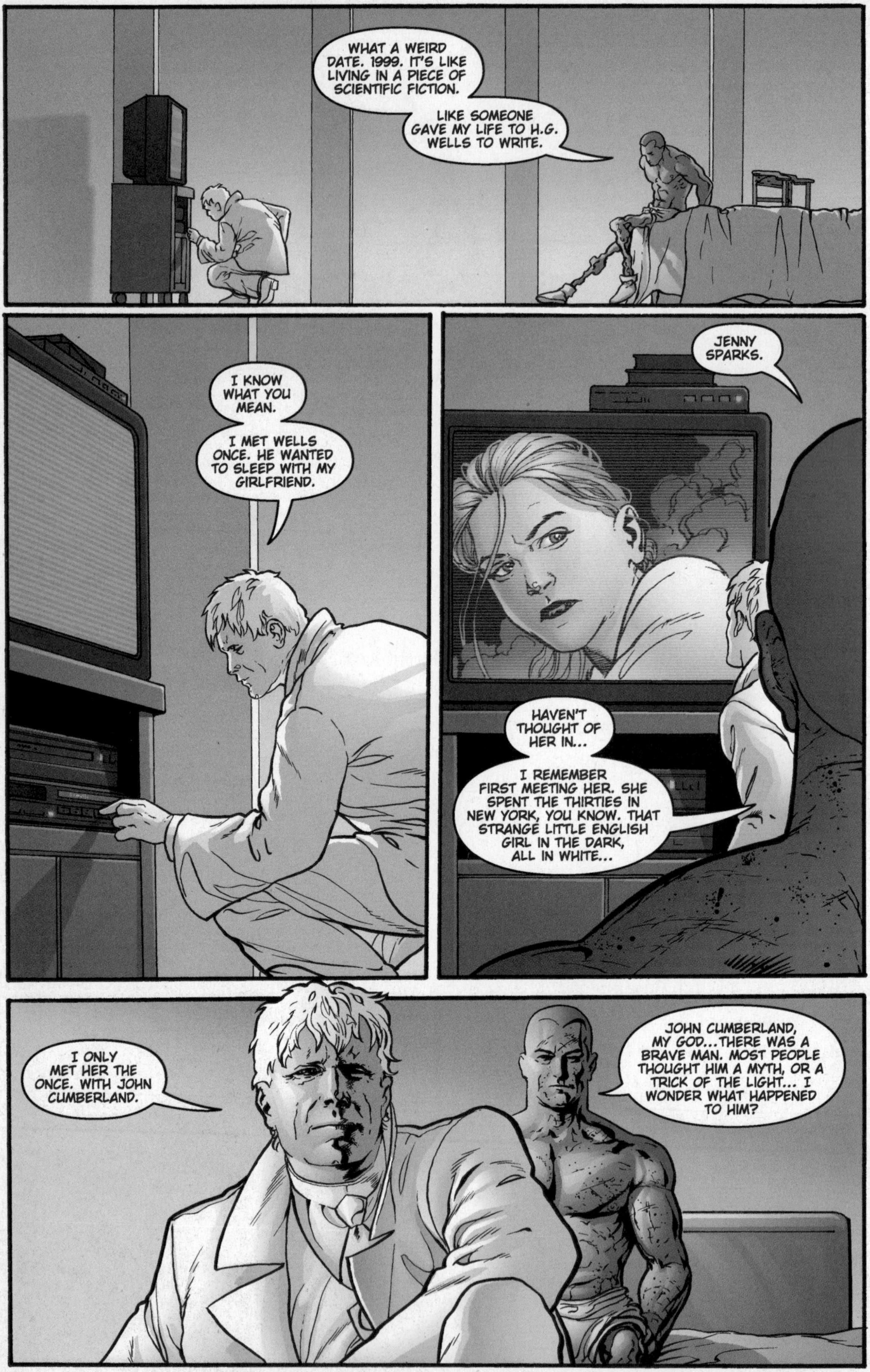
WHAT A WEIRD DATE. 1999. IT'S LIKE LIVING IN A PIECE OF SCIENTIFIC FICTION.
LIKE SOMEONE GAVE MY LIFE TO H.G. WELLS TO WRITE.
I KNOW WHAT YOU MEAN.
I MET WELLS ONCE. HE WANTED TO SLEEP WITH MY GIRLFRIEND.
JENNY SPARKS.
HAVEN'T THOUGHT OF HER IN...
I REMEMBER FIRST MEETING HER. SHE SPENT THE THIRTIES IN NEW YORK, YOU KNOW. THAT STRANGE LITTLE ENGLISH GIRL IN THE DARK, ALL IN WHITE...
I ONLY MET HER THE ONCE. WITH JOHN CUMBERLAND.
JOHN CUMBERLAND, MY GOD...THERE WAS A BRAVE MAN. MOST PEOPLE THOUGHT HIM A MYTH, OR A TRICK OF THE LIGHT... I WONDER WHAT HAPPENED TO HIM?

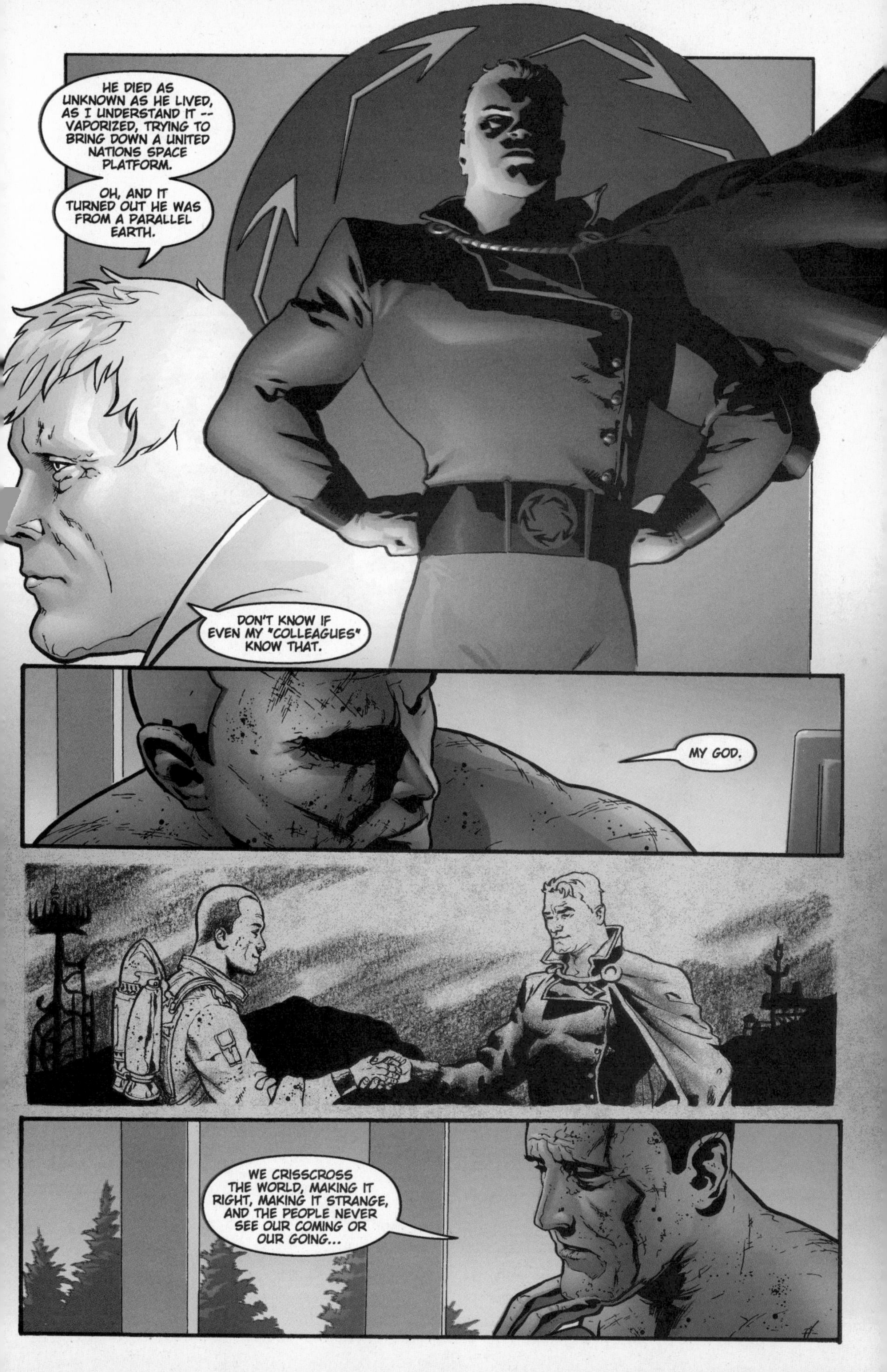
HE DIED AS UNKNOWN AS HE LIVED, AS I UNDERSTAND IT -- VAPORIZED, TRYING TO BRING DOWN A UNITED NATIONS SPACE PLATFORM.
OH, AND IT TURNED OUT HE WAS FROM A PARALLEL EARTH.
DON'T KNOW IF EVEN MY "COLLEAGUES" KNOW THAT.
MY GOD.
WE CRISSCROSS THE WORLD, MAKING IT RIGHT, MAKING IT STRANGE, AND THE PEOPLE NEVER SEE OUR COMING OR OUR GOING...

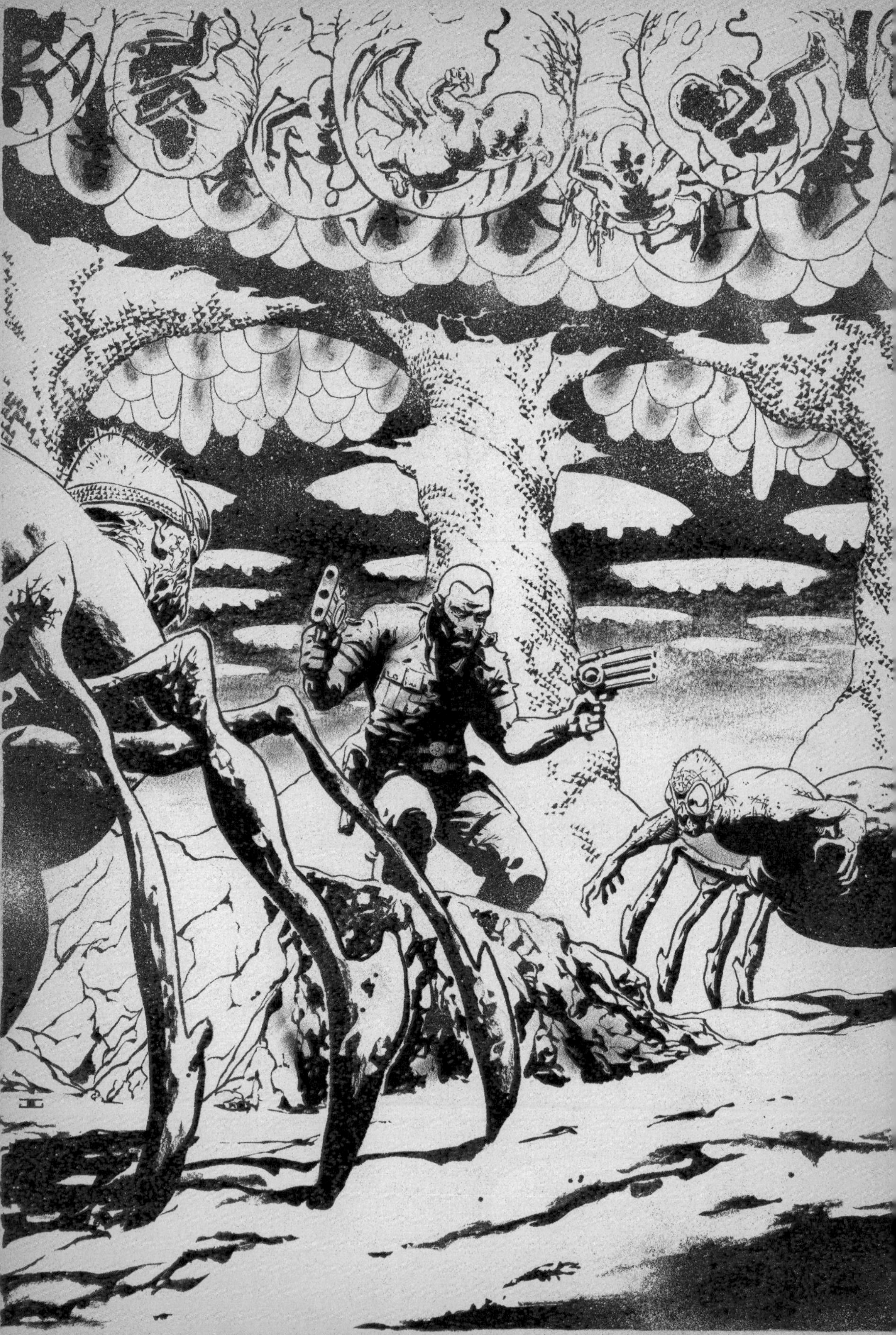

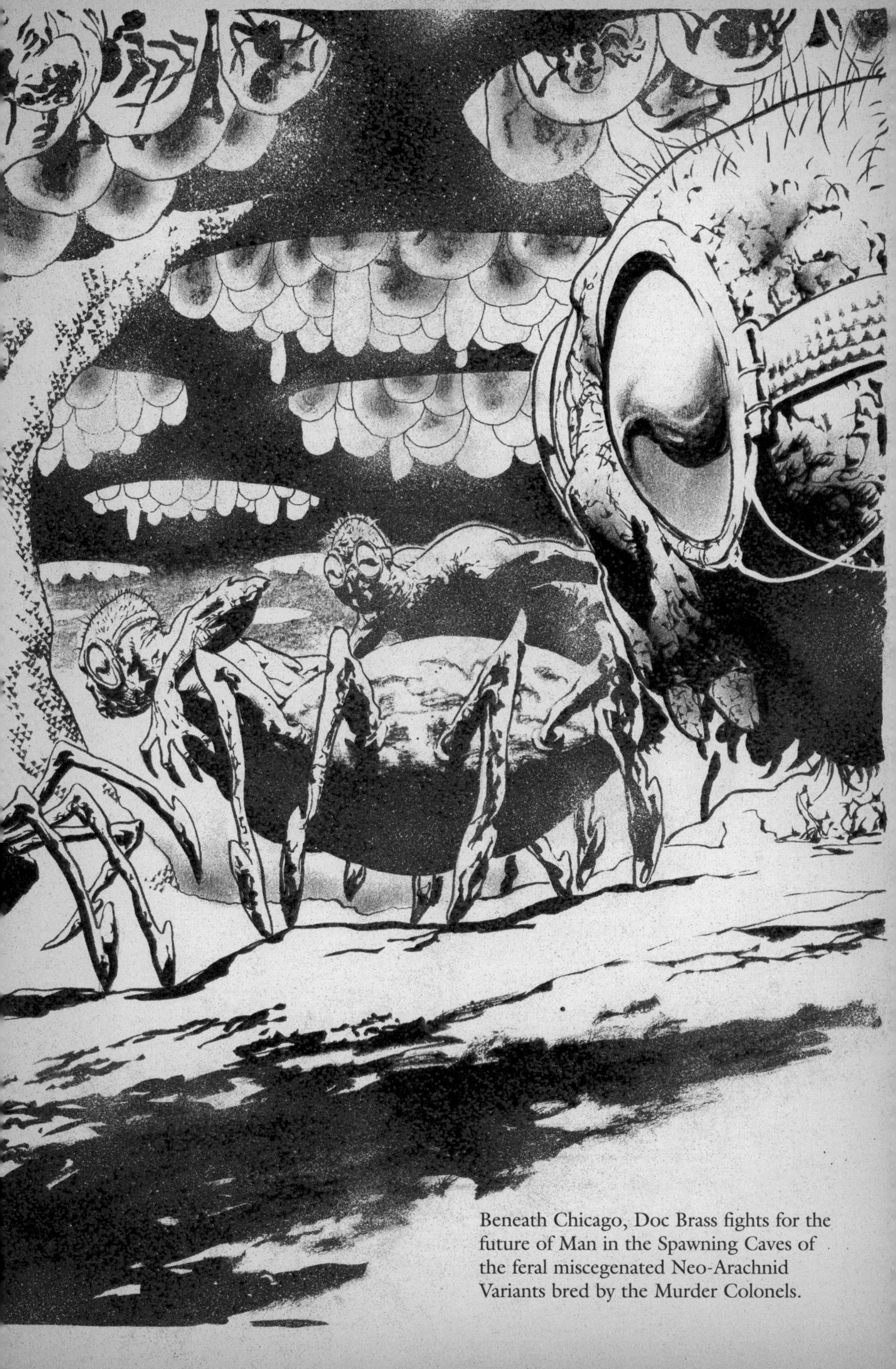

Beneath Chicago, Doc Brass fights for the future of Man in the Spawning Caves of the feral miscegenated Neo-Arachnid Variants bred by the Murder Colonels.

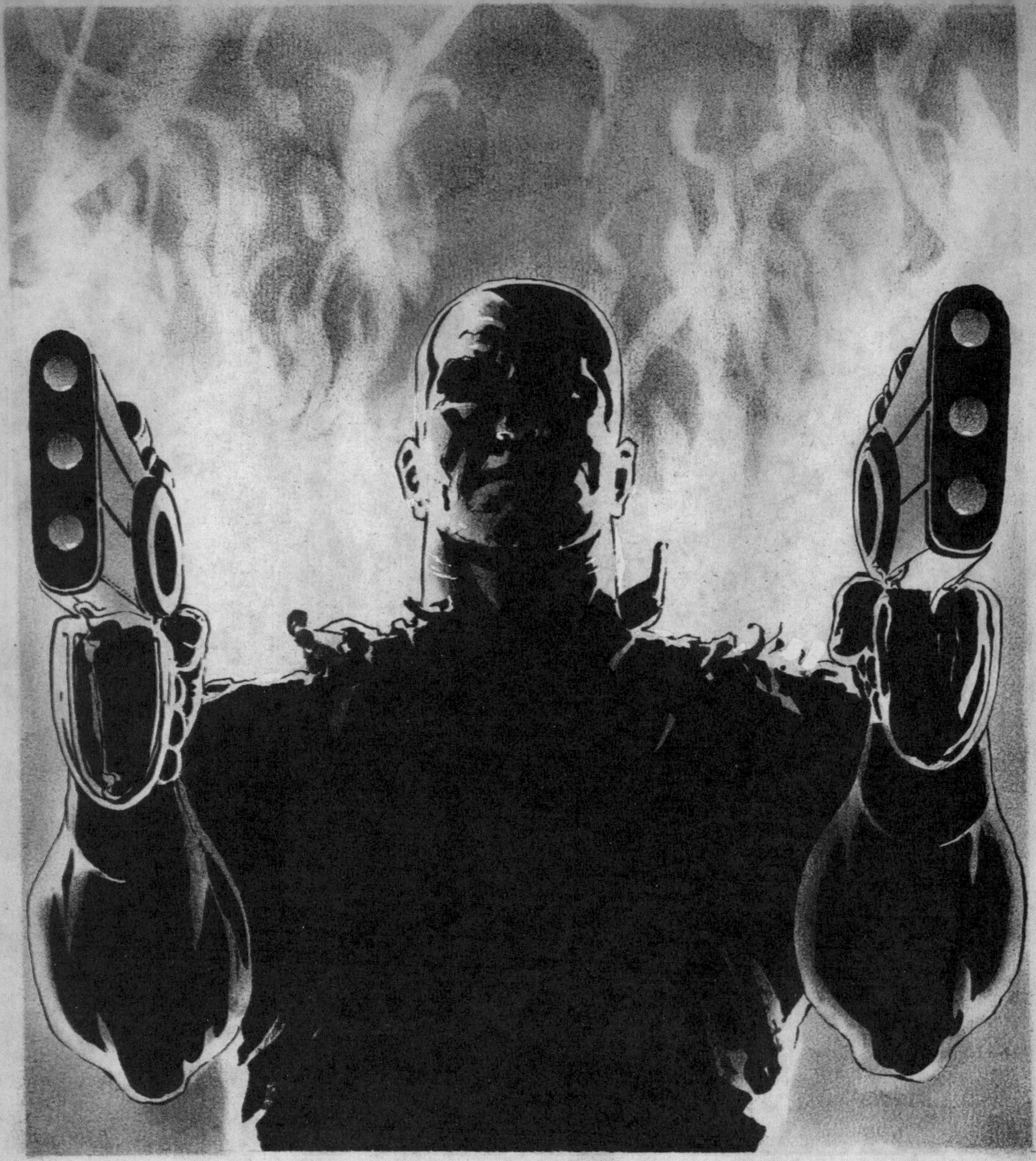

The Caged Horrors Of Nelia-Sai spat acid and shrieked like stuck babies, but Doc Brass stood fast, dealing hot righteous death with his marvelous turbopistols.

The sickening UnderEngland Junta unleashed its Black Royalty, torching the very sky and driving good men mad, and Doc Brass held his ground, taking the pain and the flame and killing hard.

The Emperors Of America advanced upon him and poisoned the ground and invented new ways to torture and despoil and murder with every step they took, but Doc Brass stayed right there and put his guns upon the monsters and saw to it that they went no further --

-- because somebody had to.

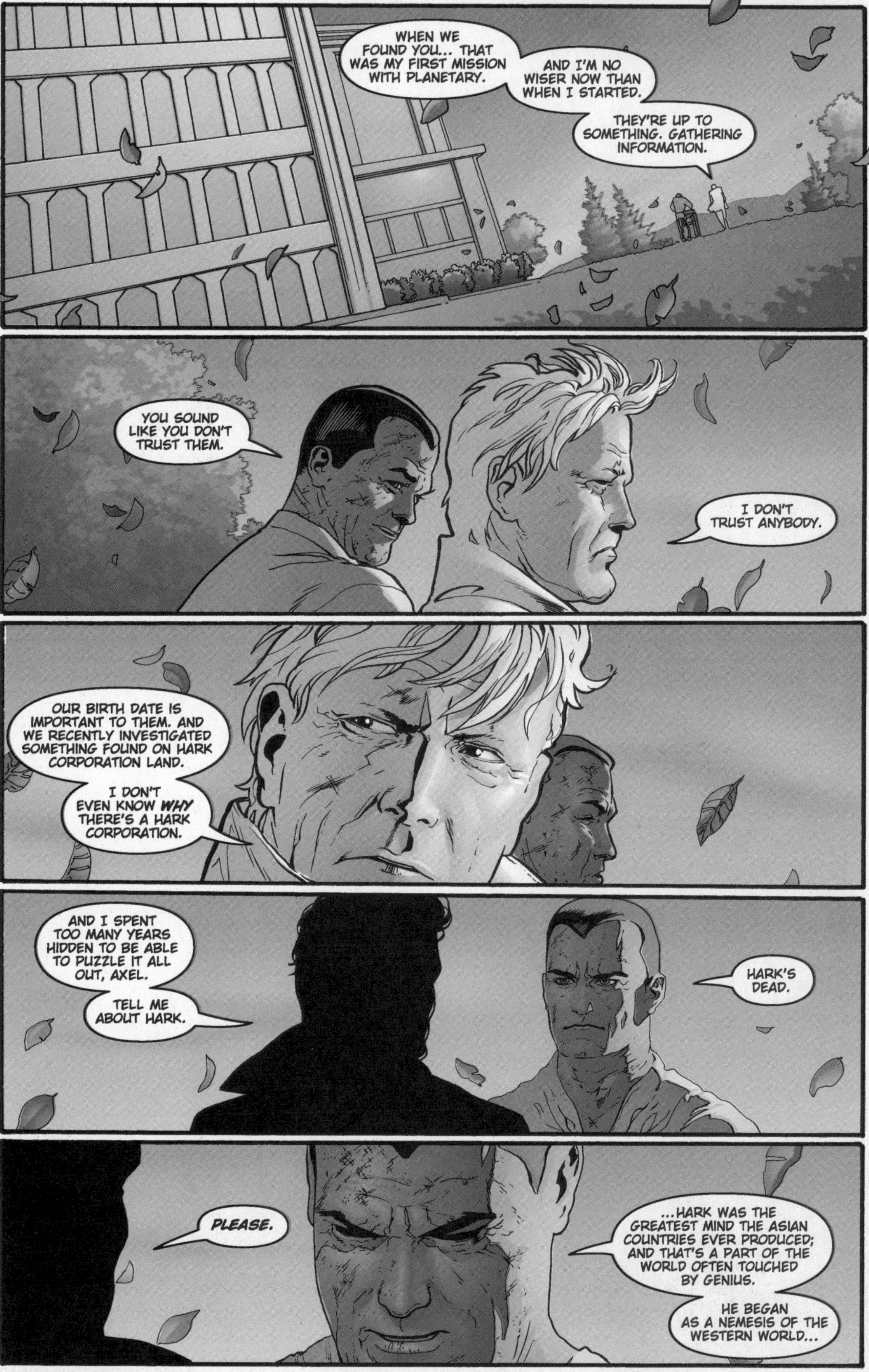
WHEN WE FOUND YOU... THAT WAS MY FIRST MISSION WITH PLANETARY.
AND I'M NO WISER NOW THAN WHEN I STARTED.
THEY'RE UP TO SOMETHING. GATHERING INFORMATION.
YOU SOUND LIKE YOU DON'T TRUST THEM.
I DON'T TRUST ANYBODY.
OUR BIRTH DATE IS IMPORTANT TO THEM. AND WE RECENTLY INVESTIGATED SOMETHING FOUND ON HARK CORPORATION LAND.
I DON'T EVEN KNOW *WHY* THERE'S A HARK CORPORATION.
AND I SPENT TOO MANY YEARS HIDDEN TO BE ABLE TO PUZZLE IT ALL OUT, AXEL.
TELL ME ABOUT HARK.
HARK'S DEAD.
PLEASE.
...HARK WAS THE GREATEST MIND THE ASIAN COUNTRIES EVER PRODUCED; AND THAT'S A PART OF THE WORLD OFTEN TOUCHED BY GENIUS.
HE BEGAN AS A NEMESIS OF THE WESTERN WORLD...

The careful training and calculated breeding of almost three hundred years had rendered Axel Brass capable of masking any emotion, even the extremes of grief and agony. Today, for the first time anybody could name...Axel Brass let the mask of years drop.

Hark's strange eyes narrowed, his sharp Oriental features otherwise composed. Here was a man of equal control -- the very pinnacle of the ingenuity of the East, contained in this tall, frightening figure. Hark had been the terror of the Occident since the turn of the century, bedeviling first Britannia, and then America herself.

"Hark," Brass said, "it doesn't have to be like this. We don't have to die here. And be sure, we will both die here, if we allow it."

Hark's sinister visage remained still.

"Damn it, Hark! We're not your enemy! America doesn't hate you! It just doesn't understand you! We're on the same side!"

Hark's own mask slipped, in the face of Brass' passion.

"We both want a better world for our people! That isn't mutually exclusive! For God's sake, man -- *we're all on the same planet!*"

Anna Hark coiled herself into her father's life. She imagined herself a beautiful snake on a brightly patterned rug. If that snake moved carefully, and was still at the right moments, then to the casual eye there was no snake, only a beautiful bright rug.

The world was just a gaudy pattern, and she a lovely, coiled thing of venom.

Her father's inventions, her father's money; soon, this could be a corporation, in the Western mold. She would hide herself in the warp and weft of America, grow rich, and wait.

ANNA HARK

Hark understood that, indeed, he and Axel Brass could be a force to protect both the Orient and the world, while teaching the world to live with respect for its differing cultures. Hark's step into the light completed the secret society that Brass had spent ten years gathering, in imitation of the group that spawned the system that led to his own birth, in the days of Robespierre.

There was Jimmy, the secret Operator for the United States government, who knew of the wars the world never saw. The English lord raised and made greater than human by the rude beasts of the deep African jungles. The Aviator, who fought unknown things and black technologies simply to learn of them. Edison, the great inventor-adventurer of electric America. And the dark millionaire, the man in black whose guns shouted out against crime in all its forms.

Between them, they could save the world.

From itself.

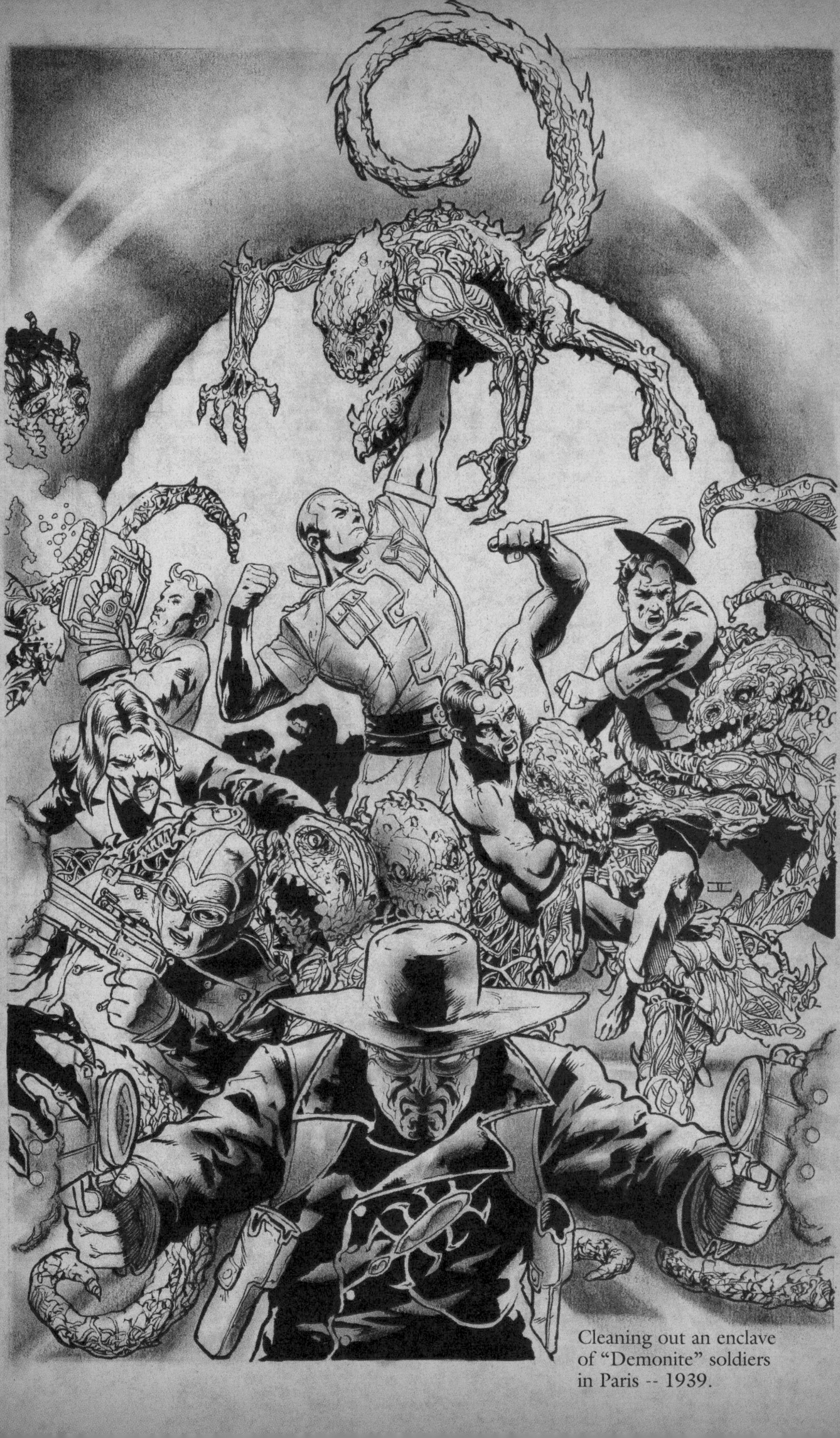

Cleaning out an enclave of "Demonite" soldiers in Paris -- 1939.

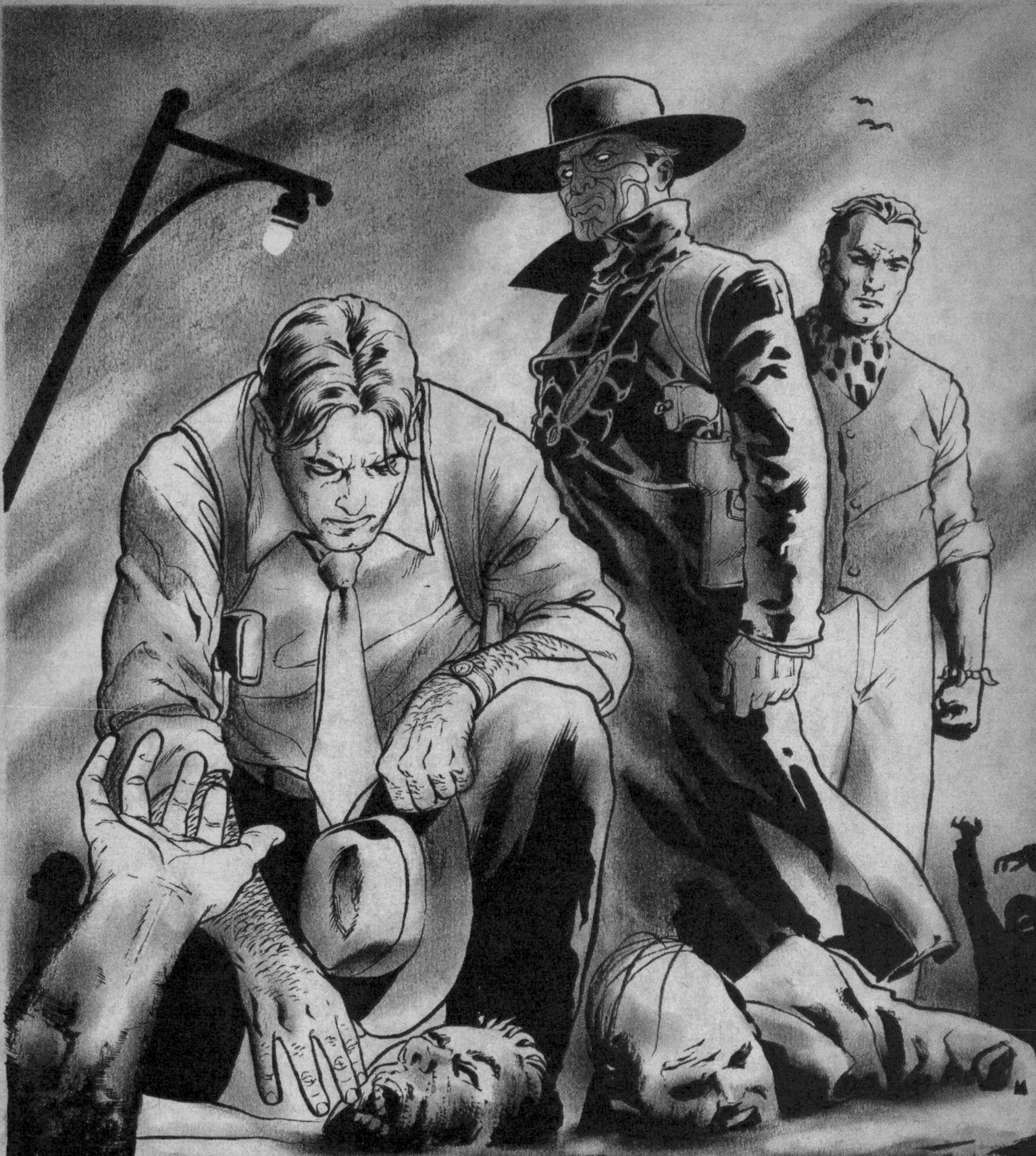

Brass and the others walked where The Charnel Ship had passed. Ahead, the air still crackled and glowed red where the Ship had sailed out from this reality, into the blood-colored tides beyond space and time.

Jimmy stared at the blasted faces underfoot, seared into the compressed and burned remains of their

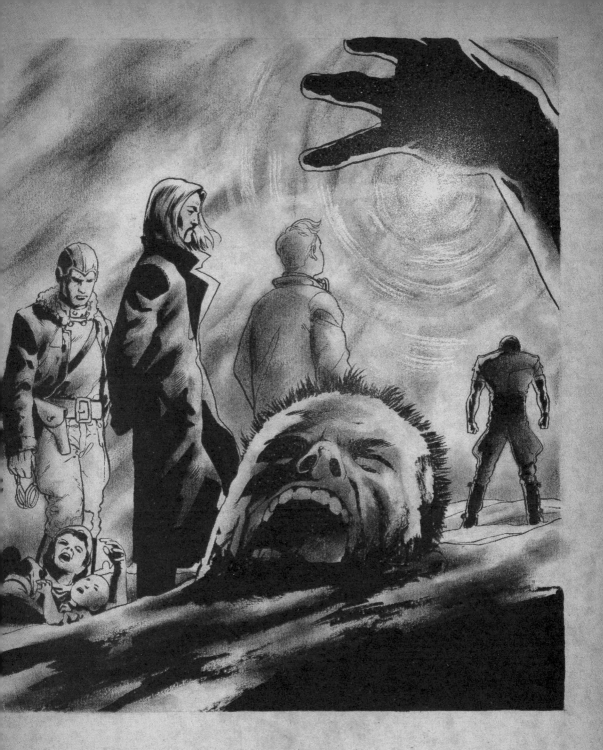

town, and balled his fists. He had only recently
saved the West Coast from invasion, in his role as
Special Operator to the Secret Service. And now
this.

Brass voiced what they were all thinking.

"We cannot allow the world to be this way."

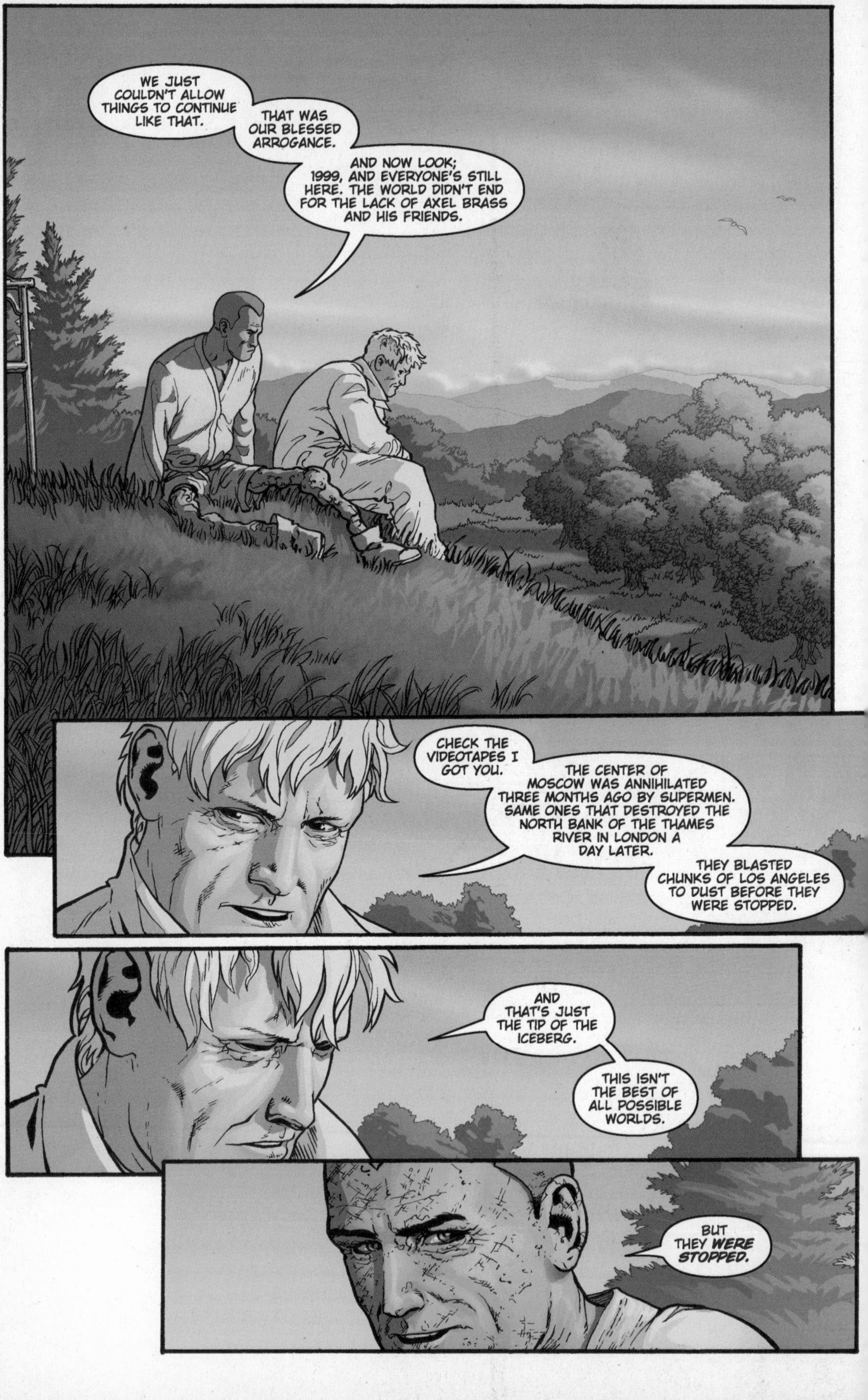
WE JUST COULDN'T ALLOW THINGS TO CONTINUE LIKE THAT.
THAT WAS OUR BLESSED ARROGANCE.
AND NOW LOOK; 1999, AND EVERYONE'S STILL HERE. THE WORLD DIDN'T END FOR THE LACK OF AXEL BRASS AND HIS FRIENDS.
CHECK THE VIDEOTAPES I GOT YOU.
THE CENTER OF MOSCOW WAS ANNIHILATED THREE MONTHS AGO BY SUPERMEN. SAME ONES THAT DESTROYED THE NORTH BANK OF THE THAMES RIVER IN LONDON A DAY LATER.
THEY BLASTED CHUNKS OF LOS ANGELES TO DUST BEFORE THEY WERE STOPPED.
AND THAT'S JUST THE TIP OF THE ICEBERG.
THIS ISN'T THE BEST OF ALL POSSIBLE WORLDS.
BUT THEY ***WERE STOPPED.***

America danced hysterically below. Axel Brass hummed a little tune to himself as he looked down on New York City's lights from his penthouse retreat. It was a tune his father always hummed, in moments of stress: "The Marseilleise."

From all across the world, tonight, Earth's secret gods were moving. From China, Hark would be departing in his "stealthy" aeroplane, that sinister thing of black angles. Jimmy would be on a train from California, provided those Things under LA had finally been quelled. Edison had already left his underground lab in downtown NYC -- he had a lot to set up at the covert gathering place in the Adirondacks. His Lordship was reported to be on a plane from Madagascar.

It was the end of 1944. Axel Brass looked down at the world and smiled. It was the end of his life's work. Everything was going to be fine. Better than fine. For everyone.

It was the end of a great many things.

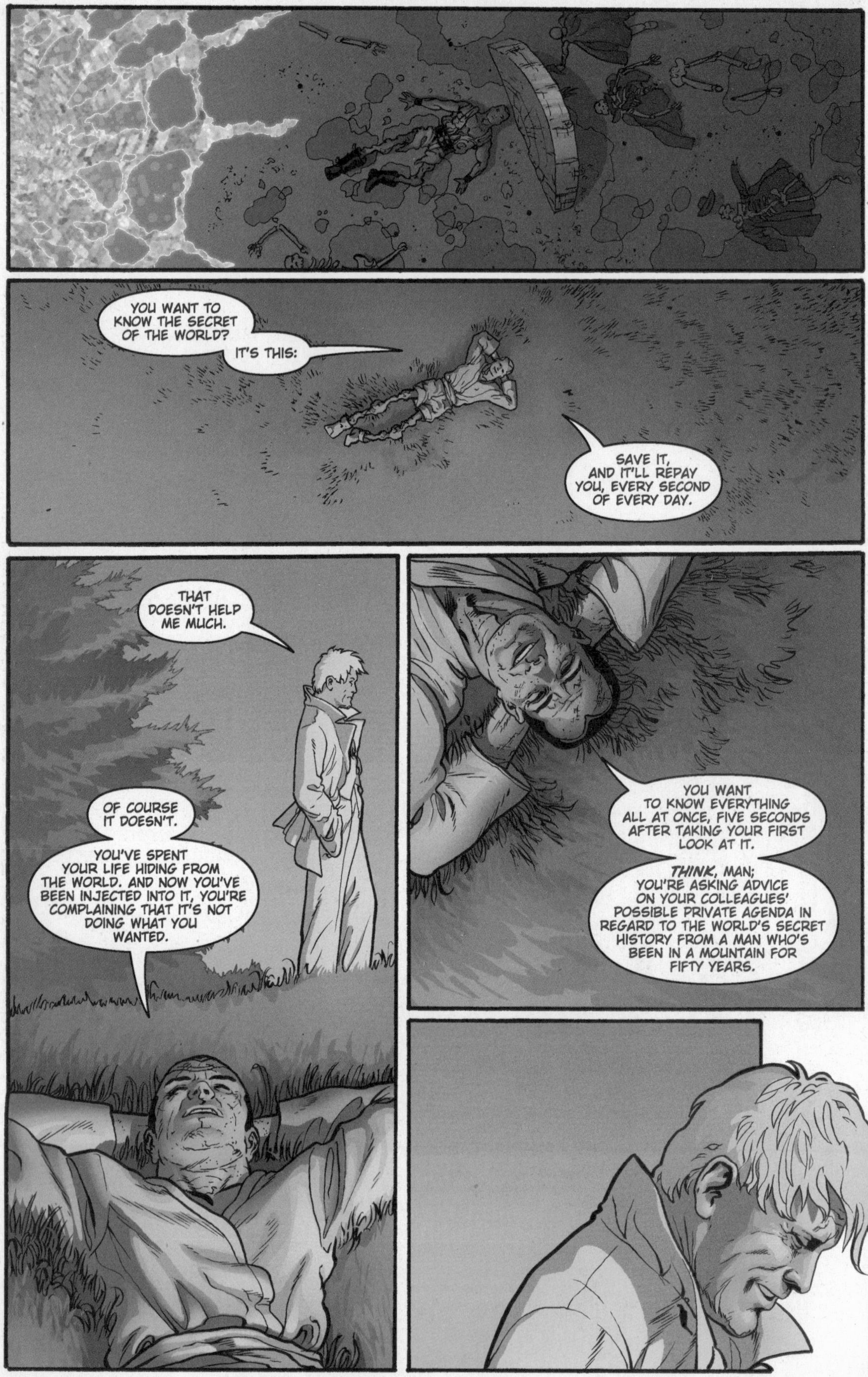
YOU WANT TO KNOW THE SECRET OF THE WORLD?
IT'S THIS:
SAVE IT, AND IT'LL REPAY YOU, EVERY SECOND OF EVERY DAY.
THAT DOESN'T HELP ME MUCH.
OF COURSE IT DOESN'T.
YOU'VE SPENT YOUR LIFE HIDING FROM THE WORLD. AND NOW YOU'VE BEEN INJECTED INTO IT, YOU'RE COMPLAINING THAT IT'S NOT DOING WHAT YOU WANTED.
YOU WANT TO KNOW EVERYTHING ALL AT ONCE, FIVE SECONDS AFTER TAKING YOUR FIRST LOOK AT IT.
THINK, MAN; YOU'RE ASKING ADVICE ON YOUR COLLEAGUES' POSSIBLE PRIVATE AGENDA IN REGARD TO THE WORLD'S SECRET HISTORY FROM A MAN WHO'S BEEN IN A MOUNTAIN FOR FIFTY YEARS.

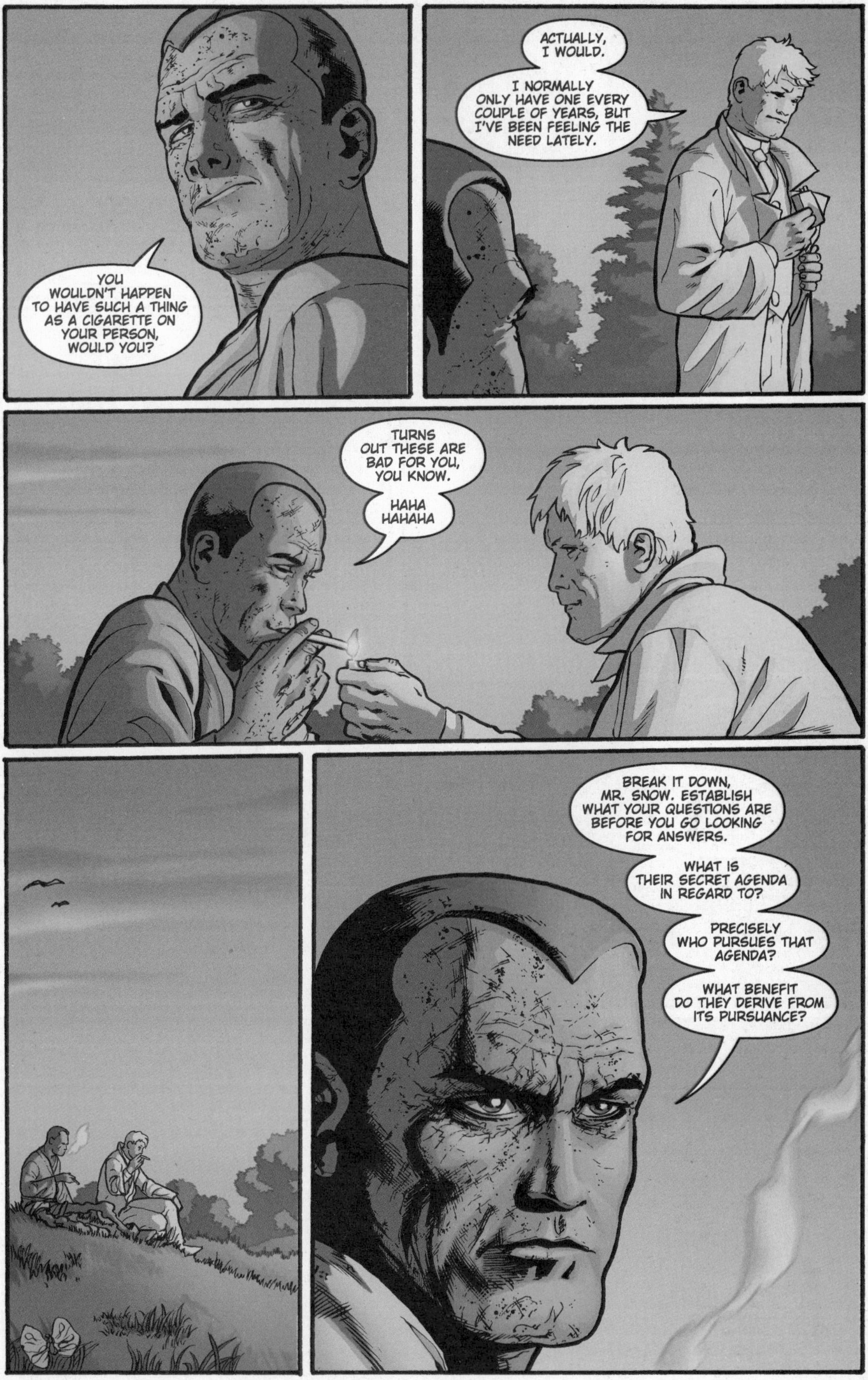
YOU WOULDN'T HAPPEN TO HAVE SUCH A THING AS A CIGARETTE ON YOUR PERSON, WOULD YOU?
ACTUALLY, I WOULD.
I NORMALLY ONLY HAVE ONE EVERY COUPLE OF YEARS, BUT I'VE BEEN FEELING THE NEED LATELY.
TURNS OUT THESE ARE BAD FOR YOU, YOU KNOW.
HAHA HAHAHA
BREAK IT DOWN, MR. SNOW. ESTABLISH WHAT YOUR QUESTIONS ARE BEFORE YOU GO LOOKING FOR ANSWERS.
WHAT IS THEIR SECRET AGENDA IN REGARD TO?
PRECISELY WHO PURSUES THAT AGENDA?
WHAT BENEFIT DO THEY DERIVE FROM ITS PURSUANCE?

THE FOURTH MAN.

WHAT?

PLANETARY'S FINANCIAL BACKER. THEY CALL HIM THE FOURTH MAN. BECAUSE THEY PROFESS NOT TO KNOW WHO HE IS.

HE OR SHE. I MEAN, THIS IS 1999. WHY NOT A SHE?

SHE.

I WONDER.

AH... YOU SHOULD'VE BEEN AROUND WITH US IN THE THIRTIES, MR. SNOW.

I CAN'T BEGIN TO TELL YOU WHAT YOU MISSED.

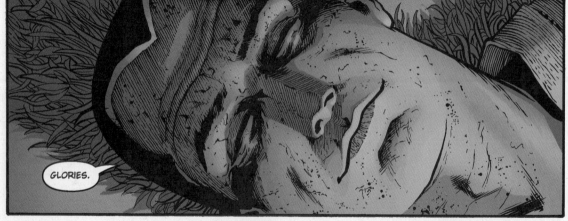

GLORIES.

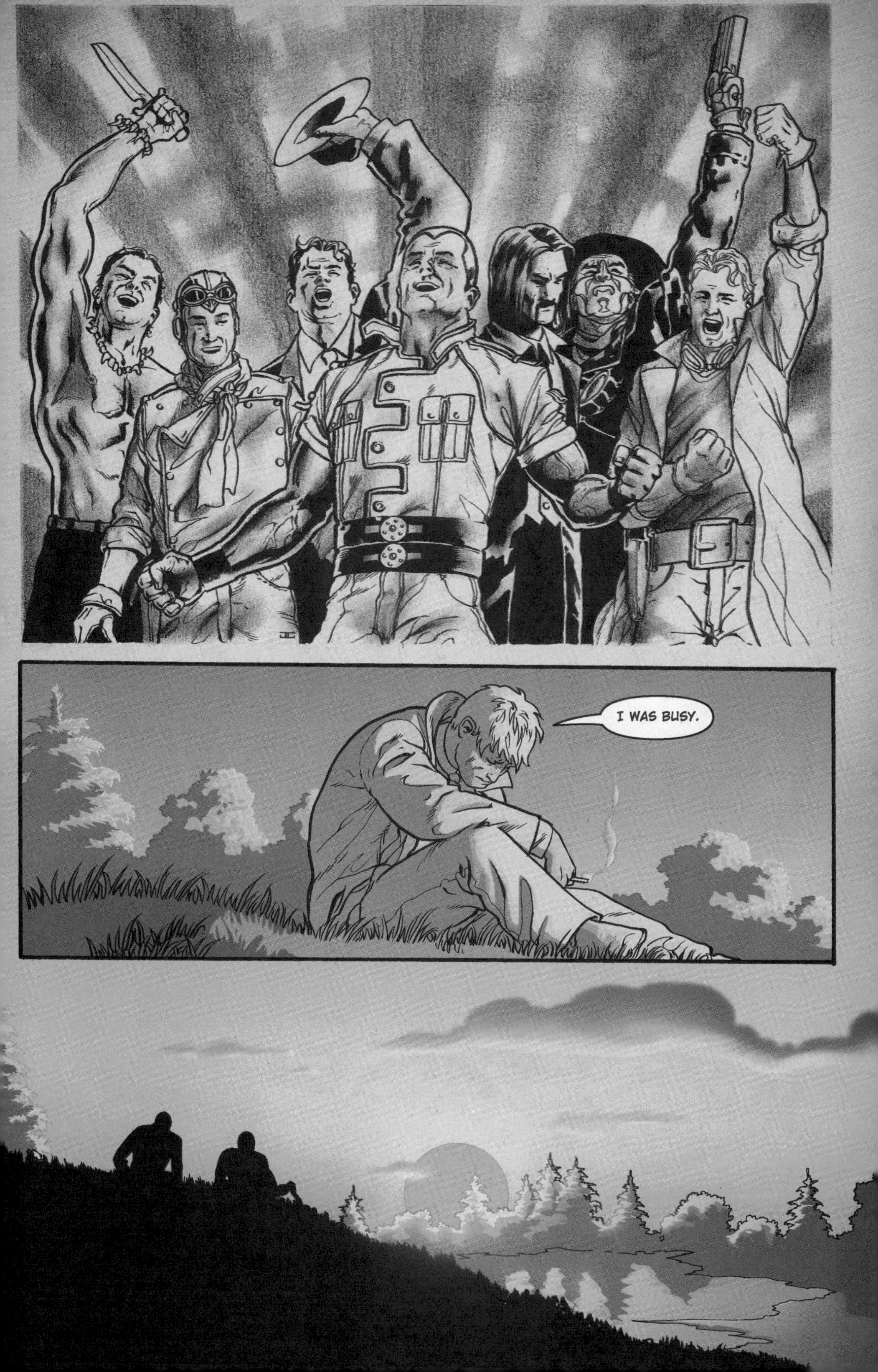
I WAS BUSY.

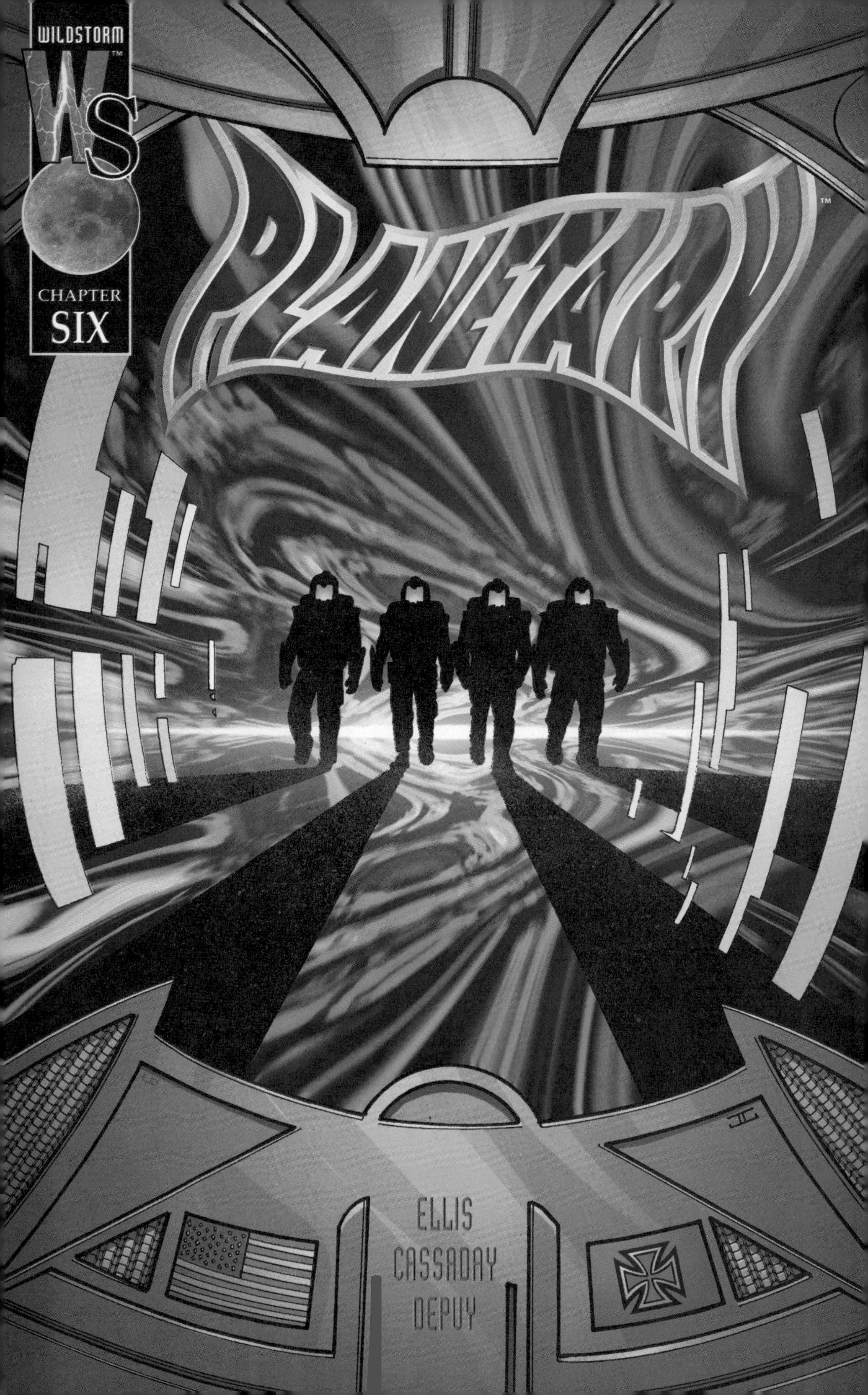
WILDSTORM
WS
CHAPTER
SIX
PLANETARY
ELLIS
CASSADAY
DEPUY

it's a strange world

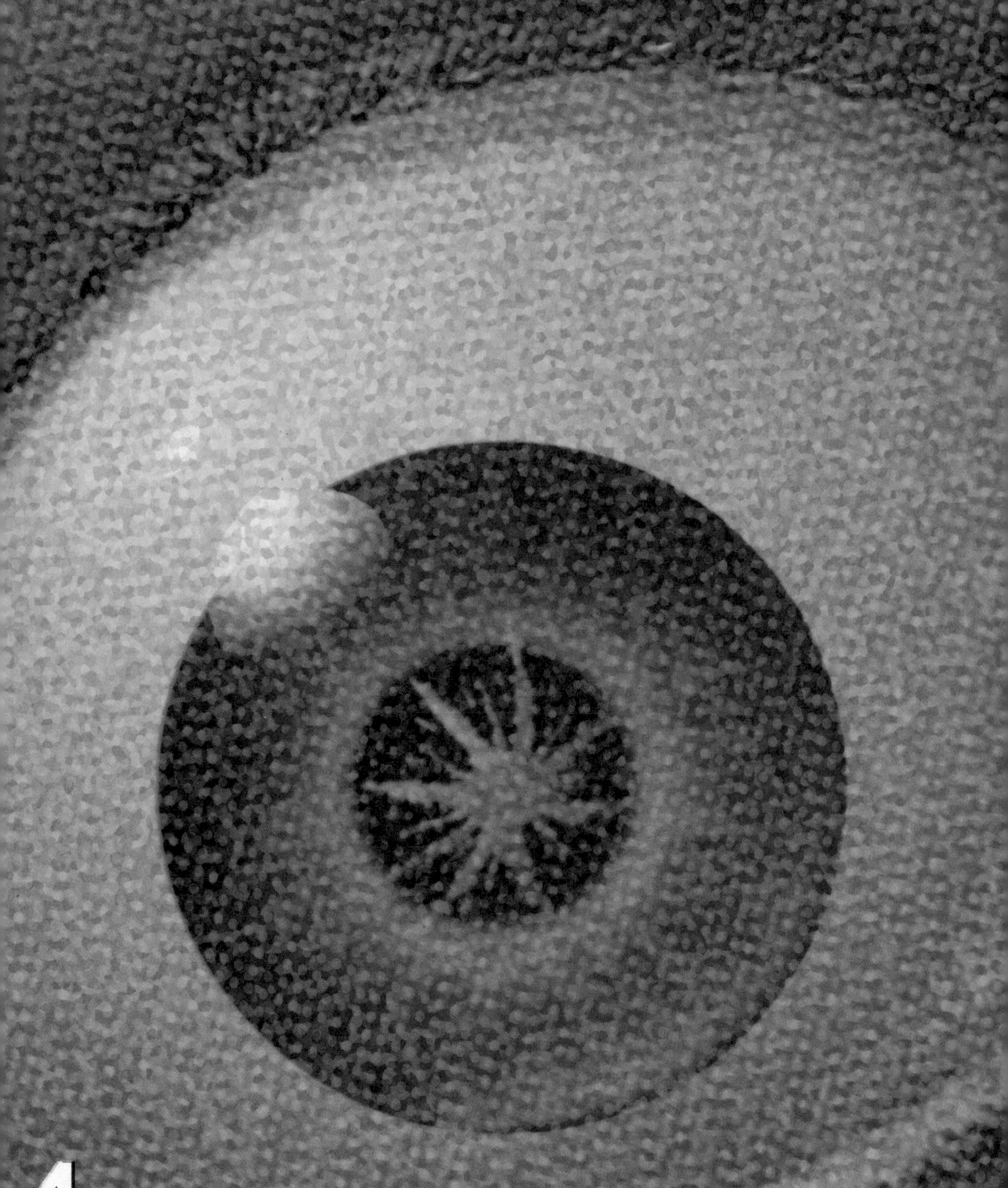

4

a planetary story

by WARREN ELLIS and JOHN CASSADAY
LAURA DePUY with DAVID BARON colors
ALI FUCHS letters
and edited by JOHN LAYMAN

Planetary created by Warren Ellis and John Cassaday

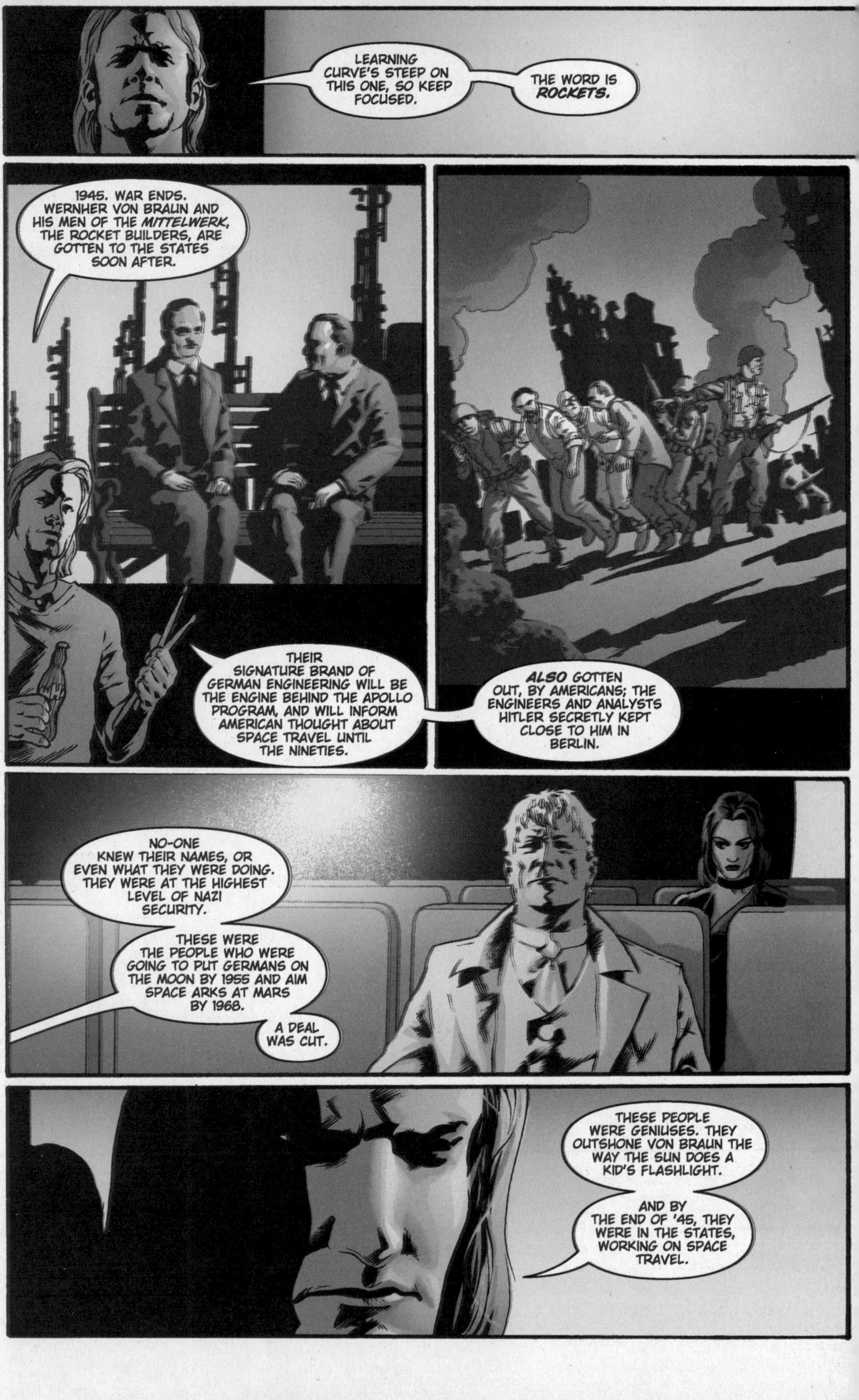
LEARNING CURVE'S STEEP ON THIS ONE, SO KEEP FOCUSED.
THE WORD IS *ROCKETS.*
1945. WAR ENDS. WERNHER VON BRAUN AND HIS MEN OF THE *MITTELWERK,* THE ROCKET BUILDERS, ARE GOTTEN TO THE STATES SOON AFTER.
THEIR SIGNATURE BRAND OF GERMAN ENGINEERING WILL BE THE ENGINE BEHIND THE APOLLO PROGRAM, AND WILL INFORM AMERICAN THOUGHT ABOUT SPACE TRAVEL UNTIL THE NINETIES.
ALSO GOTTEN OUT, BY AMERICANS; THE ENGINEERS AND ANALYSTS HITLER SECRETLY KEPT CLOSE TO HIM IN BERLIN.
NO-ONE KNEW THEIR NAMES, OR EVEN WHAT THEY WERE DOING. THEY WERE AT THE HIGHEST LEVEL OF NAZI SECURITY.
THESE WERE THE PEOPLE WHO WERE GOING TO PUT GERMANS ON THE MOON BY 1955 AND AIM SPACE ARKS AT MARS BY 1968.
A DEAL WAS CUT.
THESE PEOPLE WERE GENIUSES. THEY OUTSHONE VON BRAUN THE WAY THE SUN DOES A KID'S FLASHLIGHT.
AND BY THE END OF '45, THEY WERE IN THE STATES, WORKING ON SPACE TRAVEL.

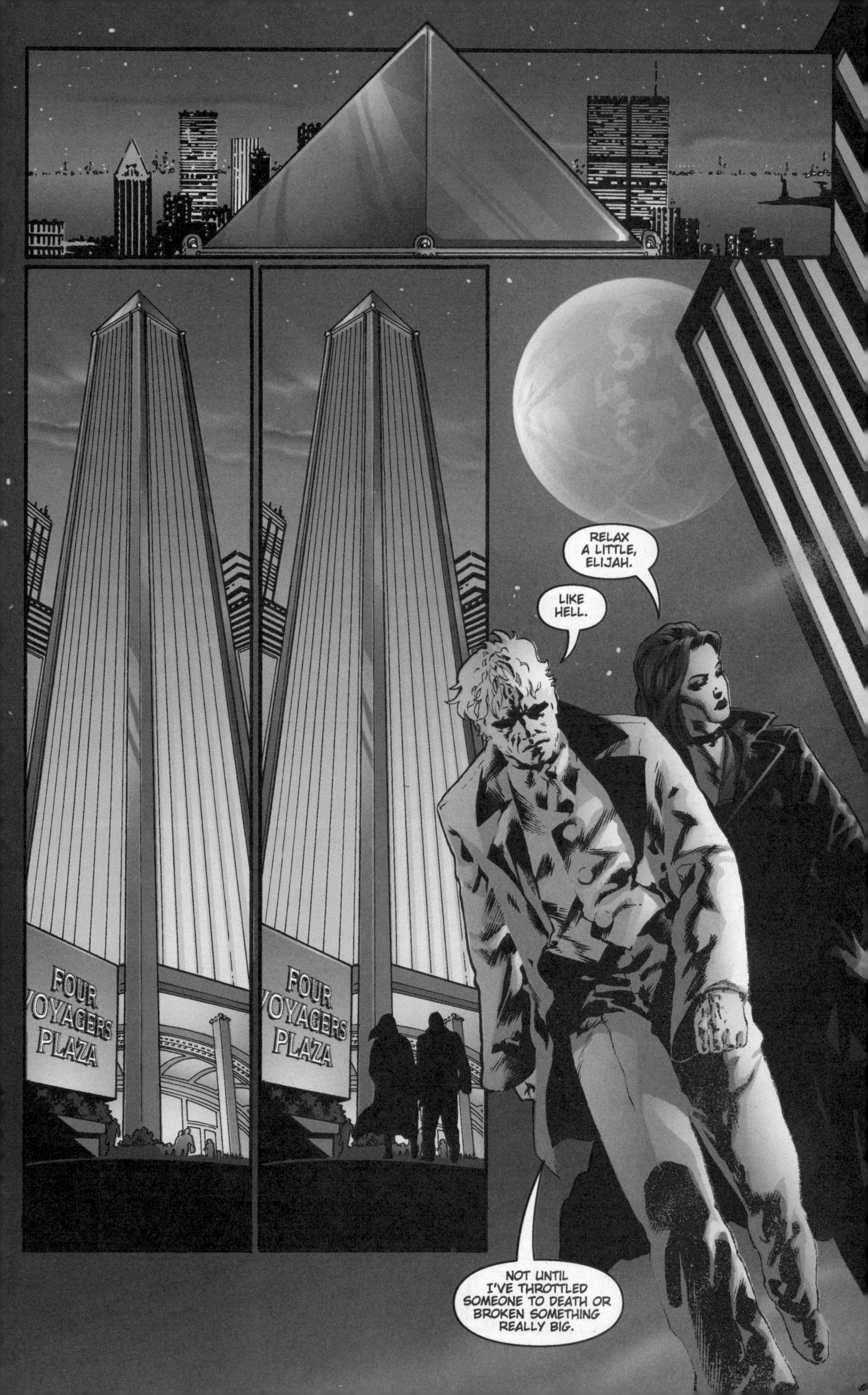
FOUR VOYAGERS PLAZA
FOUR VOYAGERS PLAZA
RELAX A LITTLE, ELIJAH.
LIKE HELL.
NOT UNTIL I'VE THROTTLED SOMEONE TO DEATH OR BROKEN SOMETHING REALLY BIG.

IT TOOK JFK AND A HIDEOUS AMOUNT OF PUBLIC MONEY FOR APOLLO TO PRODUCE THE SATURN V BOOSTER, THE ONLY ENGINE CAPABLE OF SLINGING A MAN-RATED SPACECRAFT INTO AN INTERPLANETARY INSERTION.

THE SECRET TEAM, WORKING UNDER THE CALL SIGN ARTEMIS, HAD A COMPARABLE DESIGN WORKING IN 1959.

AND THEY SENT MEN TO THE MOON IN 1961.

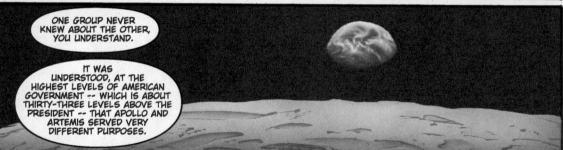

ONE GROUP NEVER KNEW ABOUT THE OTHER, YOU UNDERSTAND.

IT WAS UNDERSTOOD, AT THE HIGHEST LEVELS OF AMERICAN GOVERNMENT -- WHICH IS ABOUT THIRTY-THREE LEVELS ABOVE THE PRESIDENT -- THAT APOLLO AND ARTEMIS SERVED VERY DIFFERENT PURPOSES.

APOLLO WAS THE SHOW. IT WAS COLD WAR GLAMOR, OUR BRAVE BOYS WORKING TO BEST THE EVIL EMPIRE AND ITS SINISTER "CHIEF DESIGNER," THE ONE WHO EFFORTLESSLY HURLED THESE SPUTNIKS AND GAGARINS INTO SPACE.

ARTEMIS WAS THE WORK. IT WAS COLD WAR DIRECT, STRIKING THE VICTORIES THAT ONLY THEIR BOSS AND OUR BOSS WOULD EVER KNOW ABOUT.

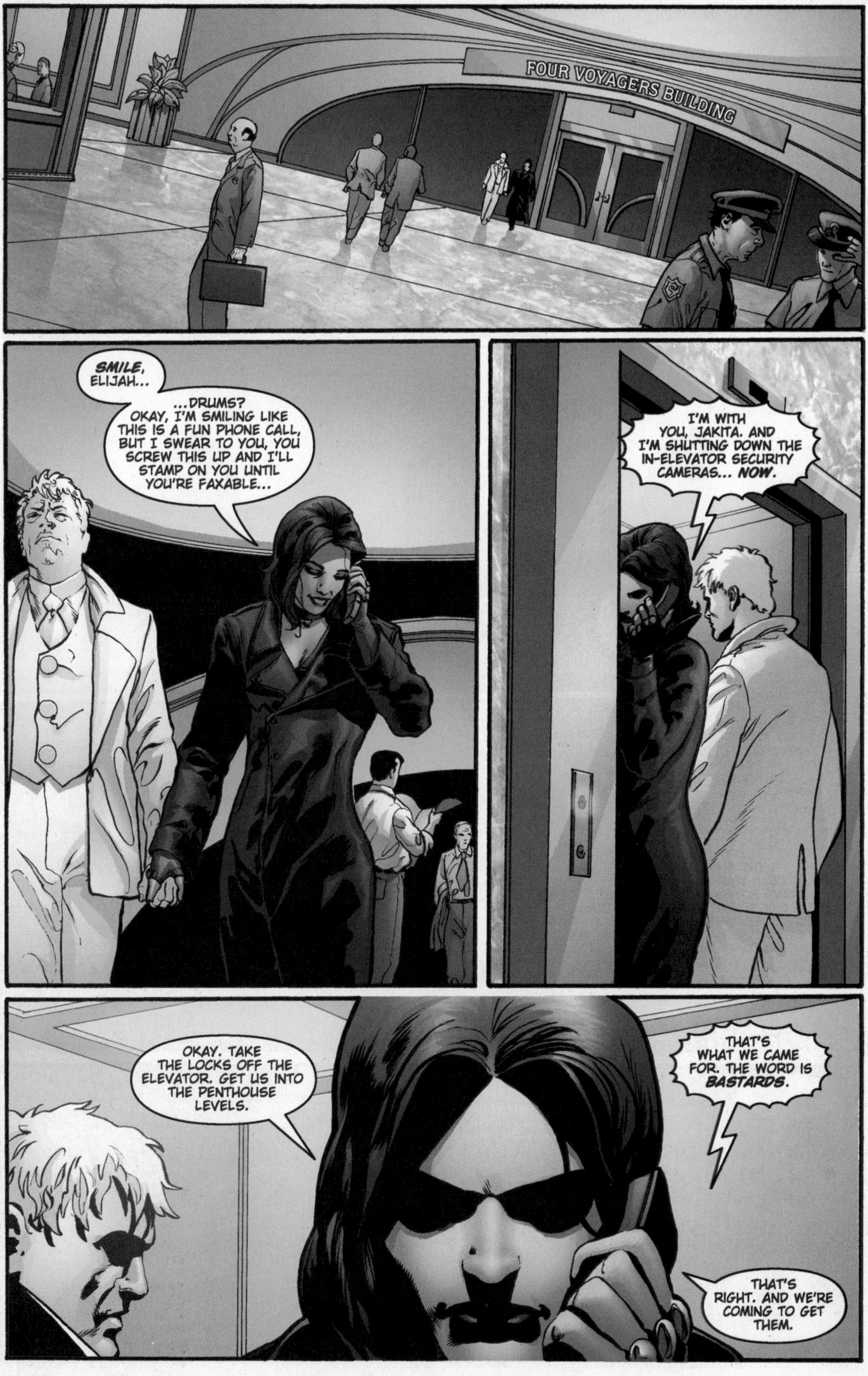
FOUR VOYAGERS BUILDING
SMILE, ELIJAH...
...DRUMS? OKAY, I'M SMILING LIKE THIS IS A FUN PHONE CALL, BUT I SWEAR TO YOU, YOU SCREW THIS UP AND I'LL STAMP ON YOU UNTIL YOU'RE FAXABLE...
I'M WITH YOU, JAKITA. AND I'M SHUTTING DOWN THE IN-ELEVATOR SECURITY CAMERAS... NOW.
OKAY. TAKE THE LOCKS OFF THE ELEVATOR. GET US INTO THE PENTHOUSE LEVELS.
THAT'S WHAT WE CAME FOR. THE WORD IS BASTARDS.
THAT'S RIGHT. AND WE'RE COMING TO GET THEM.

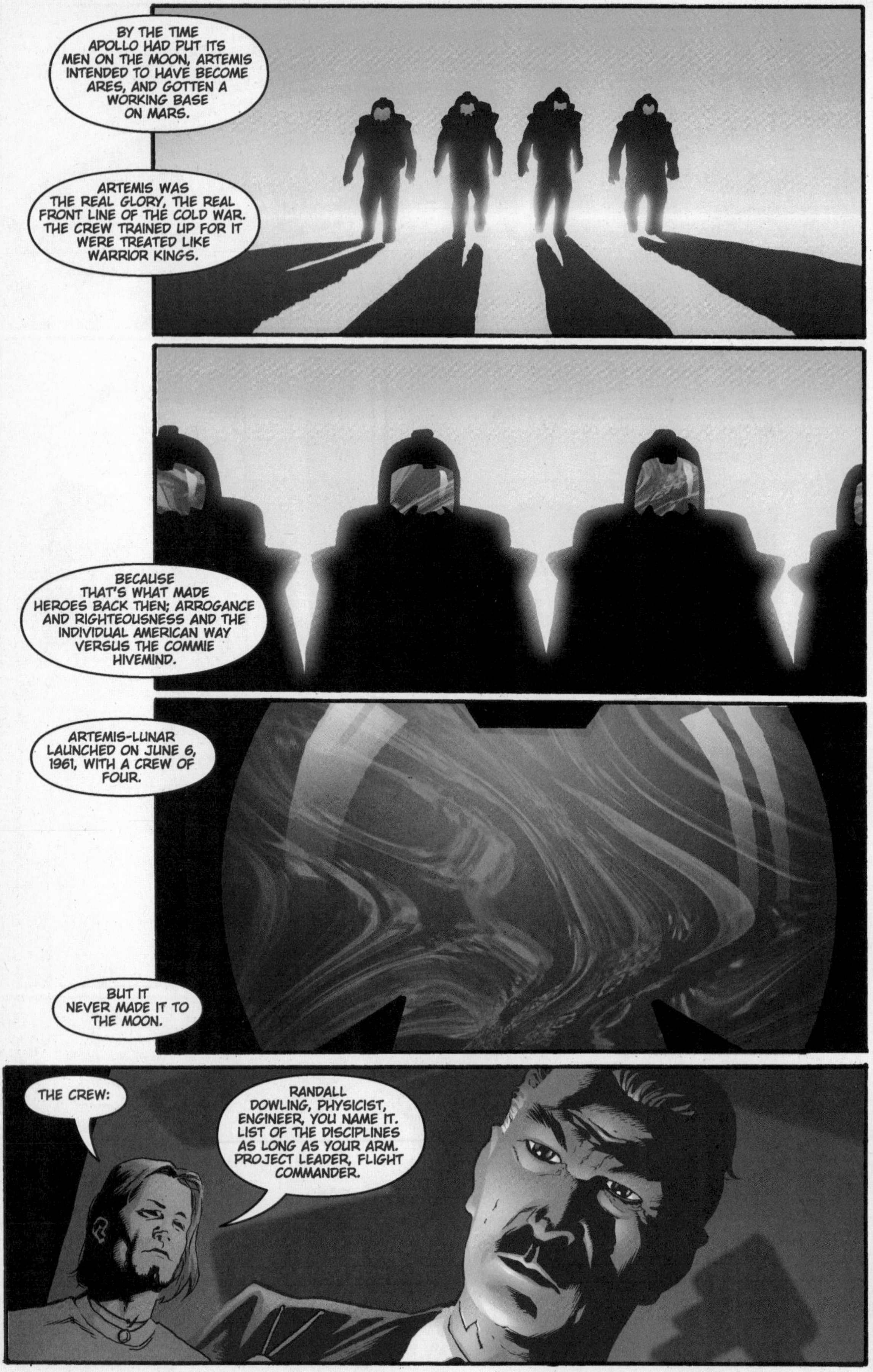
BY THE TIME APOLLO HAD PUT ITS MEN ON THE MOON, ARTEMIS INTENDED TO HAVE BECOME ARES, AND GOTTEN A WORKING BASE ON MARS.
ARTEMIS WAS THE REAL GLORY, THE REAL FRONT LINE OF THE COLD WAR. THE CREW TRAINED UP FOR IT WERE TREATED LIKE WARRIOR KINGS.
BECAUSE THAT'S WHAT MADE HEROES BACK THEN; ARROGANCE AND RIGHTEOUSNESS AND THE INDIVIDUAL AMERICAN WAY VERSUS THE COMMIE HIVEMIND.
ARTEMIS-LUNAR LAUNCHED ON JUNE 6, 1961, WITH A CREW OF FOUR.
BUT IT NEVER MADE IT TO THE MOON.
THE CREW:
RANDALL DOWLING, PHYSICIST, ENGINEER, YOU NAME IT. LIST OF THE DISCIPLINES AS LONG AS YOUR ARM. PROJECT LEADER, FLIGHT COMMANDER.

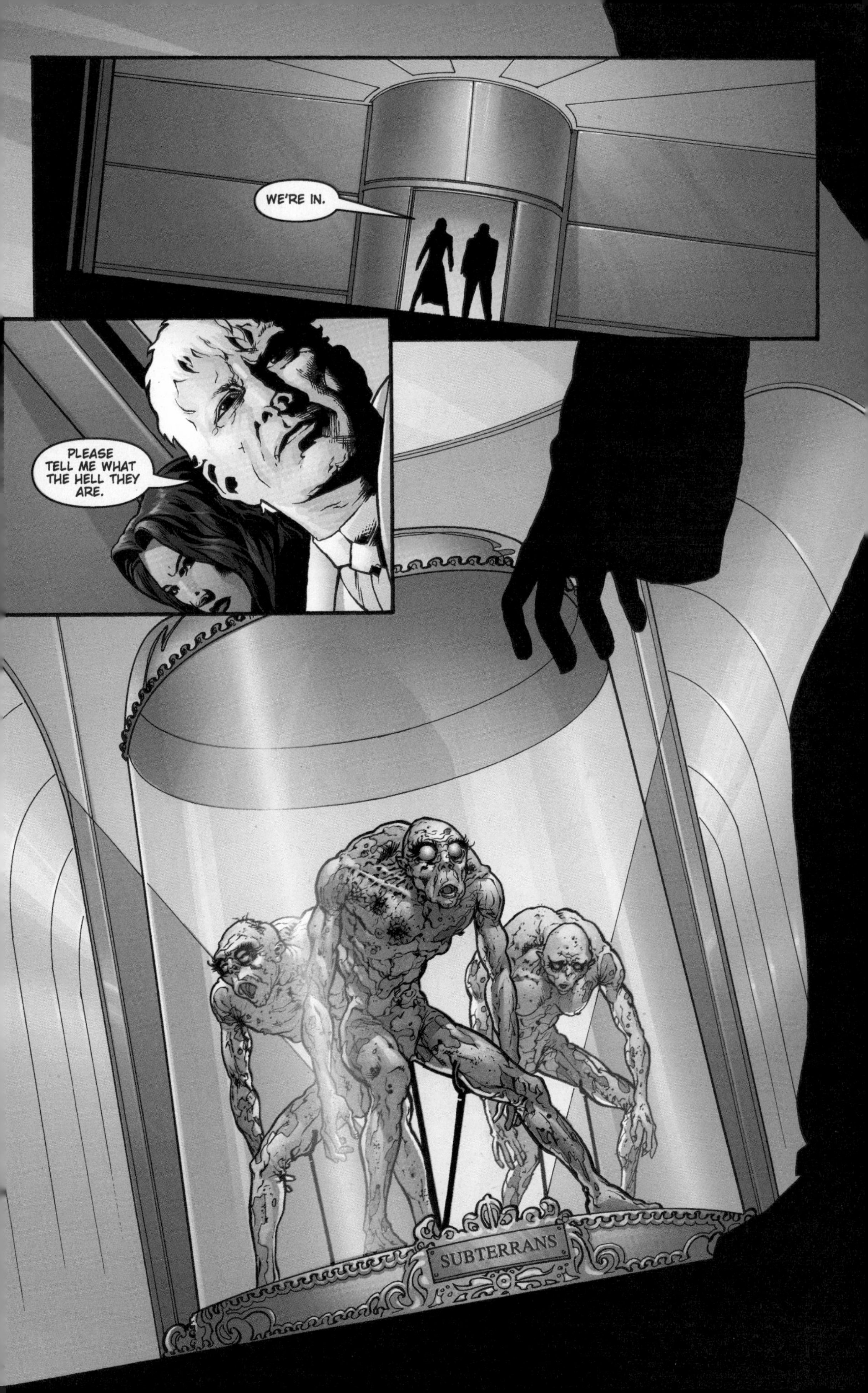
WE'RE IN.
PLEASE TELL ME WHAT THE HELL THEY ARE.
SUBTERRANS

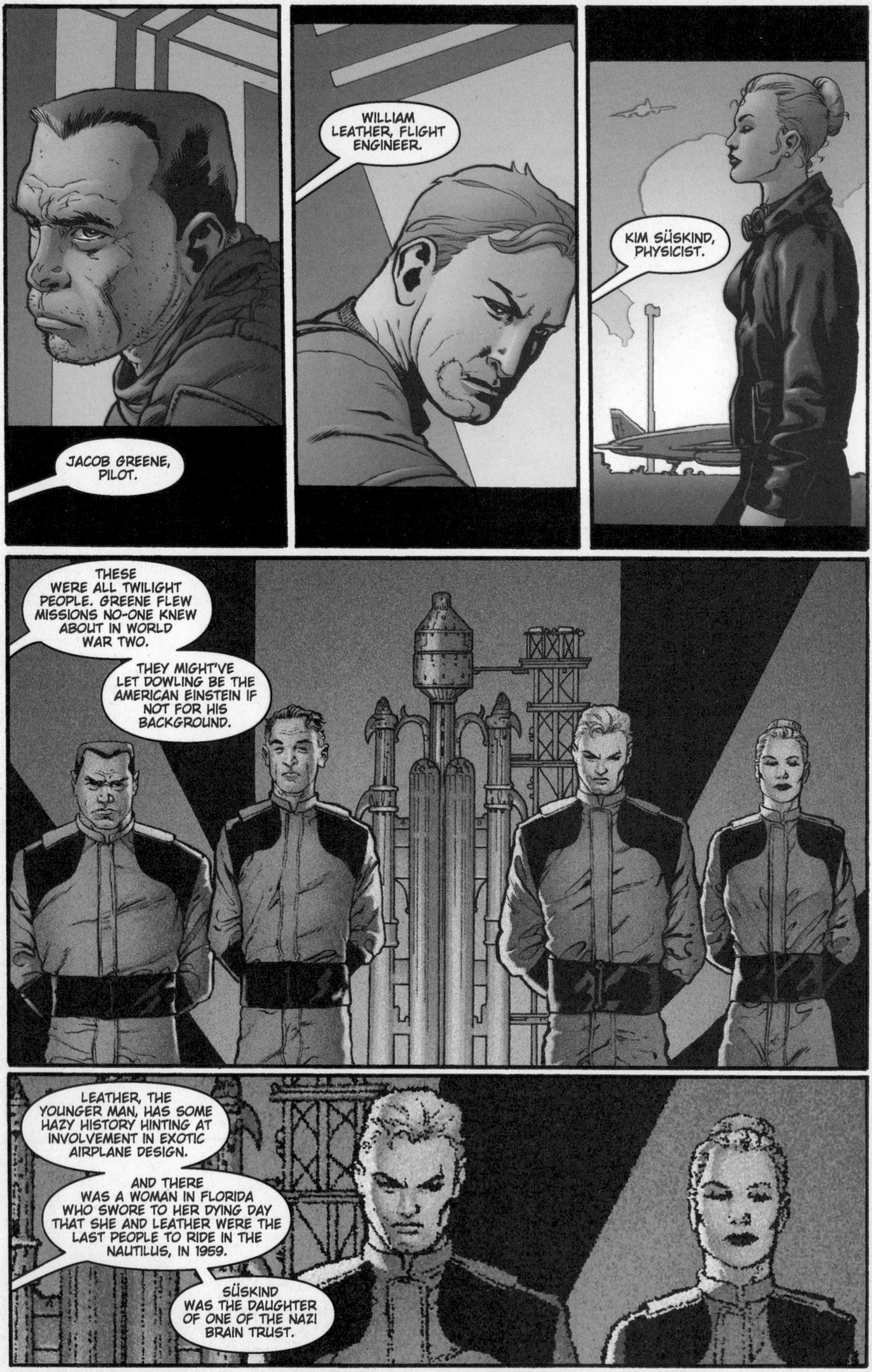
JACOB GREENE, PILOT.
WILLIAM LEATHER, FLIGHT ENGINEER.
KIM SÜSKIND, PHYSICIST.
THESE WERE ALL TWILIGHT PEOPLE. GREENE FLEW MISSIONS NO-ONE KNEW ABOUT IN WORLD WAR TWO.
THEY MIGHT'VE LET DOWLING BE THE AMERICAN EINSTEIN IF NOT FOR HIS BACKGROUND.
LEATHER, THE YOUNGER MAN, HAS SOME HAZY HISTORY HINTING AT INVOLVEMENT IN EXOTIC AIRPLANE DESIGN.
AND THERE WAS A WOMAN IN FLORIDA WHO SWORE TO HER DYING DAY THAT SHE AND LEATHER WERE THE LAST PEOPLE TO RIDE IN THE NAUTILUS, IN 1959.
SÜSKIND WAS THE DAUGHTER OF ONE OF THE NAZI BRAIN TRUST.

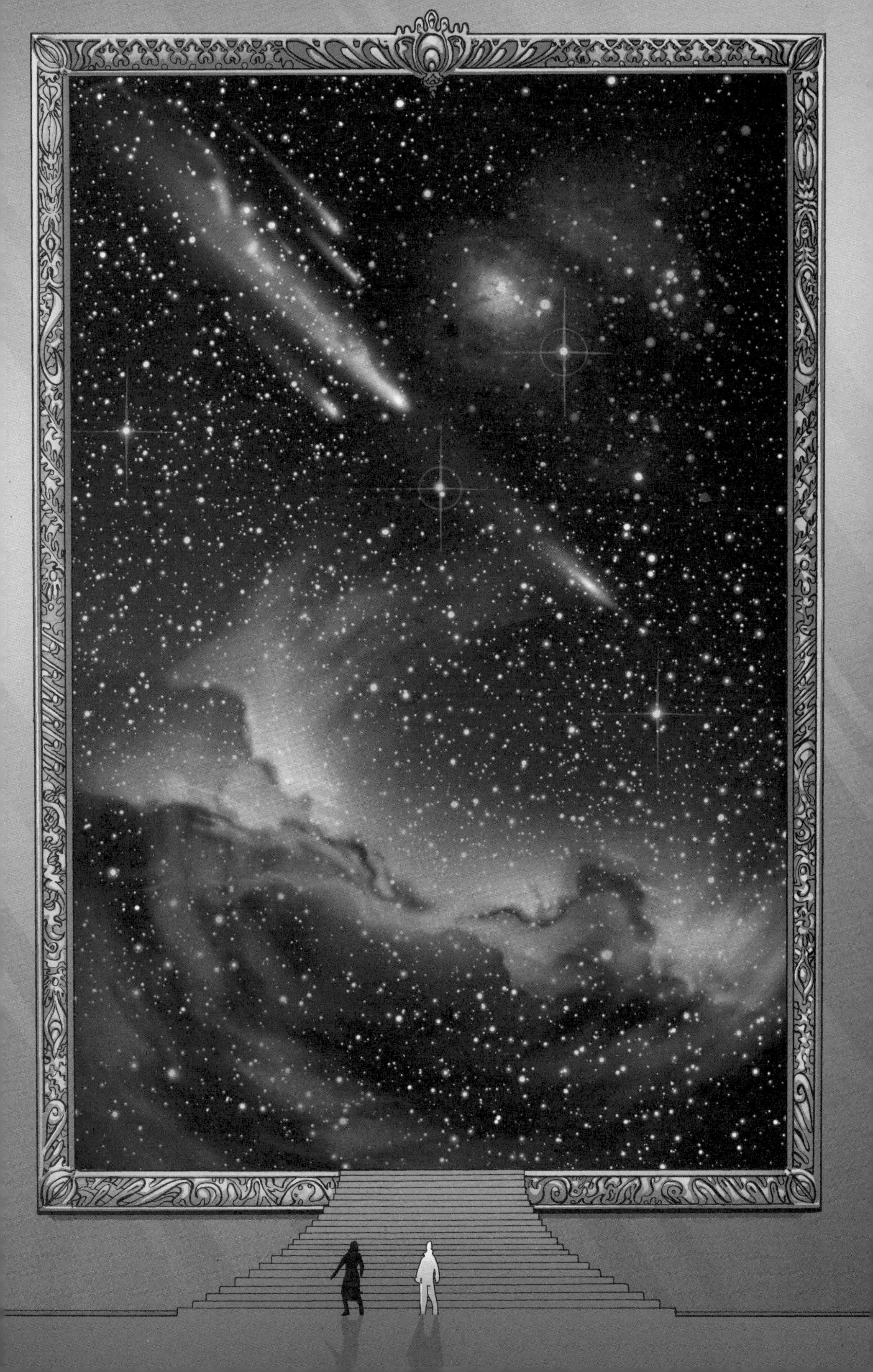

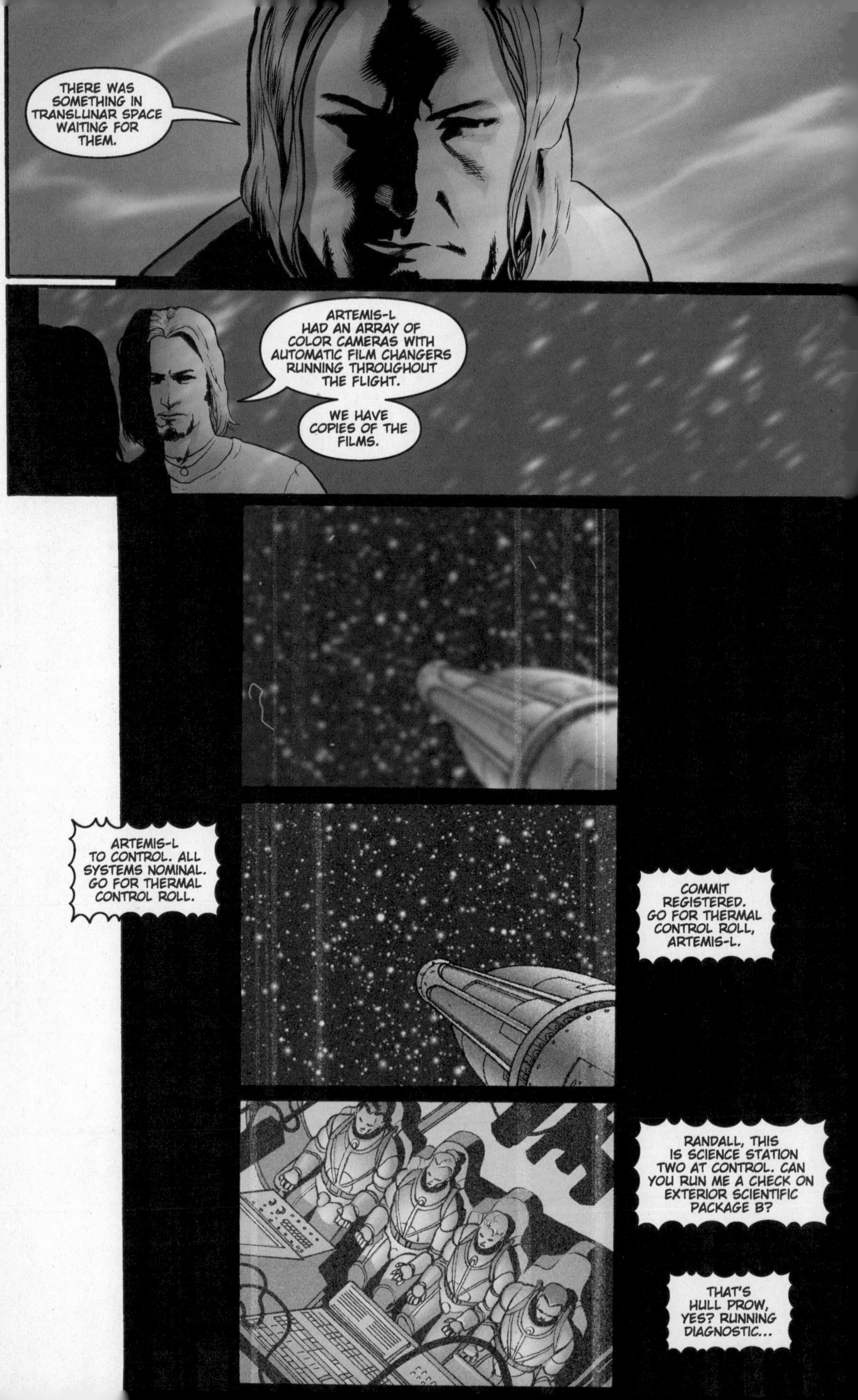
THERE WAS SOMETHING IN TRANSLUNAR SPACE WAITING FOR THEM.
ARTEMIS-L HAD AN ARRAY OF COLOR CAMERAS WITH AUTOMATIC FILM CHANGERS RUNNING THROUGHOUT THE FLIGHT.
WE HAVE COPIES OF THE FILMS.
ARTEMIS-L TO CONTROL. ALL SYSTEMS NOMINAL. GO FOR THERMAL CONTROL ROLL.
COMMIT REGISTERED. GO FOR THERMAL CONTROL ROLL, ARTEMIS-L.
RANDALL, THIS IS SCIENCE STATION TWO AT CONTROL. CAN YOU RUN ME A CHECK ON EXTERIOR SCIENTIFIC PACKAGE B?
THAT'S HULL PROW, YES? RUNNING DIAGNOSTIC...

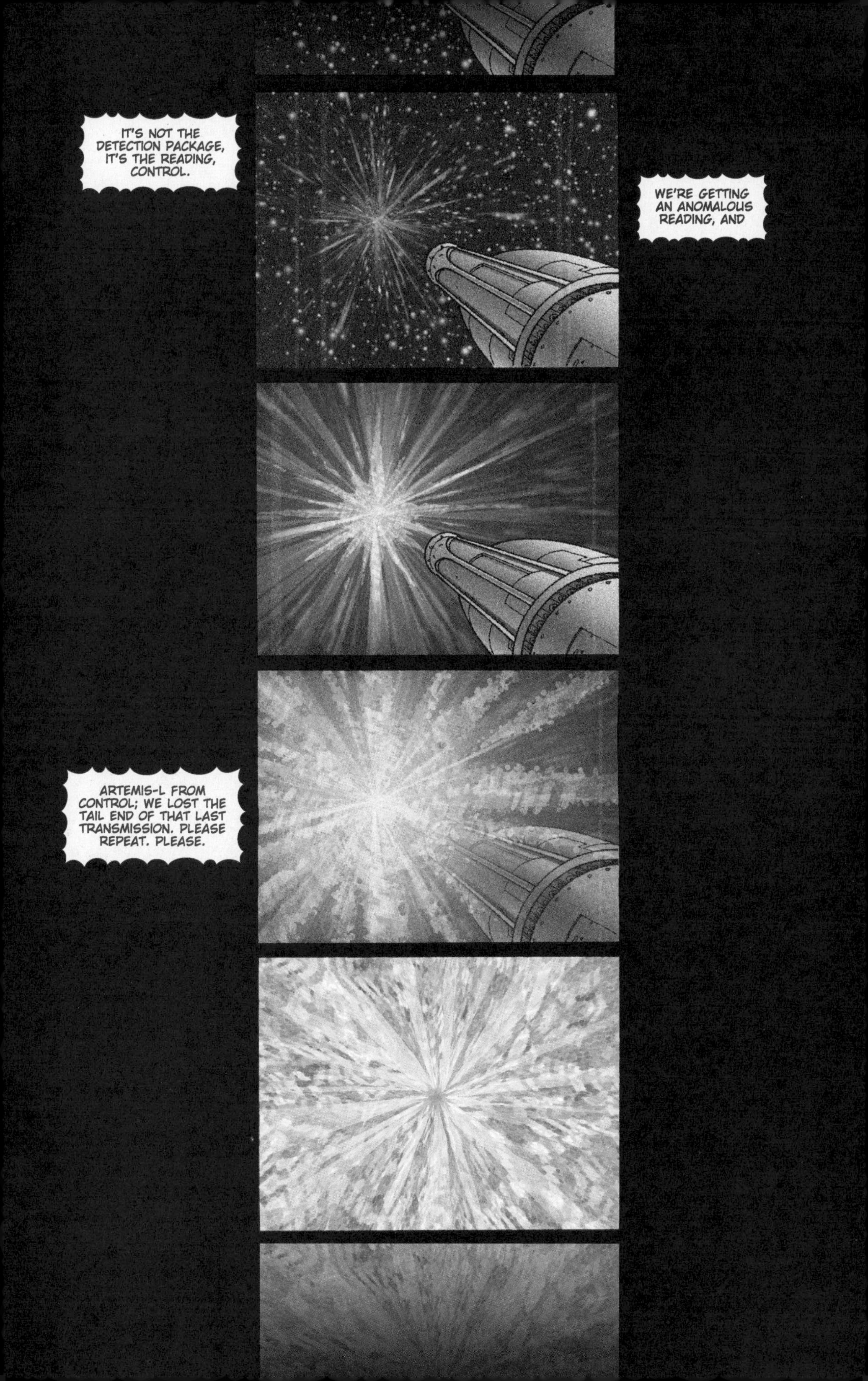
IT'S NOT THE DETECTION PACKAGE, IT'S THE READING, CONTROL.
WE'RE GETTING AN ANOMALOUS READING, AND
ARTEMIS-L FROM CONTROL; WE LOST THE TAIL END OF THAT LAST TRANSMISSION. PLEASE REPEAT. PLEASE.

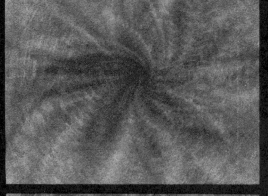

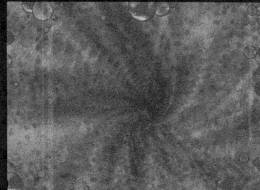

LIKE WHATEVER IT WAS HAPPENED TO ISLAND ZERO, WE KNOW WHAT THE TRANSLUNAR EVENT *WASN'T.*

THE MAJOR SUPERHUMAN PLAYERS WE KNOW OF WEREN'T INVOLVED.

THERE WAS NO EXTRATERRESTRIAL ACTIVITY IN CISLUNAR SPACE THROUGHOUT 1961 BY ANY OF THE KNOWN XENOSPECIES.

BUT WE DON'T KNOW WHAT IT *WAS.*

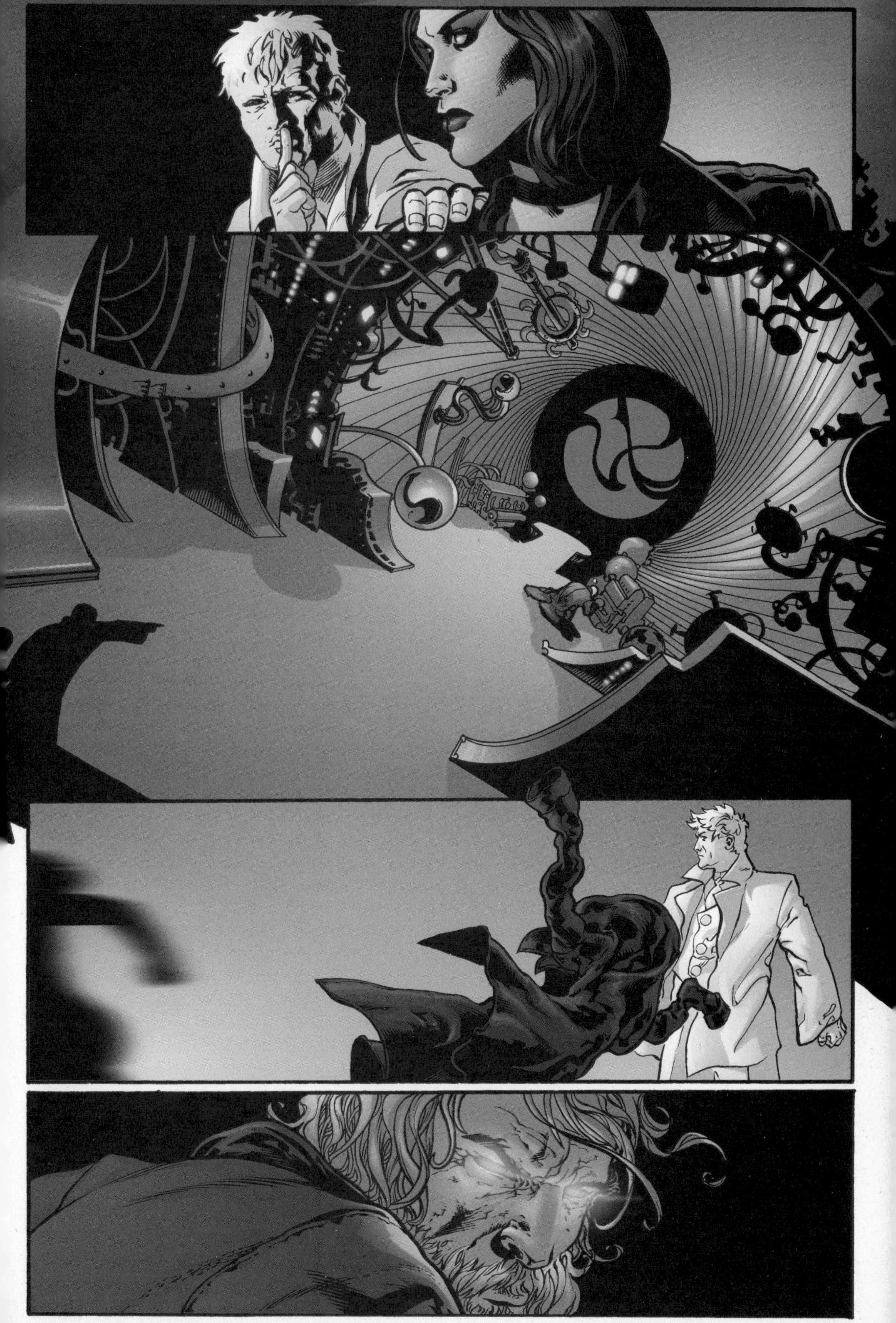

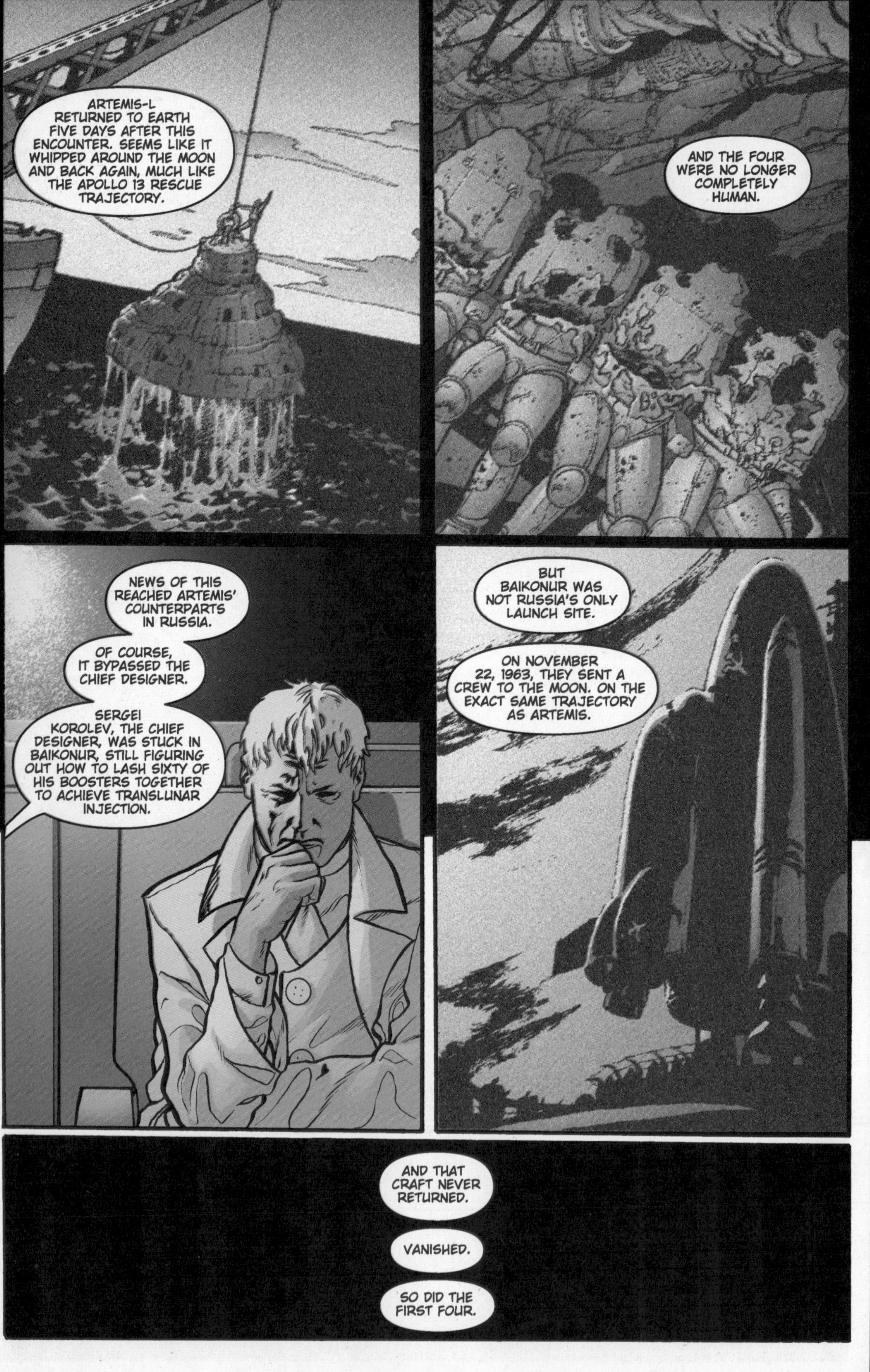
ARTEMIS-L RETURNED TO EARTH FIVE DAYS AFTER THIS ENCOUNTER. SEEMS LIKE IT WHIPPED AROUND THE MOON AND BACK AGAIN, MUCH LIKE THE APOLLO 13 RESCUE TRAJECTORY.
AND THE FOUR WERE NO LONGER COMPLETELY HUMAN.
NEWS OF THIS REACHED ARTEMIS' COUNTERPARTS IN RUSSIA.
OF COURSE, IT BYPASSED THE CHIEF DESIGNER.
SERGEI KOROLEV, THE CHIEF DESIGNER, WAS STUCK IN BAIKONUR, STILL FIGURING OUT HOW TO LASH SIXTY OF HIS BOOSTERS TOGETHER TO ACHIEVE TRANSLUNAR INJECTION.
BUT BAIKONUR WAS NOT RUSSIA'S ONLY LAUNCH SITE.
ON NOVEMBER 22, 1963, THEY SENT A CREW TO THE MOON. ON THE EXACT SAME TRAJECTORY AS ARTEMIS.
AND THAT CRAFT NEVER RETURNED.
VANISHED.
SO DID THE FIRST FOUR.

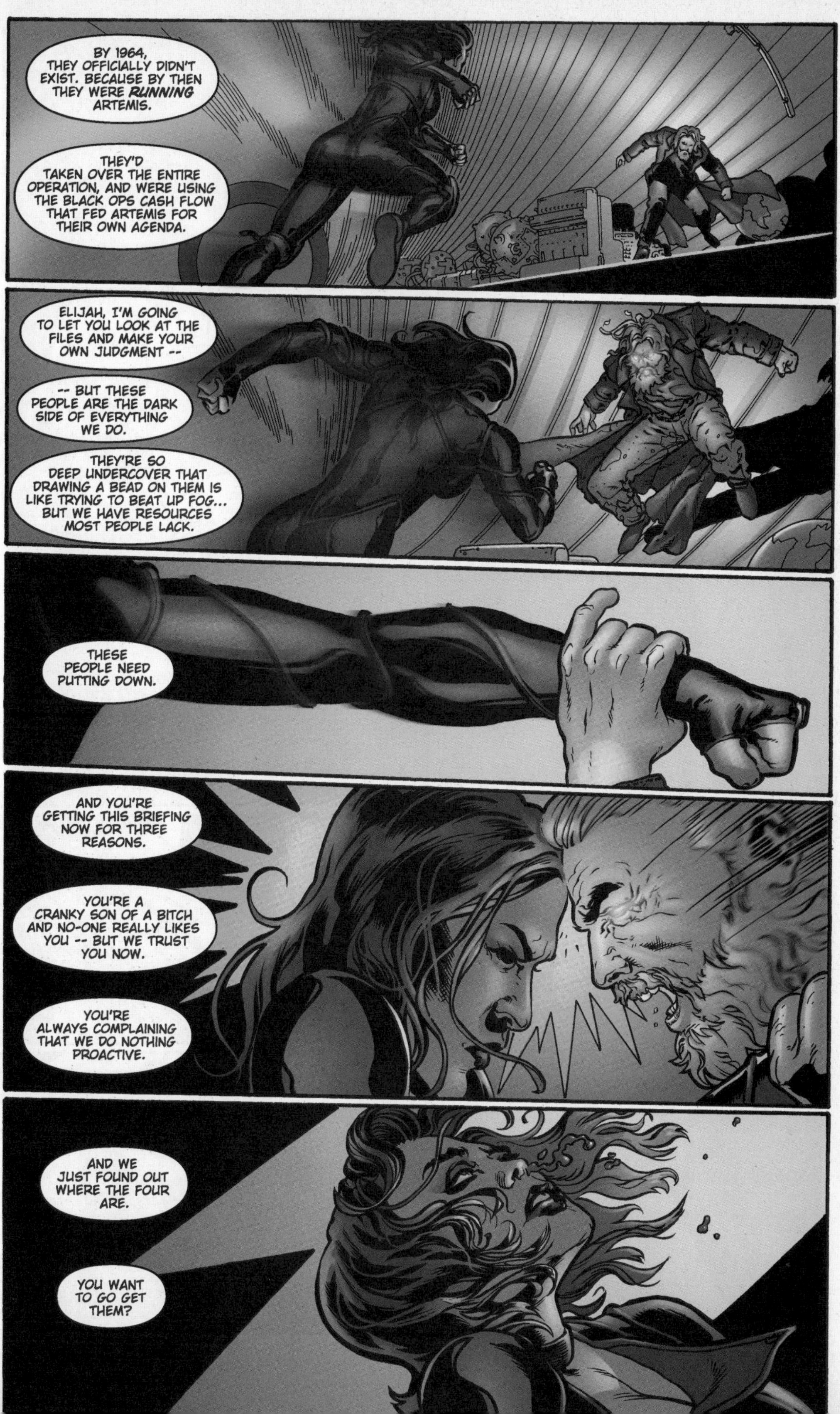
BY 1964, THEY OFFICIALLY DIDN'T EXIST. BECAUSE BY THEN THEY WERE *RUNNING* ARTEMIS.
THEY'D TAKEN OVER THE ENTIRE OPERATION, AND WERE USING THE BLACK OPS CASH FLOW THAT FED ARTEMIS FOR THEIR OWN AGENDA.
ELIJAH, I'M GOING TO LET YOU LOOK AT THE FILES AND MAKE YOUR OWN JUDGMENT --
-- BUT THESE PEOPLE ARE THE DARK SIDE OF EVERYTHING WE DO.
THEY'RE SO DEEP UNDERCOVER THAT DRAWING A BEAD ON THEM IS LIKE TRYING TO BEAT UP FOG... BUT WE HAVE RESOURCES MOST PEOPLE LACK.
THESE PEOPLE NEED PUTTING DOWN.
AND YOU'RE GETTING THIS BRIEFING NOW FOR THREE REASONS.
YOU'RE A CRANKY SON OF A BITCH AND NO-ONE REALLY LIKES YOU -- BUT WE TRUST YOU NOW.
YOU'RE ALWAYS COMPLAINING THAT WE DO NOTHING PROACTIVE.
AND WE JUST FOUND OUT WHERE THE FOUR ARE.
YOU WANT TO GO GET THEM?

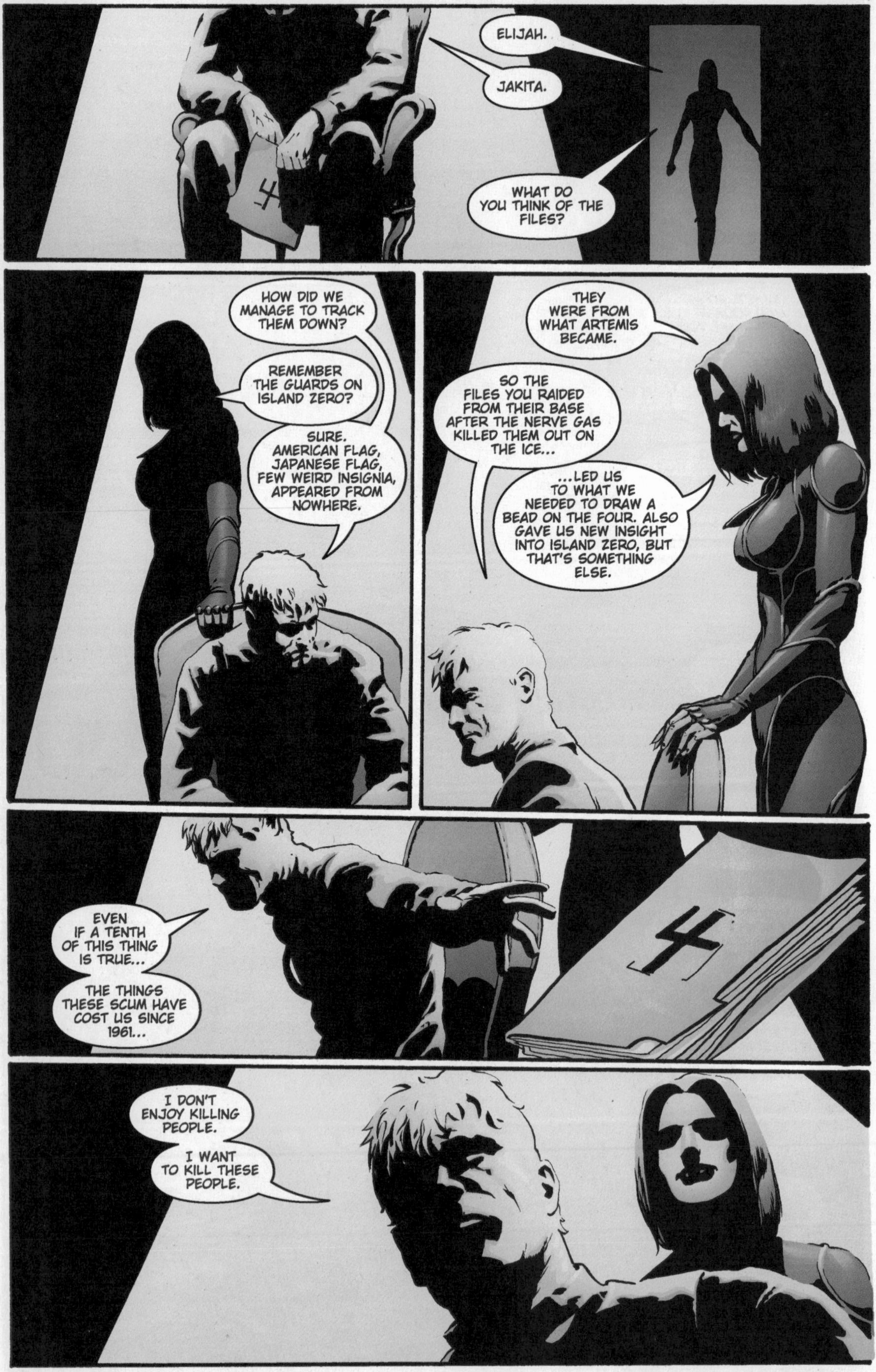
ELIJAH.
JAKITA.
WHAT DO YOU THINK OF THE FILES?
HOW DID WE MANAGE TO TRACK THEM DOWN?
REMEMBER THE GUARDS ON ISLAND ZERO?
SURE. AMERICAN FLAG, JAPANESE FLAG, FEW WEIRD INSIGNIA, APPEARED FROM NOWHERE.
THEY WERE FROM WHAT ARTEMIS BECAME.
SO THE FILES YOU RAIDED FROM THEIR BASE AFTER THE NERVE GAS KILLED THEM OUT ON THE ICE...
...LED US TO WHAT WE NEEDED TO DRAW A BEAD ON THE FOUR. ALSO GAVE US NEW INSIGHT INTO ISLAND ZERO, BUT THAT'S SOMETHING ELSE.
EVEN IF A TENTH OF THIS THING IS TRUE...
THE THINGS THESE SCUM HAVE COST US SINCE 1961...
I DON'T ENJOY KILLING PEOPLE.
I WANT TO KILL THESE PEOPLE.

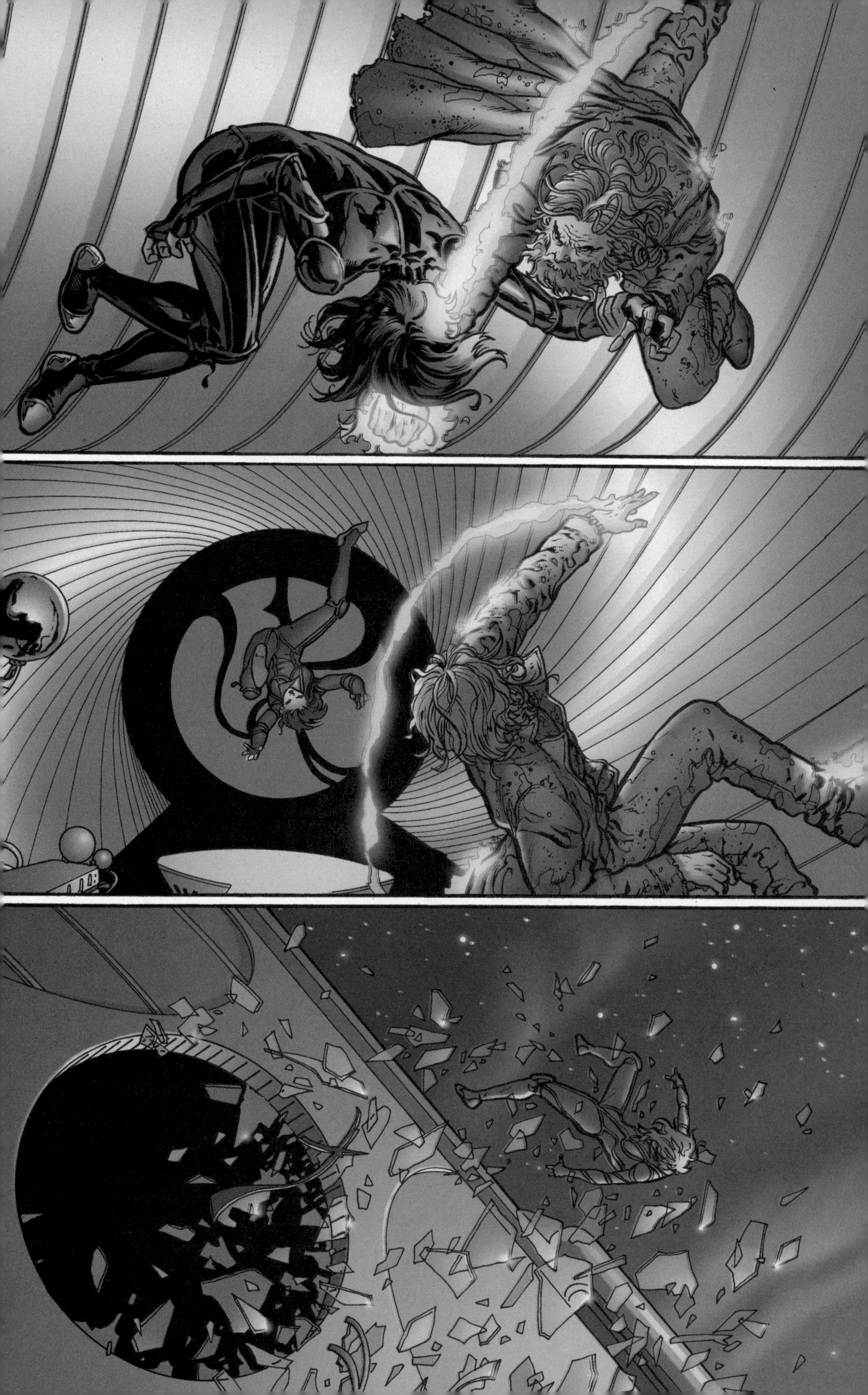

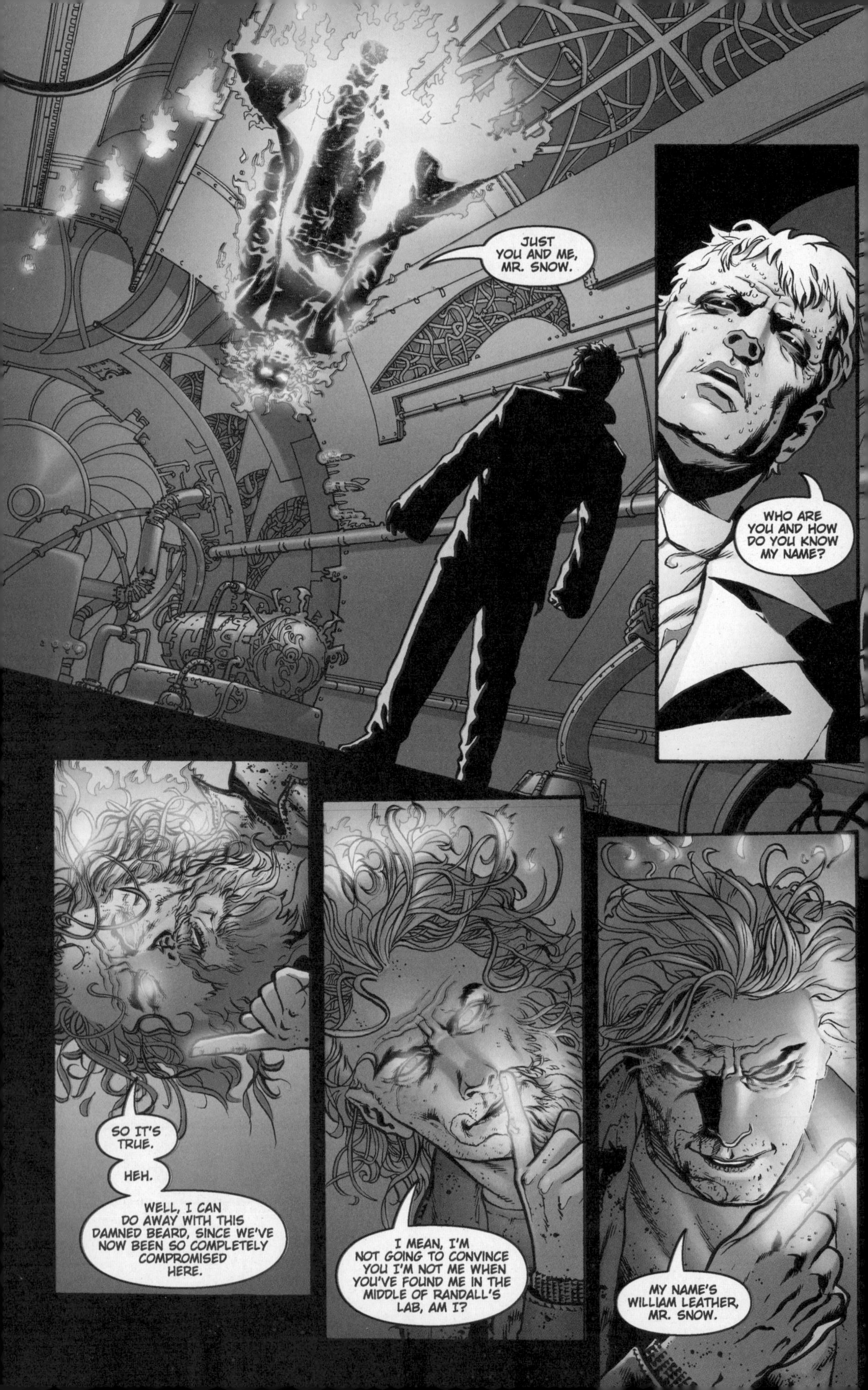
JUST YOU AND ME, MR. SNOW.
WHO ARE YOU AND HOW DO YOU KNOW MY NAME?
SO IT'S TRUE.
HEH.
WELL, I CAN DO AWAY WITH THIS DAMNED BEARD, SINCE WE'VE NOW BEEN SO COMPLETELY COMPROMISED HERE.
I MEAN, I'M NOT GOING TO CONVINCE YOU I'M NOT ME WHEN YOU'VE FOUND ME IN THE MIDDLE OF RANDALL'S LAB, AM I?
MY NAME'S WILLIAM LEATHER, MR. SNOW.

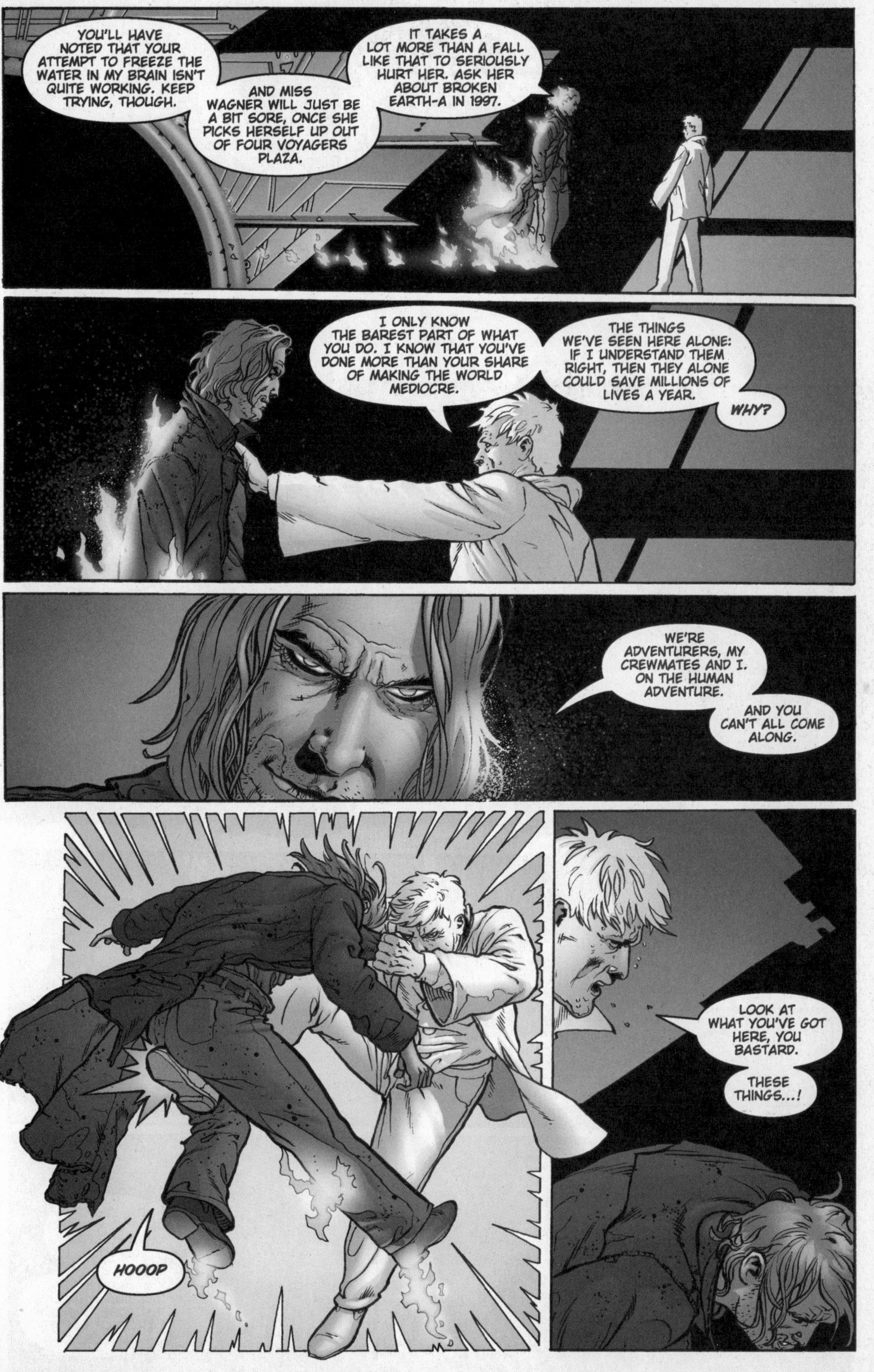
YOU'LL HAVE NOTED THAT YOUR ATTEMPT TO FREEZE THE WATER IN MY BRAIN ISN'T QUITE WORKING. KEEP TRYING, THOUGH.
AND MISS WAGNER WILL JUST BE A BIT SORE, ONCE SHE PICKS HERSELF UP OUT OF FOUR VOYAGERS PLAZA.
IT TAKES A LOT MORE THAN A FALL LIKE THAT TO SERIOUSLY HURT HER. ASK HER ABOUT BROKEN EARTH-A IN 1997.
I ONLY KNOW THE BAREST PART OF WHAT YOU DO. I KNOW THAT YOU'VE DONE MORE THAN YOUR SHARE OF MAKING THE WORLD MEDIOCRE.
THE THINGS WE'VE SEEN HERE ALONE: IF I UNDERSTAND THEM RIGHT, THEN THEY ALONE COULD SAVE MILLIONS OF LIVES A YEAR.
WHY?
WE'RE ADVENTURERS, MY CREWMATES AND I. ON THE HUMAN ADVENTURE.
AND YOU CAN'T ALL COME ALONG.
HOOOP
LOOK AT WHAT YOU'VE GOT HERE, YOU BASTARD.
THESE THINGS...!

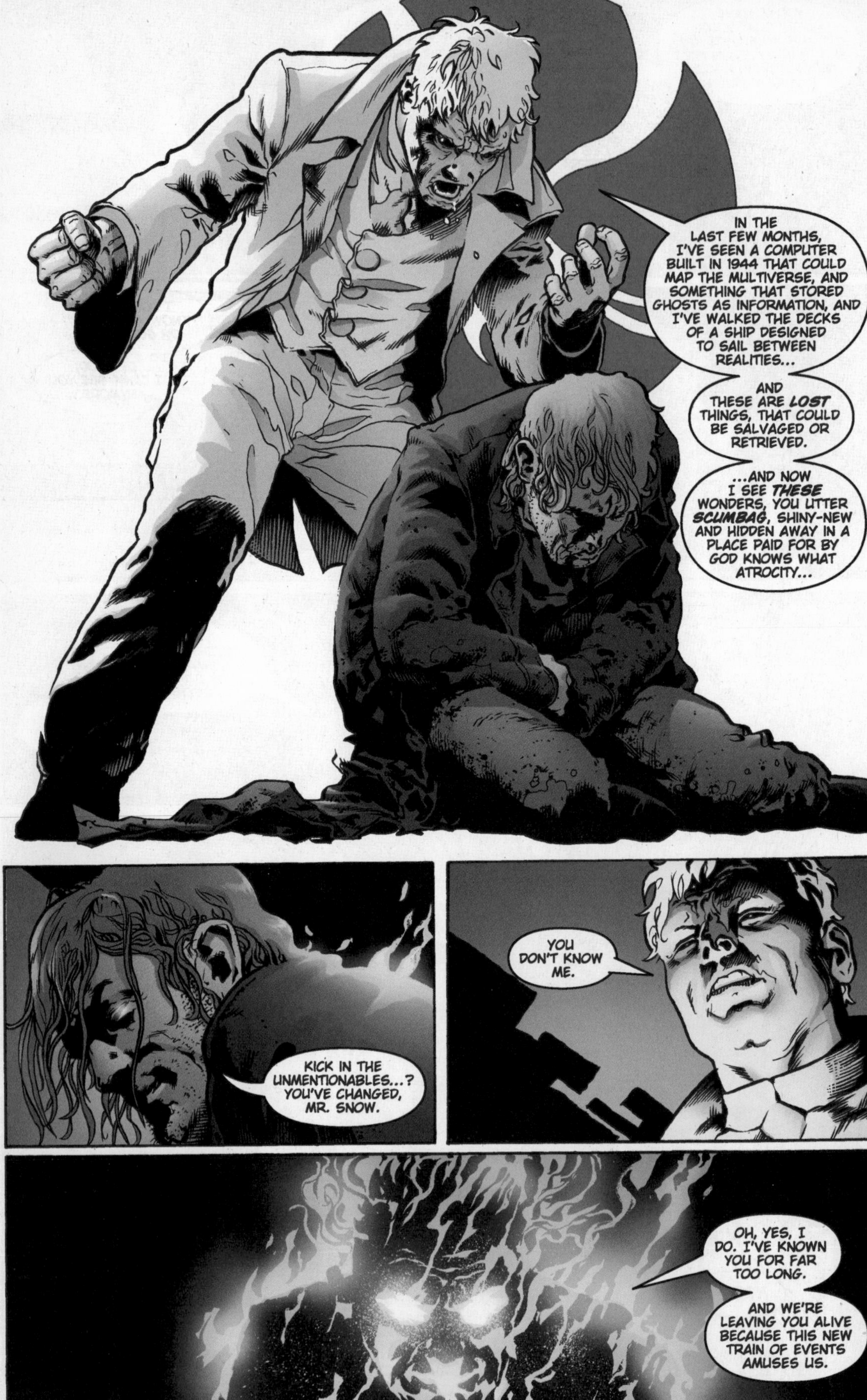

IN THE LAST FEW MONTHS, I'VE SEEN A COMPUTER BUILT IN 1944 THAT COULD MAP THE MULTIVERSE, AND SOMETHING THAT STORED GHOSTS AS INFORMATION, AND I'VE WALKED THE DECKS OF A SHIP DESIGNED TO SAIL BETWEEN REALITIES...
AND THESE ARE *LOST* THINGS, THAT COULD BE SALVAGED OR RETRIEVED.
...AND NOW I SEE *THESE* WONDERS, YOU UTTER *SCUMBAG*, SHINY-NEW AND HIDDEN AWAY IN A PLACE PAID FOR BY GOD KNOWS WHAT ATROCITY...
KICK IN THE UNMENTIONABLES...? YOU'VE CHANGED, MR. SNOW.
YOU DON'T KNOW ME.
OH, YES, I DO. I'VE KNOWN YOU FOR FAR TOO LONG.
AND WE'RE LEAVING YOU ALIVE BECAUSE THIS NEW TRAIN OF EVENTS AMUSES US.

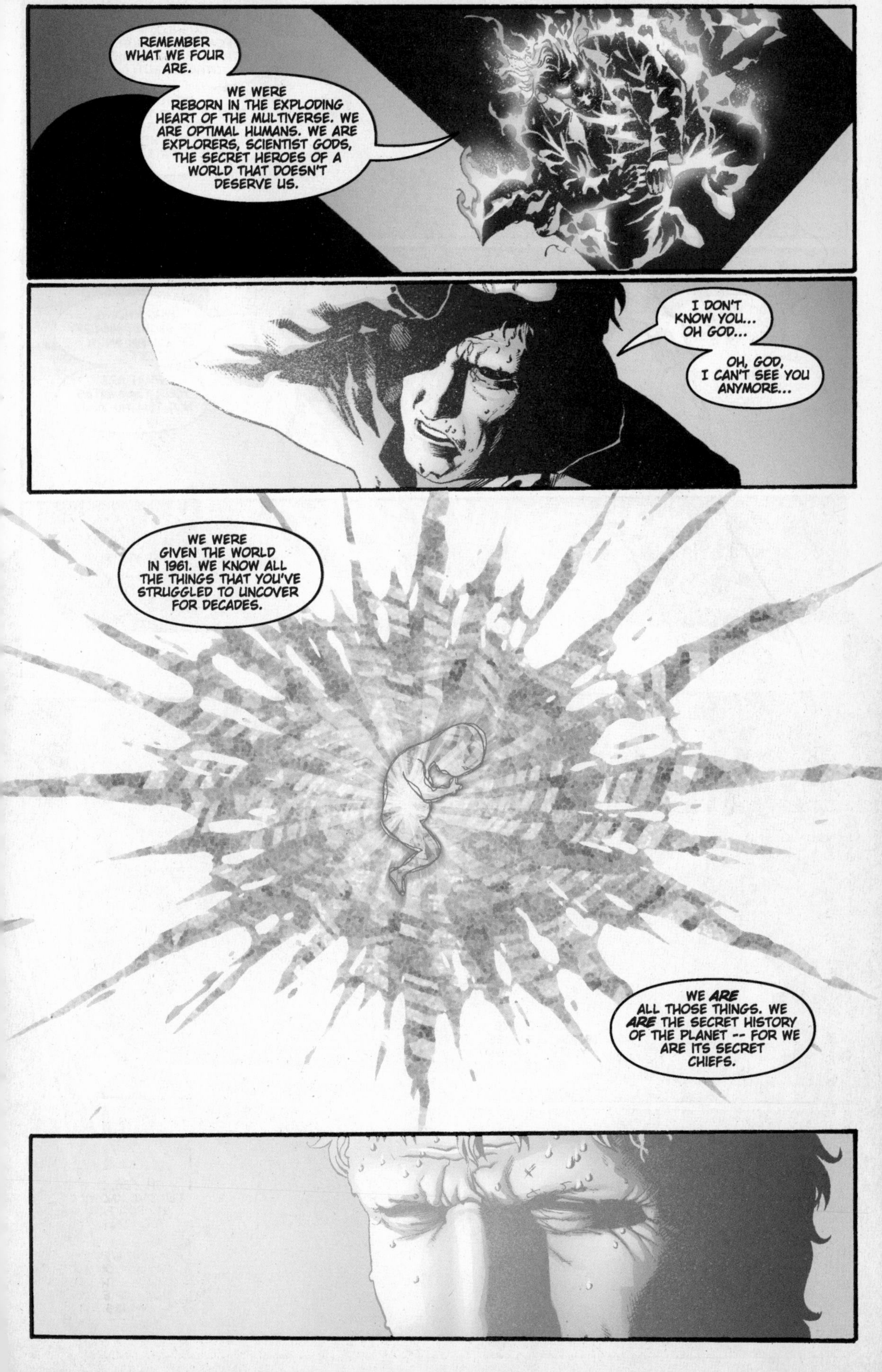
REMEMBER WHAT WE FOUR ARE.
WE WERE REBORN IN THE EXPLODING HEART OF THE MULTIVERSE. WE ARE OPTIMAL HUMANS. WE ARE EXPLORERS, SCIENTIST GODS, THE SECRET HEROES OF A WORLD THAT DOESN'T DESERVE US.
I DON'T KNOW YOU... OH GOD...
OH, GOD, I CAN'T SEE YOU ANYMORE...
WE WERE GIVEN THE WORLD IN 1961. WE KNOW ALL THE THINGS THAT YOU'VE STRUGGLED TO UNCOVER FOR DECADES.
WE *ARE* ALL THOSE THINGS. WE *ARE* THE SECRET HISTORY OF THE PLANET -- FOR WE ARE ITS SECRET CHIEFS.

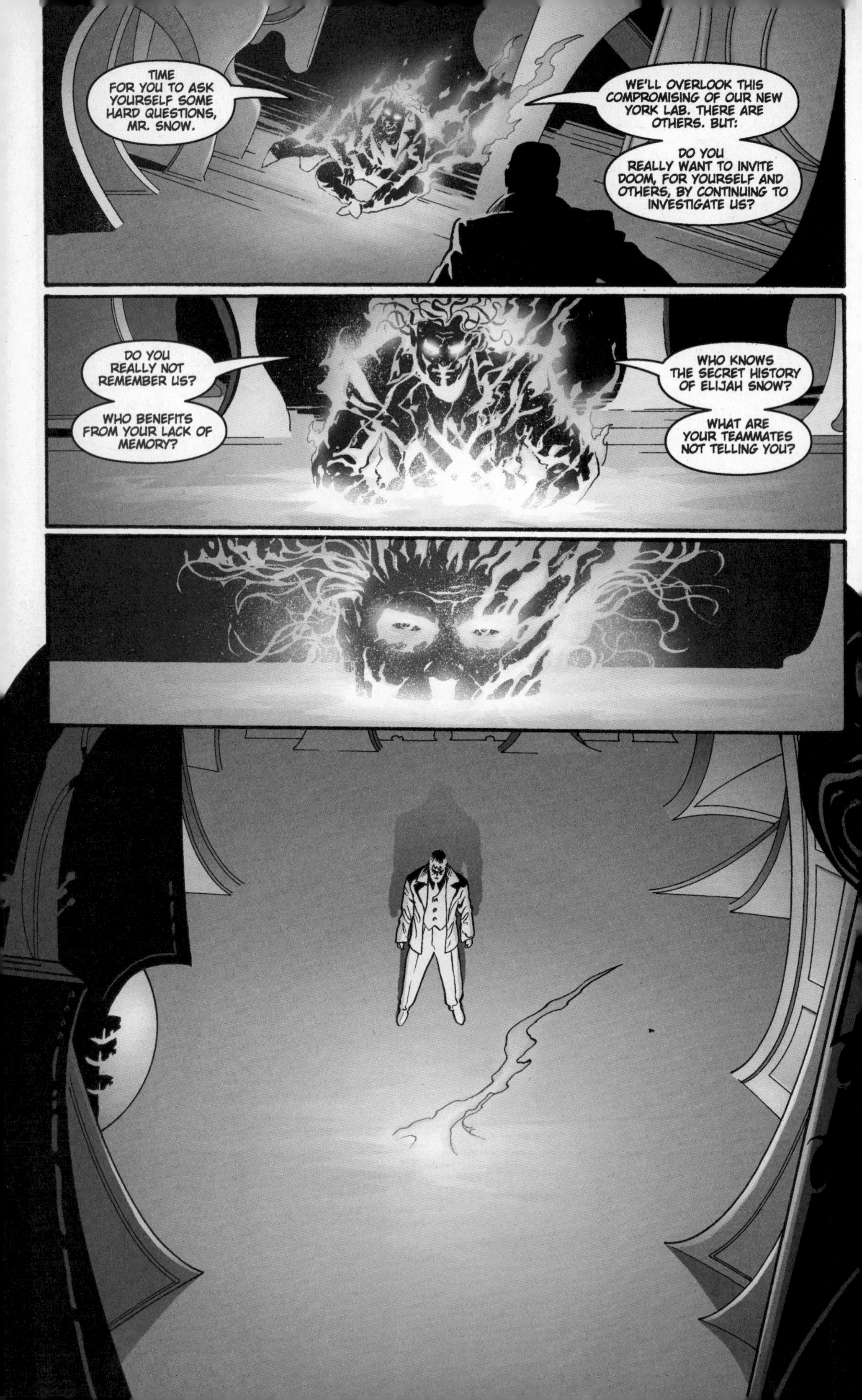
TIME FOR YOU TO ASK YOURSELF SOME HARD QUESTIONS, MR. SNOW.
WE'LL OVERLOOK THIS COMPROMISING OF OUR NEW YORK LAB. THERE ARE OTHERS. BUT:
DO YOU REALLY WANT TO INVITE DOOM, FOR YOURSELF AND OTHERS, BY CONTINUING TO INVESTIGATE US?
DO YOU REALLY NOT REMEMBER US?
WHO BENEFITS FROM YOUR LACK OF MEMORY?
WHO KNOWS THE SECRET HISTORY OF ELIJAH SNOW?
WHAT ARE YOUR TEAMMATES NOT TELLING YOU?

WILDSTORM™ PREVIEW

PLANETARY™

WARREN ELLIS • JOHN CASSADAY

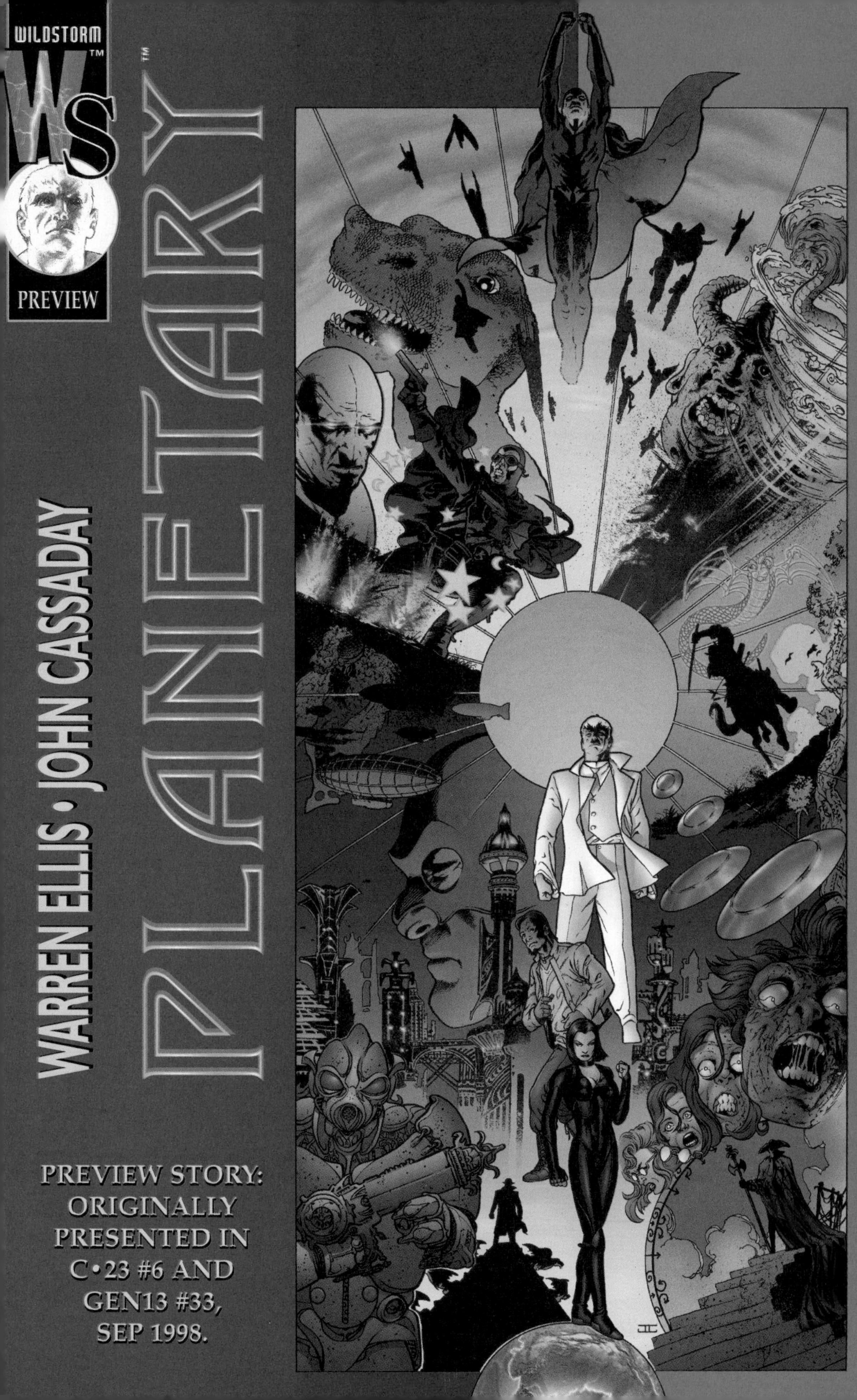

PREVIEW STORY:
ORIGINALLY
PRESENTED IN
C•23 #6 AND
GEN13 #33,
SEP 1998.

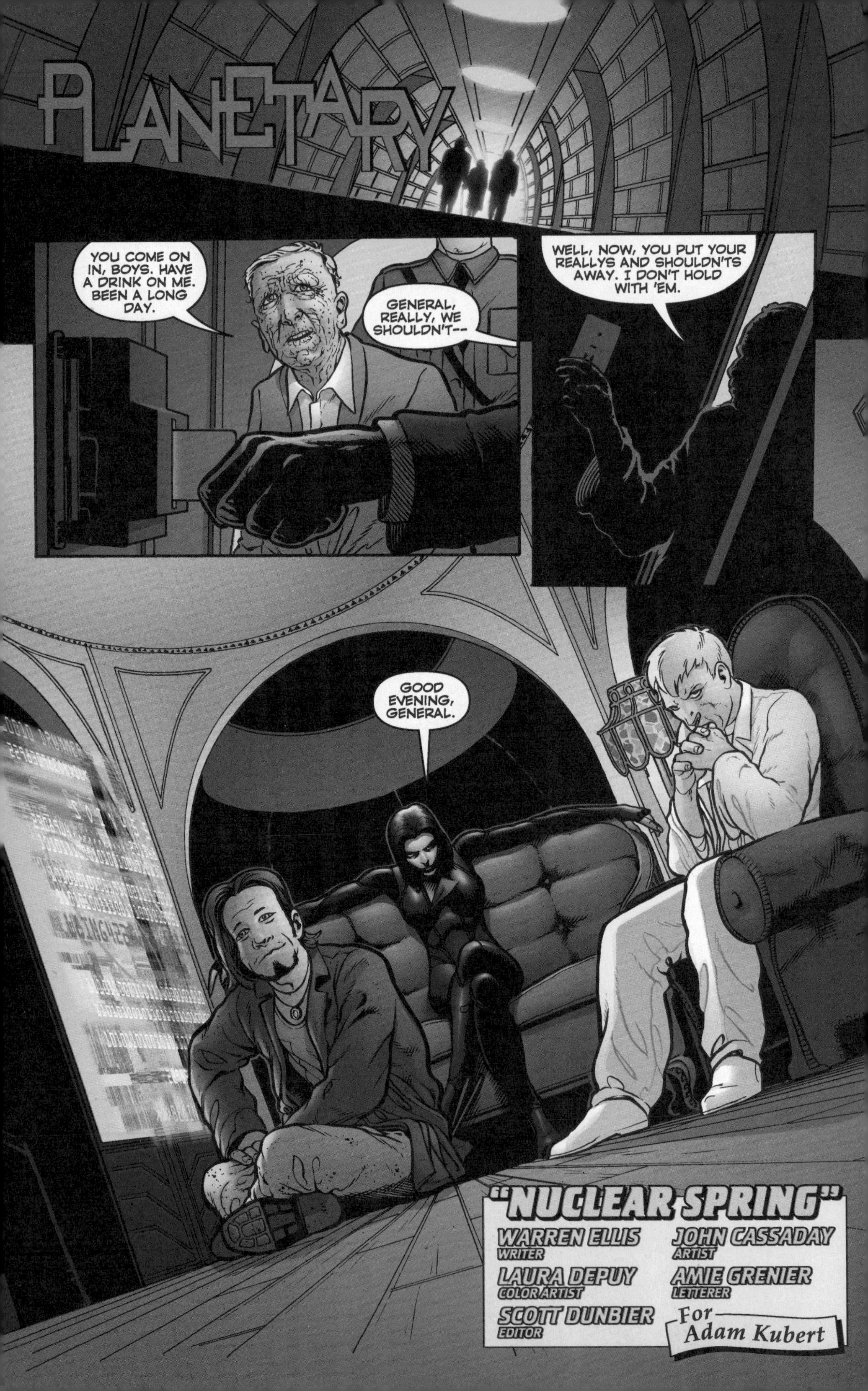
PLANETARY
YOU COME ON IN, BOYS. HAVE A DRINK ON ME. BEEN A LONG DAY.
GENERAL, REALLY, WE SHOULDN'T--
WELL, NOW, YOU PUT YOUR REALLYS AND SHOULDN'TS AWAY. I DON'T HOLD WITH 'EM.
GOOD EVENING, GENERAL.
"NUCLEAR SPRING"
WARREN ELLIS WRITER
JOHN CASSADAY ARTIST
LAURA DEPUY COLOR ARTIST
AMIE GRENIER LETTERER
SCOTT DUNBIER EDITOR
For Adam Kubert

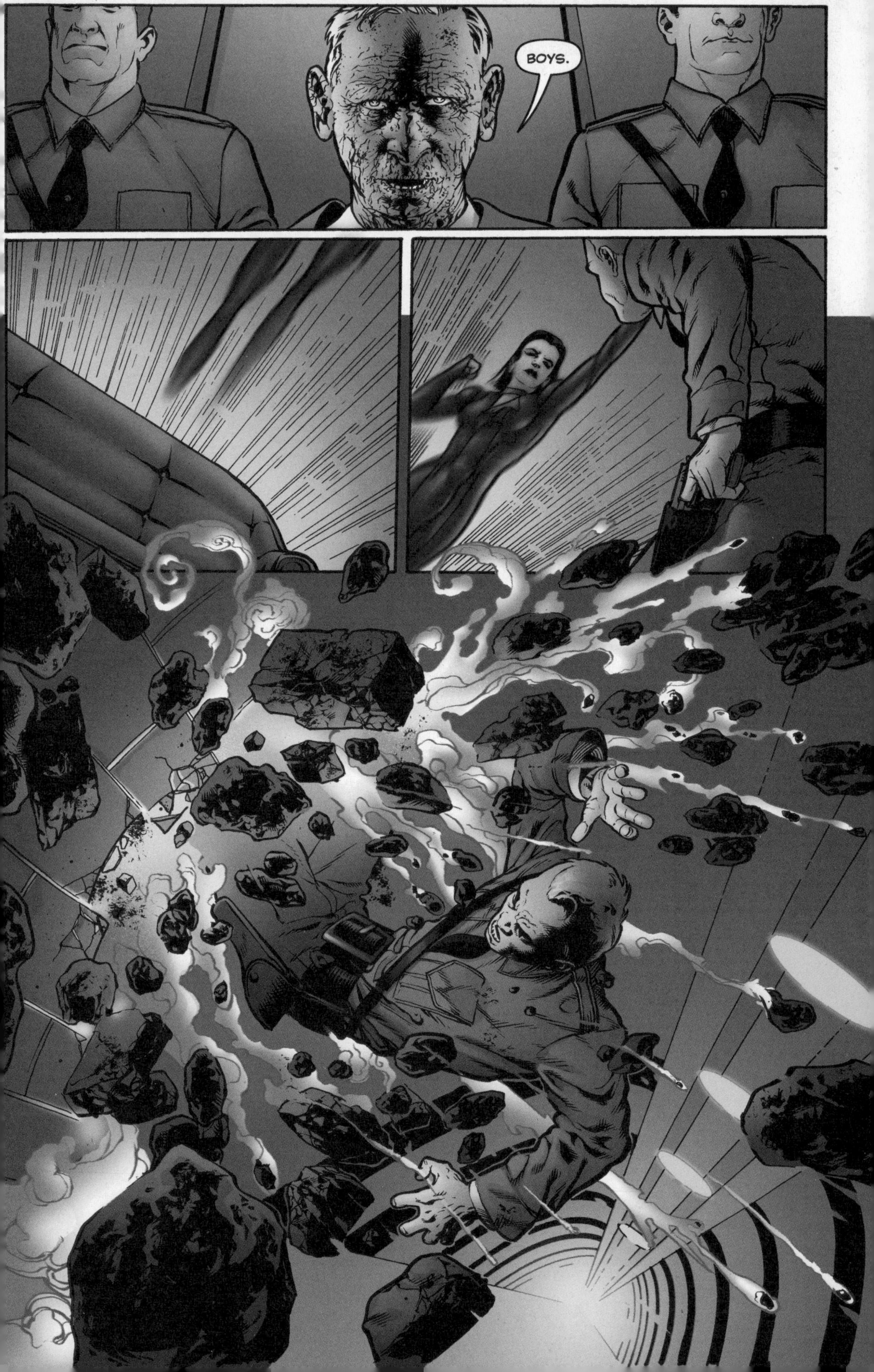
BOYS.

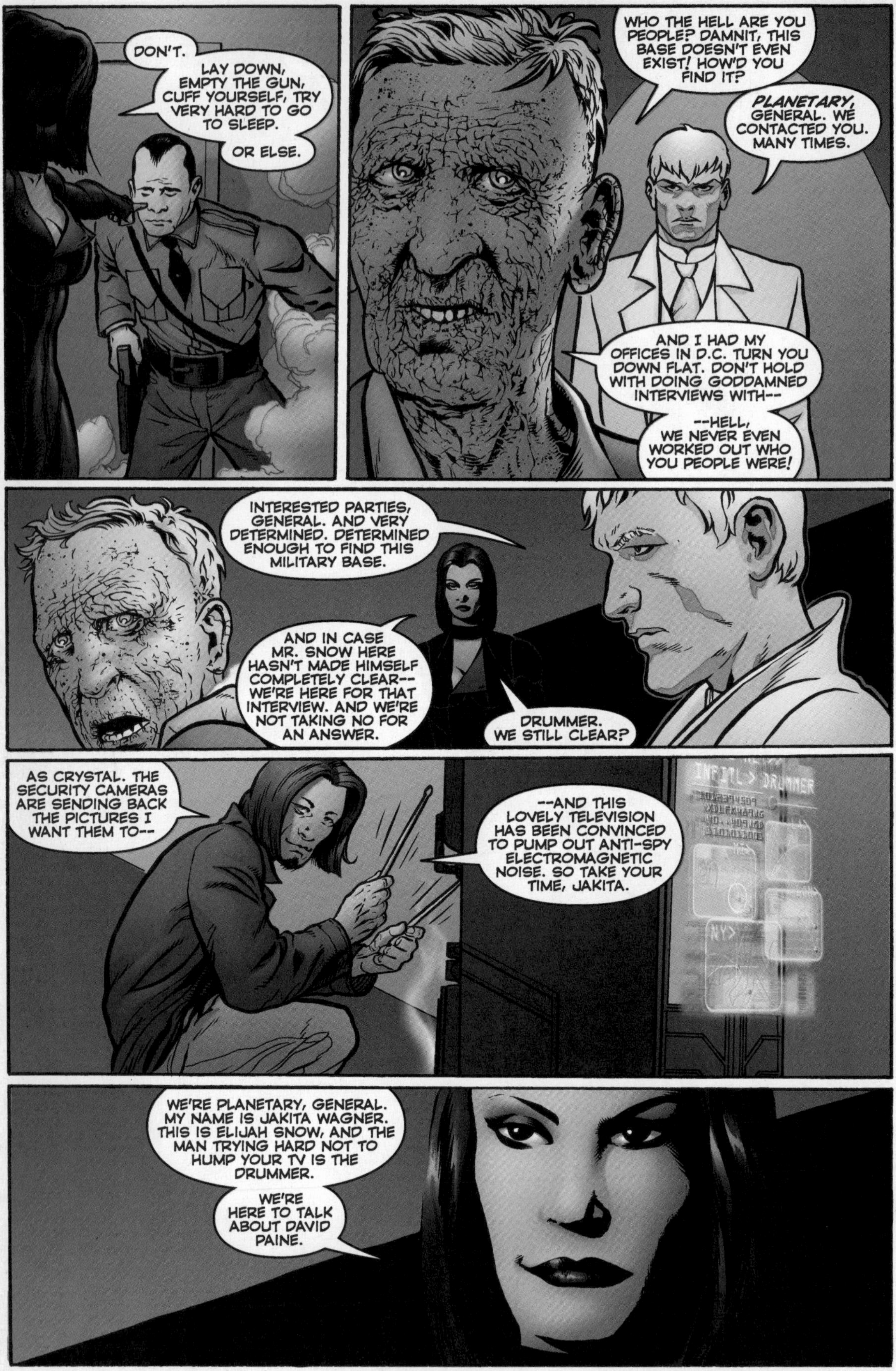
DON'T.
LAY DOWN, EMPTY THE GUN, CUFF YOURSELF, TRY VERY HARD TO GO TO SLEEP.
OR ELSE.
WHO THE HELL ARE YOU PEOPLE? DAMNIT, THIS BASE DOESN'T EVEN EXIST! HOW'D YOU FIND IT?
PLANETARY, GENERAL. WE CONTACTED YOU. MANY TIMES.
AND I HAD MY OFFICES IN D.C. TURN YOU DOWN FLAT. DON'T HOLD WITH DOING GODDAMNED INTERVIEWS WITH--
--HELL, WE NEVER EVEN WORKED OUT WHO YOU PEOPLE WERE!
INTERESTED PARTIES, GENERAL. AND VERY DETERMINED. DETERMINED ENOUGH TO FIND THIS MILITARY BASE.
AND IN CASE MR. SNOW HERE HASN'T MADE HIMSELF COMPLETELY CLEAR-- WE'RE HERE FOR THAT INTERVIEW. AND WE'RE NOT TAKING NO FOR AN ANSWER.
DRUMMER. WE STILL CLEAR?
AS CRYSTAL. THE SECURITY CAMERAS ARE SENDING BACK THE PICTURES I WANT THEM TO--
--AND THIS LOVELY TELEVISION HAS BEEN CONVINCED TO PUMP OUT ANTI-SPY ELECTROMAGNETIC NOISE. SO TAKE YOUR TIME, JAKITA.
WE'RE PLANETARY, GENERAL. MY NAME IS JAKITA WAGNER. THIS IS ELIJAH SNOW, AND THE MAN TRYING HARD NOT TO HUMP YOUR TV IS THE DRUMMER.
WE'RE HERE TO TALK ABOUT DAVID PAINE.

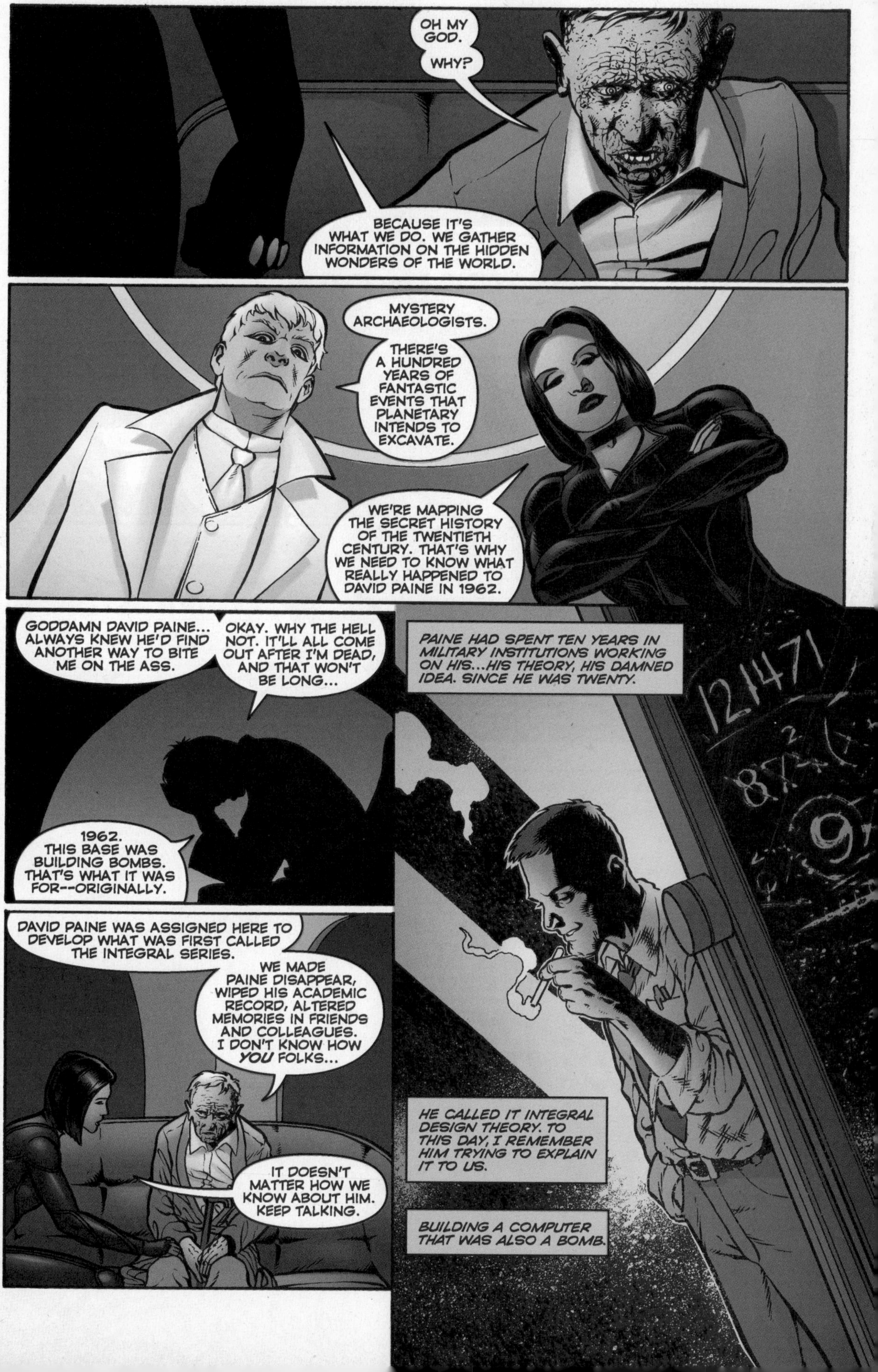

OH MY GOD.
WHY?
BECAUSE IT'S WHAT WE DO. WE GATHER INFORMATION ON THE HIDDEN WONDERS OF THE WORLD.
MYSTERY ARCHAEOLOGISTS.
THERE'S A HUNDRED YEARS OF FANTASTIC EVENTS THAT PLANETARY INTENDS TO EXCAVATE.
WE'RE MAPPING THE SECRET HISTORY OF THE TWENTIETH CENTURY. THAT'S WHY WE NEED TO KNOW WHAT REALLY HAPPENED TO DAVID PAINE IN 1962.
GODDAMN DAVID PAINE... ALWAYS KNEW HE'D FIND ANOTHER WAY TO BITE ME ON THE ASS.
OKAY. WHY THE HELL NOT. IT'LL ALL COME OUT AFTER I'M DEAD, AND THAT WON'T BE LONG...
1962. THIS BASE WAS BUILDING BOMBS. THAT'S WHAT IT WAS FOR--ORIGINALLY.
DAVID PAINE WAS ASSIGNED HERE TO DEVELOP WHAT WAS FIRST CALLED THE INTEGRAL SERIES.
WE MADE PAINE DISAPPEAR, WIPED HIS ACADEMIC RECORD, ALTERED MEMORIES IN FRIENDS AND COLLEAGUES. I DON'T KNOW HOW *YOU* FOLKS...
IT DOESN'T MATTER HOW WE KNOW ABOUT HIM. KEEP TALKING.
PAINE HAD SPENT TEN YEARS IN MILITARY INSTITUTIONS WORKING ON HIS...HIS THEORY, HIS DAMNED IDEA. SINCE HE WAS TWENTY.
HE CALLED IT INTEGRAL DESIGN THEORY. TO THIS DAY, I REMEMBER HIM TRYING TO EXPLAIN IT TO US.
BUILDING A COMPUTER THAT WAS ALSO A BOMB.

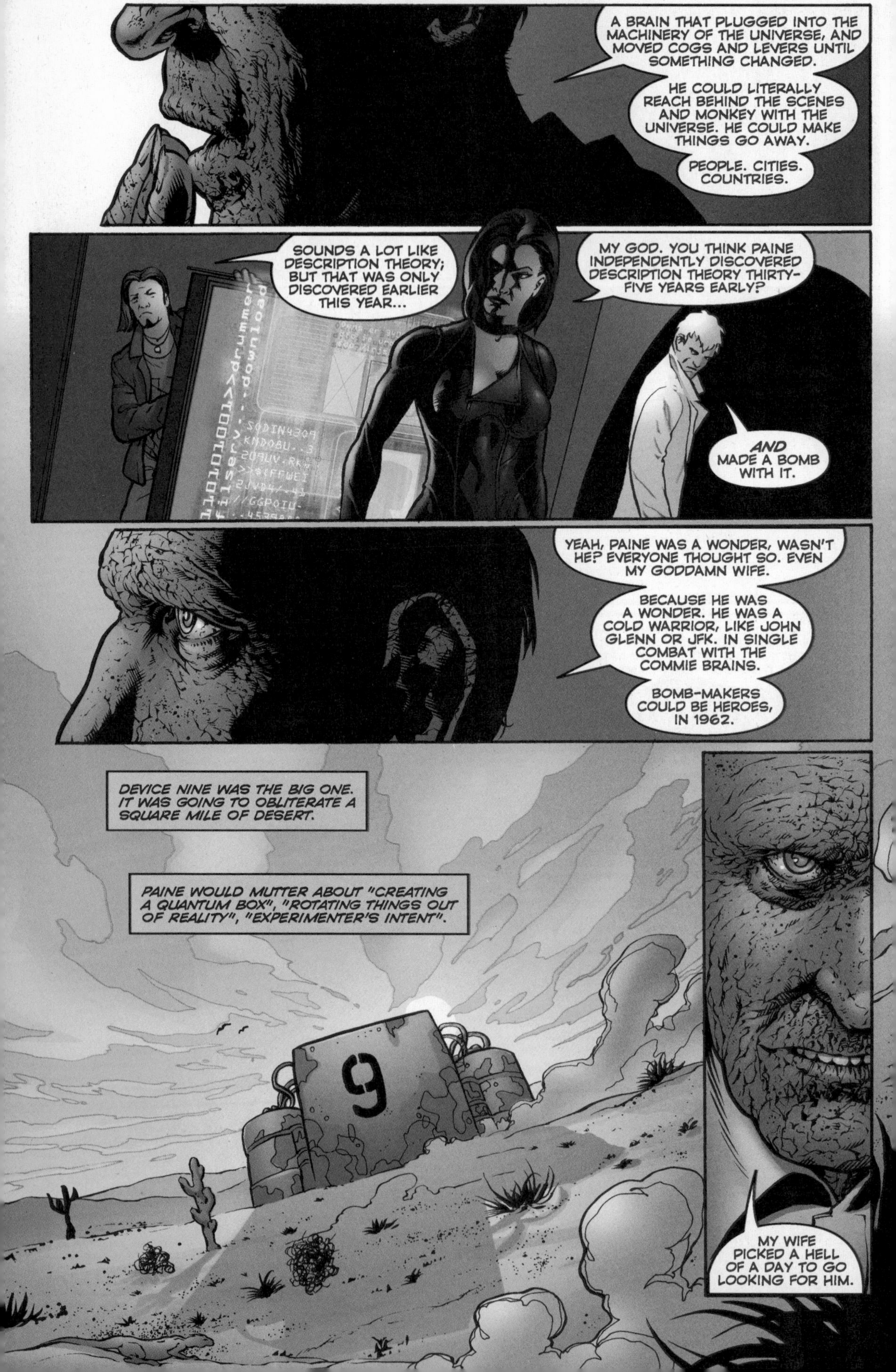
A BRAIN THAT PLUGGED INTO THE MACHINERY OF THE UNIVERSE, AND MOVED COGS AND LEVERS UNTIL SOMETHING CHANGED.
HE COULD LITERALLY REACH BEHIND THE SCENES AND MONKEY WITH THE UNIVERSE. HE COULD MAKE THINGS GO AWAY.
PEOPLE. CITIES. COUNTRIES.
SOUNDS A LOT LIKE DESCRIPTION THEORY; BUT THAT WAS ONLY DISCOVERED EARLIER THIS YEAR...
MY GOD. YOU THINK PAINE INDEPENDENTLY DISCOVERED DESCRIPTION THEORY THIRTY-FIVE YEARS EARLY?
AND MADE A BOMB WITH IT.
YEAH, PAINE WAS A WONDER, WASN'T HE? EVERYONE THOUGHT SO. EVEN MY GODDAMN WIFE.
BECAUSE HE WAS A WONDER. HE WAS A COLD WARRIOR, LIKE JOHN GLENN OR JFK. IN SINGLE COMBAT WITH THE COMMIE BRAINS.
BOMB-MAKERS COULD BE HEROES, IN 1962.
DEVICE NINE WAS THE BIG ONE. IT WAS GOING TO OBLITERATE A SQUARE MILE OF DESERT.
PAINE WOULD MUTTER ABOUT "CREATING A QUANTUM BOX", "ROTATING THINGS OUT OF REALITY", "EXPERIMENTER'S INTENT".
9
MY WIFE PICKED A HELL OF A DAY TO GO LOOKING FOR HIM.

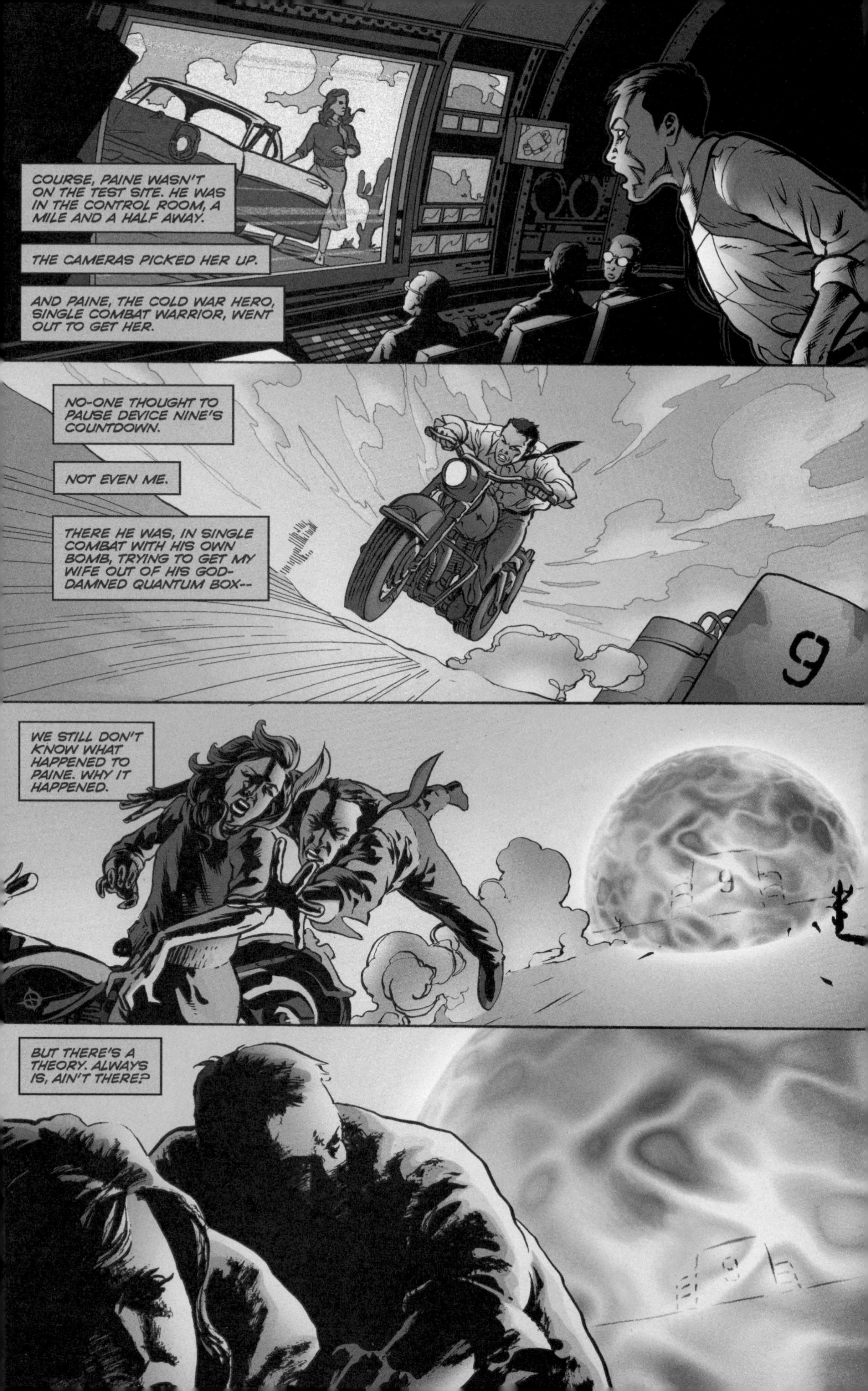
COURSE, PAINE WASN'T ON THE TEST SITE. HE WAS IN THE CONTROL ROOM, A MILE AND A HALF AWAY.
THE CAMERAS PICKED HER UP.
AND PAINE, THE COLD WAR HERO, SINGLE COMBAT WARRIOR, WENT OUT TO GET HER.
NO-ONE THOUGHT TO PAUSE DEVICE NINE'S COUNTDOWN.
NOT EVEN ME.
THERE HE WAS, IN SINGLE COMBAT WITH HIS OWN BOMB, TRYING TO GET MY WIFE OUT OF HIS GOD-DAMNED QUANTUM BOX--
9
WE STILL DON'T KNOW WHAT HAPPENED TO PAINE. WHY IT HAPPENED.
BUT THERE'S A THEORY. ALWAYS IS, AIN'T THERE?

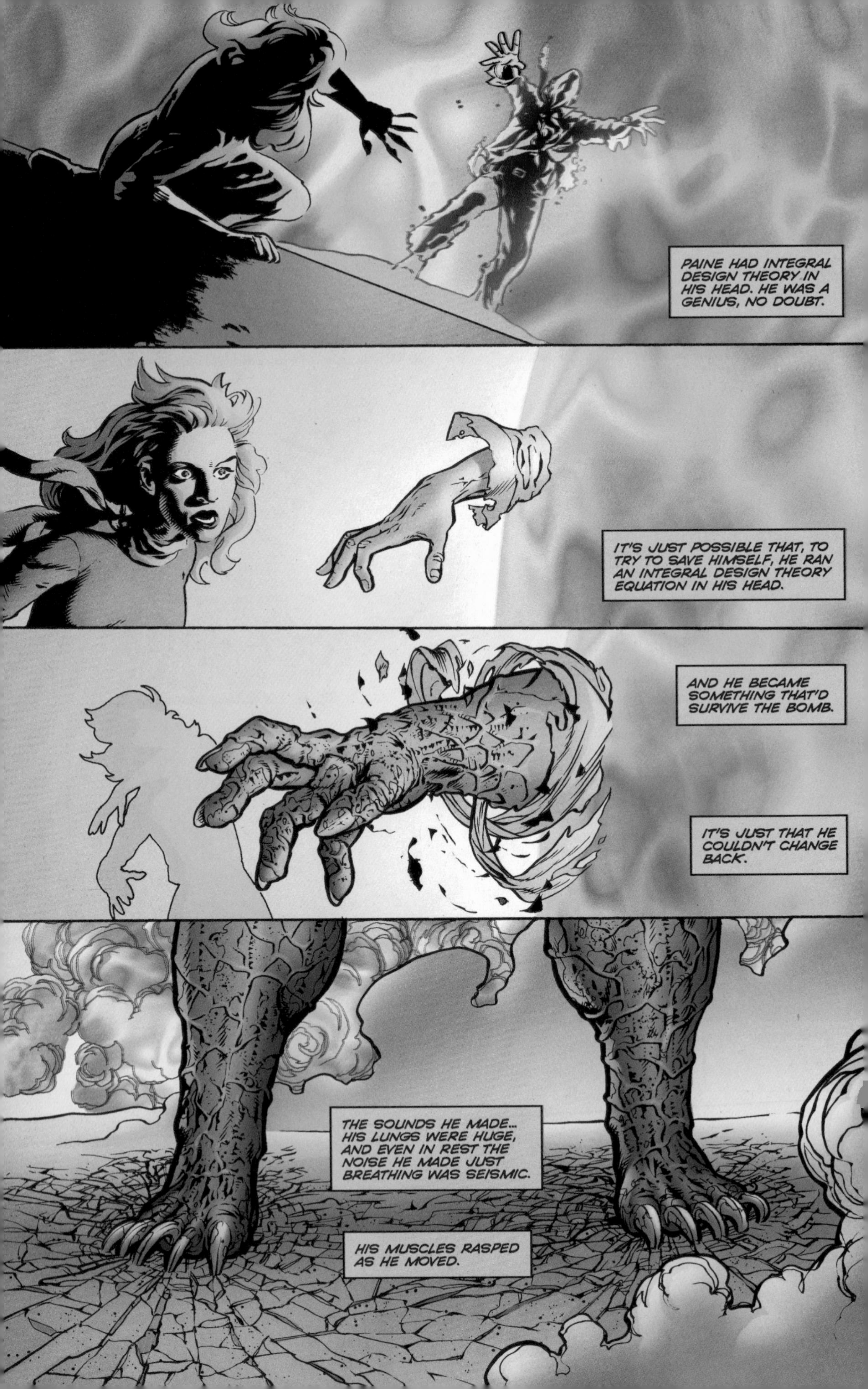
PAINE HAD INTEGRAL DESIGN THEORY IN HIS HEAD. HE WAS A GENIUS, NO DOUBT.
IT'S JUST POSSIBLE THAT, TO TRY TO SAVE HIMSELF, HE RAN AN INTEGRAL DESIGN THEORY EQUATION IN HIS HEAD.
AND HE BECAME SOMETHING THAT'D SURVIVE THE BOMB.
IT'S JUST THAT HE COULDN'T CHANGE BACK.
THE SOUNDS HE MADE... HIS LUNGS WERE HUGE, AND EVEN IN REST THE NOISE HE MADE JUST BREATHING WAS SEISMIC.
HIS MUSCLES RASPED AS HE MOVED.

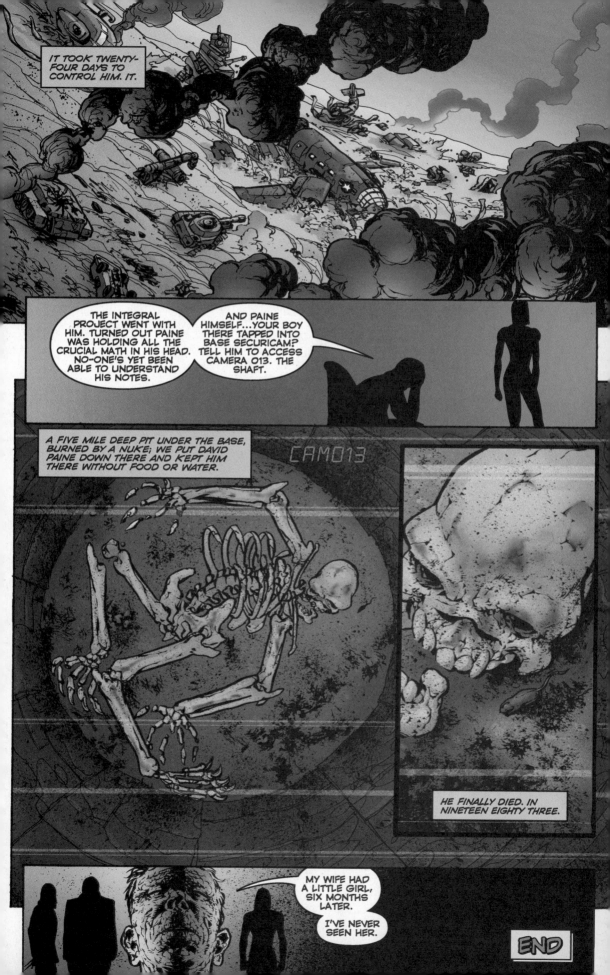

IT TOOK TWENTY-FOUR DAYS TO CONTROL HIM. IT.

THE INTEGRAL PROJECT WENT WITH HIM. TURNED OUT PAINE WAS HOLDING ALL THE CRUCIAL MATH IN HIS HEAD. NO-ONE'S YET BEEN ABLE TO UNDERSTAND HIS NOTES.

AND PAINE HIMSELF...YOUR BOY THERE TAPPED INTO BASE SECURICAM? TELL HIM TO ACCESS CAMERA 013. THE SHAFT.

A FIVE MILE DEEP PIT UNDER THE BASE, BURNED BY A NUKE; WE PUT DAVID PAINE DOWN THERE AND KEPT HIM THERE WITHOUT FOOD OR WATER.

CAM013

HE FINALLY DIED. IN NINETEEN EIGHTY THREE.

MY WIFE HAD A LITTLE GIRL, SIX MONTHS LATER.

I'VE NEVER SEEN HER.

END

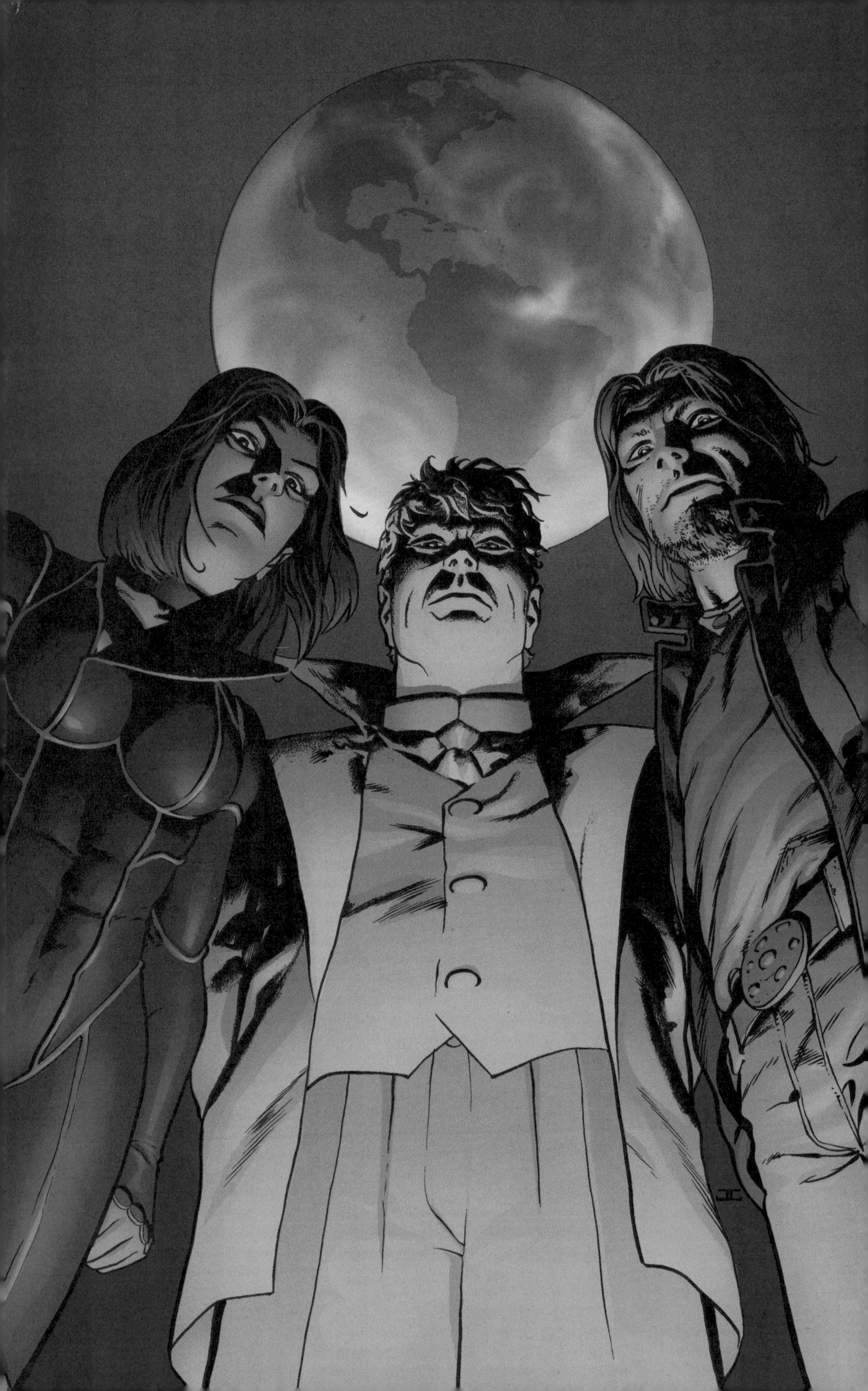

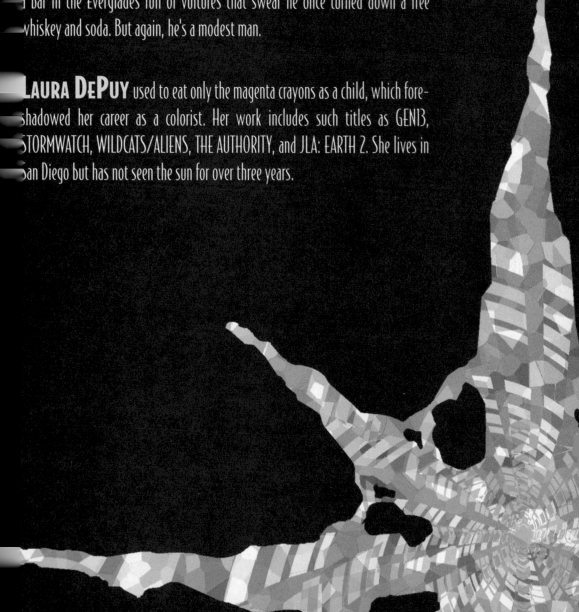

WARREN ELLIS has written LAZARUS CHURCHYARD, HELLSTORM, DV8, HELLBLAZER and THE AUTHORITY, and is beloved the world over. They call him Master Storyteller in the Viking countries. He's halfway through his 1300-page award-winning graphic novel TRANSMETROPOLITAN, serialized monthly. He lives in England with his partner Niki and their daughter Lilith.

JOHN CASSADAY is a modest man. He's too humble to mention his work on such titles as UNION JACK, X-MEN/ALPHA FLIGHT, and the critically acclaimed western DESPERADOES. He can also eat his body weight in cheddar fries. And there's a bar in the Everglades full of vultures that swear he once turned down a free whiskey and soda. But again, he's a modest man.

LAURA DEPUY used to eat only the magenta crayons as a child, which fore-shadowed her career as a colorist. Her work includes such titles as GEN13, STORMWATCH, WILDCATS/ALIENS, THE AUTHORITY, and JLA: EARTH 2. She lives in San Diego but has not seen the sun for over three years.

Battle Chasers: A Gathering of Heroes
Madureira/Sharrieff/McWeeney

Crimson: Loyalty & Loss
Augustyn/Ramos/Hope

Crimson: Heaven & Earth
Augustyn/Ramos/Hope

Deathblow: Sinners and Saints
Choi/Lee/Sale/Scott

Danger Girl: The Dangerous Collection #1-3
Campbell/Hartnell/Garner

Divine Right: Collected Edition #1-3
Lee/Williams

Gen^{13}
Choi/Lee/Campbell/Garner

Gen^{13}: #13 ABC
Choi/Lee/Campbell/Garner

Gen^{13}: Bootleg Vol. 1
Various writers and artists

Gen^{13}: Grunge the Movie
Warren

Gen^{13}: I Love New York
Arcudi/Frank/Smith

Gen^{13}: Interactive Plus
Various writers and artists

Gen^{13}: Starting Over
Choi/Lee/Campbell/Garner

Kurt Busiek's Astro City:
Life in the Big City
Busiek/Anderson

Kurt Busiek's Astro City:
Confession
Busiek/Anderson/Blyberg

Kurt Busiek's Astro City:
Family Album
Busiek/Anderson/Blyberg

Kurt Busiek's Astro City:
The Tarnished Angel
Busiek/Anderson/Blyberg

Leave It to Chance: Shaman's Rain
Robinson/Smith

Leave It to Chance: Trick or Threat
Robinson/Smith/Freeman

Voodoo: Dancing in the Dark
Moore/Lopez/Rio/Various

Ellis/Raney/Elliott/Lee

StormWatch: Force of Nature
Ellis/Raney/Elliott

StormWatch: Change or Die
Ellis/Raney/Jimenez

StormWatch: A Finer World
Ellis/Hitch/Neary

WildC.A.T.s: Gang War
Moore/Various

WildC.A.T.s: A Gathering of Eagles
Claremont/Lee/Williams

WildC.A.T.s: Homecoming
Moore/Various

WildC.A.T.s/X-Men
Various writers and artists

WildStorm Rising
Windsor-Smith/Various

OTHER COLLECTIONS OF INTEREST

Art of Chiodo
Chiodo

The Batman Adventures: Mad Love
Dini/Timm

Batman: The Dark Knight Returns
Miller/Janson/Varley

Batman: Faces
Wagner

Batman: The Killing Joke
Moore/Bolland/Higgins

Batman: Year One
Miller/Mazzucchelli/Lewis

Camelot 3000
Barr/Bolland

The Golden Age
Robinson/Smith

Green Lantern: Emerald Knights
Marz/Dixon/Banks/Various

Green Lantern: Fear Itself
Marz/Parker

JLA: New World Order
Morrison/Porter/Dell

JLA: Rock of Ages
Morrison/Porter/Dell/Various

Morrison/Semeiks/Conrad

Justice League of America: The Nail
Davis/Farmer

Kingdom Come
Waid/Ross

Ronin
Miller

Starman: Sins of the Father
Robinson/Harris/Von Grawbadger

Starman: Night and Day
Robinson/Harris/Von Grawbadger

Starman: Times Past
Harris/Jimenez/Weeks/Various

Starman: A Wicked Inclination...
Robinson/Harris/Von Grawbadger/Various

Watchmen
Moore/Gibbons

ARCHIVE EDITIONS

All Star Comics Archives Vols. 1-5
Various writers and artists

The Golden Age Flash Archives Vol. 1
Various writers and artists

The Flash Archives Vol. 1
Various writers and artists

The Golden Age Green Lantern Vol. 1
Various writers and artists

Green Lantern Archives Vols. 1-2
Various writers and artists

Justice League of America Archives Vols. 1-5
Various writers and artists

Legion of Super-Heroes Archives Vols. 1-9
Various writers and artists